THE ANCHOR OF MY LIFE

THE HISTORY OF EMOTIONS SERIES

EDITED BY

Peter N. Stearns, Carnegie-Mellon University
Jan Lewis, Rutgers University-Newark

The Anchor of My Life

Middle-Class American
Mothers and Daughters, 1880–1920

LINDA W. ROSENZWEIG

NEW YORK UNIVERSITY PRESS
NEW YORK AND LONDON

NEW YORK UNIVERSITY PRESS
New York and London

Library of Congress Cataloging-in-Publication Data
Rosenzweig, Linda W.
The anchor of my life : middle-class American mothers and
daughters, 1880–1920 / Linda W. Rosenzweig.
    p.   cm.—(The History of emotions series)
Includes bibliographical references and index.
ISBN 0-8147-7438-5
1. Mothers and daughters—United States—History.   2. Middle class
women—United States—History.   I. Title.   II. Series: History of
emotion series.
HQ755.85.R66   1993   92-44560
306.874'3—dc20   CIP

Manufactured in the United States of America

c 10 9 8 7 6 5 4 3 2 1

For My Daughters, Amy and Jane
and
in Memory of My Mother,
Helen S. Weinberg

CONTENTS

Illustrations appear as a group following p. 80

PREFACE

CONTEMPORARY historians recognize that a subjective relationship exists between researchers and their work, and that various factors predispose scholars to study particular problems. Traditionally, the influence of social and political contexts has been stressed, but more recently, the role of private and family experiences has also been acknowledged. For the social historian, whose sphere of interest encompasses ordinary human activities and relationships and familiar institutions, the links between personal life and historical subject matter can be especially close. This study is an example of such links.

I first became interested in the history of mother-daughter relationships in the context of a growing personal recognition of my own daughters as interesting people whose company I enjoyed and whose friendship I valued. A persistent curiosity about the degree to which my own thoughts and feelings had been shared by women in the past led to a preliminary survey of the literature on mother-daughter relationships. Although I found discussions of mothers and daughters by humanists, social scientists, and psychologists, I discovered no well-developed historical perspectives on this topic. While the literature treats motherhood and the socialization of girls in the context of more general considerations of women's roles, family relationships, and child-rearing styles, no focused study has examined the relations between mothers and daughters and the impact of broader developments in American society and family history on those relations. Yet the historical study of mother-daughter relationships has the potential to significantly increase our understanding of family life in the past. It can also help to evaluate the sense of tension that has been articulated by many American women in the context of contemporary feminism and new work roles, and thus enable us to examine just how new such tension really is and from what previous standards it has developed.

Where historical studies have touched on mother-daughter interactions in ancillary ways, they have postulated a golden age of sharing and harmony that was abruptly disrupted in the late nineteenth century with the rise of the "new woman" and the concurrent emergence of a female generation gap in opportunity and aspirations. The suggestion of a connection between these developments and mother-daughter relationships seems plausible: if young women enjoyed new choices and envisioned different futures, they might indeed experience new problems in their interactions with mothers whose lives had been defined more rigidly by the parameters of nineteenth-century domesticity and family life. Yet a neat "before and after" transformation in mother-daughter relationships would be unusual in light of the characteristically evolutionary patterns of change that are typically revealed in the study of social history.

This volume addresses the need for the development of a fuller historical perspective on the interactions of mothers and daughters, and for a reassessment of existing assumptions about the relationship in the past, through an investigation of American mother-daughter relationships during the four decades between 1880 and 1920. The study focuses on the experiences of middle-class mothers and daughters for several reasons. First, the pertinent sources consist primarily of documents that reflect middle-class experiences. Most of the available journals, diaries, and correspondence that record germane events, thoughts, and feelings, and thus permit the analysis of the emotional quality of women's lives, were written by literate middle-class women. The prescriptive literature from the period and relevant works of fiction also reflect this perspective. Furthermore, it seems reasonable to assume that in the case of mother-daughter relationships, as in family history more generally, middle-class patterns of behavior defined standards that were applied to the rest of society and presumably had some impact on other groups, although such standards were not necessarily internalized by them.

Obviously, middle-class female behavior patterns and values varied. The issue of representativeness poses a particularly difficult problem for the historian engaged in an effort to understand the private, emotional experiences of family life in the past. This investigation focuses primarily on mothers and daughters in the Northeast and Midwest, with some attention to comparative perspectives through an overview of English mother-daughter interactions during the same period, as a first stage in the process of developing a history of American mother-daughter relationships. The examination of the impact of regional differences on American mother-daughter relationships through an analysis of the experiences of women in the South and the West remains a subject for future research.[1]

As Tillie Olsen has observed, "Most of what has been, is, between mothers, daughters, and in motherhood, in daughterhood, has never been recorded."[2] Certainly women's personal documents cannot be assumed to provide totally reliable data regarding family interactions in the past. Diary and journal entries can be brief and incomplete, and autobiographical recollections have been filtered through memory, often over many years.[3] Correspondence may reveal more about the nature of relationships, but here too, caution is essential, since mothers and daughters in the past did not necessarily write to one another about hostile feelings. Undoubtedly, some women viewed certain concerns as too private to write about in any form. Furthermore, existing collections of family documents may reflect "editing" by family members who chose to eliminate particular material that might have divulged certain unpleasant aspects of family relationships. Similarly, prescriptive literature and literary works cannot be viewed as direct reflections of women's actual experiences.

Nevertheless, taken together, these sources reveal a great deal about women's experiences of, and attitudes toward, the mother-daughter relationship at the turn of the century and beyond, and also about the contemporary social and cultural expectations regarding the interactions of mothers and daughters. The combination of women's words to one another, and their words about one another, helps to illuminate their personal values and the values of the wider society as well. These materials testify to the relationship's complexity and its enduring centrality in women's lives. And they provide clear evidence that the years between 1880 and 1920 define a significant period in the relationship's history.

Throughout the research and writing of this book, I have enjoyed the support of several institutions. A grant from the Radcliffe Research Support Program enabled me to spend much of the fall of 1987 at the Schlesinger Library. Grants from the National Endowment for the Humanities Travel to Collections Program and the Chatham College Central Research Fund allowed me to do additional research at that library in 1988 and 1989. Additional support from Chatham's Central Research Fund helped me to spend several weeks in London at the Fawcett Library in the summer of 1987. Finally, a sabbatical during the academic year 1987–88 and a leave during the fall term, 1991, released me from teaching responsibilities at crucial periods in my work.

The assistance of a number of knowledgeable and caring librarians facilitated my work greatly. I extend my appreciation to the entire staff of the Schlesinger Library at Radcliffe College, and special thanks to Anne Engelhart and Marie-Hélène Gold. I am also grateful to Deborah Pelletier and Ann Hopkins, who introduced me to the resources of Amherst College Library's Special Collections, to Susan Boone for her kind assistance with the Sophia Smith Collection and the Smith College Archives, and to David Doughan for his gracious help at the Fawcett Library in London.

I would also like to thank several colleagues and friends who have contributed to my work in various ways. Anthony Penna awakened my interest in social history a number of years ago, for which I am immensely grateful. Richard Schoenwald has consistently offered encouragement, friendship, and wise advice, which I appreciate and value. Laurie Crumpacker and Ellen Rothman supplied relevant references at an early stage in my research. William Lenz commented on a portion of this work and guided me to several very helpful sources. Peter Karsten and Robert Corber also suggested useful materials. Robert Cooley provided invaluable assistance with the illustrations. Joan Marks offered judicious editorial suggestions and asked good questions. But my greatest debt is to Peter Stearns, for his interest in this project from its inception, his intellectual support, his generous encouragement, his unfailingly perceptive insights, and his sense of humor. I can never thank him adequately.

My family also provided important assistance. At a critical moment, Lee and Judy Weinberg convinced me that a laptop computer was a necessity, and they were right. Juliet and David Kalms offered gracious hospitality in London. Richard Rosenzweig prodded me and believed in me when I needed it most. Although illness prevented my parents from sharing this experience with me, they were a part of it in many ways. Finally, my daughters inspired and encouraged me throughout the research and the writing of this book. Amy monitored my progress with steady interest, quiet support, and reassuring confidence in my ability to fulfill my objectives. She continues to set an example for me by her conscientiousness and persistence in her own work. Jane read most of the manuscript, offered perceptive, critical comments, and issued frequent warnings about the perils of procrastination. It was a special and uniquely appropriate pleasure for me to be able to enjoy her competent assistance with the research for chapter 8, and to rely on her as a colleague in this endeavor. They are the reason for this book.

THE ANCHOR OF MY LIFE

CHAPTER 1

"THE CENTRAL PROBLEM OF
FEMALE EXPERIENCE":
INTRODUCTION

FOR many late twentieth-century feminist writers, the mother-
daughter relationship has symbolized not a source of support
and comfort, but a morass of bitterness and resentment. As
Nikki Stiller has observed, during the late 1960s and throughout the
following decade "it was rather bad form for a woman to mention
her mother favorably in public. Alienation and hostility were held to
be the hallmarks of adulthood among many who considered themselves psychologically, emotionally, and sexually liberated."[1] Indeed,
contemporary feminist discussions of the mother-daughter relationship have often stressed the negative aspects of the bond between
mothers and their female offspring, emphasizing its stifling intensity
and the concomitant implications for the limitation of individual
development, while at the same time affirming its centrality for the
lives of all women.[2] Much of the flavor of the recent impressionistic
literature on mothers and daughters is captured in a statement by
the author of a study that examines the significance of mother-
daughter ties in the life and work of Virginia Woolf: "I consider the
mother-daughter relationship the central problem of female experience. . . . fundamentally, it is a locus of tension rather than the pas-
toral haven suggested by cultural myths of motherhood."[3] But the
contemporary discourse also includes some significant theoretical work
that argues for a rather different and more positive representation
of the impact of mother-daughter interactions on the lives of both.

To a large extent, the current commentary emphasizes the daughter's point of view, attributing the difficult problems that plague the

relationship to destructive maternal behavior. This tendency to blame the mother for family problems is not new in the last third of the twentieth century. Rather, it represents the continuation of a trend that emerged with the development of the nineteenth-century emphasis on the importance of moral motherhood.[4] Thus it was foreshadowed in nineteenth-century discussions of child-rearing, in the prescriptive literature that appeared around the turn of the century, and in later discussions that have held mothers solely responsible for the maintenance of family harmony and for the physical and psychological well-being of their offspring.[5] But contemporary feminist discussions differ from their precursors in their explicit articulation of the significance of the conflict between individuality and connection in the mother-daughter relationship, and in their suggestion that mother-daughter problems derive from the societal devaluation of women.

Nancy Friday's popular book, *My Mother, My Self,* illustrates the tendency to blame the mother at its most extreme.[6] Friday argues that mothers impede daughters' development at every stage, inhibiting their individuation and denying their sexuality as their own mothers did to them. Mother-daughter interactions are inherently negative because there is an inevitable conflict between a mother's goals for her daughter and the daughter's need to attain sexual individuality. Thus Friday suggests that the problems of adult women, their failings, and their pervasive unhappiness stem directly from the mother-daughter relationship.

Other discussions of negative maternal influence stress the difficulties of mothering in a male-dominated culture. Like Friday, Judith Arcana maintains that daughters learn how to be women from their mothers, but she explicitly attributes mother-daughter conflict to the expectations imposed upon women by a male-created and male-dominated culture: "The relationship is structured, at present, upon assumptions and conclusions that are false to ourselves and for each other; that is why so many mother/daughter relationships are filled with pain."[7] The fact that mothers socialize their daughters "negatively," then, reflects the shared oppression of all women in a patriarchal society rather than their own evil intent. Arcana also argues that despite their efforts to rebel or adopt another role model, daughters unconsciously pattern themselves after their mothers.[8] This tendency results in the phenomenon Adrienne Rich has described as matrophobia, the fear of becoming one's mother. Rich suggests that women develop this fear because the mother stands for the victim in themselves, the unfree person, the martyr. Daughters experience anger at maternal powerlessness or at the fact that mothers relegate them to second-class status in favor of the male family members.[9] They seek instead mothers who, refusing to be victims themselves, acknowledge the realities of life under patriarchy, attempt to expand the limits of their own lives, and explicitly provide support to the next generation. Thus women may choose another model, a nonbiological mother, whose image appears more appropriate.[10] For Rich, as for Arcana, patriarchal society is the root of the problem.[11]

Jane Flax maintains that the mother-daughter problem centers on the dichotomy between the need for nurturance and the need for autonomy. She too emphasizes the problems associated with mothering in the context of a patriarchal society, a setting that generates conflict within the maternal role. Flax suggests that a woman's experience of this personal conflict, in turn, creates additional difficulties in her interactions with her daughter.[12] Signe Hammer, also concerned about issues of separation and individuation, indicts the societal context "in which women who were not encouraged to grow up raise daughters who are not encouraged to grow up either."[13]

Other analyses that adopt a more theoretical approach to mother-daughter issues project a less emotional tone. Nancy Chodorow's examination of the relationship between mothering and what she refers to as the social organization of gender employs a strong psychoanalytic framework that tempers the anger and hostility that permeate much of the discussion of the "my mother, my self" problem. Chodorow utilizes object-relations theory to describe and explain the fundamental characteristics of the mother-daughter relationship. Unlike classic Freudian psychodynamic theory, which attributes personality formation exclusively to the influence of instinctual drives, object-relations theory also stresses the child's social-relational experiences from earliest infancy. In our society, those experiences typically involve interactions with the mother, who has primary responsibility for child care. Because they share the same gender, mothers tend to identify with infant daughters and experience them as extensions of themselves, while they experience sons as male opposites and thus distinct from themselves. For boys, then, individuation occurs more easily than for girls, who remain more involved with their mothers psychologically. As a result, daughters alternate between total rejection of the mother who represents infantile dependence, identification with her, and identification with other female models. Hence, Chodorow asserts that mother-daughter conflict is not endemic to the relationship, but it is a function of a social structure that assigns primary parenting responsibilities, "mothering," to women.

This social structure also results in the "reproduction of mothering." Because they have been parented primarily by women, daughters develop both the capacities and the desire to be mothers themselves. The same situation produces the curtailment of nurturant capacities and needs in sons. As a result of their early social-relational experiences and the continuing attachment to their mothers, then, women define and experience themselves relationally while men experience themselves as separate and distinct from others.[14]

A second generation of analysis linking mother-daughter interactions with women's relational development has emerged since Chodorow first proposed the connection with object-relations theory. Extending the focus on social-relational experience beyond the emphasis it receives in mainstream object-relations theory (which still regards relationships as secondary to drive satisfaction and frustration), current feminist psychological research has stressed the centrality of relational development for women's lives. Hence the work of Jean Baker Miller, Carol Gilligan, and others underscores the significance of empathy and connectedness, as opposed to separation and individuation, in women's psychology generally, and specifically for the bond between mothers and daughters.[15] In more recent therapeutic and empirical discussions of the relationship, then, a less strident quality has supplanted the tone of anger and hostility that were characteristic of the dialogue of the 1960s and '70s.[16]

It is not surprising to find extensive commentary on the mother-daughter relationship in the context of the late twentieth-century feminist movement and the attendant interest in women's history and culture. Nor is it surprising to discover a negative tone in that commentary, given the changes in women's lives—the liberalization of sexual mores and the movement of women out of the home and into the work force, for example—and the alterations in women's worldviews that have been produced by these changes. But it is important to ask whether the contemporary discussions reflect the experiences of most women, either now or in the past, to ask whether the mother-daughter relationship is inherently conflictual.

It is only through focused historical inquiry that these questions can be answered and the sense of tension and antagonism that has been articulated so frequently in late twentieth-century discussions of the relationship can be fully evaluated. In the context of existing theoretical conflicts about the intrinsic nature of the mother-daughter bond, a historical perspective can provide essential evidence for the development of a fuller understanding of this basic component of women's family experiences. Historical study can illuminate the nature of mother-daughter interactions in the past, and also contribute to the further exploration and development of both existing and new theory in this area. Where theories posit universal patterns of human development that necessarily imply specific outcomes in terms of the mother-daughter relationship, as object-relations theory does, historical work can be particularly useful. The editor of a recent collection that spans nearly 250 years of mother-daughter correspondence has observed that most theories regarding the relationship "tend to conceal how often mothers and daughters inspire each other to take risks and strive for fulfillment."[17] This statement underscores the hazards of assuming congruence between the contemporary, essentially ahistorical mother-daughter literature, and the historical evolution of the relationship.

The task of assessing that congruence is complicated by the fact that like most of women's past experiences, mother-daughter relations have basically been ignored or trivialized historically. In the context of a cultural tradition that has regarded females as important only in terms of their roles as wives and mothers of men, relationships between women have not been valued. Hence the interactions of mothers and daughters have been effectively relegated to an "underground" position. It is only since the rise of the most recent wave of feminism that the mother-daughter relationship has been considered a crucial factor in a woman's path to liberation.[18] And even in this context, only a minimal amount of historical discussion of the relationship has occurred.

Despite the proliferation of research on other areas of family history, no major work has concentrated on the topic of mother-daughter relationships. To the limited extent that historians have considered mother-daughter interactions in the past, they have stressed the implications of generational differences in opportunity and behavior for mother-daughter relationships. For example, Carroll Smith-Rosenberg has pointed out that a continuity of expectation and experience linked American female generations and fostered mother-daughter intimacy until the late nineteenth century. She suggests that the changes in women's lives which accompanied urbanization and industrialization disrupted that continuity and introduced conflict, estrangement, and alienation into a previously harmonious relationship. Peter G. Filene has also noted the effect of these changes, underlining the novelty of the choices available to young women and their mothers' anxiety about, if not disapproval of, their increasingly "unladylike" patterns of behavior.[19]

The observations of these historians highlight a series of dramatic changes that peaked around the turn of the century and significantly altered the expectations and aspirations of American girls and young women. While the earlier nineteenth-century world had offered women few viable alternatives to marriage and a traditional role in the family, the world of the late nineteenth and early twentieth centuries brought new opportunities that disturbed the equilibrium of nineteenth-century domesticity and family life. The middle-class Victorian cultural image of the "angel in the house" remained the ideal, but the distance between that image and the reality of women's lives was growing rapidly.[20]

Broader horizons beckoned the "new woman." New kinds of work, for example clerical and department-store sales positions, offered more independence. Extended educational experiences—including secondary school, and college for a growing number of middle-class girls as well—enlarged the boundaries of women's lives, as did the plethora of clubs and women's associations to which they were exposed. Innovations in fashion and social behavior—shorter skirts, different hat styles, and public cigarette smoking—added to the mix.[21] At the same time, socialization toward distinctive emotional styles, especially the control of anger, differentiated girls' experiences from those of their brothers; this contrasted with earlier socialization regarding anger, which had not emphasized gender-based distinctions of this type.[22]

These changes in women's lives reflected the more general cultural and social trends of the period. The years between 1880 and 1920 witnessed the acceleration of urbanization and industrialization, major technological advances, the rise of larger and more formal organizations, and women's struggle to achieve autonomy and self-consciousness. No historical period can be characterized by one set of core values, but the division between tradition and innovation in American culture was particularly pronounced during the early years of mature industrial society, as efforts to accommodate to the scope, scale, and speed of change contrasted with an impulse to maintain earlier patterns. The extensive discussion of the "woman question," and the ambivalence on the part of social commentators who both criticized and admired the "new woman," reflected this division.[23]

The concept of the "new woman" did not define one objective reality, but symbolized different things to different people. Descriptions of this exotic image differed: The "new woman" lived her own life and made her own decisions. She rejected the conventions of femininity and interacted with men on equal terms. She was well educated and often financially independent. Her hallmark was personal freedom. She was also vulgar, unfeminine, and unladylike—and a real problem for her mother.[24]

While the era of the "new woman" witnessed both the expansion and the reform of female secondary education, this development continued an earlier nineteenth-century American trend.[25] The extension of the opportunity for higher education to women represented a more striking change. In America in 1890, approximately one of every fifty women aged eighteen to twenty-one attended college, and fewer than three thousand received degrees, as compared to thirteen thousand male recipients. Between 1890 and 1910, female college enrollment nearly tripled, and in the next decade, it more than doubled. At the turn of the century, approximately 40 percent of all undergraduate students were women.[26]

For young women, the decision to leave home and attend college represented a real departure from nineteenth-century domesticity and a clear break with the traditional female roles of their mothers and grandmothers. Superficial differences—frivolous fashions, public smoking, obvious flirting—also separated the generations, but higher education had more fundamental consequences. As a result of their removal from their parents' influence, many daughters developed a new and very unconventional mindset: as Peter Filene has observed, in college "many girls decisively grew into 'new women' as opposed to 'ladies.' "[27] For those who attended women's colleges in particular, this conversion encompassed a very new behavior—a definite tendency not to marry. Graduates of coeducational institutions married at a higher rate, but marriage was an exception for the alumnae of women's colleges. For example, only about 25 percent of Vassar, Smith, and Wellesley graduates between the ages of twenty-six and thirty-seven were married in 1903. While other factors were also involved, many college women remained single by choice, preferring the freedom of an autonomous professional life to the restraints of a more conventional family life.[28]

The female independence fostered by new educational and career opportunities disturbed contemporary observers of the social scene. Social critics who anxiously proclaimed the breakdown of the American family attributed the problems they perceived to the negligence of women who went to work, bought prepared food, and especially to the influence of higher education.[29] More than one writer commented eloquently regarding the effects of college and work experiences on the worldviews of young women. To Dorothy Dix, the "modern girl" was a "phenomenon and a problem," "a living, palpitating, feminine Fourth of July." Dix cited major differences between the ideas of young women and those of their mothers: daughters discussed things their mothers would never have mentioned, wanted to go out and work even if their parents had plenty of money, and worst of all, preferred not to rush into marriage. Thus, she concluded, "the most vital social question of today is not what we are going to do with her, but what she is going to do to us. For this girl of today is going to be the mother of tomorrow. The future of our race lies in her hands."[30] Another commentator observed that colleges produced "girl graduates who do not look upon life at all from the standpoint of their mothers," whose world had been one of "farms and homes diversified by shops and factories." In contrast, "The college-bred daughters of our day look out on a world that to them seems largely department stores and office buildings. They are less apt than girls used to be to look around for a man. They are much more apt than girls were to look for a wage-paying employment." Yet this observer remained optimistic about the possibilities for intergenerational rapprochement, for "after all the new girls are women like their mothers and have not broken with humanity, but merely with a few of its trammels."[31]

The visual arts of the period also reflected societal anxiety regarding the "new woman." In the late nineteenth-century iconography, images of aloof, elegant ladies contrasted with the reality of the changing experiences of a growing number of women, particularly those in the middle and upper classes. Thus paintings of beautiful, idealized women by artists such as Abbott Thayer and Thomas Dewing suggest that they, like other social critics, were disquieted by the new female demeanor and behavior and sought to preserve more traditional images and values regarding womanhood.[32]

The cultural anxiety concerning the "new woman" highlights the fact that during the period from 1880 to 1920, the world of daughters, particularly in middle-class families, differed from the world that their mothers and grandmothers had experienced earlier in the nineteenth century. Not all middle-class young women adopted the new and controversial posture of worldliness and self-sufficiency, but few could avoid some exposure to "modern" ideas.[33] Hence the suggestion that mother-daughter relationships deteriorated in this context seems plausible. Signe Hammer has observed that "a mother does not merely pass on the messages of her culture; she also passes on her responses to the messages she received from her mother. Thus, every transaction between mother and daughter is in a sense a transaction among three generations."[34] It is not difficult to imagine that these cross-generational transactions and the cultural messages they conveyed might have been rendered especially problematic during the period between 1880 and 1920. Research by James R. McGovern suggests that the first two decades of the twentieth century witnessed the genesis of the female emancipation in morals and manners that social and cultural historians have typically attributed to the influence of World War I and its aftermath during the 1920s.[35] It is possible, then, that the potential for mother-daughter tension was particularly high during the two decades after the turn of the century. Against this background, the era of the "new woman" certainly offers a suitable launching point for an investigation of the historical roots of the contemporary mother-daughter relationship and for an analysis of the ahistorical generalizations that typify many current discussions of this topic.

Such an investigation appropriately begins with a brief overview of earlier mother-daughter interactions. During the colonial period, mother-daughter relationships were characterized by what Mary Beth Norton has described as "egalitarian friendship." Daughters assisted their mothers with domestic tasks, while mothers instructed them in household skills, gave advice, and received companionship in return. Both valued the relationship, often describing one another as friends and companions. Occasionally women even expressed clear preferences for female offspring. And mothers and adult daughters experienced great anguish and a profound sense of loss at one another's deaths.[36]

Close mother-daughter relationships continued in post-Revolutionary America.[37] Evidence of maternal aspirations for the education of daughters in the new republic attests to women's hopes that their offspring would have better opportunities for schooling than they themselves had been offered, and that the latter would take advantage of those opportunities.[38] Continuing mother-daughter engagement enhanced the lives of women of both generations as they aged. Mothers provided important moral and practical guidance, and daughters acknowledged their special obligations for the care of aging parents. When young women married and shared more of their mothers' experiences, the relationship grew closer. Despite their advancing years, mothers continued to assume care-taking responsibilities for their daughters, nursing them through childbirth and illnesses and caring for grandchildren as well. Like their colonial predecessors, republican mothers and daughters experienced deep and lasting grief over one another's deaths.[39] These ties endured, and as they grew older, women often reflected thoughtfully and sympathetically on the events of their mothers' lives.[40]

Powerful mother-daughter bonds in the late eighteenth and early nineteenth centuries are also revealed by the tendency of women who held property in their own right to leave their estates or significant portions thereof to their daughters. Although men occasionally favored sons, they tended to divide their estates among their survivors, while women who had property to leave clearly favored their daughters, sometimes quite explicitly, as, for example: " 'I love all my children alike but my daughters I feel most attached to and think they ought to have what I own at my death, and therefore this disposition.' "[41]

Despite the evidence of strong mother-daughter ties earlier in the American past, interestingly it is mid-nineteenth-century intimacy that has most often been contrasted to more modern patterns of mother-daughter interaction. Thus some contemporary commentary that has incorporated the prevalent assumption that guilt and antagonism define the modern mother-daughter relationship also argues for the existence of a historical alternative, as revealed in the nineteenth-century "female world of love and ritual."[42] The suggestion of a major modification in the nature of the relationship since the middle of the last century raises important questions about the chronology of change, and also bears on the relevance of theoretical discussions that posit more universal claims.

It is not surprising to find strong links between middle-class mothers and their daughters in the context of the rise of nineteenth-century domesticity and the evolution of women's sphere. The first two-thirds of the century witnessed the valorization of the home as the woman's realm, and the concomitant development of the twin perceptions of women's expertise in homemaking and child-rearing. The ideal of nurturing motherhood and the concept of maternal love dominated the cultural discourse on the home during the antebellum period. Thus literature urging the importance of the bond between the "imperial" mother and her offspring conveyed a conception of motherhood as the main standard of femininity and as women's *raison d'être*.[43]

Because the nineteenth-century domestic ideal designated the home as women's realm, separate and apart from the world of men, mothers controlled their own lives and the lives of their children in a way they had not done during earlier periods. This power, described as a kind of "domestic feminism," has been documented with reference to women's exercise of control over sex and reproduction within marriage.[44] Whether the rise of domestic feminism symbolized progress for women or simply reinforced their exclusion from real power by amplifying notions of female exceptionalism, it created a context that could foster close mother-daughter relationships.[45] Although they went to school, middle-class girls were socialized within the confines of the female world of women's sphere to fulfill their ordained roles as wives and mothers and to practice the virtues encompassed by those roles. Against the dominant ideological background of nineteenth-century domesticity and with few other viable options, young women remained closely linked to their models and partners in this process, their mothers.

Other sources of information about nineteenth-century mother-daughter relationships corroborate the evidence presented by Smith-Rosenberg in her portrayal of a tightly knit female world with strong mother-daughter ties as the centerpiece. Letters and diaries clearly reveal that mothers and daughters maintained close and frequent contact when they were separated. They shared family news, expressed their concerns over one another's health, and discussed their daily activities, which sometimes included vocational as well as domestic matters.

Daughters who traveled shared the details of their journeys with their mothers. When Aurelia Smith visited relatives, she immediately conveyed the family news to her mother and urged her to answer as soon possible: "As I promised to write you soon after my arrival I will proceed to fullfill my agreement. . . . Write soon after you get this, Mother if your able write me all about your health."* After three weeks, Aurelia's anxiety was palpable: "Just imagine yourself two hundred miles from home and your mother sick would you not be anxious to hear often? Mother please write a few lines if your able."[46] Maria Avery and Fannie Russell also wrote lengthy accounts to their mothers when they visited friends and family.[47]

Young women who attended boarding school described their surroundings and discussed their feelings about being away from home. One unhappy daughter who wanted to leave school decided that people would think she had been dismissed if she left before the end of the term. Resigned to her fate, she sought her mother's advice about her courses. Although she wanted her father's opinion as well,

---

*Quoted material has been reproduced in the text with the original spelling and punctuation. Because the repeated use of *sic* to denote grammatical or spelling errors can be distracting and intrusive for the reader, this device has been omitted.

she obviously felt more comfortable corresponding with her mother. "I would like to write to father if I could think of a thing to say to him," she commented. Some weeks later, she confided to her mother that the situation at school had improved. Despite a variety of inconveniences, including bed bugs, she wrote, "I am glad that I did not go home. It just begins to seem a *little like home here.*"[48] The adjustment to school proved to be less traumatic for another young woman, although she would have liked to have "a desent looking glass" and "another pair of cloth shoes." She too looked forward to "a good long letter from home."[49]

Daughters who left home to take jobs described their work and their experiences to their mothers. Typically, these young women were teachers who would return home at the end of the school term.[50] Less frequently, a daughter's letters might relate her adventures in another occupation.[51] Correspondence with their mothers was vitally important to these daughters as it was to their younger counterparts at boarding school. Augusta Sewall enjoyed her mother's letters so much that she would have liked to receive them "two or three times a week" since "everything seems so fresh and new from home."[52]

Letters also provided an important link when mothers traveled. During her mother's extended trip to Europe, Emily Perkins Hale felt her absence keenly and looked forward to her return. Her letters contained detailed reports on her own activities and especially news of her daughter Ellen. In addition to her obvious delight in Ellen's development—"I wish you could hear her say her little Mother Goose things"—Emily reiterated her eagerness to see her mother and revealed the latter's importance to her: "I hardly dare to think yet how happy I shall be to have you really back again, but really I know I shall enjoy it more than I ever could have done before. It really seems to me sometimes, as if it was like losing my mother, and having her come to life again; for there is such a full sense of the delight it will be when I once get you again."[53]

Daughters often articulated their mothers' importance to them through expressions of concern over maternal health. Hannah Chandler ardently urged her mother to "be careful of your health—your Life is precious to us Children—long may it be granted to me especially—or I should be miserable without you—."[54] Sarah Watson

Dana, at school in Philadelphia, begged her mother not to write to her "unless you *are* well enough," noting affectionately, "I *can* believe, and do, that you love me, as never did Mother before you."[55] Middle-aged daughters also found the idea of maternal illness distressing. Augusta Sewall expressed her anxiety over her mother's physical problems as well as her determination to fulfill her own obligations to care for her. "I was so sorry to hear such an unfortunate account of your sickness. You don't know how badly it made me feel," she wrote on one occasion. Several months later, she clearly articulated her commitment to the nineteenth-century concept of a daughter's filial obligations, assuring her mother that she was prepared to come home and help her. Although her husband might be disappointed if she had to "go home to stay," he would understand: "There is a right and a wrong about all these things. I hope I shall not neglect doing for you so I shall have it to regret in after years, and you must not conceal your wants from me to that extent to produce such results. Now if you want me say so, and we will consult and make plans."[56]

Mothers reciprocated daughters' feelings of attachment and affection, sometimes expressing their own feelings quite eloquently. Abby Sewall, who had been a teacher herself, was glad to hear that her daughter found her teaching position satisfactory, but she looked forward to the end of the term. "I get along very well with the [domestic] work," she wrote, "yet I want my little girl at home as much as possible, no one can fill her place in the house or in my heart."[57] Mrs. Sewall found that Augusta's journeys back and forth during the school year reminded her of her own youth and her attachment to her own mother. Her poignant recollections attest to an enduring recognition of the value of the mother-daughter relationship and exemplify Signe Hammer's conception of a "transaction across three generations":

When she gives me the parting kiss, I often think of my own dear mother, and what my feelings were on parting with her, and how anxious I was to go home and see her. then I think did my mother have such feelings as I have, but she always had one or more daughters left when I was gone, then again I think how soon any girl may like me, be an orphan have no home to come to, and no mother to see.[58]

Some mothers recognized a daughter's worth in a more mundane or less effusive manner. When Anna Weston was away from home, her mother felt her absence at a very practical level: "You may readily suppose we missed you as we needed your assistance. . . . I hope my dear child if you live to come home you will be prepared to assist me in every department in house keeping—I need assistance and *you* are the only one I have to look to for it and I do hope I shall not be *disappointed.*"[59] Similarly, a laconic tone characterizes the record of the relationship between Melissa Carter and her mother, whose diaries document their frequent contact but make no reference to the nature of their feelings for one another. Melissa's mother regularly chronicled her interactions with her married daughter who lived some distance away—"Melissa Baby Born Wrote a letter to Melissa"; "found Melissa comfortable"; "Melissa went home"—but she expressed no explicit emotion in these brief diary entries.[60] Her daughter also carefully recorded their regular correspondence as well as the occasional exchange of gifts and their visits with each other.[61] She noted her mother's arrival two days after the birth of her daughter Ada ("Mother came this morning") and her departure eleven days later ("Mother went Home in the Stage"), but she offered no comment on these events.[62] The apparent reticence of these two women probably reflects their conception of a diary as a brief daily record of activities as opposed to an introspective narrative, and thus does not indicate any lack of mother-daughter affection. Despite the absence of concrete expressions of affection, the centrality of the relationship to their daily lives is clearly evident in the constancy of their contacts and the frequency of their references to one another.[63]

These examples, and others as well, certainly underscore the importance of the bonds between nineteenth-century American middle-class mothers and daughters.[64] Those bonds could even extend far enough to encompass maternal support for a daughter's professed desire for a career and her defiance of her father's wishes.[65] But the case for untroubled, harmonious relationships prior to the era of the "new woman" has been overstated: while Smith-Rosenberg found no evidence of discord in her study of the female world in the first two-thirds of the nineteenth century, other sources reveal the presence of both minor and more fundamental mother-daughter tensions during this period.

Various evidence indicates that mothers and daughters did not necessarily function as one another's closest confidantes. After she completed her studies at an academy in Hartford, Connecticut, Rebeccah Root missed the friends she had made there and longed to talk to someone in whom she could confide freely. At home, she lacked that opportunity: "Here is Mama but I cannot say any thing to her although the best of Mothers . . . I often think if I could see you or Harriet a few moments I should feel much more contented," she wrote to a friend.[66] In the same vein, Nancy Theriot suggests that the adult writings of Grace Dodge and Stella Gilman on the subject of mother-daughter relationships reflect their own personal experiences of a " 'lack of confidence' " between mothers and daughters.[67]

Ellen Rothman's study of courtship patterns in nineteenth-century America corroborates the suggestion that daughters did not necessarily share their most important secrets with their mothers. Despite the years young women spent in domestic apprenticeship, Rothman found little evidence to suggest that the bonds of domesticity encompassed maternal roles as daughters' confidantes or advisers in matters of courtship during the antebellum period. Her discussion of the close relationships enjoyed by nineteenth-century courting couples argues that it was only during a brief period in the last quarter of the century that mothers became fully and directly involved in this very important segment of their daughters' emotional lives.[68]

Even where daughters did confide in their mothers, conflict could arise. The mother of Kate Hodges was delighted when her daughter sought her parents' permission to correspond with young men while she was away at school, and she urged her to "continue to make us your confidants."[69] But she was disturbed by other aspects of Kate's behavior. "Do try & not write so much about *wants*. You are nicely fixed out & *really* need nothing save what I expected to get for you," she wrote sternly. Other letters reiterated Mrs. Hodges's instructions to her daughter to reduce the number and level of her requests, indicating that Kate's demands were a source of friction and conflict.[70] Apparently even her desire for more mail from home created problems, as evidenced by her mother's tone on this subject: "I feel rather hurt that you should think I fail in my duty toward you because I do not write twice a week. I think I deserve some credit for writing once a week punctually. I shall not be able to do more."[71]

Unmarried adult daughters who asserted any significant degree of personal independence might also experience conflict with their mothers. Since nineteenth-century family culture held that single women were obliged to serve the needs of parents and family members, those who wished to pursue other vocational interests could face strong opposition.[72] Cornelia Hancock refused her mother's request to leave her nursing job and come home: "I think you should all have sufficient control over your tempers not to be mad with me for doing what seems to me to be best," she wrote.[73] Emily Howland found the life of a domestic daughter unfulfilling and defended her desire to take a teaching position in a school for young black women in Washington, D.C.: "If I am different from the stereotyped kind [of daughter] I can't help it," she told her mother. "I know thy health is very poor but I can do nothing for it, and as long as no one would think of its deterring me from marrying and leaving home forever if I choose, . . . it certainly can no more be urged against my taking a few years or months perhaps, for a benevolent enterprise."[74] Fidelia Fiske also faced her mother's adamant opposition when she felt the call to pursue missionary work in Persia. Mrs. Fiske resisted her daughter's determined appeals on the grounds that Fidelia's most important Christian duty was to fulfill her obligations to her family.[75]

While acrimonious conflict over the competing claims of family obligations and personal ambitions did not necessarily characterize the relationships of the majority of single daughters and their mothers, a tract published in 1865 suggests that such conflict was not unusual by the mid-nineteenth century. Arguing that adult daughters should be allowed to lead their own lives even if their services were needed at home, Mary A. Dodge wrote:

No human being has a right to appropriate another human being's life— even if they be mother and daughter. You say that she owes life itself to her parents. True, but in such a way that it confers an additional obligation on them to give her every opportunity to make the most of life, and not in such a way as to justify them in monopolizing it, nor in such a way as to render her accountable to them alone for its use.[76]

The articulation of these sentiments highlights the relevance of this issue as one potential source of major mother-daughter tension in the decades before 1880.

An interesting additional issue pertaining to the expectations placed on single daughters arises from the fact that ironically, while Victorian culture exalted the cult of domesticity, it also implied that marriage was unpalatable. One could not be a wife and also fulfill any sort of vocational aspirations. To women raised to view sex as a necessary evil and to believe that they would have more in common with other women than with men, the possibility of remaining single, or of deferring marriage, might appear attractive despite the attendant economic and social difficulties.[77] To their mothers, however, the decision not to marry might seem threatening, a negation of their own lives and efforts. Hence the efforts of unmarried daughters to pursue their own interests could meet with adamant opposition.

Other substantial difficulties disrupted mother-daughter harmony as well. Alice James, highly intelligent and chronically ill, felt "emotionally undernourished" by her practical, Victorian mother, and apparently experienced significant relief when the latter died.[78] Although Marilla Turrill lived across the street from her mother, they did not speak to one another. " 'I have no friends here, not even Mother,' " she wrote to her brother. In the same letter, she described her mother as "deranged," commenting sarcastically, "No doubt she [her mother] would send her love if we were on speaking terms." Nevertheless, Marilla tried to keep in touch with her mother and even provided her with financial assistance after she was deserted by her husband.[79] Electa Loomis also experienced significant communication problems with her daughter, Ann, who apparently seldom wrote or visited her. More than a hint of sarcasm appears in a letter to Ann: "We should be glad to see you Mary & Elizabeth I never expect to see again they have not the means but you who have your thousand I should think would come once more & see how lonely and desolate every thing looks about home will you not be so good as to answer this letter."[80] While older mothers rarely accused daughters of actual abuse, many, like Mrs. Loomis, reproached them for their failure to write and visit often enough.[81]

The case of Emily Dickinson offers an intriguing example of a particularly troubled and extremely complex nineteenth-century mother-daughter relationship. Dickinson explicitly rejected her passive mother in both her letters and poems, writing on one occasion, "I never had a mother."[82] But her feelings were ambivalent. Although she regarded her invalid mother as a completely inadequate role model, and portrayed her as inconsequential and even ludicrous, she mourned her death.[83] This conscious and deliberate rejection apparently reflected the concerted effort of an ambitious daughter to avoid the destiny represented by her mother, that of the dutiful, domestic wife and mother. But Dickinson's reaction to her mother's death suggests that she also cared about her; through mourning, she may have expressed feelings of immediate loss, and also a sense of extended deprivation of the kind of maternal support and guidance that she had craved. In a certain sense, Dickinson's pursuit of a different destiny from that of her mother documents the pervasive influence of the mother-daughter relationship, albeit a negative influence.[84]

In contrast to Mrs. Dickinson, Hannah Blackwell provided a model of competence and strength for her ambitious daughters. But their relationships with her lacked warmth and intimacy. Although Mrs. Blackwell encouraged their achievements, she preferred to keep her female offspring under her control. She discouraged them from taking any interest in personal appearance or relationships with young men. On one occasion she arranged for her daughter Elizabeth to take a job she did not want. Later, when she disapproved of Elizabeth's decision to join the Episcopal church, she tried to force her to change her mind by crying and talking about her soul.[85] As a result of this sort of interaction, her daughters found it necessary to reject her demands for closeness and conformity and maintain their emotional distance from her. Emily Blackwell described this distance in a reference to her own feelings during a period when she nursed her mother through a serious illness: "I wished to act according to the laws of justice and right, if I could not lay aside my strong natural repugnance toward those to whom I am not drawn."[86] Obviously Emily Dickinson, the Blackwell sisters, and Alice James as well represent extreme examples rather than typical nineteenth-century daughters. Their talents and ambitions clearly distinguished them from the majority of their peers. But their experiences as daughters, and those of many of their less illustrious counterparts as well, indicate that the universe of mother-daughter relationships before the era of the "new woman" was not necessarily the halcyon world that has been portrayed. The evidence suggests a more complex picture, colored by tension as well as harmony.

Unquestionably, many mothers and daughters enjoyed close companionship and relied on one another for moral, emotional, and even financial support.[87] Their strong bonds continued the tradition and heritage of the colonial and early republican eras. Certainly the nineteenth-century social and cultural environment, with its emphasis on domesticity and on discrete male and female spheres, fostered such relationships. Many women worked constantly and diligently to fulfill their maternal obligations; they devoted themselves to their offspring, and their interactions with their daughters were gratifying to both. Proximity and a commonality of interests undoubtedly promoted and strengthened intergenerational ties between female family members. Indeed, in some instances, those ties apparently were so close that daughters identified with their mothers' experiences of ill health, developing the symptoms of anemia and weakness characteristic of "chlorosis," an ailment that seems to have mirrored the neurasthenic conditions that plagued many middle-class, nineteenth-century adult women.[88] Thus mother-daughter intimacy could encompass the sharing of invalidism as well as domestic roles and interests.

As the phenomena of sickly women and "chlorotic" girls suggest, the lives of middle-class Victorian females were not free of conflict and tension. The "cult of true womanhood" prescribed a set of expectations that would have been difficult, if not impossible, for most wives and mothers to meet.[89] Contradictions between this cultural ideal and the reality of their lives must have seemed especially troublesome to women who realized that they could not live up to the abstract image of the self-sacrificing wife and mother, but might still judge themselves by this standard.[90] This situation was further complicated by the fact that mothers were expected to socialize their daughters to fulfill the same image. In this context, it is hardly surprising to learn that conflict as well as intimacy characterized mother-daughter interactions prior to 1880. A recent analysis of the relationships between nineteenth-century cultural patterns and family patterns by Steven Mintz argues that broader cultural tensions were reflected in specific conflicts within individual Victorian families.[91] Certainly in the case of mother-daughter relationships, the pressure of the cultural prescriptions for women contributed to the development of tension, while at the same time, the cult of domesticity supported intimacy.

Thus, although the earlier tradition of female friendship and closeness continued into the nineteenth century, mother-daughter relationships before the appearance of the "new woman" were not always smooth and untroubled. This conclusion raises several interesting issues. Were the problems experienced by middle-class mothers and daughters prior to 1880 harbingers of a full-blown conflict that developed later? Did conflict rather than harmony dominate mother-daughter relationships during the late nineteenth and early twentieth centuries? How did the relationship evolve after 1920? And finally, is conflict endemic to the modern mother-daughter relationship?

The assumptions of the existing historiography, which accentuates the problematic nature of mother-daughter interactions in the late nineteenth and early twentieth centuries, together with laments about more recent difficulties between mothers and daughters, suggest the need for serious attention to the decades between 1880 and 1920, and to the later twentieth century, as possible watersheds in the history of the relationship. It is important to ascertain whether these periods witness major change between a halcyon past and a more troubled present, or whether they confirm the validity of a more universalistic approach to the history of the mother-daughter relationship. The quest for answers to these questions defines the focus of the chapters that follow.

CHAPTER 2

"MY GIRLS' MOTHERS": THE EMOTIONOLOGY OF MOTHER-DAUGHTER RELATIONSHIPS, 1880–1920

I N 1917 a contributor to the popular women's magazine, *Good Housekeeping*, made the following assertion:

> In the lifetime of girls even twenty years old, the tradition of what girls should be and do in the world has changed as much as heretofore in a century. It used to be that girls looked forward with confidence to domestic life as their destiny. That is still the destiny of most of them, but it is a destiny that in this generation seems to be modified for all, and avoided by very many. . . .
>
> The mothers of these modern girls are very much like hens that have hatched out ducks. Whether they believe in current feminine aspirations or not makes not very much difference.[1]

This perception of an emerging female generation gap highlights the climate of change and transition that pervaded women's lives between 1880 and 1920 and offered daughters the vision of a new future for themselves—a future that looked decisively different from the future their mothers had been offered as they had entered adulthood. It was this disruption of generational continuity and the apparent attendant tension that concerned the author of the *Good Housekeeping* commentary, and contributors to other contemporary popular periodicals as well. Throughout the late nineteenth and early twentieth centuries, articles, editorials, and advice columns implied that serious problems existed in the area of mother-daughter relationships. Here was a translation into women's family relationships of a concern about adolescence that was spreading around 1900, but with a potential for socially derived misunderstanding added in.

Several major themes defined the parameters of this apparent crisis. Much of the commentary centered on a perceived lack of intergenerational communication with regard to both trivial and more serious matters, and addressed the relative obligations of mothers and daughters in this area. Writers also deplored the absence of proper discipline and training for young women as reflected in their demeanor and conduct toward their mothers, and more generally as well. And they stressed the need for mutual respect and consideration on the part of adult daughters and their mothers. Some of this advice reflected traditional domestic ideology, but other discussions acknowledged and responded to the new social and cultural climate of the era, and the associated changes in women's lives.

The periodical literature portrayed daughters as more of a problem than sons. One observer believed that women were "much more in a state of becoming, of transition, than men," and that a "general law of cross-inheritance," interpreted to mean that a daughter rarely shared her mother's temperament or preferences, further complicated the situation: "If the mother starved for a college education and has yearned all her life to make some small slit of an entrance into the realm of ideas, she invariably has a daughter with an absorbed interest in hairdressing and refrigerators."[2] Whether or not this description had any basis in reality, it clearly reflected the societal perception of a female generation gap. And the potential for incompatibility posited by such a perception provided the focus for extensive discussion of the mother-daughter relationship in popular periodicals.

The commentary on communication problems frequently attributed daughters' failures to confide in their mothers to maternal behaviors and attitudes. In 1884, the first year of its existence, the *Ladies Home Journal* took a firm stand on this matter: "It is the companionable mothers who are the only ones to keep their girls' confidences. The severely critical mothers are not of this clan, nor those who are impatient of a child's many failures and shortcomings."[3] Subsequent issues offered advice along similar lines. For example, mothers were told to avoid sending a daughter to boarding school, which would make her "reticent and disinclined to talk of things nearest her heart." This sort of reluctance to communicate would not be surprising if a girl was sent away to live, eat, study, walk, and "worst of all, *talk* together" with other girls, it was suggested.[4]

It was also important for a mother to take an interest in what her daughter was doing; to remember what it was like to be eighteen; to keep herself young; and to avoid "sighing" and melancholy moods.[5] Mothers who failed to keep up with the times risked losing daughters' respect, and thus their confidence. The age of sixteen could be a particularly critical time for the relationship: "Anything that tends to make a girl look down upon her mother is fatal to the best interests of both." Hence, "antiquated" ideas must be avoided, and a mother's attire should be up to date.[6]

On the other hand, daughters should not have unlimited freedom, and communication could be especially important in this context. A mother, as the "social head of the household," ought to supervise her daughter's friendships and associations. Where a mother and daughter shared "an intimacy of exchange of thought," however, the daughter could "safely enjoy much freedom, because she is constantly, Minerva like, protected by an aegis."[7] Nevertheless, as this image suggested, no aspect of a girl's life should be exempt from her mother's scrutiny; mothers must accept and fulfill their responsibilities for preparing their daughters to lead "self-reliant, helpful, valuable lives."[8] They must trust their daughters, show them affection, and explain their reasons when they found it necessary to refuse their requests.[9] Daughters were urged to do their part to improve communication: "Never be ashamed to tell her, who should be your best friend and confidant, of all you think and feel. It is very strange that so many young girls will tell every person before 'mother' that which is most important she should know," one writer advised. "Have no secrets that you would not be willing to trust to your mother. She is your best friend, and is ever devoted to your honor and interest." Another suggested, "Take as much care to cultivate the friendship of your mother as you would that of a stranger. . . . It's a thousand times more worth having and she'll always put you first."[10] The tenuousness and superficiality of school friendships were contrasted with the fact that "in all the wide world there is no friend like a loving mother."[11] If a mother appeared to be unreceptive to her daughter's confidences, the daughter should make an effort to break down the wall between them; a daughter who had never confided in her mother should not be surprised if her mother was not instantly sympathetic when she finally did try to talk to her.[12]

In exhortations reminiscent of earlier nineteenth-century sentimentality, daughters were also advised to devote more attention to their mothers, to try to give them pleasure, and to help them with their social duties. One writer urged her readers: "Dear girls, if your mother is still spared you, you cannot cherish her too lovingly or honor her birthdays too much." She recalled a mother who had saved a poem written for her by her daughter; after her death, the family found the poem with the "garments she had prepared, years before" for her burial.[13] In another article, the same writer appealed to daughters to increase both the number of occasions and the length of time spent with their mothers, and to endeavor not to move far away from them after marriage. "We seem to need our mother all through life, and the old hungry ache for her is just the same even after we ourselves have grown grayheaded," she observed.[14] A mother would take pleasure in her daughter's presence, in her confidences, in her solicitousness, in her assistance with social duties such as pouring tea and arranging flowers, and in the opportunity to meet "any young man" her daughter met. Indeed that opportunity should be automatic as it was "due to her position."[15] It was also a mother's right to be called "Mamma" no matter how old her daughter was; by addressing her mother in this way, a girl would give her "that pleasure which it should be your duty, every day you live, to give her."[16]

Similarly intense discussions identified proper discipline and training as another matter for serious concern. Late nineteenth-century periodicals characterized American daughters as forward and overindulged, and castigated their mothers for the fact that American girls were not as well behaved as their European counterparts. Disrespectful daughters were viewed as "vulgar." A mother who was "all she ought to be" would see to it that her daughter would respect her, but unfortunately all American mothers did not have "this art."[17] One writer complained about mothers who sacrificed their own youth, appearance, health, and well-being to serve their daughters' needs, and were criticized or ignored in return. "The American girl is taught that she is a young princess from her cradle to the altar," she commented. "It is a great misfortune when she forgets that the mother of a princess must be a queen, or queen regent, and should so be treated."[18] The cause of this misfortune was clear; the mothers themselves were responsible: "The recklessness of some of our countrywomen, in regard to their girls, is terrible. The advantage the girls take of it is more terrible still."[19]

Popular magazines continued to address the theme of discourteous American daughters after the turn of the century. In 1910 an article in *Harper's Bazaar* criticized the tendency of the American daughter to "discipline and train and instruct her mother whenever she condescends to lift her down off the shelf where, as a general thing, she keeps her deposited."[20] Editorials in the *Ladies Home Journal* deplored the fact that American mothers tolerated rude behavior, failed to teach their offspring the skills of housewifery, and sent them out into the world with the feeling that they could have fun, go anywhere, and be the best dressed in the group. Given the negligence of her mother, one could not blame the American girl for the situation, according to the magazine's conservative editor, Edward Bok. "It is too much to say, as has recently been said, that American motherhood has failed," he observed, "but who will say, on the other hand, that American motherhood has succeeded?" The influential and outspoken Bok rejected the notion that anything more than maternal negligence was involved where difficult daughters were concerned: "The parent is on trial: not the times or the conditions," he maintained.[21]

The first decades of the new century also introduced a new emphasis in the popular periodicals, a concern about maternal reluctance to answer daughters' biological, intellectual, and religious questions. An earlier discussion of this problem had reminded mothers discreetly that they needed to win their daughters' confidence from early childhood in order to be able to discuss with them "things a mother should tell a girl." It was important to answer a daughter's questions directly, to tell her what she wanted to know about "the mysteries of life which trouble her innocent soul," and to tell her "simply and truthfully all that you wish your mother had told you."[22] Later discussions offered more graphic advice. Young women whose mothers failed to equip them with basic information regarding the facts of life could suffer grave difficulties. Lack of knowledge and misinformation led girls into serious trouble. This situation was not confined to the "so-called ignorant classes," but pertained to highly educated daughters as well. A physician warned mothers that ignorance rather than curiosity "ruins little girls."[23]

An anonymous contributor to *Harper's Bazaar* related her personal frustration and resentment over her own mother's avoidance of vital questions and concerns, and the tendency of other mothers to behave in the same fashion: "I do not think I am exaggerating when I say that the average mother in this country—the average, educated, intelligent mother—avoids participating in the intellectual development of her daughters." This young woman reported that she had experienced no problems with her mother until she started "to think." Although she acquired a "bare and almost fragmentary knowledge of the ordinary physiological facts of life," her mother had never alluded to "the relation of the sexes" in her presence. The mental awakening she experienced in college generated a multitude of questions she wanted to discuss, but her mother consistently steered their conversations into more comfortable areas: "She seemed . . . to be living on the inside of a crystal ball. I could see her and communicate with her, but as it were, by signs."[24] Other accounts supported this daughter's indictment of maternal reticence and described the degradation of young women who were the rebellious victims of unsatisfied curiosity.[25]

Early twentieth-century periodicals also indicated that the female generation gap continued, and indeed might widen, as young women grew up. Numerous discussions addressed the failure of college-educated daughters and their mothers to respect each others' values and points of view and the impatience of adult daughters with the whims of aging mothers. Some authors lamented the disappearance of the "home daughter" and the fate of mothers who pined away at home for their career-oriented offspring.[26] Others advised parents to recognize that a young woman who had attended college could not be expected to resume the role of the dependent daughter-at-home, and urged mothers to support their daughters in their search for fulfilling activity; a wise and experienced mother could offer vital assistance when new female aspirations clashed with "the inevitable and indispensable incidents of life."[27]

Additional guidance directed daughters to use tact, kindness, and patience rather than criticism in their interactions with aging (middle-aged!) mothers, to pay attention to them, to compliment them, and to accept their foibles rather than try to change them.[28] A minister observed that young women should fulfill their family obligations, but noted that God was the final authority to which they must answer for their decisions.[29] Some authors stressed the traditional obligations of daughters to respect and abide by their mothers' judgments regarding social occasions and acquaintances, and to heed their advice in matters of courtship and marriage.[30] Earlier commentary regarding maternal involvement in courtship had offered similar guidance, as, for example, with regard to a reader's question concerning elopement: "If you take my advice you will go directly to your mother, tell her plainly about this man, and do nothing until she has made his acquaintance and decided for you."[31] One editorial deplored the lack of deference demonstrated by a young woman who treated her mother as if she were a "painted post," ignoring her in a friend's presence. Its author reiterated the necessity for respect and esteem, even where a mother, "by some unhappy combination of circumstances . . . is not equal to her daughter's advancement—brought about, remember, by the mother's sacrifice usually."[32]

While daughters were certainly admonished to do their part to ease the strains in the mother-daughter relationship, on balance the periodical literature tended to portray them as the aggrieved parties rather than as the individuals responsible for maintaining intergenerational harmony. In 1894 an article entitled "The Mother of My Girl" had alluded with dismay to the many letters from readers that caused its author to wonder "what the mothers all over the world are doing" regarding their obligations to their daughters. In the same vein, an editorial in *The Independent* in September 1901 observed that "the unnatural burden of filial obligations and scruples imposed by some mothers is the prime factor of the secret antagonism existing between them [mothers and daughters]. . . . As a matter of fact, there is less need of confidences between the two than is generally supposed,—and much more need of confidence."[33] Mothers were primarily responsible for the prevalence of conflict and dissension, then, and it was their duty to build close relationships with young daughters and to foster independence in grown ones. This process must begin long before a daughter reached adolescence, and a mother must always be ready to listen: "If there isn't time for Baby's bath and the confidences of the little girl of nine, it is better to let some one else bathe the baby." In cases of maternal "despotism," where adult women remained enslaved to the wishes of "imperious" mothers, permanent alienation could be the result.[34]

Mothers were also blamed for the deteriorating health of daughters who became anemic as a result of academic pressures, excessive social life, and improper diet.[35] And they were accused both of failing to provide daughters with the "womanly training" the public schools did not offer, and of refusing to support daughters' efforts to practice the type of domestic science that they learned in school.[36] A mother whose love was "petty and possessive" might have a "narrowing" influence; on the other hand, one whose interests were "scattered," who was busy with clubs and social work, might be at fault where a daughter turned out to be " 'progressive.' "[37] It is hardly surprising that this climate of contradictory criticism also encompassed the confessions of mothers who lamented their own deficiencies as parents, as well as those of daughters who regretted their filial negligence.[38]

The tendency to depict daughters as the victims of maternal ineptness reflected the more general trend toward the promulgation of "scientific" child-rearing advice designed to foster the development of mothers as experts at their jobs. It suggested a marketing strategy too, an effort to address the perceived concerns of young women and thus to sell more magazines. As the reference to the content of letters directed to the author of "The Mother of My Girl" indicates, reader response also may have encouraged the continued publication of this point of view.[39] But these explanations omit any consideration of another important factor which must be taken into account in assessing the propensity for mother blaming: the nature of the role played by the personal opinions and idiosyncrasies of individual writers and editors. For example, for several years the column in which the "Mother of My Girl" article appeared was actually written by Edward Bok under the pseudonym Ruth Ashmore. No doubt the material published in this column, like the content of his signed editorials, reflected his own conservative biases at least as much as it articulated broader societal concerns.[40] Thus in this instance, and undoubtedly in many other cases as well, the nature of the prescriptive literature probably offers more evidence about the values of the writer than about any broader cultural or societal values.[41]

Who read the advice proffered by Edward Bok and his counterparts? How large an audience did their prescriptions reach? At the turn of the century, the major women's magazines were characterized by low prices, mass production, and national distribution. When Bok assumed the editorship of the *Ladies Home Journal* in 1889, it was an established periodical with a circulation of about 440,000. By 1893 this figure had increased to 700,000, at a cost of ten cents per copy, and it passed the million mark in 1904. The Ruth Ashmore column, "Side Talks with Girls," elicited some 158,000 letters from readers over a period of sixteen years, and employed three stenographers; although he had started it, Bok turned over the responsibility for this department to a female colleague because the letters seemed too intimate for his eyes.[42] The extensive circulation and apparent reader response suggest that the *Ladies Home Journal* published articles about matters of concern to many middle-class American women. As one study of popular periodicals describes it, the content was "neither highbrow or lowbrow, it rode the large middle ground of public taste."[43]

Other women's magazines followed similar patterns. *Woman's Home Companion,* first published in 1885 under the title *Ladies Home Companion* and retitled in 1897, achieved a circulation of 737,000 by 1912. In 1920, the circulation reached 2,598,000, with advertising revenues of $8,500,000. Like the *Ladies Home Journal,* it published both fiction and nonfiction, articles about food and fashion, practical advice for the homemaker, consumer advice, and the like. The *Delineator,* which first appeared in 1873, dealt with fashion until 1894, when it broadened its focus. Fiction appeared in its pages in 1897, and by the early twentieth century it also included general nonfiction articles. Its circulation reached 480,000 in 1900 and grew to slightly more than a million by 1920. *Good Housekeeping* and *Harper's Bazar* (later *Bazaar*) were also founded in the late nineteenth century. The latter was modeled on a women's periodical published in Berlin; it appeared weekly until 1901, when it became a monthly publication. At the turn of the century, the former emphasized topics such as simplified housekeeping, canning fruits, preparing Sunday dinners, fashions, and child rearing; eventually it included more "scientific" home economics material derived from investigations conducted first at the Good Housekeeping Experiment Station, and later in the laboratories and kitchens of the Good Housekeeping Bureau and Good Housekeeping Institute.[44]

The public associated these women's magazines, and other popular periodicals, with the powerful editors whose personalities were strongly reflected in their publications. Edward Bok's editorial tenure lasted for thirty years. Other leading magazines also retained influential editors whose opinions shaped the unique character of each one.[45] Bok was strongly antifeminist, and the pages of the *Ladies Home Journal* articulated his conservative point of view. *Good Housekeeping* and *Harper's Bazar* were more progressive, but these publications also stressed the obligations of wifehood and motherhood, albeit in the context of a "scientific" approach to home economics and parenting. Both emphasized women's roles as enlightened consumers. *Bazar* also concerned itself with matters beyond household affairs, including fashion, "society," and arts and letters. It supported women's suffrage and other reforms, but it rejected feminist aspirations for careers outside the home.[46] If circulation figures offer any accurate interpretation of reader response to periodical literature, apparently a large, presumably female audience was receptive to the spectrum of ideas, including those concerning the interactions of mothers and daughters, represented in these publications.

Popular advice manuals of the period echo many of the same themes addressed in the periodicals—for example, the importance of open communication between mothers and daughters, the assignment of responsibility for the maintenance of intergenerational harmony primarily to mothers, and the necessity of acknowledging the needs of adult daughters. A dichotomy between traditional and more progressive points of view is clearly reflected in the nature of the advice proffered to mothers by the authors of these manuals. The sheer volume of coverage in this literature, like the extensive treatment of mother-daughter issues in contemporary magazines, suggests that such problems were of great interest to middle-class, female readers.

The advice manuals emphatically labeled mother-daughter communication as a key problem and underscored maternal obligations in this area. "It is not enough that we encourage our children to talk freely to us. . . . We must prove ourselves worthy and able to give counsel no less than sympathy; must not have 'settled down' below the level of their requirements," the well-known writer Marion Harland reminded her readers in a tone reminiscent of much of the periodical literature.[47] In a volume dedicated "To the one who has made my life most complete and ever been my dearest comrade My Daughter," Gabrielle E. Jackson emphasized "the mutual understanding which may and should be as inseparable from a mother's and daughter's intercourse as are life and breathing." Toward the creation of this understanding, she urged mothers to respect daughters; to take their concerns and interests seriously; to involve them in decorating and caring for their rooms; and to talk to them about the books they read. It was essential to make a daughter feel that she could depend on her mother no matter what might happen: "She does not know it at seven—she does not analyze it and put the feeling into words; at twenty-seven it will have become her second creed."[48] Jackson criticized the fact that while many mothers loved their daughters devotedly, they frequently failed to make companions of them. In her opinion, the mother's responsibility was clear:

There should be no one upon earth to whom that daughter should feel so ready to go with every thought, every hope, every plan. If she does not, it is her mother's fault. Never for a single instant should she feel that her interests are separated from her mother's. No matter how trivial they may seem to the maturer eyes of that mother, she is failing pitifully in her duty if she allows her daughter to suspect it. Indeed she should not permit herself so to regard them.[49]

In another volume entitled improbably *A series of don'ts for mothers, who may, or may not, stand in need of them,* the same author offered similar advice, stressing the importance of fostering open communication, providing emotional support, refraining from criticism, and maintaining a youthful outlook. Here again, the tendency to blame mothers for the existence of problems was unambiguous: "Don't forget that if your daughter is boisterous abroad there must be something amiss at home."[50]

Caroline W. Latimer offered a more sophisticated and distinctly modern interpretation of the apparent reluctance of daughters to confide in their mothers. She suggested that reticence on the part of a young woman reflected not an intentional desire to shut her mother out, but a temporary inability to understand and express coherently the multitude of confusing new ideas, questions, and aspirations passing through her mind during adolescence. While she recognized the potential for hurt feelings on the part of a mother who might suddenly find herself excluded by an adolescent daughter, she counseled patience and restraint: "If a girl finds that her confidence is not forced and is sensible of that silent comprehension and sympathy which demands no recognition, she will give her confidence again fully and freely as she did before; but interference with the process of self-evolution just at this period will certainly impair confidence for the future."[51] Here again, mothers were expected to assume full responsibility for fostering open communication with their daughters. Parents who managed to refrain from interfering in every detail of a daughter's life and tempered their natural concern with tact and attention to personal freedom would be amply rewarded, however, for they would secure "that lifelong friendship with their daughter, which is one of life's most precious possessions."[52]

Dorothy Canfield Fisher also urged a more modern approach to mother-daughter relationships. In an acknowledgment of the changing times, she noted: "The jangling of many keys is in our ears. These are twentieth-century days. Let us take heed how we force locks, rather than open them." Fisher advised mothers to consider the possibility that an unruly daughter might need, "instead of exhortations to submission, a number of innocent outlets to her desire for gayety and fun: to be allowed to bring her friends home with her, for example; to be taken to the theater; to go on walks with her mother."[53] She observed that mother-daughter ties are not always close despite the blood relationship, and she argued that compatibility between parents and their mature offspring must be based on "spiritual affinity," or at least "mutual respect." Parents who proved to be "unworthy of respect" then could expect to have strained relationships with their children.[54] With regard specifically to women's expectations for their future roles in their daughters' lives, Fisher reminded her readers:

Our daughters do not look forward to matrimony with the fixity of intention of our grandmothers. It may very easily happen that they will prefer some other form of service to the blessed old way of family life, so dear to us. In any case we will almost certainly not become grandmothers until after our children have had several years of independent life and have achieved a maturity of character and an experience of affairs which make them able and eager to cope themselves with their own domestic problems.

Hence she suggested that mothers should prepare to occupy themselves with other activities rather than anticipate active involvement in the upbringing of their grandchildren; the mother who can live constructively without her children is "the very one they will want in their lives," she noted.[55]

Fisher's recognition of the changes occurring in women's lives was echoed in other progressive commentary that clearly mirrored the new emphasis on college education for women. In 1910 Caroline Latimer observed that while female college students had been viewed by their friends with "mingled admiration and disapproval" thirty years earlier, families now routinely considered the option of higher education for their daughters. She also reassured parents that most young women who went to college managed to remain healthy.[56] Other authors pointed out that a mother's job became more difficult if her daughter went away to college. It was vital for her to keep in touch with all aspects of her daughter's college activities for "college life is, unquestionably, a critical test of the mother's hold upon the daughter and the daughter's love for the mother." Hence mothers should write regularly to their daughters, relating "every little happening of the home life," make their college friends welcome at home, and visit the college whenever possible to "make them feel that you are in a sense one of them."[57] Additional problems surfaced when daughters finished college. Young women were not likely to return after four busy, happy years and settle comfortably into home routines; they were often deeply unhappy, and they needed to have constructive activities. Noting that "the breaking up of mental and physical habits that have in four years' time become a kind of second nature" is very painful and difficult, Helen Ekin Starrett advised parents to help their daughters to plan for this transition by encouraging them to find satisfying occupations such as teaching or settlement work even if this necessitated their leaving home.[58] While Starrett acknowledged that marriage might be the ideal solution, she pointed out that families could not depend on this occurring within a year or two of a daughter's college graduation. In the absence of thoughtful preparation for this period, a young woman could be "confronted with blank nothingness." She also advocated paid employment, even for young women from comfortable families.[59]

A similarly untraditional tone characterized Margaret Sangster's approach to the issues surrounding the impact of college on daughters' lives. She applauded the benefits of higher education for young women—"the mental discipline, the balance of faculties, the admirable poise gained in college." A college education could broaden a daughter's horizons and prepare her to be self-supporting or to pursue further professional study. It would also defer her marriage, which would allow her to have a pleasant girlhood.[60] While a young woman with a college diploma might be more interested in pursuing a career than in marrying, this should not be construed as a tragedy, she advised, since many professional opportunities awaited "the unmarried girl" who was "not only wanted, but clamored for today."[61] Sangster recommended that daughters who did remain at home after college should be treated as adults; a daughter should not be "hampered by an overbearing mother," compelled to ask permission to buy a dress or have a tea party, or expected to defer to her brothers as was the case in some families. She should be permitted to receive wages or have an expense allowance, or she should be given carte blanche to spend her father's money.[62]

Like the periodical literature, advice manuals reproved mothers for their daughters' ignorance of, or misinformation about, puberty and the facts of life. Rejecting traditional female reticence about such matters, they criticized maternal reluctance to discuss these issues and maternal inclinations to protect daughters from such knowledge or to invent silly stories rather than provide accurate information, both tendencies that forced young women to learn about these matters from servants and schoolmates. No suitable source of information would be available if a mother failed her daughter in this regard because no other "decent" woman would discuss the subject with her. Thus what should be a daughter's "dower, bearing the seal of the Divine Father" too often became a "foul secret."[63] Marion Harland indicted not only the contemporary generation of mothers for their shortcomings in this area, but their predecessors as well, projecting a clearly untraditional point of view on this sensitive issue: "The pseudo delicacy that drives the pure-hearted child away from the one who should be her confidante and teacher, to the prurient whisperings of the school-fellow who stays all night with her almost every week, or the vulgar gossiping of servant girls, is no new idiosyncrasy of well-meaning mothers. Scruples and habits have come down to them (again) 'by ordinary generation.' "[64] Gabrielle Jackson shared the same concern, advising mothers not to keep daughters "in a moral 'straight-jacket,' lest sooner or later you meet with a rude awakening."[65] While young girls would not be harmed by reading things they did not understand, another writer observed, adolescent daughters should be guided to appropriate literature about relations between men and women. Once again, "The important thing in this matter, as in all matters involving the question of sex, is that the relation between a girl and her mother shall be of such a nature that she will seek the explanation of things half understood from the legitimate source and thus learn the right way of regarding them."[66]

Straightforward advice of this sort suggests that some authors realistically acknowledged the changes in women's lives and their implications, as they addressed an audience in need of new guidelines. However, other writers projected a distinctly more conservative tone. Articulating a point of view reminiscent of earlier nineteenth-century ideology, Aline Lydia Hoffman argued that "our lot, our principal office is, then, maternity. . . . Motherhood is the paramount duty of woman, *the beginning and the end of her social duty.*" Thus motherhood was a woman's primary vocation, whether with regard to her own children or to all "mankind." For daughters who did not marry, Hoffman envisioned "a future of complete contentment in the motherhood which consists in their self-devotion to humanity and to their suffering and afflicted neighbors." To this end, she maintained that it was a mother's duty to tell her daughter about her responsibilities for the happiness of others, to "teach her early to forget self, to be useful, to help others, and thereby fulfill her destiny."[67] With regard to sex education, Hoffman found the issue of enlightening daughters "on certain matters of which they know nothing, or, to speak more correctly, matters of which we are agreed to assume that they know nothing," a difficult one. She noted that "one's instinct" was to avoid such discussions, in which case men would have to become more moral. Nevertheless, she conceded the necessity of instructing the next generation of mothers in the realities of life, at least until males had indeed progressed in the moral realm. It would be unjust, she concluded, "to bind our daughters to a destiny for themselves, and above all, to seal the future of their children by a contract, the nature and conditions which they are ignorant."[68]

James C. Fernald shared Hoffman's traditional point of view. He argued that the home remained the appropriate sphere for women, and he favored domestic education for daughters rather than the sort of advanced education that would render their mothers irrelevant to their lives, like the "slave 'mamma' of old Southern days, cherished by those entering a different and loftier existence, but not imagined capable to instruct, and not to be obeyed, except temporarily and under protest."[69] Fernald advised against permitting young women to "rush" to the cities where they would encounter a variety of temptations. He maintained that girls from good homes should not compete for jobs with poor girls who really needed the token wages they might be paid. Instead, they should remain at home "and help the dear mother who cared so tenderly for [them] in the weary loving years gone by," thus preventing her from becoming a broken old woman by the time she reached her mid-forties.[70] Frederic William Farrer also stressed the importance of women's traditional roles as wives or as single daughters who cared for their fathers and helped their mothers at home. With regard to those who did not conform to these expectations, he remarked: "Few things shock us more in the records of history than the mention of *bad* daughters. Happily they are not numerous."[71]

The impact of conservative ideology can also be discerned in advice literature that directly reflected the influence of the professionalization of motherhood. For example, Ellen Key's call for a renaissance of motherhood emphasized the value of serious, organized education, including a year of social service work, as the appropriate preparation for this important task. But her conception of motherhood remained traditional. She deplored the notion of the working mother who left the care of her children to others, an idea she considered "the death of home-life and family life." And she viewed the aspirations of the "new woman" with trepidation: "And has our race ever been afflicted by a more dangerous disease than the one which at present rages among women: the sick yearning to be 'freed' from the most essential attribute of their sex? In motherliness, the most indispensable human qualities have their root."[72] Elizabeth

Macfarlane Chesser also advocated proper training for motherhood and women's sphere. Although she acknowledged the trend toward providing higher education for daughters as well as sons, and asserted the value of a full opportunity for mental development, she favored a specialized curriculum to prepare young women for maternity. Chesser proposed that since no one knew which girls would eventually be mothers, all of them should be required to study home economics before attending college.[73]

Even Helen Ekin Starrett, whose logical, reasoned recommendations for assisting daughters to make the transition from college to the future suggested a rather progressive frame of reference, maintained an essentially traditional position with regard to young women's destinies. While she urged the wisdom of proper preparation for some sort of nondomestic work for pragmatic reasons—in case a woman never married or experienced a temporary family emergency —Starrett stressed the primacy of preparation to assume the duties of the mistress of a home.[74] Independent women could be impressive, she conceded, but, she reminded her readers, "it is probable that we all feel, when planning for the future of our daughters, that if they are called upon to fulfil the whole of woman's natural destiny, if they become wives and mothers, their normal condition, and that which would be the most favorable to their own happiness and complete and harmonious development, would be that of being cared for." Indeed, she continued, "there is no rightly-constituted woman who under the right conditions does not enjoy having all her temporal wants supplied and being cared for and protected."[75] Thus a conservative bias remained discernible even in so-called "scientific" advice for mothers. A volume published as late as 1925, which advocated the gradual allocation of more freedom to girls, warned against treating daughters as if they were friends and contemporaries: "Perhaps the most difficult thing of all for mothers who are young and vital and who feel like sisters to their daughters, is to learn that this is not altogether a wholesome relationship. The generations are distinct and are meant to be distinct, and there comes a time . . . when the daughter does not need a sister but a mother."[76] The author of this volume also believed that young women should be encouraged to do something useful rather than to "drift" after they finished school. Her definition of "useful" remained very traditional, however, as she observed in this context that those with artistic talent were particularly fortunate since art can be easily integrated with home activities. Employment in businesses such as bookstores and dress shops might be acceptable, but a woman must give up this type of work in order to raise a family.[77]

While all advice manuals certainly did not offer identical guidance regarding mother-daughter relationships, the themes of maternal expertise and professionalism, still conceptualized within the framework of domesticity, characterized most discussions. This trend reflected the stress on child study in discussions of family life more generally during the period following 1870. The publication of numerous books and monographs focusing on child development between 1880 and 1900, and the establishment of child-study programs at various universities, highlighted the emphasis on developing new, scientific knowledge about children and implementing that knowledge in the context of family life. The founding of discussion groups such as the Society for the Study of Child Nature in 1888 in New York, which met weekly to consider questions such as "Should a desire for the right of franchise be inculcated in daughters?" illustrated the influence of the child-study movement.[78] However, the interest in child study could generate conservative as well as liberal advice.

Although the distinction was not always clear, for the most part the prescriptive literature presented two different perspectives on the mother-daughter issue. The double emphasis, on the importance of avoiding conflict in the putatively harmonious mother-daughter relationship and the responsibilities of mothers for responding appropriately to daughters' needs, and the striking contrast between traditional and modernist views mirrored the intensity of the cultural dialectic between tradition and innovation, the "divided mind" of the era.[79] This literature also reflected societal anxiety about the changes that challenged the tenets of the nineteenth-century cult of domesticity and threatened to dismantle the barriers between the separate spheres. As Mary Ryan has noted, American women in the past "have been subjected to the most excessive amounts and extreme forms of instructions, all of which have sought to escort them into roles that provide vital services to the social order."[80] In the case of the period-

icals and advice manuals, the subtext in the "instructions" was concerned with the preservation of the integrity of women's sphere and
the traditional image of femininity. The maintenance of harmonious
mother-daughter relationships would enable mothers to continue to
train daughters to fulfill their domestic roles; mother-daughter conflict would threaten that continuity and would also disclose the presence of unacceptable anger.

Whether the tone was conservative or liberal, however, both the
substance and the frequency of the discussions of mother-daughter
relationships in the periodical and advice literature emphasized the
centrality of the issue and implied that tension and discord between
mothers and daughters troubled more than a few middle-class American families during this period of transition in women's lives. Given
the extent of the changes occurring in American society, the character of the prescriptive literature is certainly not surprising. Nor does
it reflect a different image of mother-daughter interactions from that
suggested by historians who have previously considered mother-
daughter relationships in this era. This literature was also undeniably
popular. These sources, then, would seem to support the contention
that unprecedented conflict intruded upon the mother-daughter relationship during the period 1880–1920—and indeed perhaps determined the nature of that relationship in the twentieth century.

Certainly periodicals, advice manuals, and other cultural documents cannot be assumed to reflect actual family behavior and experiences, but they can often mirror real concerns.[81] The correspondence between the social and cultural background of change in
women's experiences and the tone of the prescriptive literature suggests that the decades of the late nineteenth and early twentieth
centuries may represent a turning point in female family relationships, in fact as well as in perception. Did mother-daughter relationships in middle-class families develop a new element of conflict during these years of transition? Does this conflict foreshadow the sense
of tension and ambivalence in the relationship that would be articulated both formally and informally by even more American women
in late twentieth-century society? The following chapter will consider
these possibilities further through an examination of the fictional
treatment of mother-daughter relationships during the years between 1880 and 1920.

CHAPTER 3

"CULTURAL WORK": MOTHER-
DAUGHTER RELATIONSHIPS
IN NOVELS

WHEN Sylvia Marshall's grand tour of Europe is cut short
by the news of the death of her mother in Dorothy Canfield Fisher's *The Bent Twig*, the young woman is overcome
by grief: "How could her mother be dead? What did it mean to have
her mother dead? . . . She said the grim words over and over, the
sound of them was horrifying to her, but in her heart she did not
believe them. Her mother, *her* mother could not die!"[1] As she explains to her aunt's stepson, her mother's death severs a bond that
has been crucial in shaping her life: " 'Oh, what I would have been—
I can't bear to *think* of what kind of woman I would have been
without my mother!' The idea was terrible to her."[2]

While Sylvia recognizes her mother's influence as a positive force
in her development, the protagonist of May Sinclair's *Mary Olivier: A
Life*, published four years after *The Bent Twig*, regards maternal influence as a destructive rather than a nurturing presence in her life.
Mary Olivier describes her view of the unique nature of the mother-
daughter relationship to her favorite brother as they discuss family
matters:

It's different for you. . . . Ever since I began to grow up I felt there was
something about Mamma that would kill me if I let it. I've had to fight for
every single thing I've ever wanted. . . . She doesn't know she hates me. . . .
And of course she loved me when I was little. She'd love me now if I stayed
little so that she could do what she liked with me. . . . It's your real self she
hates—the thing she can't see and touch and get at—the thing that makes
you different. Even when I was little she hated it and tried to crush it.[3]

41

The sentiments expressed by these fictional daughters represent opposite emotional extremes on the continuum of mother-daughter relationships during the period between 1880 and 1920. Like prescriptive literature, novels cannot be presumed to mirror the reality of women's experiences, but through the examination of fictional portrayals of the mother-daughter relationship, the historian can develop insights on another level. In her recent study of nineteenth-century American fiction, Jane Tompkins has suggested that literary texts should be viewed as "powerful examples of the way a culture thinks about itself, articulating and proposing solutions for the problems that shape a particular historical moment." She argues that while novels do not necessarily represent attempts to express eternal verities, they do perform a kind of "cultural work" within a specific historical situation: a novel's plot and characters offer society a way to think about itself; they define aspects of social reality shared by author and reader; and they dramatize conflicts and recommend resolutions.[4]

Although Tompkins's framework stems from an effort to redefine the nature of the literary canon, to refocus literary study, and to change the criteria by which literature is evaluated, her work resonates importantly for the historian, particularly for the historian who studies women's experiences. Tompkins views the formulaic plots, stereotyped characters, common language, and conventional devices typical of the genre of nineteenth-century domestic fiction as a form of "cultural shorthand" that offers keys to understanding the concerns of the readers of these novels and clues to their popularity.[5] Her analysis of nineteenth-century fiction in terms of its popular elements rather than in terms of the principles of contemporary literary criticism offers an implicit rationale for the use of literature as a historical source: if, as Tompkins maintains, literary texts both shape and reflect the culture from which they emerge, they contain much that is potentially useful for the social historian—not in the formal properties of the literary discourse, but in the cultural data they may reveal.

The use of fiction as a source of historical data is not a new concept. Where a dearth of material has hampered research, for example, on certain aspects of the lives of ordinary people, historians have relied on literature to fill in the gaps. Most often, they have turned to novels included in the literary canon, such as the work of Hawthorne or Dickens. Because a novel never just mirrors reality, however, the historian's use of literary evidence can be problematic.[6] As Cathy Davidson has pointed out, a novel "*is* its own artificially framed world, an organized structure with its own rules and interpretations."[7] In other words, it is a closed system created by its author. Because unlike reality, the plot, the characters, and the language never change, the manifest content of a novel remains static, while the manifest content of history changes as historians revise their presentations of the past through the discovery of new evidence and new approaches to existing data. Nevertheless, the novel can be useful to the historian because it does not exist in a vacuum; the composition, publication, circulation, and reading of the text reflect the influence of cultural forces.[8]

Recent revisionist literary studies have focused the historian's attention on the importance of popular novels as opposed to those included in the canon, particularly nineteenth-century women's fiction, in both expressing and shaping the social context of the era.[9] Thus, for example, Mary Ryan has incorporated fictional sources into her historical overview of nineteenth-century American discussions of domesticity on the grounds that novels reached a large national audience, identified the "most talked-about aspects" of domesticity, and recorded how "raw individual experience . . . was sorted out, evaluated, assigned relative importance, and given a human and social meaning." Ryan contends that although the literary depiction of women and the family cannot be considered social realism, "it is a valid and intricate representation of women's past."[10]

The contention that nineteenth-century American women's literature performed important "cultural work" by both describing and changing the social context that produced it suggests that these novels contain interesting evidence regarding the history of mother-daughter relationships. An investigation of the treatment of mother-daughter interactions in late nineteenth- and early twentieth-century works can help to illuminate the nature of women's perceptions, and possibly their experiences, of the relationship. Such a study must consider several fundamental questions: How did earlier nineteenth-century novelists portray this aspect of family life? How did novels that appeared at the turn of the century and in the early decades of the twentieth century deal with the topic? And finally, do these depictions reflect the nature of women's actual experiences?

The numerous popular women's novels published between 1820 and 1870, representative of the genre known as domestic fiction, typically relate the story of a young heroine faced with the task of making her own way in the world without the emotional or the financial support she had expected to be able to depend upon to help her meet life's challenges. Frequently the heroine is an orphan. When mothers are present, they usually appear as passive, incompetent, ignorant, or emotionally and intellectually undeveloped—as negative role models or "targets of disidentification."[11] Often the heroine suffers at the hands of those more powerful than she, but usually her mother is not the oppressor. In many instances, it is actually the loss of her mother that triggers her difficulties, and the memory of her mother that enables her to endure them.[12]

In one sense, the silencing or devaluing of mothers in nineteenth-century domestic fiction contradicts Victorian family ideology, which glorified the ideal of motherhood.[13] But this ideology also posited the sacrifice of selfhood in favor of the maternal role. Hence the failings of fictional mothers mirror women's difficulties in a world where rigidly defined female and maternal roles effectively foreclosed self-development and involvement outside the home, and their absence functions as an emblem of this powerlessness.[14] The image of the absent or ineffective mother may also symbolize the personal experiences of female authors who lost their own mothers or found them unsupportive. Through these types of maternal images, then, nineteenth-century novels emphasized the negative aspects of the female world described by Carroll Smith-Rosenberg, thus articulating and proposing solutions for the problems of many participants in that world.[15]

By the end of the nineteenth century, women's fiction was characterized more by fragmentation and variety than by the uniformity that had typified the genre of domestic fiction.[16] This transition reflected the extensive changes that were taking place in women's lives. While much of their work still portrayed submissive, domestic types, novelists began to introduce the "new woman" in the 1880s and '90s, and to focus on the conflicting claims of motherhood and the desire for self-expression.[17] The "fallen woman" also functioned as a major literary character in the popular fiction of the late nineteenth century, reflecting the contemporary concern with public morals.[18] The mother-daughter relationship, no longer represented primarily through the exclusion of the mother, also provided the theme for a number of nineteenth- and early twentieth-century novels.[19]

An examination of fourteen representative novels published between 1879 and 1927 reveals that these works articulated key issues pertaining to the mother-daughter relationship through a juxtaposition of elements of the nineteenth-century concept of motherhood with the reality of the changes occurring in women's lives at the turn of the century and in the decades that followed.[20] Several recurring themes in these novels suggest the complexity of the relationship. Each text examines the importance of mothers to daughters and vice versa, and each considers the impact of societal prescriptions for women on their relationship. The authors portray maternal sacrifice, maternal ineptness, and mother-daughter communication problems, usually from the daughter's point of view. In most cases, the novelists do not describe supportive mothers who function as devoted mentors for successful "new women." Nor do they focus primarily on comfortable, contented mother-daughter dyads who share domestic insights and family news. Rather, the fiction addresses itself more to the examination of unresolved dilemmas generated by the disruption of continuity in women's experiences—in other words, to "cultural work" that remained to be accomplished. Just as other novels of the era offered readers insights regarding the impact of the changes in women's lives through a focus on gender relationships generally or on sex specifically, these employed the mother-daughter relationship to a similar end.[21]

The earliest example, Elizabeth Stuart Phelps Ward's *The Story of Avis*, which was first published in 1879, encompasses most of the themes contained in the other novels examined. This work shares with its nineteenth-century predecessors the device of a heroine who is a motherless young woman, but it also heralds the rise of more modern mother-daughter issues. Thus it sets the stage appropriately for this analysis of literary evidence.

Avis is brought up by her father and his sister, Aunt Chloe, who serves as a sort of surrogate mother, a kind and caring but very conventional person who finds it impossible to imagine "that any woman could make home happy without being able to make good Graham bread." Neither she nor Avis's devoted father can understand the young girl's desire to "be" an artist. As she ponders the contrast between her aunt's efforts to prepare her for a life of domesticity and her own desire for a different life, Avis wonders "if in the feeling that other girls had about their mothers lay hidden the wine which she found missing from her youth. For a soul which loved her so that it could not *help* believing in her, Avis could have dared the world. But only mothers, she supposed, ever cared for a perplexed and solitary girl like that."[22] Despite her mother's absence, the novel consistently invokes her image and emphasizes her importance. Avis echoes her mother's youth in her decision to marry Philip Ostrander, a scholar similar to her father. Like her mother, she discovers that marriage effectively ends her ability to express herself, as the responsibility of caring for a husband and two children curtails her creative ability. As he tries to understand his daughter's discontent, her father consistently invokes the memory of his wife: " 'If her mother had lived,' he thought, 'this might somehow have been spared.' Whenever Avis was in any trouble, he always said, 'If her mother had lived'—."[23] This device tells the reader, and the historian, that the author (and the contemporary culture) perceived this function as an essential component of the mother-daughter relationship.

Avis's feelings for her husband's mother and for her own daughter further emphasize the importance of the mother-daughter relationship and also highlight her reluctant recognition of the nature of the male-dominated society in which she lives. She is distraught when she learns about Philip's cavalier dismissal of his mother's desire to share her own wedding slippers with her new daughter-in-law, and she intently ponders the contrast between her own reaction to her mother-in-law's gesture and that of her husband: "Perhaps Philip could not be expected to know what a sacredness it would have added to her marriage-day to have worn it [the slippers]. Perhaps no man could. Perhaps this was one of the differences, one of the things that it meant to be a man, not to understand such matters. Gently she tried to think so."[24]

Although she feels guilty about her reaction, Avis expresses disappointment when her first child is a son: "If I had a daughter, I should fall down and worship her," she tells her father. This wish is fulfilled with the birth of a second child to whom she gives her mother-in-law's name, Waitstill, clearly a name with symbolic significance pertaining to her developing perception of the reality of women's position. Through the myriad of difficulties Avis subsequently faces—the illness and death of her son, her husband's infidelity, and eventually his death as well, a sequence of events that essentially removes the men from her life and creates a female community—she is sustained by her daughter's presence and by her own faith that women's lot will improve: "It would be easier for her daughter to be alive, and be a woman, than it had been for her: so much as this, she understood; more than this she felt herself too spent to question. She folded her arms about the little girl, and laid her cheek upon her hair, and closed her eyes. She had the child, she had the child."[25]

The novel's depiction of its female characters, including the dead mother's image, underscores a number of issues relevant to the status of women and to the mother-daughter relationship in the late nineteenth century. Despite her creativity and her aspirations, Avis finds herself in the same situation as her aunt and her mother-in-law; she is essentially a prisoner of domestic demands and male prescriptions for women's roles. In her emerging desire for another kind of life, she reflects the aspirations of the first generation of "new woman." Her father's conviction that his wife would have understood Avis highlights the significance of the mother as a model and also the idea of a supportive female community. Avis's own recognition that she has missed something very important—that only one's mother can offer unconditional love and support—mirrors a basic feeling also expressed by both young and adult daughters in real life.[26] Hence this theme, which is developed further through her devotion to her own daughter and her faith that women's lives will be easier in the next generation, provides interesting evidence about what was regarded as necessary in the mother-daughter relationship.

Like the prescriptive literature of the period, this novel also addresses the disruption of the continuity of expectations for women through the juxtaposition of Aunt Chloe's fear that her niece "would never be a credit to her . . . and *her* life's work would simply be thrown away," and Avis's lack of interest in domestic affairs. The threat of mother-daughter conflict growing out of generational discontinuity is clear: "Aunt Chloe was of quite as unselfish a temper as the most of us; but she found it hard sometimes to trace the exact distinction between Avis's good and her own glory."[27] The novel's conclusion is not optimistic about the possibility that mothers will be able to help daughters avoid the problems they have faced: even as Avis hopes and believes that life will be easier for her daughter, the child hands her a book and asks her to read. The story she has chosen, the tale of Sir Lancelot and Sir Galahad, represents a warning that her generation, like her mother's, remains vulnerable to an ideology that teaches women that their ultimate destiny will be fulfilled by a knight on a white horse.[28]

Through the portrayal of three dissimilar relationships, Mary Wilkins Freeman's *Pembroke,* first published in 1894, suggests that nineteenth-century gender ideology could affect mother-daughter interactions in fundamentally different ways. Charlotte Barnard's mother cannot bring herself to defy her husband when he orders her daughter's fiancé, Barnabas Thayer, to leave their home, thus terminating the engagement: "It's jest his way," she observes. She is tearful and distraught as she looks at Charlotte "with piteous appeal," seeking both her acquiescence and her understanding.

As Mrs. Barnard laments her daughter's situation, she also voices discontent with the nature of her own life: "I can't help it. . . . I feel worse about you than if it was myself, an' there's so much to put up with besides. I don't feel as if I could put up with things much longer, nohow."[29] Her inability to challenge her husband despite her sympathy for Charlotte illustrates the extent to which she has assimilated a socially assigned role. The dispirited comment about putting up with "things" reveals her recognition of a growing dissatisfaction for which she knows no remedy.

Because she is unable to reestablish her relationship with Barnabas in a socially acceptable fashion, Charlotte defies both her mother and social convention to assist him after his mother's death and nurse him when he is ill himself. When she finally gives her unused wedding clothes to her old-maid aunt whose long-term suitor has literally rescued her en route to the poor house, it is her mother who cries over the "poor slighted wedding clothes" and bemoans the fact that Charlotte has refused the attentions of another suitor. Despite her concern for her daughter, like the silent mothers in earlier nineteenth-century novels Mrs. Barnard cannot challenge the conventions that define her life. To do so would threaten her relationship with her husband and would also negate the meaning of her own existence. Charlotte expresses no overt resentment over her mother's ineffectual behavior, but she quietly and resolutely pursues her own course.

The relationship between Charlotte's cousin, Rose Berry, and her mother, who are linked by a common frame of reference, presents a striking contrast to that of Mrs. Barnard and Charlotte. Rose accepts the role she has been assigned and aspires to a conventional domestic life. When the newly available Barnabas Thayer does not reciprocate her interest, she is content to marry another man, an employee in her family's store. Rose and her mother are united by their shared acceptance of the constraints of domesticity and of the mysterious foibles of the opposite sex, as in their reaction to Mr. Berry's sudden change of heart regarding his previous insistence on charging friends to pick cherries in the family's orchard: " 'Father says I can have a cherry party, and they needn't pay anything.' 'He didn't!' 'Yes, he did.' They looked into each other's eyes, with silent renewals of doubt and affirmation." [30]

The novel's third mother-daughter combination, Deborah Thayer (the mother of Charlotte Barnard's stubborn fiancé) and Rebecca (who is in love with Rose Berry's brother William), presents another variant of the relationship. Unlike Mrs. Barnard and Mrs. Berry, Mrs. Thayer, a stern, rigid woman with a henpecked husband, displays no understanding whatsoever of her daughter's needs and desires. As a result, Rebecca Thayer is driven to the very behavior that her mother fears the most.

Mrs. Thayer consistently accuses Rebecca of unbecoming behavior, but never really suspects that she is actually sneaking out of the house at night to meet William Berry. She adamantly defends her maternal right to interfere in her daughter's life. [31] Eventually the young woman is forced into marriage, although paradoxically, despite the intensity of their clandestine relationship, she has resisted William's urging for some time. Rebecca's actions reflect her distress and confusion over the total absence of maternal understanding, which has compelled her to carry on a secret liaison. She punishes both herself and her mother by refusing, for as long as she possibly can, to legitimate her union.

By illustrating several ways in which societal prescriptions for women could shape mother-daughter interactions, *Pembroke,* which appeared fifteen years after *The Story of Avis,* suggests the presence of increasing complexity in the relationship over time. Charlotte Barnard's weak, passive mother has been rendered completely ineffectual, while Rebecca Thayer's domineering mother has become a destructive force in her daughter's life, and Rose Berry's mother has raised a clone of herself. Rose is content to conform to the expectations of her mother and society in traditional nineteenth-century fashion, but both Charlotte and Rebecca ultimately defy their mothers, subtly yet conclusively. For Charlotte, defiance results in a sort of victory, for she remains her own person in the face of both male stubbornness and maternal ineffectiveness. Rebecca's situation remains unresolved until after the deaths of her first child and both of her parents, when she finally seems to have achieved a degree of contentment on her own terms.

A completely different picture of mother-daughter interactions in this transitional era emerges in Sarah Orne Jewett's *The Country of the Pointed Firs.* Here the relationship is characterized by the empathetic communication and mutual understanding that exist between sixty-seven-year-old Mrs. Almira Todd and her mother Mrs. Blackett, who is still healthy and active at the age of eighty-seven. Their intimacy is revealed as the novel's narrator and Mrs. Todd arrive by boat on the island where Mrs. Blackett lives, and the daughter discerns, with evident pleasure, a tiny figure waving to them. " 'How do you suppose she knows it's me?' said Mrs. Todd, with a tender smile on her broad face. 'There, you never get over bein' a child long's you have a mother to go to.' " Mother and daughter greet one another, ostensibly without emotion, but the narrator notes that "they stood and beamed in each other's faces."[32]

The women tease one another affectionately about being out of breath as they proceed up the steep hill from the water to Mrs. Blackett's house. Mrs. Todd is surprised and proud to find that her mother has managed to turn the parlor carpet with only minimal assistance from her son: "There, what do you think o' havin' such a mother as that for eighty-six years old?" she exclaims while her mother assumes "a sudden look of youth."[33] When the narrator expresses her own pleasure at being on the island, Mrs. Blackett cordially invites her to return any time, but she observes without rancor that her daughter would be restless if she had to live there: "You wanted more scope, didn't you, you Almiry." Although she concedes that "folks wonders that we don't live together," and that eventually the "time o' sickness an' failin' " may force them to do so, she relishes her own independence and does not resent her daughter's autonomy.[34]

Unlike the mother-daughter interactions depicted in *The Story of Avis* and *Pembroke*, the constraints of patriarchal society do not seem to intrude on the relationship between Mrs. Todd and Mrs. Blackett. The male characters in the novel remain peripheral to the female community, even in the context of a family reunion that Josephine Donovan has described as a "matriarchal happening," where Mrs. Blackett is the center of attention. Donovan suggests that this novel responded to the transitions occurring in women's lives at the turn of the century by expressing the desire of late nineteenth-century women to preserve "a transcending matriarchal realm," the female world of love and ritual documented by Carroll Smith-Rosenberg. As an example of imaginative realism, *The Country of the Pointed Firs* contains figures and forces that represent "something beyond themselves."[35] Thus the perfect harmony and the wordless communication between mother and daughter represent and extol the tightly knit female community, whose core was the mother-daughter relationship, that existed before the advent of the "new woman." Unlike *Pembroke*, this novel, published in 1896, also highlights the strength of that relationship, as Mrs. Blackett's comfortable acceptance of her daughter's desire for "more scope" suggests that generational differences in opportunity and aspirations need not invariably weaken the mother-daughter bond.

Two later novels, both published in 1915, echo Jewett's theme of maternal tolerance and support for daughters' aspirations, but like *The Story of Avis* and *Pembroke*, they highlight the disruption of the traditional female community. Willa Cather's *The Song of the Lark* and Dorothy Canfield Fisher's *The Bent Twig* depict both strengths in the mother-daughter relationship and challenges to it in the context of the changes that were taking place in women's lives. These novels portray supportive fictional mothers, but they also emphasize the complexity of the relationship even when conflict is not the dominant mode of interaction.

The Song of the Lark relates the experiences of Thea Kronberg, a talented young woman whose devoted mother always found her more interesting than any of her other children and "took her more seriously, without thinking much about why she did so."[36] Mrs. Kronberg has no qualms about her decision to send Thea to Chicago to study music when the opportunity arises, and her husband defers to her judgment. But she also realizes that the experience will change her daughter: " 'She won't come back a little girl,' Mrs. Kronberg said to her husband."[37]

This prediction is correct. On her first visit home, Thea definitely seems different, although she is still receptive to her mother's interest and attention: "There was no sham about her mother. . . . She liked her mother."[38] The change is even more obvious when Thea spends the summer at home. As always, her mother defends her, but the rest of the family finds her demeanor incomprehensible. She realizes that she no longer has anything in common with her siblings, who seem now to be "among the people whom she had always recognized as her natural enemies. Their ambitions and sacred proprieties were meaningless to her." She perceives too that even her mother, whom she still cares for, remains an integral part of the family while she herself is no longer involved, and this perception creates a barrier between them: "In the nature of things, her mother had to be on both sides."[39]

In response to this sense of emotional distance, Thea effectively withdraws from the family, and thus from the traditional female world of domesticity. This withdrawal presages the dilemma she ultimately confronts as she is forced to choose between her mother and her career in a particularly painful manner. When Mrs. Kronberg collapses after her husband's death, Thea is in Germany, where she is performing the role of Elizabeth in Tannhäuser for the first time, and she cannot leave: "She wanted to go to her mother more than she wanted anything else in the world, but, unless she failed—which she would not—she absolutely could not leave Dresden for six months. It was not that she chose to stay; she had to stay—or lose everything. . . . As soon as she was free, she would go to Moonstone and take her mother back to Germany with her."

The decision to remain in Dresden effectively insures Thea's professional future, yet it is disastrous in a personal sense. Her mother, recognizing the reality of the situation, observes: "The children you don't especially need, you have always with you, like the poor. But the bright ones get away from you. They have their own way to make in the world."[40] Mrs. Kronberg's memories are not enough to sustain her, and she dies without seeing her daughter again. Although Thea's career prospers, her personal life is empty, and the impact of her mother's death endures: "I've only a few friends, but I can lose every one of them, if it has to be," she comments. "I learned how to lose when my mother died."[41]

In *The Song of the Lark*, the strong mother-daughter bonds portrayed in *The Country of the Pointed Firs* are complicated by factors outside the domestic setting, reflecting the changes imposed by societal developments during the nearly twenty years that separate the publication of these works. Mrs. Kronberg recognizes that Thea has moved into a wider world, and she sadly acknowledges the implications of this transition. The novel does not resolve Thea's dilemma with a last-minute dash to her mother's bedside and a happy ending. Rather, it traces her movement away from her family, which culminates in the conflict between her obligations to the mother who has supported and fostered her aspirations, and her commitment to the professional life her mother has helped her to achieve.

Thea's story, which moves beyond the hints of change in women's aspirations and experiences suggested in the earlier novels, distills the essence of the "new woman's" struggle to reconcile a growing sense of her own potential as an independent individual with her family ties, especially her feelings for her mother. Through Mrs. Kronberg's plaintive recognition and acceptance of the reality that "the bright ones get away from you," the novel also depicts the combination of pride and pain that a mother might experience if she understood and fostered a talented daughter's ambitions. While *The Song of the Lark* suggests that conflict did not necessarily define mother-daughter relationships in the era of the "new woman," the novel also indicates that the cost of maternal mentoring could be significant for both mothers and daughters.

Like Thea Kronberg, Sylvia Marshall, the college-student heroine of Dorothy Canfield Fisher's *The Bent Twig*, enjoys the assistance and encouragement of a frank, approachable mother who trusts her and respects her privacy. Sylvia loves her and admires her strength, yet she regards her mother as a difficult role model, and in some ways identifies more with her father: "I couldn't live like her, without wanting to smash everything up. She's somebody that Seneca would have liked."[42]

The novel traces Sylvia's painful development as she gradually rejects the materialistic, superficial values embraced by the social set at the university, and also by her fashionable, widowed aunt, and learns to appreciate the more substantial and fundamental values espoused by her mother. Like Thea Kronberg, Sylvia is in Europe when she learns that her mother has died, but unlike Thea, she returns home immediately to look after her distraught father and to come to terms with a loss that seems incomprehensible at first.

As Sylvia remembers her relationship with her mother, she views their interactions with a new maturity: "All the time I was growing up, I was blind, I didn't see anything. I don't feel remorseful, I suppose that is the way children have to be. But I didn't see her. There were so many minor differences between us . . . tastes, interests. I always said hatefully to myself that mother didn't understand me. And it was true too. As if it matters! What if she didn't!"[43] She finds meaning in her own existence as she develops an understanding of the meaning of her mother's life: "She lived her life. And there it is now, there it always will be for me, food for me to live on. I thought she had died. But she has never been so living for me. She's part of me now, for always. And just because I see the meaning of her life, why there's the meaning of mine as clear as morning."[44] In this novel, maternal influence triumphs as the heroine belatedly but decisively acknowledges the importance of the positive model provided by a competent, supportive mother who understands the pressures experienced by her daughter. Sylvia's final decision to marry a man who, like her mother, cares more for nature and beauty than for material possessions, completes the young woman's development.[45] Thus *The Bent Twig,* like various contemporary advice manuals, conveys the message that even in the context of dangerous outside influences, a capable mother can maintain a healthy connection with her daughter.

With the exception of *Pembroke,* the preceding examples affirm the centrality of the mother-daughter relationship for women's lives in relatively positive terms up to, and even after, the turn of the century. But other works that appeared concurrently offer a sharp contrast in their manifestly negative portrayals of mother-daughter interactions. Mary Austin's *A Woman of Genius* presents a graphic picture of an almost unbridgeable gap between the heroine, Olivia, an aspiring actress, and the conventional, distant, uncommunicative mother who offers her untraditional daughter neither affection nor understanding. Their tastes and interests differ completely, and Olivia's efforts to converse with her mother about things that bother her—relationships with boys and later, the connection between marriage and maternity—are singularly unsuccessful.[46]

After her mother suffers a serious stroke, their communication improves, although Olivia realizes that they will never be fully in touch with one another: "It grew upon me during the days of my mother's illness that there was a kind of intrinsic worth in her which I, with all my powers, must forever and inalienably miss." Nevertheless, they finally develop a common bond: "We were two women, together at last, my mother and I, and could have speech with one another."[47] Their new ability to communicate prompts her mother to confess the fear that Olivia's rebellious behavior stems from the fact that she had not wanted another child when her daughter was born: "You cried all the time when you were little, Olivia, and it was I that was crying in you. I've expected some punishment would come of it." However, Olivia assures her that she understands and that she is comfortable with her own unconventional traits.[48] This conversation represents their final reconciliation, for although her mother lives for nearly two years, ironically another stroke deprives her of the ability to speak before Olivia sees her again.

Unlike *The Song of the Lark* in which the heroine enjoys the support of a mother who is instrumental in her professional development, this novel weaves overt mother-daughter antagonism into the larger conflict between women's new career aspirations and traditional domestic values. Olivia resents her mother's preferential treatment of her brother. She is unhappy in the conventional marriage she entered as a result of maternal pressure, and she is frustrated by her own inability to seriously pursue an acting career. After her husband's death, she rejects the opportunity to marry her first real love and care for his children in favor of the chance to devote herself to the stage. Although she eventually understands her mother more clearly, and recognizes that the conflict between conventional expectations and her chosen way of life is not just a product of her mother's narrowness, Olivia never really identifies with her. The distance between them mirrors the generation gap that characterized the female world at the turn of the century.

The absence of maternal support and a positive maternal model does not deter Olivia permanently from achieving her goals, but it has disastrous effects on Lily Bart, the protagonist of Edith Wharton's *The House of Mirth,* published in 1905. Completely dominated by her mother's materialistic values and fear of "dinginess," the beautiful young woman spends her entire adult life traveling to the homes of frivolous friends, playing bridge, helping with social duties, and searching for the right wealthy man to marry. Although Lily has a sense that there are other values—for example, she sympathizes with her father's interest in poetry—she is unable to move beyond the influence of a mother who resents her husband's financial limitations and regards her daughter's beauty as a social commodity.[49]

To Mrs. Bart, the worst fate in the world is "to live like pigs," which is the way she characterizes the lives of relatives who inhabit dingy houses and employ frumpy maids. Lily takes pride in her mother's ability to avoid this fate despite the family's precarious finances. After her husband's bankruptcy further curtails her ability to maintain her standards, Mrs. Bart is consoled only by her daughter's beauty, "the last asset in their fortunes, the nucleus around which their life was to be rebuilt." But she soon recognizes the futility of this hope and dies "of a deep disgust" two years after her husband's death, but not before adjuring Lily to avoid dinginess at all costs: "Don't let it creep up on you and drag you down. Fight your way out of it somehow—you're young and can do it."[50]

Because she is so susceptible to her mother's influence, Lily cannot move beyond the latter's materialistic aspirations to build an independent life for herself. After she learns the small size of a legacy she has expected from her aunt, she can no longer face her empty life. She finally escapes, not in the way her mother had hoped, but through an overdose of sleeping medicine that kills her. *The House of Mirth* places the responsibility for a daughter's failings more directly in her mother's lap than any of the other novels examined. Mrs. Bart's shallow example leads Lily to ruin her own life, and finally to end it, as through her suicide she fulfills her mother's adjuration to "fight your way out of it somehow." Through the portrayal of Lily's empty existence, the novel indicts Mrs. Bart for her espousal of the vapid social values that ultimately destroy her daughter, but the conspicuous absence of integrity that distinguishes most of the other characters indicts the society that fosters those values as well.

The protagonists' mothers in Ellen Glasgow's *Virginia* and *Life with Gabriella* also serve as negative role models, "specters of the expected female," to the detriment of their daughters' own lives.[51] Virginia Pendleton never questions her mother's self-sacrificing martyrdom: "She let her mother slave over her because she had been born into a world where the slaving of mothers was a part of the natural order, and she had not yet become independent enough to question the morality of the commonplace."[52] Nor does she ever achieve that independence. Instead, she systematically destroys her own personhood and alienates her husband by replicating her mother's single-minded devotion to motherhood with the latter's encouragement and approval. Dimly recognizing her own predicament, Virginia observes, "Something has gone out of me."[53]

While Mrs. Pendleton succeeds at least as a model of maternal martyrdom, the widowed mother of the heroine in *Life with Gabriella* is completely inept: "Though Mrs. Carr worked every instant of her time, except the few hours when she lay in bed trying to sleep, and the few minutes when she sat at the table trying to eat, nothing that she began was ever finished until Gabriella took it out of her hands.

She did her best ... yet through some tragic perversity of fate her best seemed always to fall short of the simplest requirements of life."[54] Unlike Virginia Pendleton, who accepts her mother's injunction that it is a woman's duty to sacrifice herself, Gabriella rejects the traditional feminine values that her mother represents. Despite her own difficulties, which include a broken marriage and the problem of supporting herself and two children, Gabriella rarely becomes discouraged. She copes successfully while her mother remains dependent on the charity of relatives.

Neither Virginia nor Gabriella engages in conflict with her mother, and both remain sympathetic, attentive daughters. When her mother dies, Virginia remembers her childhood fear of losing her, and she realizes that this loss will always be with her in the future: "Whatever the years brought to her, they could never bring a love like her mother's. ... 'I have my children still left—but for my children I could not live!' " she thinks. For Gabriella as well, the thought of her mother's death "had been the most terrible nightmare of her childhood." This memory restrains her when she is tempted to speak crossly to Mrs. Carr.[55]

Both novels chart mother-daughter conflict through the next generation as their protagonists experience serious difficulties with their own daughters. Virginia is distressed by her oldest daughter Lucy's decision to marry a man she barely knows, by the apparent lack of sentiment and romance involved, and by Lucy's careless dismissal of these concerns. She feels as if there are "profound disturbances beneath the familiar surface of life."[56] She is equally puzzled by her younger daughter Jenny's desire to go to college and by her efforts to explain modern ideas about women's roles. Jenny's regular letters reflect her sense of duty rather than any genuine rapport with Virginia, while Lucy's infrequent communications appear only when she needs something from her mother.[57] The yawning gulf of misunderstanding between these young women and their mother testifies to Mrs. Pendleton's strong, negative influence as a role model for Virginia. In embracing her own mother's old-fashioned ideas, she has distanced herself irreparably from Lucy and Jenny, to whom such ideas are completely incomprehensible.

Despite her own ostensibly untraditional ideas, Gabriella also has no rapport with her spoiled, beautiful daughter Fanny, who, like her grandmother, lacks her mother's strength of character: "They were so different that there was little real sympathy between them, and confidences from daughter to mother must spring, she knew, from fulness of sympathy." Like the bewildered Virginia, whose only comfort is her son Harry, Gabriella too develops a strong bond with her son Archibald. Unlike Virginia, however, she also establishes a new, adult relationship on her own terms with an attractive though unpolished man.[58] Through the protagonists' troubled relationships with their own daughters, these novels highlight the long-term negative impact of the social ideology that engendered the impotence demonstrated by their mothers.

Two later novels by Edith Wharton, *The Old Maid* and *The Mother's Recompense,* published respectively in 1924 and 1925, examine the effects of such ideology from the point of view of mothers rather than daughters. In *The Old Maid,* a young woman who has borne a child outside of marriage is forced to give up both her own independence and her claim to her daughter in order for the latter to be accepted by society.[59] The combination of the social stigma attached to her behavior, and her love for her child, compels Charlotte Lovell to accept the offer of her wealthy widowed cousin, Delia Ralston, to provide a home for herself and the little girl, Tina, who has no idea who her real mother is. Ironically, as she grows up in the Ralston home, the little girl regards Charlotte as an old maid aunt and actually thinks affectionately of Delia as her mother. When her cousin (who was once in love with the child's father) convinces Charlotte to agree to a formal adoption in order to elevate her daughter's status from that of a "foundling," she feels as though she has been robbed of her child, although she realizes that she really has no other choice.

On the eve of Tina's wedding, Delia proposes to offer her adopted daughter some motherly advice concerning her "new duties and responsibilities," but Charlotte insists that it is her right to initiate this discussion. Yet she can find no way to approach Tina without revealing the secret both women have kept for over twenty years, and she concedes: "It's no use. You were right: there's nothing I can say. You're her real mother. Go to her. It's not your fault—or mine."[60] Hence, as her daughter is about to embark on the respectable married life made possible only by her natural mother's sacrifices, Charlotte recognizes that neither she nor Delia is responsible for the situation. They are captives of the hypocritical, patriarchal social system that has effectively determined the nature of her relationship with Tina from the moment she was born. Her only compensation for her selflessness lies in the secret knowledge that, as a good mother should, she has insured her daughter's happiness through her sacrifices, and in Delia's request to Tina that she give her last kiss to "Aunt" Charlotte before she leaves home as a bride.

Like *The Old Maid, The Mother's Recompense* also examines the mother-daughter relationship through the theme of maternal sacrifice precipitated by a woman's unconventional behavior. Kate Clephane has resided as an expatriate on the French Riviera since she left her husband and three-year-old daughter Anne to live with another man. She returns at Anne's invitation and finds a beautiful, mature, sympathetic young woman determined to restore her mother to her rightful place. Their reunion proceeds smoothly. Kate finds peace and joy in her daughter's presence, and Anne takes pleasure in her mother's attractive appearance and in the opportunity to confide in her.[61]

Although it appears that Kate has been reinstated both as a mother and as a member of respectable society despite her earlier reckless behavior, this resolution is only temporary. Her transgressions return to haunt her when a young man with whom she has had a serious love affair reappears as Anne's fiancé. Like Charlotte Lovell in *The Old Maid*, Kate faces an agonizing dilemma; she realizes that she will lose the daughter whose life she has reentered so recently whether she tells the truth or keeps this terrible secret. Kate's unsuccessful attempts to separate the young couple inevitably engender her daughter's hostility, and their newly established rapport is irreparably damaged as the distraught young woman exclaims: "You don't know me; you don't understand me. What right have you to interfere with my happiness. . . . It was my own fault to imagine that we could ever live like mother and daughter. A relation like that can't be improvised in a day."[62]

Kate finds it impossible to keep her secret and still remain part of her daughter's life.[63] Like Charlotte Lovell, she realizes that she can retain her daughter only by giving her up, and she returns to the same rootless existence she had endured earlier. Despite previous indications to the contrary, her recompense is not the return to a comfortable life at home, but the contrasting fates of permanent separation, both physical and emotional, from the daughter who has become so important to her, and the preservation of her independence and her private past.

Three final examples offer interesting literary representations of the mother-daughter relationship in settings that differ significantly from those depicted in the other novels examined. Mary Wilkins Freeman's *The Portion of Labor,* published in 1901, resembles *The Song of the Lark* and *The Bent Twig* in some aspects of its presentation of a mother-daughter relationship, but it differs significantly from these novels in its focus on the problems of working-class people whose lives center on the shoe factory in which they are employed, and its pervasive emphasis on the theme of maternal sacrifice. Like Sylvia Marshall, who is influenced by her attractive aunt, Freeman's protagonist, Ellen, is drawn to a beautiful, sophisticated woman, Cynthia Lennox, whose image contrasts with that of Fanny, her plain, hardworking mother. Like Thea Kronberg, Ellen faces a choice between family loyalty and her own future, in this case the opportunity for a college education, which Miss Lennox has offered to provide. But Ellen's dilemma is complicated by her mother's consuming desire to keep her beautiful daughter out of the factory no matter what the cost.

Fanny's willingness to sacrifice her own personhood for her daughter's welfare echoes the nineteenth-century ideology of motherhood: " 'What, after all, did it matter?' she asked herself, 'if a woman was growing old, if she had to work hard, if she did not know where the next dollar was coming from, if all the direct personal savor was fast passing out of existence, when one had a daughter who looked like that?' "[64] She ardently wishes that she herself were different so she could be more of an asset to this marvelous young woman.[65]

As Ellen considers her benefactor's offer to pay for her education, she reassures her mother (and herself as well) that "there is nobody in the whole world to me like my own mother. . . . It isn't being beautiful, nor speaking in a soft voice, nor dressing well, it's the being you—you. You know I love you best . . . and I always will."[66] Despite

Fanny's fervent hopes to the contrary, Ellen finds it impossible to repudiate either her mother or her class by accepting Miss Lennox's sponsorship, and she decides to go to work in the factory. Her mother responds by stoically preparing Ellen's favorite stew for dinner.[67]

The novel's resolution demonstrates that Fanny's ambitions for her daughter reflect traditional maternal aspirations for a daughter's future rather than any recognition on her part of the existence of genuinely new possibilities for women's advancement. She is "openly and shamelessly triumphant" when Robert Lloyd, the nephew of the factory owner, calls on Ellen. Her distress when their romance founders as a result of Ellen's participation in a strike reflects her empathy for her daughter's suffering—the "realization of her state of mind, of which a mother alone is capable"—and also her own fear that Ellen will lose this chance to better herself through a good marriage. Fanny's acceptance of the conventional social ideology regarding women's roles is clearly apparent as she considers the possibility that Ellen and Robert might marry: "It would be a splendid thing for her," she tells her husband. His terse reply, "It would be a splendid thing for him," intimates the nature of his concerns as he considers the possibility of his daughter's marriage to the boss's nephew. But his wife's concerns are different, and she insists: "It'll be a great thing for her. . . . It'll be a splendid thing for her, you know that."[68] Thus Fanny's disappointment over Ellen's decision to forgo college is mitigated by the promise of her bright future with Robert Lloyd. Her earlier dreams for her daughter have been fulfilled through a different route, as it appears that the young woman will still escape from the trials of working-class poverty to live happily ever after, and her mother's sacrifices will not have been in vain.

This novel suggests that the addition of working-class economic concerns to the elements that defined the interactions of middle-class mothers and daughters intensified the complexity of the relationship. Issues of sacrifice and survival could take precedence over those of ideology for working-class mothers, while loyalty to class as well as to family might concern their daughters. Nevertheless, deep and abiding affection could also be present.

Anzia Yezierska's novel *Bread-Givers* depicts the working-class mother-daughter relationship from another perspective through its formulaic portrayal of the struggles of an immigrant Jewish family.[69] Here the selfless, long-suffering mother would do anything for her daughter, Sara, who has left the family to seek a job and an education. All she asks in return is an occasional visit, but the young woman begrudges any time spent away from her studies. When Sara has finally established herself professionally as a teacher (and as an American) and finds the time to visit her mother, she, like Thea Kronberg in *The Song of the Lark,* discovers it is too late. The exhausted woman, who has sacrificed her entire life to be a "bread-giver" for her husband and children, is dying of blood poisoning. Belatedly, Sara recognizes her mother's love and devotion, and she regrets her own failure "to give Mother the understanding of her deeper self during her lifetime."[70] The mother's recompense in this case is posthumous; her daughter eventually becomes a bread-giver herself, assuming responsibility for her selfish father and his manipulative second wife.

Like *The Portion of Labor, Bread-Givers* differs from the other novels examined in its portrayal of the mother-daughter relationship in a working-class context, and also in its focus on an immigrant subculture. While neither of these works reflects the experiences of middle-class American mothers and their daughters, both offer revealing presentations of the themes of maternal sacrifice and the conflict between a daughter's aspirations and her family obligations.

Finally, an English novel provides the most intense and concentrated portrait of the mother-daughter relationship of any of the works examined. In May Sinclair's *Mary Olivier: A Life,* a daughter who feels rejected and unloved by her domineering, yet outwardly gentle mother consciously recognizes that her essential selfhood is threatened by their relationship.[71] Mary Olivier reflects, "She was powerful and rather cruel. . . . If you didn't take care she would get hold of you and never rest till she had broken you, or turned and twisted you to her own will." Yet her feelings remain ambivalent:

She hated her mother. She adored and hated her. Mamma had married for her own pleasure, for her passion. She had brought you into the world, without asking your leave, for her own pleasure. She had brought you into the world to be unhappy. She had planned for you to do the things that she did. She cared for you only as long as you were doing them. When you left off and did other things she left off caring. . . . She hated her mother and she adored her.[72]

Mary's intuitive recognition of the problems of separation and individuation and her allusion to the psychological impact of maternal sexuality foreshadow the commentary offered by some late twentieth-century scholars.[73] Eventually she discusses her ambivalent feelings with her mother, who replies that she never knew Mary loved her, and that she had always been afraid of her daughter because she was so different from her sons. Like Mary's thoughts about their relationship, Mrs. Olivier's reply anticipates more recent discussions of mother-daughter interactions in works of both fiction and nonfiction: "I felt as if you knew everything I was thinking. . . . I didn't like your being clever. . . . I was jealous of you, Mary. And I was afraid for my life you'd find it out."[74] Sinclair's sophisticated understanding of the depth and complexity of the mother-daughter relationship is equally clear in the novel's conclusion: despite, or because of, their difficulties, Mary never leaves her mother, and she is devastated by her death.

What conclusions about the history of mother-daughter relationships at the turn of the century, and beyond, can be drawn from the examination of these fourteen novels? Several related questions suggest a structure for the analysis of their collective historical contribution: What is directly apparent about the portrayal of the relationship in these works? What is implied by that portrayal? What is the relationship between the authors' own experiences and their fictional presentations of this aspect of women's lives? How did the contemporary audience view and understand the images of mother-daughter interactions in the novels?

Clearly, mothers are central to the lives of the fictional daughters. Even in absentia, they play important roles, as illustrated by *The Story of Avis*. Neither Virginia Pendleton nor Gabriella Carr can bear the thought of losing her mother, and maternal deaths have serious major consequences in *Pembroke*, *The Song of the Lark*, *A Woman of Genius*, *The Bent Twig*, *The House of Mirth*, *Bread-Givers*, and *Mary Olivier*. In some instances, a mother's support for unconventional behavior is crucial to a daughter's ability to fulfill her own desires, as with Thea Kronberg's musical ambitions and Almira Todd's more general need for "more scope." In other cases, the absence of such support hampers a daughter's progress but does not curtail her development completely; this situation describes the experience of Olivia in *A Woman of Genius*. The conflict between a daughter's aspirations and her obligations to her mother can be emotionally wrenching, as in *The Portion of Labor,* and often irreconcilable, as in *The Song of the Lark* and *Bread-Givers.*

Mothers provide both positive and negative role models in these novels. Occasionally they may intercede with their husbands on their daughters' behalf, as Mrs. Kronberg does in *The Song of the Lark.* Sylvia Marshall and Almira Todd have strong, salutary maternal examples to follow, while the protagonists of *Pembroke, Virginia, Life with Gabriella,* and *The House of Mirth* are far less fortunate in this regard. These characters suffer serious problems as a result of their mothers' failings. Like the images of maternal ineffectiveness, representations of maternal sacrifice rather than maternal mentoring recur in these novels, highlighting the impact of the dominant social ideology of gender. Unconventional behavior on the part of both mothers and daughters in the novels results in various forms of social and emotional punishment.

In several instances, negative maternal qualities contrast strongly with more favorable paternal images. While his wife ignores him after his financial failure, Lily Bart feels a special empathy for her "neutrally-tinted father" who reads poetry and fills "an intermediate space between the butler and the man who came to wind the clocks."[75] In *A Woman of Genius,* Olivia recalls "romping" with her father, who was much more relaxed with his children than his wife was. She also remembers that she never experienced any real mothering as a child.[76] Even Sylvia Marshall, who "loved her mother passionately and jealously," feels a special kinship with her father, whose "mind was more like her own," and a certain distance from her immensely competent mother.[77] Similarly Ellen, in *The Portion of Labor,* identifies more fully with her father's feelings although she loves her mother, and he, in turn, suffers more in his anxiety over his daughter than his wife does.[78] The suggestion that an ambitious young woman might identify with her father rather than her mother, no matter how capable the latter might be, testifies to the dominance of an ideology that categorized men as powerful achievers and their wives as nurturing caregivers.

The mother-daughter interactions depicted in these novels underscore the complexity of the relationship during a period of considerable turmoil in women's lives. Despite their differences, little or no overt anger is expressed by either generation toward the other, a circumstance that reflects the nineteenth-century emphasis on the suppression of female anger.[79] Instead, these portraits emphasize the enduring negative impact of nineteenth-century prescriptions for women as both mothers and daughters confronted a range of changes and new opportunities around the turn of the century. To a large extent, the novels represent a collective indictment of the social values that reduced women effectively to ciphers or forced them to choose between impossible alternatives in order to preserve their own personhood. For the most part, neither mothers nor daughters are held fully responsible for their failings; they are both compelled by circumstances over which they have no control. The painful inability of mothers to recognize the limitations of their own lives is reflected in the difficulties experienced by their daughters as they attempt to come to terms with society's expectations for them or to challenge those expectations.[80] Generally, these mothers continue to adhere to the ideology of maternal sacrifice—an ideology that is no longer viable in the era of the "new woman."

With the exception of *The Bent Twig*, the texts portray neither independent college daughters nor strong, supportive mothers. The mothers in the novels generally do not actively assist their daughters to pursue new avenues. Of the two instances where young women display significant professional aspirations, *The Song of the Lark* and *A Woman of Genius*, only one depicts a mother who understands her daughter's ambitions. (Although the daughters in *The Portion of Labor* and *Bread-Givers* also work, they represent the special circumstances of working class and immigrant life.) Consistently, then, like the prescriptive literature, the novels imply that the pressure experienced by many mothers and daughters as they confronted the changes in women's lives during the late nineteenth and early twentieth centuries formidably challenged their abilities to respond to these changes and altered the nature of their relationships.

This inference seems to reflect in part the writers' own experiences, which necessarily colored their interpretations of the interaction between the changing times and the mother-daughter relationship. As heiresses of the earlier "literary domestics" and prominent representatives of the vanguard of "new women" who challenged Victorian standards, the authors of these novels encountered in their own lives instances of both the general and the particular experiences of their characters.[81] The hostility directed toward female authors in the late nineteenth century has been well documented; this shared experience certainly suggests a reason for the pervasive tendency in these works to represent mother-daughter conflict as an inevitable outcome of social prescriptions for women.[82]

The influence of more specific components of individual authors' lives is clearly discernible in the novels as well. For example, Elizabeth Stuart Phelps Ward was eight years old when she lost her mother, who was also a popular novelist. Ward's original name, Mary Gray, was changed after her mother's death.[83] The latter's struggle to combine marriage with a creative career, and Ward's own reaction to the drudgery of domesticity as well as her identification with her mother, are reflected in the character of Avis.[84] Similarly, through Olivia, the protagonist of *A Woman of Genius,* Mary Austin articulated her personal feelings of rejection by her mother, while Willa Cather recorded the importance of her own mother's support for her aspirations through Mrs. Kronberg's behavior in *The Song of the Lark.*[85] The fact that Ellen Glasgow lived and wrote in traditional Virginia society is evident in the maternal images depicted in *Virginia* and *Life with Gabriella,* and the rather preachy image of maternal rectitude conveyed by *The Bent Twig* mirrors Dorothy Canfield Fisher's point of view as the author of advice literature as well as fiction.[86] Finally, Anzia Yezierska's personal experiences in an immigrant family obviously informed her treatment of the interactions in *Bread-Givers,* and Edith Wharton's lack of communication with her own mother contributed to the mother-daughter portraits in *The Old Maid* and *The Mother's Recompense.*[87]

While it is impossible to ascertain precisely how readers of these novels responded to their contents, it is probable that the contemporary audience recognized some personal relevance in the experiences portrayed. Like the discussions of mother-daughter relationships in popular periodical and advice literature, the fictional portraits must have spoken directly to the concerns of large numbers of women as they grappled with the growing recognition of a new and uncomfortable female generation gap. For example, when *The House of Mirth* was serialized in *Scribner's* between January and November 1905, Edith Wharton was deluged with mail from readers who were experiencing great anxiety over the decline and fall of Lily Bart.[88] No doubt some readers discovered reflections of the actual reality of their own lives in these works. For those who found it easier to accommodate to the changing circumstances, novels like these may have appeared to exaggerate the situation. Nevertheless, because they addressed issues that certainly troubled many women, the novels probably functioned widely as a nonthreatening outlet for uncomfortable personal tensions that might otherwise have been unexpressed. In their representations of various ramifications of the mother-daughter relationship, then, these works offered assurance to women that their own problems were not unique, but they also warned them in no uncertain terms that those problems were not easily resolved. The message concerning the connection between women's prescribed status and mother-daughter interactions was more subtle, but it certainly must have reached a portion of the contemporary audience as well.

For the most part, the novels communicated the same concerns as those articulated in the prescriptive literature. Although the discourse was more nuanced and complex, these texts also identified the mother-daughter relationship as particularly important in the context of the major social and cultural changes that were taking place. They too portrayed the relationship as a source of tension and conflict, and they frequently attributed the problem to maternal inadequacies. While the issues were presented at a more sophisticated level, the message was essentially similar.

These literary texts reflect the historical circumstances and the contemporary cultural discourse of the late nineteenth and early twentieth centuries. In a sense, their very existence defines their contribution to the history of mother-daughter relationships, for they challenge what has been referred to as the "lost tradition," the conspicuous absence of emphasis on mother-daughter interactions in Western literature.[89] Their shared thematic elements identify and underscore dominant mother-daughter issues throughout the era of the "new woman."

Through their fictional portrayals of the mother-daughter relationship, the novels raise questions and articulate concerns that most women, and even social commentators, would have found too disturbing to address openly. The presence of certain common themes suggests the existence of continuing areas of concern for women at the turn of the century and beyond. But an element of chronological progression is also discernible in the movement from the emphasis on a motherless, and therefore, bereft daughter in *The Story of Avis,* to the presentations of a mutually supportive mother-daughter dyad in *The Country of the Pointed Firs* and variants of both positive and negative interactions in other works, and finally to the portrayal of a troubled and ambivalent daughter in *Mary Olivier.* The latter work, which appeared in 1919, stresses several psychodynamic aspects of the mother-daughter relationship to which considerable attention has been directed in the post-Freudian twentieth century—specifically, issues of anger, jealousy, separation, individuation. *The Mother's Recompense,* published in 1925, also anticipates later literature through its subtle intimations regarding fundamental psychosexual issues.[90] These two novels presage the stress on the psychology of mother-daughter conflict that distinguishes women's fiction after the 1920s. Viewed chronologically, the fourteen novels examined suggest that changes in the nature of the cultural discourse concerning the mother-daughter relationship may herald changes in women's actual experiences.[91] But this suggestion recalls Peter Laslett's warning that historical generalizations derived from literary sources may "make people believe that what was the entirely exceptional, was in fact the perfectly normal."[92] Hence it is important to view the novels not as precise reflections of reality, but as examples of the contemporary cultural discourse concerning important problems and possible solutions for them. To establish what was "normal" and what was "exceptional" in middle-class mother-daughter relationships between 1880 and 1920, to learn how women themselves viewed and solved the problems defined through literary texts, the historian must turn to other sources, those in which mothers and daughters recorded their personal experiences, thoughts, and feelings.

CHAPTER 4

"A GIRL'S BEST FRIEND": ADOLESCENT DAUGHTERS AND THEIR MOTHERS

FOR Edna Ormsby, the birth of a daughter on December 20, 1891, represented an auspicious occasion. "She is perfect in every way and promises to be a bright child for which we feel that we can not be thankful enough to the Good Father," Mrs. Ormsby wrote in her diary. "I hope and pray that she may live to be a noble godfearing woman and a 'woman's woman.' If she might be permitted to do some great service for the uplifting of her sisters I shall feel that I have not lived in vain," she continued. "If she might only *do* the work that I have dreamed of how glad I should be. . . . We named the baby Esther by common consent. I had thought of that long before and when Fulton [her husband] suggested it and Mother liked it the matter was settled."[1] With these succinct observations, Mrs. Ormsby embarked on the task of raising a daughter.

By the time Esther was born, the era of the "new woman" had been launched by the first generation of young women to pursue higher education and various professional paths. In this setting, the challenge of guiding a daughter safely through childhood and adolescence to maturity and adulthood could be a formidable one for a conscientious mother. As Mrs. Ormsby's comments indicate, it might also suggest an opportunity for the vicarious fulfillment of maternal aspirations through the potential achievements of the next generation.

Over a period of about nineteen years, Edna Ormsby recorded her efforts to meet the challenge of raising a daughter well, and her thoughts and feelings about the mother-daughter relationship, in the diary she titled "The Book of Esther." The concerns she expressed mirrored the contemporary cultural expectations for middle-class mothers as they fulfilled their assigned responsibility for socializing their daughters. Reminiscent of prescriptive literature that urged the importance of friendship between mother and daughter, Mrs. Ormsby noted fervently: "I hope that we will be companionable and that her mamma will always be her closest confidant until there is a 'nearer and dearer one still than all others.' "[2] As Esther developed from babyhood to adolescence, her mother worried intensely about her mood changes, her attachment to other children, and her headaches. She played piano duets with her daughter, removed her from kindergarten when it seemed to tax her strength, and nursed her when she experienced what appears to have been an emotional breakdown around the age of fifteen.[3] She also took great pride in Esther's appearance: "None of her pictures do her justice because her expression is so brilliant and in her pictures she wears an unnatural look."[4] And she reflected thoughtfully on her own reactions to Esther's progress:

Her development has been very interesting and in most ways very gratifying to me. She is said to be one of the most popular girls who has ever attended the [high] school. . . . There seems to be an elusive spiritual quality about her that makes her very charming to both her boy and girl friends. . . . She is the life and music of the home and brings much young and pleasant company. . . . She has so much admiration and attention I am a little worried some times. I try to teach her to be in the world but not too much of it.[5]

Mrs. Ormsby's diary offers no evidence of Esther's response to the intensity of her mother's concern over both major and minor aspects of her growth and development, but it highlights the dedication and seriousness with which a middle-class woman approached her maternal responsibilities. Not surprisingly, it also suggests that mother-daughter relationships acquired a new complexity as young women entered adolescence. Edna Ormsby's account of her daughter's life between the ages of twelve and nineteen indicates that these were particularly difficult years for both mother and daughter. At the age of thirteen, Esther "did the least work and got into more mischief and gave [her mother] more trouble than ever in her life. . . . None of it very bad but she was very disorderly in her mental and personal habits."[6] Following a "very trying time in her development," her parents considered delaying her enrollment in high school for a year, but they changed their minds. However, after only one month of secondary education, "which she enjoyed very much," she suffered a "severe nervous shock" which kept her out of school for a year and a half, until her health was restored through the intervention of a Christian Science practitioner. The final entry in the diary reports that Esther's recovery was complete, she was able to go back to high school, and she planned to attend college as well.[7]

While it is impossible to determine the nature of Esther Ormsby's health problems or to attribute her difficulties to middle-class family dynamics, her mother's account clearly implies that a new element of tension characterized their relationship as the young woman moved from childhood to adolescence. They were hardly unique in this respect. Although historians can glean only an impressionistic sense of relationships between mothers and young children since the thoughts and feelings of the latter are rarely accessible through written sources, the experiences and emotions of adolescent daughters, as well as those of their mothers, can be documented more readily.[8] The reactions of late nineteenth- and early twentieth-century adolescents indicate that mother-daughter conflict was not an unusual occurrence as little girls grew into young women. At first glance, there is a striking resemblance between the sense of emergency conveyed by the emphasis on communication with adolescent daughters that characterized the periodical and advice literature, and historical evidence that also suggests at least a limited sense of crisis in the relationship. But that evidence actually reveals a more complex scenario in which tensions between adolescent daughters and their mothers form only one element.

The diary of Mary Anderson Boit offers a classic example of the trials and tribulations of a young teenager whose difficulties with her mother strike the late twentieth-century reader as almost timeless in nature. At the age of thirteen, Mary sulked when her mother expected her to take her "water proof and rubbers" to school in case of rain. She "called mamma horrid names" because she would not let her wear longer dresses, she lied when her mother asked her if she had crimped her hair, and she objected to being served "only bread & butter, cake & organe marmalad" when she had hoped to have "toasted crackers" for tea.[9] Mary felt that she and her siblings were rigidly constrained: "We can not do anything in this house as soon as we start to have any fun we are stopped. . . . It seems as though we were kept in a glass case & everything else in this house," she lamented.

Her feelings were complicated. She tried to understand her mother's position: "I am sure I never seem to be able to do anything to suit Mamma but she must get very tired having four children to look after," she observed.[10] Several weeks later, after another altercation, she noted contritely: "She [mother] has said many a time she would have nothing more to do with me & that she had given up trying to make a lady of me as she never could now I am really going to try to improve in all my bad habits." On the same day, Mary also dreamed about her mother's death and recorded her distress in her diary: "I cried & cried so as if I never would stop it seemed so real. . . . I don't like to dream of my dear sweet mamma it makes me feel so sad."[11] She alluded to her own bad habits again on the day before her fourteenth birthday, when she wrote, "Poor Mamma she has so many trials & cares with four unruly children especially from me I am so horrid I should think she would lose her patience with me much more than she does," and she expressed the hope that she would be able to "cure [her] faults."[12] Yet a few months later, much to her own chagrin, Mary found herself "up in the garret in disgrace" once again as a consequence of her objectionable behavior: "She said I had always been ungrateful & rude. . . . I said I had not been rude since spring but had been trying not to be & she would not believe me . . . but I know well enough that sometimes this spring it was very hard for me to consider my answer back when she scolded me. . . . I do hate to be in disgrace with Mamma it makes me feel dreadfully."[13]

Clearly, this young woman's relationship with her mother was very important to her, but despite what she viewed as her own heroic efforts, their interactions were far from harmonious. Whether or not her mother recognized the problem, Mary was disturbed by what she perceived as a serious lack of communication between them: "I am really afraid of Mamma as I do not dare to talke to her the way I would like to I am sure she would call me sentimental. If I told her how I felt about very many things & that makes me so mad."[14] This poignant confession by an articulate adolescent daughter attests to her desire to confide in her mother and to her distress over her inability to do so.

An even more poignant disclosure by another introspective teenager offers further evidence of the significance a young woman might place on her interactions with her mother, and also of her reluctance to reveal all of her feelings even to this most important figure in her life. Sixteen-year-old Harriet Burton wrote the following in her diary on February 29, 1890: "Can it be only a month since my mother died. Oh when I need her most. I could talk to her more than to anyone, even then I never opened all my heart, but O my dear dear Mother if I could but see you now, if I could but tell you all, if you could but *comfort me* and *love me*. . . . Oh My Mother! If I could only have someone to talk to, there is no one—no one. I feel *so* alone." As a result of her mother's death, she felt isolated, left with no one to love and no one who loved her.[15] Maud Nathan, who also lost her mother when she was sixteen, echoed similar sentiments when, as an adult, she recalled her bereavement: "I was blessed with a wonderful mother, the cherished memory of whom has abided with me through all my life. When my mother passed away in my early youth, it seemed as though the rest of my journey must be made in darkness, in sorrow, in gloom."[16] Like the frustration Mary Anderson Boit experienced as a result of her inability to communicate with her mother, the loneliness Harriet Burton expressed and the grief Maud Nathan remembered reflected the central role a mother could play in the emotional life of an adolescent daughter.

That role was also reflected in less traumatic contexts, for example, in letters from Mary and Emily Hills to their mother. "I would great deal rather be at home and never see anything but dusting all my life than to stay here twenty-four hours longer . . . do *please* let me come *home*," Mary, the older sister and the first to go away to school, begged on September 17, 1886.[17] "I am glad you enjoy my letters but I am sure you can not look forward to them as much as I do to yours for I feel as if I were at the other end of the world from Amherst," she wrote several weeks later.[18] She particularly missed her mother during her first term at school: "Sometimes it seems as if I would go wild because I want to see *you* so much," she told her. And she looked forward eagerly to their first reunion: "I know I shall tag you every step you take for I am going to make the most of my time with you."[19] Emily was also homesick when she joined her sister at boarding school: "I am trying to improve my time Mamma but I do think all the time of you," she wrote. "Please notice," she urged in another letter, "that I have not said anything about being homesick, but you know how I feel."[20] And in typical younger-sister fashion, she complained: "I must say I cannot get used to the girls here and I wish I might be with Mamie [Mary] all the time."[21] Emily also confided her feelings about growing up: "I cannot realize that the eighteenth year I have so long anticipated is so nearly here and that I can soon go to the 'Promenade,' but I feel so little like a young lady."[22] She and her sister also sought their mother's advice about traditional matters such as clothing and appropriate Christmas gifts for family members.[23]

Both girls relied on receiving frequent mail from home. Mary was particularly distressed when she expected to hear from her mother and no letter appeared. Both also worried about the effects of their mother's busy schedule on her health.[24] They also complained to her about each other. Mary especially objected to the privileges granted to her younger sister: "I suppose Papa told you of how jealous I was when I heard you are going to allow Emily to go to the Phi Psi musical for it did not seem at all like you to let a *child* like her go to any such thing."[25] She thought that her sister received more mail from home: "I feel as if the family had quite forgotten my existence," she lamented, "for all the letters come addressed to Emily. . . . Good night Mamma. Do not neglect me any more but write soon."[26] Emily in turn protested to her mother that "Mamie takes all the news," and offered self-righteous criticism of her sister's behavior: "Mamie's stockings came today and I am positively ashamed of her; tell Papa he ought to take the postage from her allowance. Can this be her twentieth year and she guilty of this act!"[27]

It was not unusual for adolescent daughters to experience anxiety and confusion as they puzzled over their complicated feelings about their mothers. Alice Blackwell adored her mother, the prominent abolitionist and suffragist, Lucy Stone and identified strongly with her. She defended her against any criticism of her professional activities and even declared her intention of writing her biography, observing: "I am uncommonly proud of being Lucy Stone's daughter." Yet the diary she kept between the ages of fifteen and seventeen attests to frequent disagreements and communication problems between them.[28] Alice lamented her mother's resemblance to "Aunt Sarah, snarling all the time," objected to Lucy Stone's "scratching out something in my diary," and resented when she "hid a library book and made me feel cross."[29] On one occasion, after she had been asked to get some apples from the cellar and bake them for her father, she bitterly resented her mother's response to her inquiries about candles and the oven : "Mamma jumped up and said it was less trouble to go for them herself, and that *She was so ASHAMED OF ALICE* that she did not want any one to say anything or talk or something."[30]

But Alice and her mother were not always at odds with one another. After a particularly exhausting and unsatisfactory shopping excursion, they shared a sense of amused frustration:

Went shopping in Boston with Mamma. We mutually begged each other to put on our tombstones

"Died of shopping with an unreasonable mother"
"Died of shopping with an impracticable daughter"[31]

On another occasion, Alice nursed her mother through a severe headache. She also recorded her mother's absences when the latter traveled in the course of her suffragist activities, attended meetings and lectures with her, and expressed her pride in Lucy Stone's accomplishments.[32] Their conflicts apparently did not reflect any real estrangement, and as an adult, Alice devoted her life to carrying on her mother's work.

A later, but similar, example illustrates the same combination of intimacy and conflict that characterized the relationship between Alice and Lucy Stone. Marion Taylor loved her mother "more than anybody else in the world," but she felt uncomfortable about showing her feelings: "I never kiss her and I'd feel dreadfully silly if I hugged or anything."[33] Like Mary Hills, she was jealous of her mother's affection for her younger sister: "Mother loves the baby best."[34] Frequent references in her diary highlight other areas of discord. "Mother doesn't approve of my writing—she doesn't like the stories ... but I do love to write and if I get an idea for a story I just have got to write it down," she noted.[35] Her mother also criticized her lack of interest in clothes, her tendency to use "affected" speech and mannerisms, and her impatience with her sister. "I just paused in my writing to lend my ear to a lecture from mother," she confided to her diary on one occasion. "I say snappy things to Caroline all the time and mother says I'm getting to be an awful (lemon) old maid."[36] Marion was particularly distressed by her mother's attitude about a proposed eighth-grade graduation party: "Mother says I can't go with any boy! It isn't the *boy* that I want to go for but all the other girls are going with them and I don't want to be the *only one* and a left out. I simply won't go to the party at all if I can't go like the other girls! Maybe fourteen *is* too young but I don't care."[37] Nevertheless, she took her mother's opinions seriously and identified with her— "I'm like mother—I have to express my feelings on paper every once in a while," she commented.[38]

Other adolescent daughters were also the recipients of the sort of maternal "lectures" and unsolicited advice that distressed Marion Taylor. Frequent letters from her mother provided such guidance to Mary Almy who was traveling in Europe with her sister during the summer of 1909. In one such letter, Mrs. Almy inquired: "Pussy dear, *have* you tried a bicycle? Do make the time for it, if you can. If you could manage to ride ten miles without fatigue, I feel pretty sure you would feel repaid for the trouble." In another letter she wondered, "I know that you do both wipe out your drawers occasionally, but have you ever taken the drawers out and wiped under & behind them, as should be done always once a year?" A few weeks later she commented, "I am glad you got a dress at Libertys but am surprised you didn't get it lighter, and dye it when it soiled. I don't doubt it is charming."[39]

Mrs. Almy's concerns focused on trivial matters, and her daughters were probably not unduly distressed by her suggestions. But sixteen-year-old Josephine Herbst thought she could never please her mother: "I've tried but it don't work. The more I try—I've given up. Whenever I dust M. [Mother] or someone looks at me, when I neglect for one day to get dinner a heap of abuse is piled on me."[40] Annie Winsor Allen probably felt the same way when her mother exhorted her to be "fastidious" about her own room and personal grooming, and criticized her desultory response to a request to clean another room at home, referring to "how superficially, if at all, you had attended to it when I asked you to do so."[41] Yet, as the preceding examples demonstrate, superficial conflicts of this nature did not necessarily define the essence of the mother-daughter relationship for young women, nor did they represent the most troubling issues for mothers and daughters generally.

In 1925 a group of graduate students reported that as adolescents, they had found ideas about sex and religion the most difficult to discuss with their mothers, while problems of dress were the least difficult to talk about.[42] Although these findings pertained to a very small, select sample of highly educated, middle-class young women, numerous references to maternal advice and indulgence with regard to daughters' clothing suggest that it was indeed easy and natural for adolescent young women to consult their mothers about matters of dress. While other aspects of teenaged daughters' experiences in the era of the "new woman," such as extended secondary education, might differ from the experiences of their mothers, here was a shared female interest that linked the generations. Some mothers apparently enjoyed the role of fashion consultant and took pleasure in dressing their daughters attractively, while the latter were equally pleased by maternal interest in this aspect of their lives. For example, Maud Rittenhouse was delighted that her mother proposed to buy her "the lovely crushed cream rose . . . to wear to the grand reception"; she was equally pleased with "a charming new cream-colored lace bunting" and a "fluffy pink lawn piling on lace" with "a dainty bonnet to match."[43] Letters from daughters who were away at boarding school or college often contained descriptions of new clothes as well as requests for advice (and financial assistance) regarding shopping excursions. Both the tone and frequency of such discussions reflected the assumption that these were matters of mutual interest, and indeed that mothers expected to be involved in such decisions.[44]

Although mothers and daughters clearly shared an interest in this area, clothes could be a serious matter. Carey Thomas's sensible Quaker mother did not believe in following fashion and tried to dress her daughters plainly. But when fifteen-year-old Carey refused to attend a literary society meeting on the grounds that she would be the only person in a dress without an overskirt, Mrs. Thomas relented: "My mother was so distressed by this incident that she immediately bought me dresses with overskirts and from this time dressed me and my younger sisters like other children," her daughter re-

membered. "She was the most logical of persons and really reasonable. She was convinced that she had done wrong and the battle was
fought once and for all."[45] Another mother was greatly distressed by
her daughter's apparent carelessness about her appearance when she
had appropriate new outfits from which to choose. "How could you
wear your old blue dress about *anywhere?*" Annie Winsor Allen's
mother asked her daughter, who was traveling in England in 1885.
"After all the pains we took (Aunt E.) to supply you with plenty of
suitable costumes it is trying to have you going about in that thing
that was not fit to wear out of your bathroom? How did it happen?"[46]

As the 1925 survey suggested, adolescent daughters and their
mothers communicated far less comfortably about matters pertaining
to sex than they did about wearing apparel. This finding underscores
an issue of relevance to earlier generations of mothers and daughters
as well. Intergenerational communication problems regarding the
"facts of life" were not new to the mother-daughter relationship in
the early decades of the twentieth century. During the previous century, sexuality was generally considered an inappropriate subject for
discussion, and even private letters and diaries tended to refer to
pregnancy in cryptic terms, if at all.[47] Nineteenth-century physicians
had deplored maternal reluctance to prepare daughters for the physical changes of puberty and described the difficulties experienced by
young women whose prudish mothers kept them ignorant of what to
expect.[48] Prescriptive literature directed to women also addressed
this problem.[49] A survey of married women conducted by Dr. Clelia
Mosher between 1892 and 1920 provided additional corroboration.
Of a total of forty-five respondents, forty-three born before 1890 and
thirty-three born before 1870, only fourteen had discussed sexual
physiology before marriage, and only six of those had discussed the
topic with their mothers. One woman who was married in 1882
reported that her mother, who was herself a physician, refused to tell
her anything. The mother of another woman said that such things
were not even to be thought about let alone discussed. While one
respondent did report a frank conversation with her mother and
another received information from both her mother and friends,
apparently most women, like the mother of Mary Ezit Bulkley, regarded the subject as taboo.[50]

These experiences were not unique. Josephine Herbst was completely unprepared when she began to menstruate at the age of eleven. Her mother only cautioned her to be more careful during her period and expressed her own feeling that it had happened too soon. Although she tried to get more information, she found that the library had little to offer and she was uncomfortable about herself.[51] An entry in Marion Taylor's diary suggests that she felt unable to ask her mother about such matters: "There are so many things I don't understand—things about life—I don't like to ask mother—it's my funny disposition but I can't make myself ask her," she wrote.[52] After a disturbing conversation on the subject with another young woman, Maud Rittenhouse finally discussed sex, at the age of seventeen, not with her mother but with a married friend who was sensitive to her concerns: "Alice could not change the inevitable to be sure," she wrote in her diary, "but she talked in such a delicate and sweet, womanly way with me, . . . that although I cried some I didn't feel utterly wounded to the heart's core as I had after Eva's shocks." Nevertheless, she noted that she lay awake very late "trying to be brave enough to face what seemed horrible realities."[53]

Although it was considered appropriate for a mother to have "a little talk" with her daughter before she was married, most women apparently were reluctant to provide any substantial information on the subject of marital relationships. Some felt that "prenuptial revelations" would tarnish a young girl's innocence. Frances Parkinson Keys, married in 1904, recalled her anxiety and puzzlement as a nineteen-year-old bride who knew almost nothing about the physical aspects of marriage because her mother was too embarrassed to enlighten her.[54] Edith Wharton had a similar experience when, at the age of twenty-four, in 1895, she asked her mother to tell her "what marriage was really like." Her mother found this a ridiculous question and would tell her only that she must have seen enough pictures and statues to recognize the difference between men and women: "You can't be as stupid as you pretend," she chided. Obviously such conversations provided no reassurance for apprehensive young women. Wharton's biography indicates that her mother's response, which was not unusual among society mothers of the day, also had a long-term negative impact on her life.[55]

Maternal reticence regarding the "facts of life" even characterized women who tended to be more understanding and sympathetic than

Left: Anne Bent Ware Winsor (mother of Annie Winsor Allen) and daughter Mary. (The Schlesinger Library, Radcliffe College)

Above: Mary Simkhovitch with her daughter Helena. (The Schlesinger Library, Radcliffe College)

Left: Mary Kenney O'Sullivan and her daughter. (The Schlesinger Library, Radcliffe College)

Left: Ethel Sturges Dummer with daughters Marion and Katherine, 1894. (The Schlesinger Library, Radcliffe College)

Below: Mrs. Hugh Cabot (Mary Anderson Boit) and daughter Mary, on "the grand tour," 1924. (The Schlesinger Library, Radcliffe College)

Minnie Roop Millette with daughter Nancy, dressed for Hallowe'en. (The Schlesinger Library, Radcliffe College)

Our first walk in the Park June 25. 1911

Jessie Tarbox Beals and infant daughter Nanette, 1911. (The Schlesinger Library, Radcliffe College)

Below: Jessie Tarbox Beals and
Nanette. (The Schlesinger Library,
Radcliffe College)

Facing: Jessie Tarbox Beals and a
very grown-up Nanette. (The
Schlesinger Library, Radcliffe College)

Above: Charlotte Perkins Gilman with photograph of her mother, 1915. (The Schlesinger Library, Radcliffe College)

Right: Charlotte Perkins Gilman and her daughter, 1893. (The Schlesinger Library, Radcliffe College)

Mrs. C.W.Mcc Sbran at her first convention 1901 in Racine

Catharine McCullough Spratt
attending her first women's convention, on her mother's lap,
1901. (The Schlesinger Library,
Radcliffe College)

Facing: Mrs. Mayer and Daughter,
oil on canvas. Ammi Phillips. (The
Metropolitan Museum of Art, Gift
of Edgar Williams and Bernice
Chrysler Garbisch, 1962)

Above: The Bedroom, oil on canvas,
c. 1660. Pieter de Hooch. (National
Gallery of Art, Washington, D.C.,
Widener Collection)

Below: Mother and Children,
1874. Pierre Auguste Renoir.
(Copyright © The Frick Collection, New York)

Right: The Bellelli Family: Detail,
1860–62, oil. Edgar Degas.
(Paris, Musée d'Orsay)

The Stocking, 1890. Mary Cassatt.
(The George A. Lucas Collection
of The Maryland Institute, College
of Art, on indefinite loan to The
Baltimore Museum of Art.
L.33.53.516)

Mother and Child on Beach, oil on canvas, c. 1860–70. Jean Baptiste Camille Corot. (Philadelphia Museum of Art, The John G. Johnson Collection)

Emma and Her Children, oil on canvas, 1923. George Wesley Bellows. (Gift of Subscribers and the John Lowell Gardner Fund. Courtesy Museum of Fine Arts, Boston)

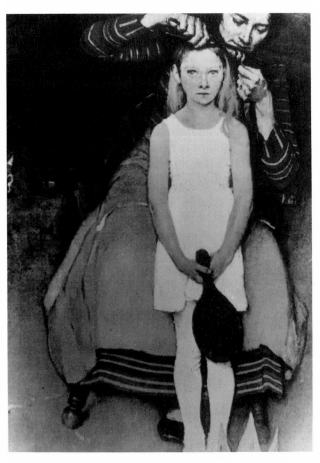

After Supper She Curled Donna May's Hair up on an Iron, illustration, Saturday Evening Post, December 18, 1937. Norman Rockwell. (Printed by permission of the Estate of Norman Rockwell. Copyright © 1937, Estate of Norman Rockwell)

Above: Portrait of Mrs. Burckhardt and Her Daughter, oil on canvas, 1885. John Singer Sargent. (Private Collection. Photograph courtesy of Kennedy Galleries, Inc., New York)

Right: Portrait of Countess Livia da Porto Thiene and Her Daughter Porzia, c. 1556. Paolo Veronese. (Walters Art Gallery, Baltimore)

The Crochet Lesson, pastel, 1913.
Mary Cassatt. (Bonfini Press, Brus-
sels)

Edith Wharton's mother. While Carey Thomas's mother was willing to compromise on matters of dress to save her daughter from the agony and embarrassment of being unfashionable, she apparently could not bring herself to save her from ignorance and distress regarding sex. When Carey and two friends decided that they needed more information about these matters, they proceeded to investigate independently: "I had gotten Mrs.____ *What Women Should Know* and about fifteen of father's medical books (he was in New York) and we began and read till 11:30. The reason we wished to was it seemed to us we were old enough to know all about the different forces of life. . . . After all in purely natural phenomena what can be degrading?" Despite this rational approach, the young women evidently learned more than they either needed or wanted to know: "But positively after we had done we did not say much, we could not, the revelations of vice and hateful disgusting things that we had not the faintest conception ever existed were too much, but I went to bed sick."[56] This reaction, like Maud Rittenhouse's reference to "horrible realities," underscores the lack of mother-daughter communication on this topic. Yet apparently Maud's mother did discuss some delicate matters with her, as the following observation indicates: "Today I am *soul-sick* over some things Mama told me. She has been working with dauntless energy and determination in social purity work. She told me of some of the things that compelled her to do it, that taught her the fearful need."[57]

Even when mothers were willing to talk about these matters, the discussions were not necessarily candid or productive. One young woman was indignant because her mother defended the notion of a double standard of chastity for men and women. She refused to accept the argument that a wife must keep her husband happy or he will seek satisfaction elsewhere, and she insisted that she would leave such a man.[58] After her engagement, Helen Swett discussed birth control indirectly with her mother, who hoped that her daughter would not find herself in a position where she would have to work when she was "not in a condition to do so." In response to her daughter's observation that it was not necessary to have a family until one was ready to do so, her mother replied that this "was a matter some people could regulate and others could not" and that she herself had been one of the latter. But Helen and her fiancé had already discussed this matter, and she felt certain that they would have more success with family planning, although she "thought it better not to rouse her [mother's] curiosity by making any boasts."[59] In contrast, however, Mary Smith Costelloe told her mother in 1888 quite directly that she and her husband were using abstinence as a means of birth control, which suggests that some mothers, and married daughters at least, felt more comfortable about discussing these matters.[60]

While the biological aspects of gender relations were generally avoided, late nineteenth- and early twentieth-century mothers and daughters did talk about other components of courtship and marriage. In her survey of the history of courtship in America, Ellen Rothman argues that during the first two-thirds of the nineteenth century, young women did not share the details of their interactions with the opposite sex with their mothers, who had to care for large families and thus could not devote much attention to these concerns. Rothman suggests that this situation changed in the decades after the Civil War, as young women began to seek maternal advice about these matters, and smaller families allowed mothers the luxury of developing the sort of intimate relations with their daughters that would foster such confidences.[61]

Clear evidence of confidential mother-daughter interactions supports the contention that the last decades of the nineteenth century witnessed this type of communication. From the age of sixteen, Maud Rittenhouse shared the intricate details of her romantic relationships with her devoted mother, who encouraged her patiently and with good humor, invited her male friends to dinner, advised when it was appropriate to write to them, and even visited one young man when he was ill. Maud relied on her mother's judgment in matters of the heart. She shared the love letters she received, confided her feelings of doubt and confusion, and hoped that her mother would think well of her suitors.[62] Although on at least one occasion her patience threatened to give out, Mrs. Rittenhouse remained a model of sympathy and understanding, and a source of unfailing support while her daughter agonized at length over her feelings for one long-suffering young man: "About Elmer it seems so sad, but Maud I do not believe you will ever love him as you ought, to marry him. . . . Feeling as you do you must not let things go on as they have done. . . . Do not think dear child that I am censuring you. . . . Somehow I have never felt that you could love him, much as I have wanted you to. God help you to do right, my dear dear little daughter."[63] When Maud finally decided to marry another young man, her mother was delighted with her choice: "When I told Mama this morning she fairly cried with happiness, for she loves him dearly," she noted with pleasure. "Mama is almost more frantic over him than I."[64]

Although she was more restrained in her confidences, Ella Lyman also relied on her mother's guidance as she struggled to understand her feelings for Richard Cabot. In a troubled letter marked *"Private,"* she confided: "I wanted to tell you that Richard loves me;—perhaps you knew it before. . . . I have *not* accepted him I could not then & cannot now; it means too much. . . . He is my best friend. . . . We have many interests in common & strong ties and I trust him utterly, but I do not love him as I love you & Papa." She took comfort in her mother's understanding answer: "Thank you, dearest Mamma for your lovely note. It was just like you, and will help me very much."[65] Their discussion about Richard was lengthy and serious. Ella found it very difficult to contemplate the idea of separation from her home and parents, and although she desperately wanted her mother's guidance, she hesitated to worry her. "You told me to tell you everything & now that I have you must not let it make you worried or I shall regret it," she wrote anxiously. It was easier for her to put her feelings in writing than to talk about them as her anxiety escalated: "I am going to write all this to you, because if I tried to speak I am afraid I should break down & not say all I want. . . . I must decide today whether I can let Richard go away or not. I don't want to have him go and then be always sorry for it, nor to give him all the added extra loneliness & suffering." Undoubtedly her mother did worry, despite Ella's injunction to the contrary, as she contemplated her answer to her daughter's request for advice on her dilemma: "I don't want marriage in itself & rather dread it, but only Richard's love & the service of God. Do you think now dearest that I ought to wait or not? I feel first one way & then the other & I want your help though I cannot bear to add anxiety to my lovely delicate mother."[66] Her "lovely delicate mother" was indeed long-suffering, as Ella's courtship extended over a period of almost six years until she finally married Richard Cabot in 1894.

Like Ella Lyman, Affa Miner was uncertain about the nature of her feelings when she received a proposal of marriage, and she too sought her mother's guidance. "Mr. Tuttle has opened his mind to Affa but she does not seem to reciprocate—entirely. I do not know what will be the result," Mrs. Miner wrote to another daughter. "It is now left in an uncertain state—I told her to take time & consider upon it. She thinks his manners are [unclear] but he will improve all the time by going into society &c &c."[67]

While all late nineteenth-century mothers were not called upon to help daughters cope with as many suitors as Maud Rittenhouse acquired or doubts as profound as Ella Lyman and Affa Miner experienced, it was not unusual for them to be consulted on matters of the heart. Ellen Hale kept her mother well informed with regard to her preferences among the males of her acquaintance. After an encounter with a young man whose interest had previously distressed her, she reported: "Well, he said and did nothing to give me the least uneasiness, from which I augur well for the future."[68] Mrs. Hale acknowledged her daughter's negative opinion of another gentleman when she shared the news of an acquaintance's engagement. "Only think of Lily Rogers being engaged, and to the very man you dreaded!" she exclaimed.[69]

Both of the Hills sisters discussed their relationships with the opposite sex with their mother. "I received a very nice letter from John H. last week," Mary reported. "Do you think there is any harm in my writing to him? If you do I won't but of course I do not write anything that he could have any cause to make fun of." A few months later she asked the same question again: "You haven't written me yet about my writing to John I only hope you will say I can for of course I wont write anything that I wouldn't want anyone to see and he wants to write very much." A year later, she confided her concern over the fact that "Mr. W." would be jealous if she paid attention to other young men. "You see don't you Mamma how it is? . . . I don't feel as if I had had any really gay young lady times and I do want to have some next winter and I don't want Mr. W. to feel that he is being slighted all the time," she explained.[70] Emily Hills shared the news of her engagement with her mother before she told anyone else: "Here is something which may not wholly surprise you, but perhaps you will be glad to know the truth from me and keep it to your self please while I write you what Dr. Perry and I decide about having an announcement made of our engagement . . . and I beg of you *don't* please even tell papa until I write you again. . . . You can not disapprove I am very sure and I think you will find him an ideal son-in-law." She also confided her intention to see a "*woman physician* to find out what is the matter (if) [with] me," and she added: "I have ever so much to talk with you about but I don't like to put it on paper."[71] On her wedding day, she told her mother in confidence where she would be spending the first night of her honeymoon: "Announce this at the breakfast table tomorrow morning, and do not tell anyone but Papa when you go to bed tonight," she requested.[72]

Although middle-class protocol regarding the propriety of corresponding and socializing with male friends relaxed somewhat after the turn of the century, young women might still seek their mothers' advice in this area. Some mothers responded to daughters' ideas and attitudes about men with ambivalence or disapproval. Even those who might sympathize with unconventional aspirations in other areas could react in a more traditional manner where relationships with the opposite sex were concerned. While a mother might understand and foster a daughter's interest in education, for example, at the same time she could disapprove of behavior that violated the established Victorian social conventions surrounding gender relationships, even when a young woman was long past adolescence.[73] Annie Winsor Allen's mother wrote testily to her daughter, aged twenty-seven: "I don't see why you should go to Church with a young man any more than to a concert; . . . I'd rather you'd go to the Tuckermans' with your Uncle."[74] Josephine Herbst's mother encouraged her daughters to pursue everything they desired—career, marriage, family— and stressed the need for excitement in life. Yet when Josephine wrote from college that she had gone on a night picnic in a ravine with a young man, her mother's ambivalent reply revealed her own reluctance to sanction behavior that so clearly violated the conventional code of ladylike behavior: "Do you go *alone* with a young man on moonlight picnics in deep ravines? That sounds nice but surely it is not the thing to do."[75]

Even Ethel Sturges Dummer, a particularly tolerant and understanding mother, could be apprehensive about her daughters' more casual interactions with young men.[76] When her youngest daughter Frances reported a conversation she had with another young woman about "flirting," and asked her mother if it was wrong for the friend, whose own mother "has not her confidence," to engage in this activity, Mrs. Dummer was alarmed by the nature of the question. Frances hastened to reassure her: "Mother dear—You are all off the track if you think I have been having an 'Affair' as you call it. . . . There was never any question in my mind as to spooning being wrong for me, I never would think of doing it." With regard to her friend's defense of flirting, she continued: "And I dont think either, that it would lower my standard if I tried just to understand, not to accept her point of view. . . . No-[body] ever tried to take any liberties with me. . . . Neither have I ever thought that I was in love or that anybody was in love with me."[77]

The sort of maternal apprehension to which Frances Dummer was responding mirrored a more general societal concern about deteriorating morals during the first two decades of the twentieth century. Organized efforts to control public morals, including the behavior of women, during the Progressive era reflected major changes in sexual behavior as young women adopted habits of dress and conduct that would have been unthinkable throughout most of the nineteenth century. These changes also included the blurring of the distinctions between young and middle-aged women in "silhouette, dress, and cosmetics."[78] Yet the value system did not keep pace with the changes, and conventional moral values continued to define the life-styles of most middle-class American women.[79] Hence while mothers might embrace, or at least acquiesce in, daughters' desires for higher education and interesting jobs, they might be more reluctant to lend their support to unconventional behavior with men, either because they actually disapproved or because they felt constrained to uphold social expectations in this particularly delicate area.[80]

While conventional middle-class values certainly determined in part the nature of mother-daughter interactions regarding the opposite sex, other factors also came into play. For example, Marion Taylor's feelings about men were complicated by the fact that her divorced father objected to fulfilling his financial obligations to the family, and she contrasted his recalcitrance unfavorably with her mother's dedication and support.[81] At the age of fourteen, Marion "thought men were like animals," and her mother "nearly had a fit." The following year she had "designs on every male" she saw, and her

mother teased her about her search for the "model boy." Marion
hoped to meet a man who would share her intellectual interests, but
her mother maintained that a woman must "submerge her personality" after marriage and that no man would "read and talk about
serious things with a woman." They argued frequently about Marion's "romantic tendencies": "I never tell her anything about my
affairs in that line because she lectures me every time I do. . . . She
says that if I'm getting silly and boy-struck, there isn't any use planning for college. Just because a girl of 18 who has never known any
boys in her life wants to know some she talks that way! It makes me
so mad that I am rendered fairly speechless."[82]

No doubt her mother's contradictory reactions to such expressions
of growing interest in young men reflected her own negative experience of marriage and the fear that her daughter might make a
mistake as she had. They probably also reflected the confusion many
women must have experienced in a cultural climate that directed new
attention to women as individuals and simultaneously articulated
support for older Victorian social mores. It is difficult, if not impossible, to imagine conventional nineteenth-century mothers offering
such mixed messages about the importance of men.

Annie Winsor Allen's mother focused not on the importance of
men, but on the importance of her daughter when she told her
future son-in-law bluntly: "I find it hard to believe thoroughly in
spite of all I know, that any man can be quite good enough to give
her to. Still I assure you that I am well satisfied and content with her
decision."[83] Mrs. Winsor revealed her own concern with middle-class
standards of propriety in her definite objections to other aspects of
Annie's marriage plans—she thought it was unfortunate that the
engagement and the wedding should be planned so close together
and that the young couple should be able to "evade the wishes of the
old and absent" as they made their arrangements. "Darling don't be
vexed with me," she begged. "Of course I know it is all for you to
decide but I know you are a little wild and I can't help wanting to
save you from mistakes. Love to Joe—I don't think you need show
him all I write," she added.[84]

Ellen Rothman contends that the tendency to seek maternal advice
about love and marriage was confined to only a brief historical period, and it declined among young women who came of age after

1900 in the context of an increasingly urban society that encompassed new leisure outlets such as the automobile, and the influence of an expanding peer culture. She offers some evidence to support this suggestion, but points out correctly that this new reticence was certainly not universal.[85] No doubt many girls shared Marion Taylor's aversion to maternal lectures on the subject of male-female interactions, but others, like Frances Dummer, continued to seek their mothers' advice on this subject despite the potential for awkwardness and disapproval. This aspect of mother-daughter interactions seems to mirror the transitional character of an era in which both young and mature women were involved in the confusing process of choosing between the traditional and modern values to which their culture exposed them.

The foregoing examples suggest that a blend of tension and intimacy defined the relationships of adolescent daughters and their mothers in middle-class American families during the decades between 1880 and 1920. Illustrations of conflict, many times over superficial matters, and reticence, often with regard to more substantive issues, indicate that mother-daughter interactions could be a source of anxiety and stress for both generations. But other evidence documents instances of close communication and sympathetic understanding, which imply that a mother could indeed be a "girl's best friend," as the title of a contemporary magazine article suggested.[86] In either case, these examples clearly underscore the importance attributed to the relationship by adolescent daughters as they confronted the countless dilemmas that characterize the process of the transition from girlhood to adulthood.

A certain element of intergenerational tension would appear to be almost unavoidable as young women begin to test their changing perceptions of self and personhood, and their mothers begin to acknowledge, often reluctantly, the resulting inevitable alteration of their culturally prescribed supervisory roles.[87] Several characteristics of nineteenth-century American child-rearing probably contributed to this predisposition toward conflict specifically during the period 1880–1920. Middle-class parents seem to have utilized a combination of permissiveness, affection, little or no physical coercion, and the expectation that rules would be internalized to socialize young children.[88] Although this pattern may have succeeded earlier in the nineteenth century, a daughter entering adolescence in the era of the "new woman" might question many of the rules she had automatically followed as a child, and thus experience considerable confusion. A negative maternal reaction to this new behavior could inject additional confusion and might also produce major mother-daughter conflict. Against a historical background marked by major transitions in women's roles and experiences, and by intense cultural anxiety over the implications of those transitions, then, the experience of adolescence might be especially difficult for both mothers and daughters.

While the social and cultural matrix almost certainly fostered the development of some degree of mother-daughter conflict throughout the four decades preceding 1920, the impact must have been particularly pronounced before the turn of the century, when mothers' own experiences of Victorian socialization still contrasted sharply with the new ideas and behaviors to which their daughters were exposed. Such a situation may describe the relationship between Mary Anderson Boit and her mother, whose comments about giving up her efforts "to make a lady" of her early adolescent daughter suggest a lingering Victorian mentality. Similarly, the influence of nineteenth-century socialization regarding the necessity to avoid open discussions of sex clearly contributed directly to maternal reluctance to educate daughters about this component of love and marriage, although they were apparently comfortable dealing with other aspects of courtship. That influence may have also caused mothers to feel guilty about their own sexual feelings, which in turn could make them even more unwilling to recognize and acknowledge their daughters' natural curiosity about this delicate area.

Other cultural factors could also cause problems. Some post-Civil War advice about caring for young children advocated the importance of unrestricted, active childhoods for girls as well as boys, but young women were expected to conform to more feminine roles as they reached adolescence. If mothers followed this advice, it could lead to major conflict, as the shock of the transition to the sex-linked restrictions of adolescence in the late nineteenth-century context of changing female images would very likely produce a rebellious daughter.[89] The trend toward "scientific" motherhood and the new emphasis on the significance of adolescence, particularly as it was experienced by girls, may have given mothers new impetus to fuss at daughters and worry about insignificant aspects of their behavior.

Most likely, women experienced a significant amount of apprehension and ambivalence about many different issues that arose as their daughters entered their teens and moved toward young adulthood. On one hand, a mother might fear that new and corrupt influences would violate everything she had been brought up to believe with regard to the proper socialization of young women. Conversely, she might find the idea of new freedom enticing or at least partially attractive, for her daughter and for herself as well, but she could also be uncertain. The resulting maternal confusion could easily send mixed messages to an adolescent daughter who was already confused by her own thoughts and feelings, and thus create or escalate intergenerational tensions.

How important was the antagonism between mothers and adolescent daughters? And how did they resolve their difficulties? In the context of the smaller, isolated nuclear family that typified middle-class life at the turn of the century and beyond, adolescent daughters recognized and acknowledged the centrality of the mother-daughter relationship to their lives. They worried about the tensions they felt, and they valued the intimacy they developed. Despite their conflicts, most mothers and daughters apparently shared at least a few interests, and some communicated easily about a wide range of issues. However, in other cases the tensions remained unresolved, as Edith Wharton's experience suggests. Often, the issues that provoked conflict were not really significant, and the relationship remained intact. But the resolution of mother-daughter conflict might become more difficult when adolescent daughters became young adults and chose to engage in activities for which there was no prior precedent in female experience, such as higher education and professional careers. The next chapter will examine the impact of this new, and potentially more serious, test of the complicated bonds between mothers and daughters.

CHAPTER 5

"I AM SO GLAD YOU COULD GO TO COLLEGE": THE "NEW WOMAN" AND HER MOTHER

WHEN Louise Marion Bosworth entered Wellesley College in 1902, she joined the ranks of the small, but significant, vanguard of middle-class young women who attended college between 1880 and 1920. These "new women" constituted a group whose untraditional behavior clearly and conclusively refuted conventional standards and expectations for daughters—a group whose activities seemed particularly likely to generate major mother-daughter conflict of the sort that elicited so much attention in the contemporary periodical and advice literature. It would not have been surprising to find that the mothers of these young women objected to the new path their offspring proposed to follow. But Eleanora Wheeler Bosworth was delighted that her daughter had the opportunity for higher education: "Oh Louise, I believe you have a future before you," she wrote on December 3, 1902. "I am proud, proud, proud of my girlie. . . . I am so glad you could go to college. . . . I feel sorry for these girls who have a mother so narrow, that they have to wait until they are married before they can do the things that young people love to do."[1]

Mrs. Bosworth was not alone in her enthusiasm for her daughter's educational and professional aspirations. Support for daughters' goals and objectives in the face of contradictory societal imperatives had characterized American mothers' attitudes as early as the eighteenth century, when Eliza Lucas Pinckney "took equal pride in her daughter's Latin and in her management of the dairy," despite the prevailing concern that too much education would lead women to neglect

91

their domestic roles.[2] The family experiences of Louise Bosworth and many of the other young women whose educational and professional endeavors collectively provoked so much public controversy around the turn of the century reflected the continuation of this trend. While tension and conflict certainly were not absent from the mother-daughter relationship during this period, particularly during the years of adolescence, American mothers essentially functioned more as mentors for college-bound daughters than as restrictive or critical influences on their activities. Although women missed their daughters when they left home, worried about their health and well-being, and complained about various aspects of their behavior, maternal encouragement and confidence actually played a vital enabling role in the process of daughters' taking advantage of the new options available to them.

Louise Bosworth became a "college daughter" in the early years of the new century, approximately halfway through the 1880–1920 period. In 1902 a college education was not quite as unusual for a woman as it had been twenty years earlier, but it was far from a commonplace experience. Typically, it was not the elite upper class American families, the wealthy "Brahmins," who sent their daughters to college, but it was members of the growing middle class who blazed this new trail for women. Family backing, particularly that of an enthusiastic mother, could be crucial for a daughter as she embarked on the new and distinctly untraditional path to higher education and possibly a professional career.[3]

Eleanora Bosworth provided such support. Her strong advocacy of college for her daughter pervaded their correspondence. "I hope you will work hard if you are able and be able to graduate [from preparatory school] this year. Because if you are thinking of ever going to college you ought to be getting started," she advised Louise on October 18, 1901.[4] Her interest in her daughter's academic progress did not preclude attention to more mundane matters: "Your marks I copied off. I wanted to keep the original to compare with the future ones. I am delighted that it is so grand. Do you not take English? I feel you ought to. I presume you explained that to me, but I have forgotten. You would better mark your pillow cases."[5] Mrs. Bosworth's enthusiasm, sometimes accompanied by a wistful desire to share her daughter's new life, continued as Louise studied at

Wellesley: "I feel greatly interested in all your talk about your college life, and the faculty, and hope you will tell me all you do and all about it," she commented. "You girls must have great times. What a pity mothers can't go to college with their daughters. What fun they might have together."[6] She anxiously awaited letters from Louise and another daughter—"It is the only way I live without you both from day to day." She also worried incessantly about the headaches (which plagued her as well), the upset stomachs, and the academic burdens Louise described in her letters home.[7]

Mrs. Bosworth's support for her daughter's endeavors as well as her attention to Louise's more prosaic needs continued after her daughter finished college. While her husband measured professional success more in terms of salary, she took great pride in Louise's developing career in social work: "I enjoyed reading the clipping you sent. . . . I feel proud that I have a child who can do so much good. Every one is not fitted for it, and few would care to do it. . . . I am trying to fix your dress and write at once and tell me exactly how large your belt is and hips. (the Japanese crepe.)"[8] Her daughter continued to seek her advice and assistance on both personal and professional matters.[9] As late as 1928, Mrs. Bosworth anxiously exhorted Louise to take better care of herself, although the tone of her advice suggests that Louise, by then forty-seven years old, had outgrown her reliance on her mother's guidance: "There is no use giving you advise about being moderate. And the publicity you had when you were ill is dreadful. I cannot imagine people being so inconsiderate as to flock in to your room that way, or the room where you were."[10]

The relationship between Louise Bosworth and her mother offers one representative example of the combination of emotional and practical support for daughters' untraditional educational and professional choices that was provided by more than a few middle-class American mothers between 1880 and 1920.[11] A range of mother-daughter conflicts certainly existed, but such conflict was balanced, if not outweighed, by powerful support and mutual caring, even in families where daughters' aspirations and experiences differed significantly from those of their mothers—and occasionally also where upper-class social mores were emphatically disregarded.[12] This situation resulted in interactions characterized more by understanding between college daughters and their mothers than by alienation. The nature of such understanding ranged from convincing inflexible fathers that higher education was an appropriate choice for their daughters as well as their sons, to actually accompanying daughters to college and even to graduate school. Tensions certainly occurred, but fundamental, systematic conflict did not define the relationship between middle-class women and daughters who went to college. Thus although the picture of mother-daughter relationships painted by the popular periodical and advice literature may have captured some of the experiences of younger daughters, it did not provide an accurate portrayal of the interactions between college students and their mothers.

Anne Bent Ware Winsor and her daughter, Annie Winsor Allen, offer an interesting first-generation case. A collection of nearly thirty years' worth of letters reveals a demanding, critical mother who complained and nagged incessantly, and a patient daughter who found their relationship stressful, but loved and understood her mother. When Mrs. Winsor scolded her for looking down while speaking, Annie, aged twenty-one, replied: "I am so afraid of the criticysm, correction or dissatisfaction that may be in your face and eyes that I do not dare to look up. . . . I am so afraid you will not like my way of doing things, my opinions and my tastes that I seem indifferent and offish . . . it is because I care so much to please you that I despair and grow discouraged." [13]

Annie not only wanted to please her mother; she was also willing to humor, support, and reassure her: "I cannot imagine myself wishing to prevent my mother from showing her full share of interest in me . . . I want you to understand me and not to worry silently," she told her. [14] Mrs. Winsor took her at her word and continued to express that "full share of interest," feeling free, for example, to ask her daughter, now about thirty-four years old, "Do you realize that you are habitually stooping a great deal? It's very unbecoming and will soon become so fixed that you can't cure it, unless you set about it at once." [15]

On the surface this relationship appears to have been a *Ladies Home Journal* classic, but it was more complicated. While Mrs. Winsor criticized and complained, she also consistently expressed warm affection for her daughter, encouraged her studies at Radcliffe, and applauded her success as an educator and a contributor (under the pen name Marion Sprague) to the *Ladies Home Journal*. And Annie remained communicative, affectionate, supportive, and tolerant of her mother's needs.[16]

M. Carey Thomas, one of Annie's contemporaries and the future president of Bryn Mawr College, described her relationship with her mother in her journal when she was twenty-two years old:

> I have just had a talk with Mother and I do believe I shall shoot myself. . . .
> There is no use living and then Mother would see in the morning that she
> had been cruel. She says I outrage her every feeling, that it is the greatest
> living grief to her to have me in the house . . . that I make the other children
> unbelieving, that I barely tolerate Father, and that I am utterly and entirely
> selfish. . . . O heavens what a religion that makes a mother cast her daughter
> off![17]

This young woman's problems with her mother stemmed from weightier issues than posture and personal appearance. Even as a young girl, she resisted any notion of traditional female roles and activities, devoting herself to her studies. She seriously questioned her family's religious beliefs and eventually rebelled against her strict Quaker upbringing. Her journal records her anguish over the tension in their relationship as the conflict with her mother escalated when she lived at home following two years of study at Cornell.[18]

But the journal also documents her mother's decisive encouragement of her educational aspirations in the face of her father's religiously based opposition: "Many and dreadful are the talks we have had upon this subject, but Mother, my own splendid mother, helped me in this as she always has in everything and sympathized with me," she had written four years earlier.[19] It was her mother too who borrowed money to send her abroad for graduate study, whose health she worried over while she was in Europe, and with whom she ecstatically shared the triumph of the successful completion of her dissertation and her comprehensive exams, asking on November 25, 1882: "Mother, is it not too splendid to be true?"[20] Carey recognized and appreciated her mother's assistance, wrote to her faithfully, and articulated her affection and respect for her: "Dear, dear Mother thee does not realize how I desire that you may be proud of me and find me a comfort. Thee must not think that because I am not a missionary in your sense that I have no missionary spirit. . . . I love you so much that I want you to be satisfied with me as I am satisfied with you."[21] She apparently thought of her mother as a career woman due to her involvement in religious affairs and various charitable endeavors and respected her for those activities: "My experience has been these are the mothers [women with jobs outside the domestic sphere] whose opinions their daughters care for."[22] Here, as with Annie Winsor Allen, mother-daughter conflict, which in the case of Carey Thomas involved fundamental value issues, was offset by strong maternal support and reciprocal daughterly devotion.

Like Carey Thomas in the previous generation, Hilda Worthington Smith, born in 1888, was committed to her studies. She argued frequently with her mother about her clothes, her interpersonal skills, and her sense of responsibility. Her journals abound with entries like the following: "Mother made me wear a horrid new grown up hat. Mother gave me a lecture on Cordiality. Only without lantern slides"; "Got another lecture from Mother & Auntie Bell for looking like a graven image when I speak to strangers! I don't."[23] The loss of a piece of jewelry provoked more conflict: "Mother most sick over the pearl pin she sent down with my class supper dress & which I never saw here, & says I must have thrown it away," Hilda recorded. "She talks as if I did it (whatever I did with it,) on purpose."[24]

At first glance, this relationship, like that of Annie Winsor Allen and her mother, recalls the difficulties recounted in the popular women's magazines, but these superficial tensions did not define Hilda Worthington Smith's relationship with her mother. Mrs. Smith, who, like Carey Thomas's mother, had been deprived of the higher education she herself had desired, understood and supported her daughter's aspirations.[25] She provided both moral support and laundry service for Hilda when she enrolled at Bryn Mawr, and she encouraged her to complete a fifth year of study there as well as two years of graduate study in social work. "I was sure your speech *would* be a success. Did you add anything to it? Write me any more said about it! When does the next one come?" she wrote enthusiastically to her college daughter on one occasion. "It has just occurred to me to ask if your study curtains are not *very very* dirty. If so send them with with [sic] laundry—I will send your laundry back Thurs.," she advised in another letter.[26]

In this instance, maternal support was somewhat ambivalent, as

Mrs. Smith often objected vigorously to any plans proposed by her children that would result in their living away from her. Her ambivalence seems to reflect more the fact that she was widowed at an early age than any fundamental disapproval of her daughter's activities, but in her journal, Hilda complained about her mother's attitude more than once, commenting, for example: "It seems as if I should never get anywhere, but should stay at home with Mother. *She* hasn't enough to do, & realizes it sadly."[27] Nevertheless, Mrs. Smith took great pride in her daughter's achievements: "It delights me," she told her, "that you are as Father was, above his fellows, & that you have so much quiet power as he had with the same humility.... I only want you to know that your Mother appreciates and rejoices over it all."[28] And with her mother's blessing, Hilda became a successful social worker, labor educator, and an administrator at Bryn Mawr, where the two eventually lived together. Some twenty pages of her journal record her grief and her sense of loss over her mother's illness and death from pneumonia on Christmas morning, 1917: "I cannot *bear* to have her gone. I think I was more of a companion to her than the others [her siblings], we had read so much & done so many things together," she wrote.[29]

Among the letters of condolence Hilda Worthington Smith received is one of particular interest, written by M. Carey Thomas (whom she knew from Bryn Mawr) on January 20, 1918:

Ever since I heard of your Mother's death I have been wishing to write to tell you how deeply I sympathized with you, but I have hesitated because I remember as if it were yesterday—and it is thirty years ago—how hard it was for me to get letters about my Mother after she died. There is nothing in the world quite like one's Mother's death and I think one never ceases to miss her however long one survives her. It must be a comfort for you to remember how good a daughter you were. People have often spoken to me about your care for her.[30]

Neither of these women was a "traditional" daughter. Neither ever married. Both were outstandingly successful, independent, professional people. Annie Winsor Allen followed a more traditional path in that she married and had three children of her own. She studied at Radcliffe for several years but never actually received a degree, although she pursued a career as a teacher and writer. All three of these women experienced conflict with their mothers; but this dissension was countered by the strong maternal support they relied upon as they fulfilled their educational and vocational aspirations—and by their own reciprocal appreciation and devotion.

The sources document many other intriguing instances of middle-class maternal support for daughters' untraditional activities during the four decades between 1880 and 1920. Several particularly striking late nineteenth-century examples, like that of Carey Thomas, illustrate the importance of such support for the early "new women" who ventured into higher education at a time when college education for females still generated significant controversy in American society. Vida Scudder's widowed mother took her sewing and went with her daughter to tutorial sessions at Oxford because the tutor preferred not to meet alone with female students; she had previously accompanied Vida to Northampton at the beginning of her freshman year at Smith, where she walked a mile and a half to the dormitory at 6:30 every morning for several weeks to help her daughter, who had never "done" her own hair.[31] In retrospect, Vida herself commented on the significance of her mother's support, noting her surprise that Mrs. Scudder "should so have departed from her tradition, social and other, as to send her daughter to college." She also found it remarkable that although she had never confided her secret desire to go to Harvard, her mother had decided independently to send her to the newly organized Boston Girls' Latin School to prepare for higher education.[32]

This departure from tradition had enabled Vida Scudder to take advantage of opportunities available only to a very small number of her contemporaries—four years at Smith, graduate study abroad, and eventually a distinguished career as a professor of English literature. She reciprocated her mother's support and devotion through her own choices and decisions. Although she was drawn to missionary work as her father had been, and to settlement work, she chose an academic career partly out of a sense of duty to her mother. She also accepted an appointment at Wellesley rather than one at Smith so that she would not have to "uproot" or "desert" her mother, whose home, church, and friends were in Boston. With the exception of her four years at Smith, mother and daughter never really lived apart, and Vida regretted even this period away from her mother, "so fragrant always was the time spent in her dear company." They eventually moved to a new house in Wellesley in 1912, where Mrs. Scudder enjoyed the company of her daughter's students and, ultimately, of Vida's close friend Florence Converse and her mother, until her death in 1920.[33]

Mary Kingsbury Simkhovitch's mother also traveled with her when she went abroad for graduate study: "Girls were not free then to take trips by themselves, and in any case, it was a great adventure for us both, for I was to study in Berlin for a whole year," Mary explained in her autobiography.[34] Her mother had supported her previous educational efforts as well, taking a detailed interest in her undergraduate work at Boston University and her earlier graduate study at Radcliffe, as well as in her work as a secondary-school teacher.[35] Mary described her as "primarily an intellectual person. Domestic duties worried rather than interested her. She was from childhood an outstanding student, both in the country school and at the Normal School."[36] As a former teacher, she retained her interest in pedagogy, and she criticized her daughter's "impatience and evident favoritism for the brightest students" when she visited her at Somerville High School.[37]

While few mothers would have had the freedom or the inclination to accompany daughters to European universities, unqualified maternal support for the "new woman's" desire for higher education and for her career aims was certainly not rare at the end of the nineteenth century. Maternal mentoring for college daughters took many forms. For Marion Talbot, a dedicated student who had discouraged the young men at Boston University who expressed interest in her, maternal advocacy extended beyond interceding with an obdurate father or offering advice on clothing and room decoration. Her mother, a former teacher who was frustrated by the limits of her own education, campaigned actively for the reform of women's education to secure broader intellectual opportunities for her daughters. When more conventional friends ostracized Marion after her college graduation in 1881, Mrs. Talbot organized the Association of Collegiate Alumnae, predecessor of the American Association of University Women, for the dual purpose of encouraging young women who wanted to go to college and expanding the opportunities available to female college graduates. Marion was eventually offered the opportunity to teach and serve as dean at the new University of Chicago.

With "many a heart pang," her mother encouraged her to accept the position, although this choice meant that her daughter would move away from Boston and also virtually insured that she would never marry.[38]

Alice Hamilton, who entered the Fort Wayne, Indiana, College of Medicine in 1890 and continued her medical education at the University of Michigan, recalled that it was from her mother that she had learned that "personal liberty was the most precious thing in life."[39] Unusually unpossessive, Mrs. Hamilton, who had a strong social conscience, encouraged her four daughters to do what they wanted to do, took pleasure in their achievements, and sometimes even provided direct assistance in their endeavors. When she visited Alice, who was living at Hull House at the time, she helped with dramatic productions and taught English to foreign visitors. Although she worried about some of her daughter's activities, for example, expressing her nervousness when Alice (at age forty-four) proposed to visit a brothel in an effort to "rescue" a prostitute, she remained supportive.[40]

In the case of Ethel Puffer Howes, a supportive mother meant an interested audience for her detailed accounts of educational, professional, and social activities as she attended Smith, studied abroad, acquired a Ph.D. in psychology from Harvard, and taught various subjects at both the high school and college levels. "I'm absolutely bursting with things to tell—and the worst of it is, I'm sure I can't under such circumstances do anything justice. How far did I get in my last letter?" Ethel wrote from Germany where she was studying in 1896. Three years later, she described at length a dinner at which Louis Brandeis and George Santayana had been present, and then consulted her mother about changing the ruffles on an old "waist" so that she could wear it for a lecture she was scheduled to give.[41]

Ethel's sister, Laura Puffer Morgan, a Smith graduate too, also discussed the details of her daily life and her work as a high school teacher with her mother: "I am convinced that you are right—some minds cannot see into Geometry," she wrote. In the same letter she reported: "Mrs. Pease thinks that your daughter is the best looking of all the high school teachers—and that too when there are two who are really pretty. It is a tribute to my gray hat and gown."[42] Laura's letters occasionally suggested the presence of tension about relatively trivial matters, as in her response to her mother's comments about a young man's interest in her: "Many thanks for your good advise but I am twenty two years old and am not quite devoid of common sense."[43] However, where education and career issues were concerned, apparently she, like her sister Ethel, enjoyed her mother's support and encouragement.

Not all college daughters in the period before 1900 sought or achieved distinguished professional careers, but those whose goals may have been less ambitious also relied upon maternal support and guidance. For young women like Carey Thomas and Marion Talbot whose feminist commitments dominated their lives, a supportive mother could serve as an ally against formidable obstacles as they challenged the behavior patterns prescribed for them by the traditions of a patriarchal society. For their peers whose aims were narrower, food packages from home and reassurance at examination time could be equally as important.

Blanche Ames consulted her mother about her assignments and sent her exam schedule home from Smith "so you can sympathize with me while I am taking them." She appreciated the fresh fruit her mother sent, asked her advice about changing roommates, and objected when her mother worried about the advisability of skating on the ice on Paradise Pond.[44] Although Blanche liked college, she was homesick, and she found it difficult to return to Smith after the Christmas holidays. In January 1895 she told her mother: "We try to reconcile ourselves to the fact that we wont be home for ages," while the following year she confided: "I think I am getting hardened to coming out here, but still I have that funny feeling somewhere in the stomach or throat or head—even if I don't go and cry."[45] She also confessed her anxiety about her academic progress: "I always keep thinking how Father and you would feel to think I was too big a fool to pass my mid years and then what would the rest of the family think of me?" she wrote.[46] And she complained about not receiving enough mail from home.[47]

Her mother's answers were warm and sympathetic. She teased Blanche about her own negligence as a correspondent and told her how much the family missed her.[48] She offered practical advice—"Do not undertake too much and get pulled down"—and she responded willingly to her daughter's requests for help: "Thinking of your themes and your request that we should think up some subjects for you, I ran over last night some . . . reminiscences and got up at seven this morning to write them out."[49] Her characteristic interest and responsiveness were augmented by expressions of unconditional support: "I must add my congratulations to all those you have already received," she wrote on one occasion, "not because of the honor that is supposed to have been conferred upon you, for I feel that you honor any position you may accept, but because it was something you desired and I wish you to have all you long for."[50]

For Josephine Wilken, as for Blanche Ames, maternal support also meant food packages—home-made candy—and academic advice. In a letter written from Smith on October 25, 1891, she included a list of suggested essay topics and asked anxiously, "Which shall I take?"[51] Josephine depended on her mother's assistance with her college financial arrangements too. Requesting the latter to send her a " 'statement of impecuniosity.' . . . that I may give it to the authorities before I leave," she reported happily, "I am to have $125 this year, instead of $100. Isn't that nice?"[52]

Maternal involvement in a daughter's academic life was far from unusual. When Charlotte Wilkinson's mother expressed her concern about her daughter's lack of interest in biology, Charlotte replied: "I'm sorry Mamma that I can't be interested but I don't think that it is honestly my fault for Professor Pillsbury is such a poor teacher. I have never found any one who got really interested in it . . . and his lectures are very vague and incomprehensible so much for Biology but Mamma I will try to work well in it."[53] Despite Professor Pillsbury's shortcomings, Charlotte unreservedly enjoyed her life at Smith. She told her mother about her studies, reassured her that she would never be "converted" by her attendance at "orthodox" prayer meetings, and confided her disappointment when she was not admitted to the college society she had hoped to join.[54] She found her mother's letters comforting and supportive, and on more than one occasion, she expressed her love and admiration, as in a birthday letter written on April 24, 1892: "I can only tell you that I love you *ever* and ever so much and that I am so glad that you're my mother and that I wish I were one bit like you."[55]

For Alice Mason Miller and her sister Helen, who attended Smith together, their mother's frequent letters were a source of prestige as well as comfort: "Mamma, you are quite famous as a correspondent, in Smith College. Helen mentioned at the table one day that you wrote two or three times a week, and the girls were very much surprised especially when they heard what long letters you send us."[56] Like other Smith women, Alice and Helen discussed their academic experiences with their mother. Helen complained that one of her professors was "perfectly horrid . . . the most vicious-looking man I ever saw."[57] She asked whether her mother would prefer that she take analytical geometry rather than chemistry.[58] Alice enjoyed telling her mother about the lectures in her music theory class and about the literature she was reading—"It is pleasant to 'talk over' what one reads, I think, especially with one's mother, and more especially if that mother happens to be you."[59] Many of the letters these young women wrote home emphasized social rather than scholarly matters as they struggled with their finances, asked for more money, and complained about each other.[60]

While Alice liked Smith, Helen was ambivalent about going to college. Her frequent references to parties and young men suggest that she was far more interested in socializing than in studying.[61] This tendency concerned her mother, but Helen assured her that she was not "grabbing at every young man I meet."[62] Mrs. Miller continued to worry, however, and wondered whether her daughter was keeping secrets from her.[63] Helen found her fellow students socially inferior in comparison to her friends at home. Although she told her mother that she appreciated the opportunity to go to Smith, she would have preferred not to be in college: "I *dont* believe in a college education for girls, and how *can* I study with any pleasure or profit," she lamented.[64]

Helen's case suggests that her mother may have valued higher education more than she did herself, and more generally, that maternal support for higher education could translate into maternal pressure on a daughter who was reluctant to attend college. While it is difficult to discern how often this situation might have occurred, it is particularly intriguing to find it before 1900 when sending a daughter to college still represented a form of social rebellion. Helen Lyman Miller had studied briefly at Northwestern University before she enrolled at Smith, and she had not been happy there either.[65] Possibly her mother was ideologically committed to providing both of her daughters the opportunity for a college education. However, Mrs. Miller's apparent insistence on the importance of finishing college also implies that despite societal reservations about higher education for women, some middle-class mothers may have regarded a college daughter as a socially prestigious asset even as early as 1878.[66]

Such an attitude would not be surprising after the turn of the century when college and career aims were no longer considered quite so revolutionary. By 1900 a female college student might be the daughter of a woman who was a college graduate herself; mother and daughter might share a common dedication to higher education.[67] Still, with under 3 percent of the college-aged female population choosing this option, college was far from the norm, and maternal support continued to play a significant part in determining which young women took advantage of it during the early decades of the twentieth century.

Ethel Sturges Dummer, the wife of a prosperous Chicago banker and herself a social welfare advocate, philanthropist, and author, provided unequivocal support for all four of her daughters in diverse ways. Her frequent, affectionate letters to her daughter Katharine, who entered Radcliffe in 1910, document a warm and open relationship.[68] Like her predecessors in the previous generation, Mrs. Dummer was interested in Katharine's academic life; she was also concerned about her welfare, anxious to provide anything she needed, and eager to know whether she was happy at college. No doubt she was gratified by her daughter's enthusiastic response to college: "I always knew I would like college and that it would be nice, but in all my anticipations, pleasant as they were, I didn't imagine that college *could* be as nice as it is. . . . Talk about Democracy, and high ideals, and earnest purposes—there is lots to education, isn't there? and many sides, and what a joy to be eager and learning fast! With a life full of love   Katharine"[69]

Her support for her daughter's desire to "take Phil. instead of Geology" was not unusual. Nor was her assistance with long-distance laundry service or the pleasure she took in providing such help.[70] However, her advocacy extended beyond what had become relatively conventional parameters after 1900. In a fascinating letter to the mother of Katharine's fiancé (which may never have been mailed), she questioned the young man's parents' preference for a postponement of the marriage of their children, arguing, on the basis of her exposure to "modern thought on sex" through her work with Juvenile Court, that "the content brought by the consummation of love is the right of these young people."[71] When his parents did not change their minds about the wedding date, she and her husband helped the young couple to elope and accompanied them.

Equally supportive of her other children's educational and personal choices, she told her daughter, Happy: "You have made at Wisconsin a record to be proud of. The thought of you, dear, makes me very humble."[72] On another occasion, she assured the same daughter: "If any plan comes up that really tempts you, you and your life and work, that which you have to offer to the world, must be considered as of most importance. . . . Your life must not be stunted by us. . . . Our love can make any leaps of time and distance."[73] She was just as understanding when her daughter Marion decided unexpectedly to get married during World War I although she was unable to attend the wedding.[74]

Not surprisingly, Mrs. Dummer's four daughters responded in kind, sharing their concerns and the details of their daily activities with their mother, and frequently expressing their appreciation for her letters and her unfailing encouragement.[75] Their voluminous correspondence reveals occasional disagreements, including an emphatic declaration by Frances, the youngest daughter: "I don't want to dislike a man just because you do. I have got to form my own opinions."[76] Essentially, however, the relationships these young women enjoyed with their mother were characterized by mutual pride, esteem, and understanding, as another letter Frances wrote from Wisconsin clearly illustrates: "Please, Mother, if there is anything you want to know just ask me because there is nothing I wouldn t tell you you know."[77]

Although Ethel Sturges Dummer may have been unusually tolerant and open-minded, she was not unique. Many of her contemporaries expressed their support for their daughters' enterprises in countless ways. Like Louise Bosworth's mother, the mother of Dorothea May Moore was passionately interested in the details of her daughter's college life.[78] Lydia Bush-Brown's mother assured her that she would respect her confidences: "If you write to me 'privately' about your health or anything else I wont impart it to a soul."[79]

Helen Landon Cass relied on her mother for advice about a tea kettle and for the vital information she needed in order to pass her college physical examination: "Will you write me *as soon as possible* telling *age & disease* of every one in the immediate family who has died," she requested anxiously. A few days later, she repeated this request, in capital letters: "DON'T FORGET ABOUT SENDING PARTICULARS CONCERNING THE DEAD PEOPLE OF OUR FAMILY—It's *important* & I need it right off." While the arrival of this information is not documented, Helen gratefully acknowledged her mother's gift of home-made jam.[80]

For the mothers of the first generation of "new women," supporting a daughter's aspirations often meant challenging entrenched traditional expectations and questioning the validity of their own lifestyles. By the early twentieth century, an untraditional daughter represented less of an anomaly, and it was not quite so problematic for a middle-class mother to take an interest in her daughter's college life.[81] But maternal advocacy could involve more than the translation of conventional mothering—providing advice on fashion and baking cookies to be shared with roommates—into untraditional environments. For example, despite the fact that Willa Cather assumed a male identity, cut her hair, and cross-dressed from the age of fourteen to eighteen, her mother encouraged her intellectual and cultural aspirations, provided her with a private attic bedroom of her own, and supported her wish to go to college over her husband's objections.[82] Although she completely subordinated her own life to her husband's wishes, the mother of Lucy Sprague Mitchell also supported her daughter's aspirations, albeit less forcefully, and Freda Kirchwey's mother approved of her daughter's unorthodox activities, including her participation, while she was a student at Barnard, on the picket lines during a shirtwaist factory workers' strike in 1913.[83]

While particularly unconventional behavior, such as that of Willa Cather, might strain a mother's ability to be supportive, distance could also threaten the bonds between mothers and daughters. Because her father's work kept him in Europe and she was sent to the United States to finish her education, Marguerite Queneau was separated from her mother for five years. Mrs. Queneau's letters reflected her determined effort to remain part of her daughter's life despite the geographic distance between them. Complaining about both the infrequency and the content of Marguerite's letters, she urged: "Do please tell me more about your *inner* self. I don't want you to grow away from me dear Margot—I love you very much and am always interested in what you think and do."[84] Unlike her husband, she thought it was important for a woman to acquire the best possible education "which is in the states." Since the family's financial situation precluded the possibility of transatlantic visits, she accepted the necessity of their separation and rejoiced in her daughter's opportunity to study home economics at the University of Minnesota.[85] Mrs. Queneau's anxious but affectionate letters testify to her eagerness to maintain her maternal role as well as to her daughter's continued willingness to seek her advice about college life.[86] Her earnest hope that they might "become acquainted before a separation through marriage or otherwise occurs" poignantly documents her recognition that distance had interfered with their relationship despite her best efforts to maintain close contact.[87]

Lucile Burdette Tuttle did not see her mother for almost three years while she was at Denison University in Granville, Ohio, and her parents were engaged in missionary work in India. Her lengthy, detailed letters reiterated her affection for her mother and related the details of her daily life.[88] Lucile was anxious to live up to her mother's example: "You don't know, 'cause I'll never be able to tell you, how very glad, glad, glad and proud, proud, proud I am that you are my Mother, and I am resolving to try and live nearer to the ideals you have held before me all these years, and to be the kind of a girl you want me to be."[89] She missed her mother and regretted the latter's inability to be present for Denison's annual "mother's day," writing wistfully about her eagerness to be able to share these occasions with her: "While I am just longing to have you here I know that you'll be here for certain my Senior Mother's Day, and you might get home early enough for my Junior one, too."[90]

Although their physical separation obviously concerned Lucile Tuttle, her letters do not suggest that any significant emotional distance intruded into her relationship with her mother. In contrast, Mrs. Queneau's obvious anxiety about maintaining communication with her daughter indicates that she perceived a similar situation to be a real problem. These examples recall the prescriptive literature that urged mothers to keep in touch with their daughters' college activities, and they reemphasize the importance placed on close mother-daughter communication as the twentieth century unfolded.

Three additional examples offer further evidence of the extent to which maternal support and mutual affirmation could define the mother-daughter relationship even as daughters became fully "modern" women. The intensity of the relationship between Crystal Eastman, a 1903 graduate of Vassar, and her mother, Annis Ford Eastman, was described by her brother Max in the following terms: "The great love of Crystal's life, never replaced by any man or woman, was our mother. . . . They asked no greater happiness than to be together; in separation they wrote to each other constantly, as often as twice a week; and yet, each rejoiced with admiration in the outgoing career of the other. No wish to retain, no glimmer of possessiveness, filial or parental, ever marred the sweet, tranquil, confident, life-enhancing flow of their friendship."[91] Mrs. Eastman, the first woman to be ordained in the Congregational Church in the state of New York, valued her daughter as her closest confidante. "I shall have so much to tell you all the rest of my life," she wrote in 1899. Crystal's esteem for her mother was equally strong: "Oh, the unhappy people who have not you for a mother! My heart goes out to them," she observed.[92] For Crystal Eastman, as for so many other "new women," maternal support included laundry service and fashion advice as well as solid encouragement for more significant endeavors. "Your card was there in the box to cheer me as I started for the bar examination this morning," she wrote to her mother on June 25, 1907. Two years later, Mrs. Eastman applauded her daughter's career choice enthusiastically: "If the *main contention* of the progressive woman is her right to a work of her own—a life work—then you are doing more to prove the rightness of that contention by making your way in a regular business—[the legal profession] than you could do by the most brilliant success as a social worker or investigator for a few years before marriage."[93]

Crystal summarized her mother's importance to her in an autobiographical essay published in *The Nation* in 1927, seventeen years after Mrs. Eastman's death, when she wrote, "My mother has always been a beacon to me."[94] Many years later, Florence Luscomb, who had studied architecture at Massachusetts Institute of Technology in the

early twentieth century, participated actively in the suffrage movement, and worked for the Woman's Trade Union League, told an
interviewer much the same thing in a slightly less elegant way: "Mother
was interested in the things that I was. In fact the reason I was
interested was because she had exposed me to those ideas when I was
young."[95]

For Virginia Gildersleeve, as for Crystal Eastman and Florence
Luscomb, maternal influence defined the course of her educational
and professional life. It was Virginia's mother who told her that she
"had brains and no nerves" so there was no reason why she should
not have as good an education as her brothers had. It was also her
mother who persuaded her shy, unsocial daughter to take the entrance examinations for Barnard even though Virginia feared that
college was "a sort of cloister" where she would never develop socially.[96] Her college debut, on her eighteenth birthday in October
1895, marked the beginning of a distinguished academic career which
encompassed the pursuit of a Master's degree and a doctorate from
Columbia, in addition to her degree from Barnard. Eventually she
taught at both institutions. In her memoirs, she highlighted her
mother's role in her educational life: "While I was in college people
asked me often why in the world I went to college, because at that
time it was not a very usual thing for a girl to do. They never believed
me when I said I went to please my mother, and I fell into the habit
of saying, 'Well, I suppose I went to get educated.' That always
perplexed and annoyed them."[97] Shortly after she accepted the position of dean at Barnard in 1911, her mother experienced a severe
attack of vertigo that lasted several months; although they employed
a nurse for the day shift, Virginia came home from her office before
the nurse left at 4:00, and her father took over at night. This routine,
reminiscent of the duties performed by countless daughters earlier
in the nineteenth century, grew easier after her parents sold their
home and found an apartment closer to Barnard.[98] Whether or not
she resented her obligations for her mother's care, Virginia's recollec-
tion of this difficult period offers no explicit suggestion of such
feelings. In her discussion of her mother's unexpected death, which
occurred in 1923, she observed, "The greatest grief I have ever
known was the realization that I had not been with her at the end.
More than any other single person she influenced my life."[99]

For Virginia Gildersleeve, as for many "new" women in the four decades before 1920, the mother-daughter relationship provided crucial reassurance and encouragement in the pursuit of untraditional educational and career paths. Despite the inevitable presence of dissension over matters such as appearance and manners that typically accompanied adolescence, with few exceptions interactions between college daughters and their mothers during the period 1880–1920 were distinguished by the absence of fundamental antagonism. This conclusion seems especially interesting with regard to those who experienced the largest generation gap—the early "new" women and their mothers for whom nineteenth-century domesticity had defined the nature of women's roles. Yet it applies equally to the next generation of daughters who sought to expand the boundaries of women's sphere and to the mothers who backed their efforts as well.[100] For in spite of obvious generational differences in the style of interaction, for example, the use of less formal, even slang expressions in correspondence, strong maternal support and mutual caring link the early twentieth-century mothers and daughters with their late Victorian predecessors.[101]

Certainly there were exceptions to the prevailing tone of harmony that characterized the relationships between middle-class mothers and daughters whose educational and professional choices defined them as "new women." However, only one conspicuous case of unmitigated and lasting mother-daughter conflict was apparent among the examples surveyed. This was the mother-daughter relationship depicted by Margaret Anderson in her autobiography. An exceedingly radical and independent young woman, with a strong interest in the work of Emma Goldman and other anarchists, she apparently had no common bond whatsoever with her mother, who wanted to suppress rather than encourage her.[102] Their relationship reached what Margaret called "our breaking point" in a confrontation following the death of her father. "Her ultimatum was that I must not live my life, think my thoughts, publish my magazine. I must live her life as dad had done," Margaret recalled.[103]

Clara Savage Littledale's conservative mother also found it difficult to understand some of her daughter's interests and activities, and she complained that Clara did not confide in her. Although she sympathized with her mother's feelings, Clara considered her expectations unrealistic.[104] Conflict over these issues distressed both mother and daughter. "She [Mrs. Savage] determined to be frank and was," Clara confided to her journal. "It was terrible and I said awful things and got hard and absolutely unfeeling and it did no good except to teach me there was nothing in trying to be frank and to make me see how hard it is for mothers. Both perfectly miserable."[105] She also remembered another equally uncomfortable occasion when a colleague whom she admired came to dinner: "I was very anxious for Mother to like her, but Mother connected her mentally with . . . rampant radicalism and *froze!* And the connection was all wrong."[106] Unlike Margaret Anderson, however, Clara Savage Littledale remained essentially devoted to her mother, with whom she lived following her graduation from Smith in 1913. Despite the demands of her career in journalism, she sewed for her mother, shopped with her, comforted her after her husband's death, and admired her domestic skills.[107]

Lella Secor seems to have found her filial obligations more onerous. A journalist, and later a peace activist during World War I, she had left home to pursue newspaper work although her mother wanted her to be a teacher. While her letters were affectionate, they occasionally highlighted areas of definite mother-daughter conflict. "I am not for one moment forgetting my home obligations, and will not consider any work which will not make it possible for me to fully meet my share of the home expenses," Lella assured her family in an obviously defensive tone.[108] In a letter to two of her sisters, she alluded to the difficulties of growing up "under a sort of system of suppression," and she commented: "I don't regret any sacrifice I have made in my effort to make Mother happy. The only thing I regret is that so much of the time our efforts have met with no result."[109] When her mother had to sell the family home, Lella offered both emotional and financial support, but she also took the opportunity to remind her that she must assume responsibility for her own well-being: "You are at liberty, as I have told you before, to do exactly as you wish. . . . I am convinced that happiness rests with you alone. No one else can make or find it for you . . . it would be feeble folly for me to attempt it for you, as I have often falsely thought I could do, had I gone home."[110]

This letter, which is signed "Lovingly your baby, Lella Faye," does not suggest that Lella felt the kind of hostility toward her mother articulated by Margaret Anderson. Nor do any of her other letters reflect that degree of anger. But her correspondence clearly indicates that she was occasionally impatient, that she was too busy to be as attentive as her mother would have liked her to be, and that, as a result, her mother felt neglected.[111] Possibly the profound sense of loss she articulated after the latter's death reflected Lella's feelings of regret over incidents of this sort as well as her genuine love for her mother.[112]

Despite the inevitable existence of a certain amount of tension, which was exhibited in different ways, then, the relationships between middle-class daughters who followed untraditional paths and the mothers who stood behind them were characterized more by tolerance and understanding than by negative, hostile interactions. While the "new" young women of the late nineteenth and early twentieth centuries to some extent repudiated the world of their mothers, as Carroll Smith-Rosenberg contends, it seems clear that their mothers did not repudiate them or their world.[113]

On the contrary, they often empowered their daughters in various ways and so authorized them to move in new directions. Although this was not the case universally, the willingness of mothers to align themselves with daughters in the face of paternal opposition undoubtedly made a crucial difference for a number of ambitious "new women." But maternal support represented more than a translation of nineteenth-century domestic bonds into a new setting: to a significant extent, women shared the achievement orientation of their daughters, and in some instances, mothers actually led the way—by inclination if not by action. In turn, many young women who went to college still saw their mothers as role models and continued to seek their advice; apparently the majority did not perceive a serious generation gap based on the new opportunities for higher education, although for a few this generational difference seemed to be a problem. This picture differs considerably from the impression conveyed by the prescriptive literature that represented college as a set of very threatening, potential problems. It also demonstrates that the period 1880–1920 is an important one in the history of mother-daughter relationships—not because it heralded the early stages of contemporary matrophobic tendencies, but because it sustained positive, supportive interactions even in the context of significant generational differences in opportunity and experience.

The middle-class women who encouraged and supported their daughters' educational and professional aspirations in the late nineteenth and early twentieth centuries might not have agreed with the thoughts of Lydia Maria Child, who commented in 1863: "I know people are accustomed to congratulate mothers when their daughters are married, but to me it has always seemed the severest trial that a woman can meet, except the death of her loved ones."[114] Probably, however, they would have applauded the view expressed by one outspoken mother in a letter written in 1910: "Daughters are wonderful luxuries; they are well worth a bad husband in my opinion: at least mine are."[115] And no doubt many other college-educated, professional daughters would have understood perfectly Clara Savage Littledale's reaction to the news that her mother was terminally ill: "My mother is desperately ill and the doctors say she can't get well, but all I can seem to do is to go and take her little brown hands in mine and sit by her. We are very unlike and I have no words to tell her how she is, after all, the anchor of my life and I would die for her if I only could. Without her I seem to have lost my base and am a-drift."[116]

CHAPTER 6

"WE NEED EACH OTHER":
ADULT DAUGHTERS AND
THEIR MOTHERS

A S Lucy Wilson Peters embarked on married life on Thanksgiving Day, November 27, 1890, she linked her own life with that of her mother in a new and adult way: she now shared her mother's wedding anniversary, and that of her maternal grandmother and an aunt as well.[1] Lucy's selection of this particular day for her wedding implicitly affirmed the importance she placed on maintaining close ties with her mother and her past as she entered a new phase of adulthood. Her recollections offer no hint about the ease or difficulty with which she adjusted to marriage, but her marriage date symbolizes the enduring connections that bound middle-class mothers and adult daughters during the late nineteenth and early twentieth centuries.

Those connections were equally as important to Blanche Ames Ames, whose marriage (to a young man with the same last name as hers) took place about ten years after that of Lucy Wilson Peters. Frequent, detailed letters to her family described the wonderful sights and interesting places Blanche encountered during her honeymoon in Europe, where she had "the best time in the world." But the reality of life as a married adult was different, and she found it hard to feel settled in her new home, as she explained to the "dearest of Mothers":

Oakes [her husband] has been troubled because he says at the first proposition of anyone to go away I am eager to go. He thinks I will never make this really my home. Of course it is not quite so bad as that, but upon thinking it over I find he is right to a certain extent, for any plan of meeting you people or going somewhere with you makes my heart go up. I thought of you again and again [on other recent journeys]. . . . And have been counting the days when I could see you, before you had forgotten all the news.[2]

For Blanche Ames Ames, Lucy Wilson Peters, and many other daughters—married and single, domestic and professional—the mother-daughter bond played a crucial supporting role in mature adulthood, as it had earlier in their lives. For their mothers as well, the relationship remained one of paramount importance. Women and adult daughters shared both family and professional experiences, relied on one another for advice and sympathy, and worried about one another's health and happiness. Conflicts occurred, but despite such factors as advancing age and geographic distance, for the most part the relationship endured as a central component in the lives of both generations as it had in the previous decades of the nineteenth century and even earlier. One devoted mother characterized this strong bond simply but accurately: "We need each other."[3]

Mothers and adult daughters regularly consulted and advised one another on countless domestic matters during the period between 1880 and 1920. For example, the dialogue on dress and personal appearance continued. "You will be pleased to learn that I'm fixing my hair now in the way you have wanted me to for so long, waved in front and combed down on the sides of my head," forty-year-old Caroline Judson Hitchcock told her mother.[4] Like many of their contemporaries, she and her sisters often wrote to their mother about the purchase or remodeling of dresses and even included fabric samples with their letters. "You will be interested in the samples heading the page, it is my new dress goods which I bought yesterday at Hartford. I hope you will like it," Caroline noted in one letter. "What dressmaker have you had at the house, Maria?" she asked in another. Mrs. Hitchcock responded with interest when her daughters wrote to her about their clothes, asking, for example: "Have you got your cloak yet and does it suit you?"[5]

Discussions about wearing apparel and accessories helped mothers keep in touch with daughters' lives. Mary Elizabeth Homer's daughter moved to Hawaii after her marriage, but she still consulted her mother about new clothes. Mrs. Homer was delighted when she received a sample of "pretty" dress material, which she approved

enthusiastically. Louise Herrick Wall's mother made a new handbag
for her and took great care to insure its safe arrival: "I sent your
bead[ed] bag there [to Portland, Oregon] by registered mail," she
wrote. "I hope you will like it. It is the prettiest one I have made I
think." And Eleanora Bosworth continued to assume responsibility
for organizing her daughter's wardrobe long after the latter had
completed her education and embarked on an independent career.[6]

Daughters routinely discussed other practical domestic concerns
with their mothers as well. As a young bride in rural Vermont, Lulu
Perry Fuller wrote about the details of her daily life. "We had a
yellow rooster for dinner yesterday. It was the first chicken that
Frank had ever dressed but it was real tender and good," she reported happily. She found other domestic tasks more daunting: "Next
week I expect to wash the parlor curtains but I haven't any idea of
how much starch to put into them."[7] Mrs. Perry's weekly letters to
her own aging mother during this period offer an interesting three-
generation comparison. In the same matter-of-fact tone found in her
daughter's letters, she reported family news and local events, and
occasionally offered comforting advice, as in the following straightforward response to a question her mother had apparently asked
her: "I shouldn't think it was any more wicked to clean house on
Decoration Day than to play baseball if one was inclined to."[8]

Mothers sought advice from adult daughters on weightier domestic matters as well, often where the welfare and behavior of other
offspring were involved. Helen Jackson Cabot Almy consulted her
oldest daughter Mary, twenty-five years old at the time, when she was
afraid she had been too lenient with another daughter: "Betty had
dinner at the Putnam's and went canoeing with Jamie. (Was I rather
foolish to let her?)."[9] Annie Winsor Allen's mother complained bitterly to her about her sister Jane's behavior: "She treats me with great
indifference usually—often with contempt & not infrequently with
displeasure & anger. She does not regard my advice of which I give
her as little as I can, nor care for my opinion which she often knows
even when I do not express it."[10] Although she regretted the necessity to discuss the faults of one of her children with another, she
greatly appreciated Annie's response to the situation, which she found
"very wise." She continued to share her concerns about Jane, and
occasionally about another daughter whose uncommunicative man-

ner distressed her.[11] Bessie Hitchcock's reply to a letter about her brother's drinking problem suggests that her mother also discussed one child's faults with another: "Your letter has nearly broken my heart! Why must you have so much trouble when you ought to be beginning to have a good time with your grown-up boys and girls."[12] Eugenie Homer Emerson replied in a similarly sympathetic manner to her mother's lament over the impending marriage of her son Tom, who was the last child to leave home, and encouraged her to take pleasure in the great happiness her brother had found.[13]

Like the behavior of siblings, other aspects of domestic life prompted mothers to confide their discontent and anxieties to their daughters. The mother of Maud Rittenhouse elicited her daughter's concern and sympathy when she complained about the tediousness of her daily routine. "What a miserable selfish creature I have been to take every advantage for cultivation, and stay away from home, while my little mother-bird wears herself out with vexing domestic problems," Maud confided to her diary.[14] Visits from family members could generate complaints similar to those of Mrs. Rittenhouse, as when Mary Hitchcock found herself cleaning and arranging things "as they will have to be when Aunt May comes which I suppose will be the last of this week. I dread her coming very much for she is in a very doleful state just now." Emily Perkins Hale also felt herself "a helpless victim" when she had to entertain a relative who, though "interesting and agreeable," had no interest in any activity but talking. As a result, Mrs. Hale told her daughter wearily: "I am so overcome with cousin Lucy's visit that I shall not write a real letter till she has gone, which I don't know when it will be!"[15]

Evidence of shared confidences between mothers and adult daughters seems to follow logically from the earlier examples that suggested that mutual support and caring characterized relationships, even in cases where factors such as adolescent behavior and untraditional ambitions might intrude on mother-daughter interactions. It is hardly surprising that the alliances formed in these contexts would remain strong as young women matured. In many instances, adult daughters probably felt even closer to their mothers than they had earlier, especially when they shared the experiences of marriage and child-rearing.

One of the strongest traditional intergenerational bonds, the experience of pregnancy and childbirth, continued to link mothers and their adult daughters as it had throughout the nineteenth century.[16] Even an unconventional daughter could take comfort in her mother's presence and appreciate her assistance both before and after the arrival of an infant: for example, despite very ambivalent feelings about her mother, Charlotte Perkins Gilman welcomed her help when she was ill during pregnancy, and following the birth of her daughter as well.[17] Certainly more domestically inclined daughters found it completely natural to share these events with their mothers from beginning to end. When Eliza Brown Moore reported her pregnancy to her mother, she asked her not to tell anyone else. Describing how her stomach rejected "everything it don't like," she alluded to the common bond this experience created between mother and daughter: "I know I can't tell you . . . news about this stage in the proceeding—for you have gone this way so many times before me."[18] Lulu Perry Fuller desperately wanted her mother to be present for the birth of her second child, and asked her husband to write to her: "Lulu says she doesn't see how she can get along without Mother and wishes I would ask her to come," he reported.[19]

Daughters relied on maternal input in this phase of their lives even where unusual distance prevented a mother's direct personal involvement. For Frances Tuttle, living in China, it was important to anticipate the possibility of pregnancy and to be prepared if it occurred. Accordingly, she asked her mother to send samples of appropriate fabric for baby dresses: "I truly hope I wont need any for years, but it isn't bad to have some knowledge along those lines."[20] A year later, she found herself pregnant; she would have preferred to wait until after the baby's birth to tell her mother, but she needed her advice. She assured her that she looked forward with pleasure to having a child even though the pregnancy had not been planned, but she did admit to being worried that she might not "know what to do with it after it arrives." "What finally decided me to tell you all this now was my perplexity over the clothes [for the baby]," she confessed to her mother. She wondered whether "hot weather babies" ought to wear flannel and how many little dresses she should make.[21]

The earlier reticence regarding her pregnancy reflected Frances's desire to spare her mother months of worry rather than any unwillingness to confide; she felt free to write in detail about her condition

in subsequent letters. "There is nothing especially private to write—
or especially public. All of my letters to you are more or less private,
however, for I tell you everything," she declared, adding that her
doctor "very much approved of the fact that I never wear a corset."[22]
Recovering from childbirth, she reiterated her sense of the common
bond of female experience in her observations on the difficulties of
giving birth and the aftermath: "I would like to pour out all my
troubles into your sympathetic ears, but I guess it would be better not
as you know them already and they are quite too fresh in my mind
for me to dwell on with safety. . . . It is a kind Providence that keeps
us from knowing before hand what is in store for us, isn't it?"[23]

News of a daughter's pregnancy could be an occasion for celebration rather than a cause for worry. When the mother of Lydia Marie
Parsons learned that her daughter was expecting a baby, she was
delighted: "I feel like pinching me to see that I am really awake for
such [a] happy message I had not looked for," she wrote. "I just cried
tears of joy, for I know now my little Darling will never be lonesome
again, and with such a dear Husband & baby why Lydia you will
come to your joys at last." Reflecting her own desire to be part of the
event, she suggested that Lydia might want to "come home" for her
confinement.[24] Her reaction to her granddaughter's birth was equally
emotional: "May she be a constant joy and pleasure to her parents,
the same as its very dear Mother has been to Daddy and me since she
was born."[25] Upon learning that Lydia was pregnant again ten years
later, she revealed very traditional feelings about the centrality of
motherhood in a woman's life: "People that have no children I imagine live a life of sham, never know the real meaning what life consists
of. . . . I know that my life always has been wrapped up entirely for
my children, and my Darling Lydia, [you] are such a wonderful
Mother, devoted like very few of them are now days."[26]

Once they arrived, grandchildren clearly played an important part
in maintaining and nurturing the connections between mothers and
daughters. Detailed discussions of their development, health, and
latest achievements pervaded women's correspondence. Affa Miner
Tuttle described the particulars of her children's activities and repeated what they said in her lengthy, frequent letters to her mother.
With one letter she enclosed a separate note dictated by her daughter
Elizabeth to her grandmother.[27] Amy Aldis Bradley, a conventional

homemaker like Affa Miner Tuttle but apparently more affluent, wrote extensively about her five children. In one letter, she assured her mother that her premature baby was doing well. In another, she reported that her daughter had discovered her toes, which were "a source of endless delight & wonder" to her. She also noted the fact that her children had whooping cough, and that she had to curtail her very active social life because she found that "so many grown people [who] havent had it are afraid of it."[28] Professional women with families were no different in their enthusiasm for sharing the details of their children's activities with their mothers. For example, Annie Winsor Allen included a whole dialogue between herself and her baby daughter Nancy, complete with phonetic spelling, in one of her letters to her mother, and enclosed a note dictated and illustrated by her daughter Dorothy in another letter.[29]

Not surprisingly, women eagerly welcomed news about their grandchildren and shared it with other members of the family.[30] Mary Pierce Poor's letters testified to the important place her grandchildren held in her life. She reported the recovery of one grandson from diphtheria with obvious relief, and she worried about the safety of her grandchildren on other occasions. "Do be careful of the boys on the fourth!!!" she urged. "Even at Cotuit there are probably the all pervasive fire crackers & probably many more deadly weapons also. So take care!"[31] Her children and grandchildren were the center of her life: "Your daily letters are daily comforts to your father & mother. To hear that the dear babies are well & the boys & their mother enjoying themselves at the seashore, which is my idea of bliss, makes us happy mortals," she declared. "I long for you & the babies. To have all three of my daughters together is my ideal life," she wrote on another occasion.[32]

Undoubtedly many women worried, as Mary Poor did, about the well-being of their grandchildren and wondered about the wisdom of their daughters' child-rearing decisions. But few seem to have been as outspoken on this subject as Annie Winsor Allen's mother. Distressed by the fact that her son-in-law, her daughter, and her new grandchild were "crowded together" in the same room, she suggested that it would be more appropriate for Joe to use the empty guest room until Annie recovered from the baby's birth. "I almost wish I didn't know the details of your *squalid* living—I never heard of such a thing except in a . . . tenement house. . . . Your ways disturb me with your lack of reserve and fresh air," she complained in a letter marked "Strictly Private." Mrs. Winsor also objected to the number of visitors who came to see the new baby.[33] And she worried about the lack of heat in her grandchildren's nursery: "Mary [another daughter] thinks you have no fireplace in your nursery. If that deficiency in building is from economy I should like nothing so well as to supply it, and I beg you will let me put in a chimney or whatever is necessary. I never could bear to think of those babies the least *under par* for want of being well *warmed up,* especially in the morning when in bath."[34] Here was clearly a potential source of conflict, but Annie apparently did not respond with anger or resentment. She was accustomed to her mother's critical disposition and understood her, and their relationship remained stable.[35]

Although there were no children to link them, other strong bonds connected mothers and unmarried adult daughters. Professional women whose careers had been facilitated by maternal support often remained very close to their mothers and even lived with them. Vida Scudder's concern for her mother's comfort and happiness shaped her own career decisions. In turn, Mrs. Scudder apparently accepted her daughter's close and, possibly, intimate relationship with a female contemporary who, along with her own mother, eventually shared their home. Hilda Worthington Smith's mother read her daughter's books, discussed social problems with her, and also lived with her for a number of years.[36] Like Vida Scudder, Mary Williams Dewson, a Wellesley graduate who enjoyed an active and successful career in the field of women's employment and in Democratic politics, lived with her mother until the latter's death. She also wrote a laudatory memoir of her which she tried earnestly, but unsuccessfully, to publish.[37]

Mothers provided continuing support and served as an interested audience for more conventional single women, such as those who taught elementary or secondary school, as well as for "new women" who pursued more revolutionary activities. Caroline Hitchcock reported to her mother in detail when the "school visitor or superintendent" visited her biology class. "When I was talking of sea-urchins he would interpose remarks on the star-fish and when I made the star-

fish my subject he talked of something still different," she complained. Her sister Lucy, describing the Christmas gifts she received
from her students, wrote: "Bess is not the only one blessed with
remarkable Christmas gifts. . . . Some of the things [I received] were
too queer for anything."[38] Helen Brewster also related her teaching
experiences to her mother, describing her kindergarten students in
detail, including one who was a "howler," and her classroom, which
needed "Japanese jack sticks" to deodorize it, and confiding her
loneliness when she moved from Hartford to a new job in Plainville,
Massachusetts: "I have been nearly crazy with homesickness for the
past week really Mother it is perfectly terrible, I can't control myself
at all. I get just sick with crying, and every little thing discourages me
so, and what do you think to crown it all I have lost my money. . . .
Good night with *literal floods* of love from The most miserable creature in the world."[39]

As in the past, unmarried daughters might still share their mothers' commitments to the family and thus, in effect, follow in their
footsteps. Representative of the end of the era of the "daughter at
home," Agnes and Lucy Poor devoted themselves in traditional nineteenth-century fashion to the needs of their parents and their married siblings.[40] Elizabeth Ellery Dana did the same: "You write as if
you were expecting me soon," she told her mother. "I want to see
you very much darling, but it would not be right to leave Charlotte
[her married sister] so with all her house on her hands."[41]

Even single daughters who traveled extensively continued to care
a great deal about events at home and to depend on frequent contact
with their mothers. "Your letters always seem too *short*," thirty-eight-
year-old Anna Gertrude Brewster wrote to her mother from Europe.
"Do put in everything, even who goes by on South street now that
the new bridge is open," she urged.[42] Although Ellen Hale lived an
independent life, traveling and studying art abroad, she too remained exceptionally close to her mother and looked forward to
receiving her letters. As their voluminous correspondence illustrates,
she also sent her mother detailed accounts of the places she visited,
the people she met, her meals, and her painting experiences.[43]

Like their earlier counterparts, late nineteenth- and early twentieth-
century mothers and adult daughters regularly discussed health is-

sues.[44] Ellen Hale frequently alluded to digestive difficulties—"I have decided not to go to the mountains till tomorrow, owing to one of those circumstances which we don't put on postal-cards, and which occurred directly after Mr. Balch's dinner." She often reported the arrival of "The Friend," noting on one occasion, "I think I am going to have a much easier time of it than last month."[45] Mrs. Hale also described her health problems and those of her own elderly mother as well: "Saturday and Sunday I had a sort of bilious turn, though today I feel pretty well," she wrote in one letter. "I wrote about Grandma's nervous twitching, but she has had no more since yesterday morning, and Dr. Hooker's medicine seems to control it," she reported in another. Reports like these distressed Ellen: "I can't help feeling a little uneasy about home affairs. You spoke of Granmamma's not being quite well in your last letter, and either then or before that of your having a cold yourself."[46]

Married daughters had their own families to look after, but they too expressed anxiety about their mothers' health problems. Distance exacerbated their concerns. Affa Miner Tuttle, who lived in Indiana, worried incessantly about her mother, particularly when she failed to hear regularly from her family in Massachusetts. "I haven't heard a word from home this week and I am beginning to get uneasy—Jean [her sister] would better send me a postal if she hasn't time for a letter just to let me know that you are no worse. . . . I do hope you are feeling well enough to get out again," she told her mother.[47] As her wistful inquiry regarding the family's Thanksgiving celebration in 1903 suggested, Affa found it particularly difficult to live so far away in view of her mother's increasing age and frailty: "I want to know now whether Mother ate dinner in the dining room. Elizabeth and I were there two years ago and Miner and I five years ago."[48] Eugenie Homer Emerson, newly married at the age of forty-two and living in Honolulu with her minister husband, also found her inability to keep up on the details of her mother's health distressing. "Mother dear, how are you and all? How I wish I could know this very minute!" she wrote. "I hope you are warmly tucked up in your bed without any pain or irritation from your exzema."[49]

When daughters experienced health problems, maternal anxieties were equally apparent. One anxious mother worried that her daughter would not take the appropriate precautions before undergoing an operation: "From what Dr. Cooper told me I am sure the local anaesthetic is something quite new. . . . The expense is not to be considered where your life and health are in the scale. And I do not want you to consider that. . . . I do not think you ought to let any etiquette have weight in regard to an operation so important as this. . . . It should be done where it can be done with the greatest safety."[50] The lingering illness of another daughter prompted her mother to suggest that she should "take the Children & come here and Stay untill you are better I think there must be something in the Location that doesnt suit you as it seems some of you are sick most of the time." This mother expressed her continuing concerns about the health of her daughter and her family a year later when she wrote: "Are you all well now I think so much about you that I dream about you when I havent heard for some time."[51]

Just as concerns about one another's health understandably increased when mothers and daughters lived far apart, distance could create other difficulties for them. While it did not impair the close and affectionate relationship Eugenie Homer Emerson and her mother had shared before her marriage, it meant that they rarely saw one another. Mrs. Homer's advancing age made it impossible for her to travel to Hawaii to visit her daughter, who deplored the necessity to rely on correspondence and particularly regretted her own inability to go home for special occasions. But her mother found a way to cope with their separation: "Give us particulars—what you have for dinner, what you do and where you go; do not think anything too small to tell. _I_ don't and it makes you seem nearer to us," she advised.[52] The same approach worked for Frances Tuttle, who kept in close touch with her mother by sharing the details of her life and missionary work in China and discussing the news from home in regular weekly letters.[53]

To some extent, geography also determined the nature of the relationship between Sophia Bledsoe Herrick and her daughter Louise Herrick Wall, who moved with her husband from the East Coast to Aberdeen, Washington, and eventually to Portland, Oregon. Visits were impractical and few, so Mrs. Herrick poured out her love and longing for her daughter in multitudinous lengthy letters.[54] But the case of Sophia Bledsoe Herrick also illustrates another feature of the relationship between some mothers and their adult daughters: although she had a successful professional career herself, Mrs. Herrick seems to have been particularly dependent on her children emotionally. She had divorced her husband because his commitment to the philosophy of the Oneida community was unacceptable to her. No doubt this accounts in part for the intensity of her attachment to Louise, which she articulated in highly emotional terms: "The world would mean nothing to me if you were not in it. And it is only by steadily turning my thoughts away from the fact of your being so many miles away that I can keep cheerful," she declared in one letter. "Virgie [another daughter] thinks I am very lugubrious at times and speaks about how your being gone affects me & I try not to make it more disagreeable than I have to her," she continued.[55] Another observation, regarding Louise's absence on Christmas Day, 1889, highlighted her feelings of loss and her need to feel connected to her daughter: "You seem more hopelessly far away because the times are so different. If I could think of you at any time as doing at all what we are doing It would seem as though you were in the same world."[56] Mrs. Herrick's response to a particularly gloomy thought Louise had expressed suggests that the latter reciprocated her mother's intense affection: "I have never had the thought you have had that we 'may go out together,' " the devoted mother replied. "Leaving you would be almost the hardest part of it. . . . It helps me to know that you feel so . . . I have never had such close and real companionship with anyone else in the world."[57]

Victoria Booth Demarest's mother, who was the daughter of the founder of the Salvation Army, also had marital problems and relied on her daughter for emotional support. Her letters, like those of Sophia Bledsoe Herrick, document the intense attachment of an emotionally needy mother to a beloved daughter. To Catherine Booth-Clibborn, her daughter, who worked with her in the religious revival movement, was a *"twin soul,"* and a "comforter companion & *Lover* & friend."[58] She consulted Victoria about her marital difficulties and asked her to intervene on her behalf; begged her to eat properly and get enough rest; worried about her personal comfort; and implored her to write more often and "tell me of your inside life darling."[59] Her affectionate tone often bordered on the infantile—for example, "Now you will have *no more crying fits* because that *spoils* little Doves!! & They do not coo & comfort their little mothers when they are sick

& cry!!" and "My own *flower* My Dimple—My Comforter My Angel Child."[60] Occasionally the tone was more like that of a lover.[61] The quality of Catherine Booth-Clibborn's entreaties to her daughter probably reflects a combination of her own personal emotional needs, her passionate commitment to preaching, and a strong desire for Victoria to carry on her work. Nevertheless, the overall impression is one of intense maternal pressure that could be destructive to a mother-daughter relationship. Yet Victoria apparently understood her mother's temperament and sympathized with her concerns. She treasured her letters, which she labeled, "A few of my mother's . . . very precious very wonderful and revealing love letters received when I was in St Cloud 1908 and in Germany 1909–1910," and "A few precious love letters from Mother 1914–15–16."[62] The diary she kept while traveling with her mother in 1914 recorded her devoted efforts to support and help her. Entries such as "I sleep with my darling. She confides her troubles to me"; "I pack for mother & get our things in order"; "Slept with Mother—she is such a darling"; and "Mother leaves for England I hate to separate from her & to have to let her travel alone She looked so pathetic when she said goodbye" offer no evidence that Victoria found anything unusual in their relationship or resented the emotional demands her mother made. Apparently their interactions were conditioned by their shared religious faith and their joint commitment to preaching, and were generally harmonious rather than hostile.[63]

The manifest absence of significant conflict in the rather strange relationship between Victoria Booth Demarest and her mother raises once again the issue of mother-daughter conflict more generally. Despite the clear generational discontinuities they represented, the educational and professional aspirations of the "new woman" did not generate the sort of fundamental mother-daughter hostility that might have been expected, given their revolutionary character. Nor did the presence of tension between adolescent daughters and their mothers create the sort of unbridgeable gap alluded to in popular magazines and advice manuals. It is not surprising, then, to find that mothers and adult daughters communicated with one another regularly and valued their relationships highly. For "new women," whose mothers had been instrumental in their abilities to achieve their ambitions, mature adulthood must have brought an increasing recognition of the significant role maternal support had played in their lives. For women whose adult lives conformed to more traditional patterns, maturity undoubtedly strengthened the sense of shared female experiences and generational connections. For older mothers, daughters were a unique source of comfort and sustenance. As one elderly mother observed: "Sons wives are not your own girls if they are ever so good, you do not feel as free with a Daughter in law as your owe [sic] child."[64]

Nevertheless, interpersonal conflict was not completely absent from the relationships of adult daughters and their mothers. Typically such conflict took the form of relatively trivial disputes over ordinary domestic matters. For Blanche Ames Ames, a proposed family visit furnished an occasion for this sort of problem: "If you and Father do not want to come to North Easton please don't, for what pleasure will there be for any of us if I know all the time, you are wishing to be at home and you on your part are simply going through the visit because you feel you must," she wrote to her mother in 1900. An unmarried daughter who cared for her mother at home, as Jean Miner did, might be sorely tried by the effort of "trying to please & do for her & not being able to suit in anything or way," and indeed could find it necessary "to just get out in order to have any nerves left stay in my room or run off." Or she might worry, as Lucy Hitchcock did, about the fact that her mother was disturbed when her sister "put little private notes" to her in family letters, and thus feel compelled to ask her to "send a separate letter" in order to avoid piquing maternal curiosity.[65] Pressure to write and visit more frequently must have also annoyed daughters, although they may have avoided articulating their objections.[66] Indeed, adult daughters who led traditional domestic lives may have experienced more of such pressure than their less conventional contemporaries whose mothers recognized and even applauded a clear difference between their own routines and those of their offspring.[67]

More complex conflict could also disturb the equilibrium between mothers and adult daughters. Ella Reeve Bloor, a thrice-married radical union organizer and suffragist, complained angrily that her daughter Helen seldom wrote to her from Europe where she was studying the violin and performing concerts, and that she told her nothing about her fiancé. Her anger was accompanied by plaintive expressions of her need for reassurance about her importance to Helen, for example: "I *wish* you'd write me a real old timer I'm your same old chum not a bit old inside, just as lively as ever Let me in to your very soul—I'll *always understand*—I got sore when I thought *you* thought old Mom didn't understand."[68] Here was a conflict generated by the insecurity, and possibly also guilt, experienced by an undomestic, unconventional mother whose own work commitments took her away from her children for extended periods. Despite this, however, she could not accept what she regarded as neglect on the part of her adult daughter. It is interesting that while Ella Reeve Bloor continued to object to her daughter's negligence as a correspondent, she also sympathized with Helen's distress over the communication difficulties she experienced with her own daughter.[69]

The troubled relationship between Laura Ingalls Wilder and her daughter, Rose Wilder Lane, offers one additional example of more serious dissension between a mother and an adult daughter. Shaped in part by their demands on each other as writers and their efforts to work together as professional colleagues, their conflict was manifested through clashing needs for mutual affirmation and autonomy. Mrs. Wilder depended on her daughter for economic security, but she found it difficult to acknowledge the latter's contributions to her welfare, while Rose sought her mother's approval and resented her demands. Although she felt that she had been deprived of maternal nurturing as a child, Rose never believed that she had done enough for her mother as an adult. A recent analysis of this relationship suggests that their struggle is reflected in the stories and articles they produced as well as in their personal papers.[70]

This example, like that of Ella Reeve Bloor, describes an atypical relationship between two unusual women. Both cases illustrate how specific circumstances and particular personal characteristics fostered problems for mothers and adult daughters. Obviously, the idiosyncrasies of individual women could affect mother-daughter interactions in other ways as well. Even within individual families, temperamental differences might allow one daughter to enjoy a close, affectionate relationship with her mother while a sister experienced serious, overt conflict with her.[71]

It is difficult to discern precisely the extent to which tensions may have intruded into the interactions of mothers and adult daughters during the period between 1880 and 1920. As in the case of younger daughters, the absence of overt references to conflict does not indicate that it did not occur. Indeed, as daughters grew older, they may have become even more reticent about recording or expressing anger, both as a result of their own socialization and out of respect for aging mothers.[72] Hence the possibility that more dissension existed than is readily apparent certainly cannot be discounted.

Mary Bulkley's recollections of the life she shared with her mother after her father died reveal that a mature daughter's patience could be strained severely despite the absence of manifest antagonism. Mary resented the degree to which maternal needs and concerns constrained her activities. She was annoyed by her mother's assumption that an unmarried daughter had no life of her own, and by her excessive anxieties. "I found out what a tyranny an overpowering and possessive affection could be. I spent my time wavering between disgust with myself and impatience and irritation at being treated in my fifties as if I were fifteen," she remembered. Their conflict was unspoken, however, and although she grew increasingly dependent on her daughter as her own health declined, Mrs. Bulkley worried primarily about her daughter's ability to manage without her after her death. This perception of their respective roles convinced Mary that she had been a good daughter even though she had resented her obligations. But in a frank and pointed statement about their relationship, she clearly revealed the complexity of a mature woman's feelings about her responsibilities for an elderly mother: "I have never really regretted what I was enabled to do for my mother, but it is to me a source of great satisfaction that I shall never have to take from any one what I gave to my mother."[73]

Despite the ambivalence reflected in Mary Bulkley's reminiscences, and in the experiences of other women as well, on balance the available evidence suggests that mothers and adult daughters recognized the vital importance of each to the other, and acknowledged it in various ways—in the frequency of their communications, in their enduring interest in the details of one another's lives, and in the articulation of their love and concern for one another. The depth and strength of this affection was often expressed in the context of birthday greetings, such as those extended by Mary Pierce Poor to her daughter Agnes on the latter's forty-first birthday: "Much love goes to you . . . on your birthday! Your father & I look upon your life as one of our greatest blessings. Indeed I do not know how we could have lived without you." Daughters could be equally eloquent, as suggested by Ellen Hale's sentiments on her mother's sixtieth birthday: "I shall think of you continually during the day—even oftener than usual. it [*sic*] won't be very long before we shall meet, and then I shall have the sixty kisses. it is easier for you to *feel* how I feel than for me to write about it,—I don't think you can imagine my affection more than it is."[74] On her own birthday in 1904, Affa Miner Tuttle wrote: "This is my birthday. So I must write and tell you that I am glad that you lived & that I lived and love you up for my birthday." Her sister, Elizabeth Garman, noted her mother's birthday in her diary even after her death, and Elizabeth Ellery Dana remembered her mother's birthday by placing flowers on her grave.[75]

To some extent, the character of the interactions between middle-class mothers and adult daughters during the period 1880–1920 represents a continuation of the trends illustrated by the relationships of younger daughters and their mothers. If discord was not the distinguishing feature during the years when young women were in the process of becoming "new women," it was probably unlikely to increase as the maturity of daughters removed the most obvious sources of potential conflict. However, it is also important to consider how broader societal influences may have shaped the nature of the relationship as both generations experienced new stages in the life cycle.

For example, early twentieth-century changes in family demographic patterns produced falling death rates and rising life expectancies. Among other things, this meant that fewer daughters lost their mothers prematurely. It also meant that women were likely to live to see their grandchildren, and to participate in the lives of their adult children for an extended period.[76] Thus daughters could expect to have the benefit of maternal guidance and support through a significant portion of their own adult years. They could also anticipate additional responsibility for an elderly mother's welfare since longer life was likely to lead to increased dependence on middle-aged offspring.

As a result of these demographic changes, the mother-daughter relationship now lasted longer than it had in the past, and thus women had an opportunity to know each other as equals and friends as well as parent and child. Possibly this prolonged contact fostered and even increased the intensity of their companionship. In the context of extended, intimate mother-daughter relationships, the impact of maternal death might be particularly devastating for a daughter who found herself bereft of her closest friend and mentor just as she was in the process of coping with the traumas of middle age, the recognition of her own mortality, and so forth. While it is also possible that relationships of longer duration resulted in more tension, and even resentment, as daughters' obligations increased, the weight of the available evidence suggests that was not generally the case. Although it is difficult to document precisely, it appears that maternal economic insecurity did not constitute a major area of concern in the middle-class families whose experiences have been considered in this chapter. Perhaps the financial independence of elderly mothers partially explains the apparent absence of tension even as daughters found themselves responsible for other aspects of mothers' welfare over a longer period of time.[77]

Extended life expectancies also meant that marriages lasted longer, and thus that co-residence between parents and adult children was relatively infrequent. While their husbands were alive, few women lived with married offspring. But when they were widowed, this changed.[78] This demographic trend may have affected mother-daughter relationships in several ways. First, the decline in co-residence could have fostered harmony by reducing the potential for tension that would be likely to exist in a household made up of three generations. Affection and mutual support could predominate in relationships where mothers and adult daughters did not challenge or compete with one another with regard to the routines and responsibilities of daily life. This situation seems to describe many of the preceding examples of interactions between mature women and their mothers. However, circumstances might change, as the shock of widowhood terminated a long marriage and an aging mother suddenly became extremely dependent on a daughter, either emotionally or physically or both. If co-residence followed a father's death, new tensions could certainly ensue.[79]

The continuation of an earlier trend in the structure of the American family also contributed to the maintenance of intimacy between mothers and adult daughters between 1880 and 1920. The closeness of the middle-class nuclear family, and its growing isolation both from other relatives and from the wider society in the course of the nineteenth century, made it especially difficult for young women to break away from their families of origin when they married. Despite the fact that marriages were founded on the basis of love and romance, it was not unusual for a nineteenth-century daughter, or for her counterparts at the turn of the century and beyond, to have difficulty adjusting to the separation from parents and siblings, and to want to remain a part of their lives, just as Blanche Ames did.[80] Undoubtedly, this situation promoted and fostered strong ties that endured as mothers aged and daughters matured into middle age.

The existence of powerful ties between older women and their daughters has been documented elsewhere, for example in the context of mid-twentieth-century English working-class families studied by Michael Young and Peter Willmott, and also earlier in the nineteenth century.[81] These studies suggest that for at least some adult daughters, the mother-daughter relationship took precedence over spousal interactions. While the foregoing examples offer no evidence that this was the case in late nineteenth- and early twentieth-century American middle-class families, other similarities can be noted. Like the English working-class daughters who moved away from their home neighborhoods, American middle-class daughters stayed in close touch with their mothers when they were separated from them geographically. While socioeconomic status (and obviously cultural differences as well) certainly distinguished the two groups of women, the sources indicate that like those interviewed by Young and Willmott, many middle-class American daughters also experienced the same domestic concerns their mothers faced, and that they found comfort in sharing those concerns. And their mothers, too, benefited from the close and enduring ties that characterized the mother-daughter relationship. Finally, as in the case of the English working-class families, the interactions of middle-class American mothers and daughters involved far more than a mere exchange of services.[82] While the precise quantities of duty and affection that defined the structure of the relationship cannot be specified, it is clear that these mothers and daughters maintained and nurtured their ties to one another throughout the life cycle.

As a young woman, Lucy Wilson Peters had acknowledged her mother's central role in her own life when she chose to be married on her parents' anniversary. As an adult, she expressed the essence of a mature daughter's love and respect after her mother's death, when she carefully copied the latter's reminiscences to preserve them. At the end of her copy she penned the following conclusion: "I shall never get over the terrible void that came into my life when my talented mother closed her eyes on February 26, 1913, to open them in heaven. It has been hard for me to copy her beautiful writing, for my eyes *would* fill, as I realized there would be no more to copy. I would not call her back though I am so lonesome."[83] Neither her devotion nor her feeling of loss was unusual.

CHAPTER 7

"THE REVOLT OF THE DAUGHTERS": MIDDLE-CLASS ENGLISH MOTHERS AND DAUGHTERS

HE preponderance of strong, mutually supportive American
mother-daughter interactions between 1880 and 1920 seems
especially striking in light of the conspicuously different patterns revealed by an investigation of middle-class English mother-
daughter relationships during the same period. Because the lives of
women in both societies were altered significantly as a result of similar social and cultural changes that marked these four decades, a
comparative examination can enhance the development of a comprehensive historical understanding of American mother-daughter relationships. Despite the potential contributions of such an approach,
relatively few cross-cultural comparisons are attempted by social historians. For example, while the use of the term "Victorian" often
implies significant overlap between American and English social and
cultural experiences, this potential linkage is tested only infrequently.[1] Given the absence of agreement regarding both the definition and the methodology of comparative history, historians' reluctance in this area is understandable. Nevertheless, a cross-cultural
consideration of late nineteenth- and early twentieth-century mother-
daughter interactions can help to define the parameters of this topic,
which has received little historical scrutiny to date. The addition of a
comparative perspective will help to distinguish between aspects of
the relationship that specifically reflect the American setting, and
those that resonate in a broader context. And it may also identify
important additional issues that merit further study.

Regardless of the possible benefits of comparison for the development of a new field like the history of mother-daughter relationships, a comparative effort can be especially risky where no established knowledge base exists as a foundation for the construction of a broader picture. In this sense, the attempt to compare English and American middle-class mother-daughter interactions may seem premature. In addition, the nature of the English middle class, which encompassed a very diverse group during the period 1880 to 1920, makes the task of comparing middle-class family interactions in the two cultures even more challenging. Membership in this varied class ranged from entrepreneurial businessmen, professionals, and managers at one end of the spectrum, to clerks and small shopkeepers at the other end. A shared set of values shaped by those at the upper levels of the class linked its members, but they were separated widely in terms of financial status and as a result, also in terms of life-style.

Although the ideal of gentility was pervasive, the majority of middle-class people lacked the resources to maintain the rigid social standards established by the small proportion of affluent families that comprised the upper middle class. Thus, despite the tendency of social historians to emphasize the central role of servants in nineteenth-century English middle-class homes, the typical middle-class household employed only one general domestic servant, and very few families enjoyed the services of specialized domestics such as cooks, parlor maids, and nurses.[2] While the circumstances of middle-class women varied widely, the same ideology and prescriptions were meted out to all of them. Yet the reality of their experiences was determined by the family budget.[3] In this context, the task of drawing generalizations about middle-class mother-daughter relationships becomes very complex.

Nevertheless, even an imperfect comparison may generate useful questions and new hypotheses to guide further research. Thus, while it may be impossible to claim that a single set of middle-class experiences resulted in a typical English mother-daughter relationship, it is not inappropriate to suggest that evidence about mother-daughter interactions in all segments of the English middle class is potentially useful and relevant to the present study. Despite the intrinsic difficulties, then, this chapter will consider the nature of relationships between untraditional daughters and their mothers across the spectrum of English middle-class families between 1880 and 1920, toward the relatively modest goal of developing the preliminary outlines of a comparative picture.[4]

Throughout the Victorian era, social observers in England vigorously debated the "Woman Question." Here, as in America, this discussion encompassed multiple issues pertaining to women's physical, political, social, economic, and educational lives. Here too, by the last decades of the nineteenth century, the debate centered increasingly on the behavior and activities of the "new woman," whose English image reflected a growing recognition and acknowledgment of the changes taking place in women's lives on both sides of the Atlantic. Although the prototypical "new woman" portrayed in print existed primarily in fiction, there was some basis for the concept in late Victorian and Edwardian social realities. New opportunities attracted middle-class young women in England as well as their counterparts across the ocean. New jobs, new fashions, new social behaviors, and particularly new educational experiences clearly distinguished their world from that of their mothers.

By the 1890s, both secondary and higher education for women were well established in England, although this was a relatively recent development. For most of the nineteenth century, women's education had been unsystematic, as Maria G. Grey, who founded the National Union for the Education of Women of All Classes in 1871, noted in 1884: "Perhaps no movement of equal importance and involving such far-reaching results ever developed so rapidly, or attained its object so completely within a fraction of the life-time of one generation. Forty years ago the question of women's education did not exist, and only within the last twenty years has it taken its place among the public and active interests of the day."[5] This assessment by an activist dedicated to women's education conveys some sense of the reaction to expanded schooling for women, and also underscores the extent of the change, especially in the area of higher education.

In the late nineteenth century, female students were permitted to study in almost all of the universities and university colleges, as well as in a number of newly formed women's colleges, although the latter institutions were viewed with suspicion. The University of London included three women's colleges: Bedford, Westfield, and Royal Holloway. Four women's colleges existed at Oxford and two at Cambridge by 1893, but these functioned more as "unofficial appendages" than as established colleges, since women were not yet permitted to pursue degrees at those august institutions.[6] The absence of reliable university statistics for the period before 1922 makes it difficult to ascertain the actual number of female students enrolled in English universities and university colleges between 1880 and 1920. In 1922–23, the first year for which such information is available, universities in Great Britain enrolled 42,512 men and 16,440 women; the latter figure represents less than 1 percent of the total female population of England and Wales between the ages of nineteen and twenty-four, as measured by the 1922 census. In contrast, approximately 7.6 percent of American women aged eighteen to twenty-one were in college in 1920.[7]

For English women as for their American sisters, the decision to leave home and attend college represented a real departure from nineteenth-century domesticity and a clear break with the traditional female roles of their mothers and grandmothers. The young women who took this step represented all levels of the middle class.[8] Like their American counterparts, many of them displayed a proclivity for remaining unmarried. For example, only 16 of the first 41 students at Girton, and a quarter of the first 750 at Lady Margaret Hall, married. An article published in the *Nineteenth Century* in 1895 noted that of 1,486 women with university educations, only 208 had married, while 680 had become teachers. The author warned English mothers that such figures indicated that highly educated women could not be expected either to choose or to attain marriage.[9]

Data of this sort fanned the flame of the Woman Question and further highlighted the image of the "new woman." Despite obvious sociocultural differences, the Anglo-American world shared a transatlantic culture and a system of values during this period. Language, traditions, and literature linked the two societies. Nineteenth-century Americans were influenced significantly by English ideas, and the English, in turn, were intensely conscious of cultural developments in the United States.[10] Both societies experienced similar changes that accelerated during the nineteenth century, among them a major transition in women's roles within the family and in the larger world as well. Part of this transition involved the development of an enhanced sense of female personal autonomy, which was generated by changing gender relations and alterations in the place of women in society. By the end of the Victorian era, literary and social influences moved regularly in both directions across the ocean. For example, G. Stanley Hall's work on adolescence influenced English as well as American thinking about young people. The discussion of the Woman Question moved back and forth as well; social critics in England, like those in the United States, seem to have been obsessed with the issue of the "new woman" and threatened by the perception of a gender upheaval of enormous magnitude.[11]

Some twenty years before the appearance of the "new woman," her predecessor in England, labeled "The Girl of the Period," had also sparked a tremendous controversy. In a widely read essay first published in 1868, Mrs. Eliza Lynn Linton castigated a stereotypical image, which, she maintained, was no longer the "fair young English girl," the modest, refined, and generous daughter of the past, but a tasteless imitation of the vulgar *demi-monde*. This essay (which was later published as a pamphlet and also appeared in 1883 in a volume entitled *The Girl of the Period and Other Social Essays*), was reprinted in America, and the *New York Times* closely followed the controversy generated in England by Mrs. Linton's message.[12]

Thus the stage was set for the wave of social furor over the Woman Question that was initiated in 1894 by a series of articles published in England in the *Nineteenth Century*. The first article, entitled "The Revolt of the Daughters," suggested that young unmarried women had the right to be considered individuals as well as daughters. The author of this revolutionary idea was herself the wife of a barrister and the mother of an aspiring young writer.[13] Other writers quickly joined the discussion, which soon moved beyond the pages of the *Nineteenth Century*. An interchange between two prominent women, published in the *North American Review*, an American journal to which many English writers contributed, established the term "new woman" as a durable phrase and concept.[14]

Much of the commentary portrayed the "new woman" as a corrupt, threatening figure who made her mother's life miserable. Many of the critics were women; Mrs. Linton herself inveighed against "The Wild Woman" in a series of articles that appeared in the *Nine-*

teenth Century in 1891–92. Yet the "new woman" was also defended by other observers.[15] The intensity of the discussion surrounding an image that essentially lacked congruence with reality suggests that conventional people of both genders in late Victorian middle-class society experienced real fears regarding the implications of the new forms of independence, including the opportunity for higher education, which were claimed by many women. Apparently the "new woman's" activities—even such relatively unthreatening activities as smoking and participating in athletics—were perceived as seriously challenging the foundations of the established patriarchal society.[16]

This challenge occurred during a period of general cultural uncertainty in England. Discord in the areas of national and international politics, science, economics, and the arts, as well as tension over gender issues, characterized pre-World War I English society and fostered a continuing conflict between liberation and control. The period that has been described by nostalgic writers as "a golden afternoon" and "a long garden party," during which the middle-class ideal of gentility reigned supreme, actually witnessed class antagonism, union issues, an armament race, serious concerns over the future of the Empire, and efforts to censor literature and the theater. As in America, conflict between old and new ideas, including those pertaining to the Woman Question, defined the cultural ambience of late Victorian and Edwardian England.

In this context, women's new aspirations could be welcomed as part of a more general liberation from the restrictions of Victorian ideas. However, they could also be perceived as evidence of a broader threat to the social order posed by the claims and demands of various groups—women, the Irish, the working class, and so on. Thus, while the perception of an incipient gender upheaval to some extent reflects the realities of female behavior during this period, it also mirrors the more general turmoil and anxiety of the era.[17]

Female aspirations for independence threatened male prerogatives both within the family and beyond its parameters. Fears of national deterioration sparked by the Boer War promoted an emphasis on the importance of women's maternal role for the preservation of the Empire; it was only through mothers that the survival of English values and ideals could be assured. National defense and security demanded that both middle-class and working-class women marry and produce children so that the country could maintain its international position and compete effectively with Germany.[18] The "new woman" who might choose college rather than marriage could hardly have been a comforting image against this background.

If the "new woman's" activities presented a threat to conventional, male-dominated society, and even to imperial hegemony, how did her pursuit of personal freedom affect her relationship with her own mother? Did public discussion of her habits and behaviors reproduce the anxieties of middle-class mothers during the late Victorian and Edwardian periods? Or did English mothers, like their American counterparts, function more as mentors than as critics for their daughters?

The contemporary English periodical and advice literature, like that in America, portrayed middle-class mother-daughter relationships as tense and troubled.[19] However, although a pronounced discrepancy between the nature of actual mother-daughter interactions during the period 1880–1920 and the images conveyed in the prescriptive literature characterizes the American evidence, the picture is less distinct with regard to English mothers and daughters during this period. Data regarding mother-daughter interactions in families representing all segments of the middle class suggest that while American mothers clearly functioned as advocates and mentors for daughters' untraditional choices during this era of transition in women's lives, their English counterparts experienced more difficulty supporting the efforts of ambitious offspring. No doubt the difficult situation of the middle-class "daughter-at-home," who was expected to devote her life only to waiting for marriage, frustrated more than a few young women and provoked conflict even where daughters were not prototypical "new women."[20] And where young women harbored distinctly untraditional desires, dissension and hostility appear to have been quite common.

The experiences of Constance Maynard, one of the first students at Girton College, offer an interesting early example of such conflict. Although she was born in 1849 and grew up during the mid-Victorian period, Constance's desires for independence and education anticipated those of the "new woman." Her ascetic and domineering mother scorned worldly pursuits and severely restricted the activities of her four daughters, who were not permitted to have a normal social life with other children. She objected to Constance's emotional response to religion and stopped her correspondence with a favorite school friend. Constance was compelled to leave school at the age of sixteen, and she spent the next seven years at home, where she and her sisters shared the household duties and the care of their mother, who was often ill.

Although physical problems removed her somewhat from its daily activities, Mrs. Maynard continued to dominate the family. Her disapproval of Constance's desire for further education and personal development manifested itself through a constant "pat pat patting down of all ambition," despite the fact that she herself highly respected classical learning. It is not surprising, then, that this young woman first sought her father's permission to pursue a college education.[21] When she finally secured the reluctant approval of both parents for her plan to enroll at Girton, in 1872, she felt that she and her fellow students were at last en route to a "real destination, even though we hardly knew what that destination was."[22]

Constance's escape to Girton was conditional; she was required to promise that she would return home and resume a more suitable life after college. She kept this promise, living the life of a daughter-at-home until 1876, when she finally accepted her first teaching position. While she lived at home, she spent a good deal of time with her mother. Their relationship was intense, and despite their differences, Mrs. Maynard confided some of the difficulties of her married life to her daughter. Although she eventually freed herself from the physical confines of her home and lived an independent life, Constance never repudiated her mother or her mother's beliefs, which shaped much of her own life.[23]

Another early Girton student, Constance Jones, also experienced the restriction of her intellectual interests. As a child, she was not permitted to read novels or Longfellow's poetry; her mother particularly objected to her reading *Ivanhoe*. Her father's sister, who sympathized fully with the desire to go to college, financed Constance's education at Girton. She graduated in 1880 and enjoyed a successful career as a logician, returning to the college to teach and eventually to serve as mistress from 1903 to 1916.[24] Her autobiography contains no hint of resentment or anger about her mother's lack of support for her aspirations; indeed, her recollections portray a sympathetic, patient, and kind parent: "It sticks in my memory that the girls [in school] sometimes talked about their mothers, and that every girl (including my sisters and I) thought her own mother more delightful than anyone else's."[25] As with any autobiographical source, it is impossible to determine Constance's real feelings about her mother's negative response to her intellectual orientation. The eldest of ten children, she remembered that she was the only one who "started life with an inexplicable love of books and hunger for knowledge."[26] Whether she deliberately omitted any mention of conflict over this issue, or unconsciously refused to acknowledge it even to herself, it is difficult to imagine that no tension was present in her relationship with her mother.

A generation after Constance Maynard and Constance Jones, Lynda Grier also coped with an unsupportive mother. A partially deaf, awkward young woman, she had no formal schooling before she enrolled as an external student at Newnham College in 1904. Although she received a scholarship to continue her education the next year, her mother never took her daughter's work seriously. Indeed, Mrs. Grier insisted on sharing Lynda's bedroom and study until she died when her daughter was forty and a highly respected professor of economics at Leeds University.[27]

Unlike Lynda Grier, whose formal education started at Newnham, Helena Sickert Swanwick had attended secondary school before she enrolled at Girton in 1882. Her mother's views on the Woman Question were inconsistent: "She believed in higher education—but not for her own daughter—and if I had to struggle to go to the High School, I was to have a much harder struggle to go to college." Because Mrs. Sickert still believed in the ideals of the good housewife and the dutiful "daughter at home," although she did take some pride in Helena's academic success, she saw no need for a college education, nor did her husband. Thus it was only through the generosity of a relative who offered to supplement the scholarship Helena had been offered that she was able to pursue higher education.[28]

When she arrived at Girton, Helena was thrilled with her college accommodations:

To begin with, I now had a study as well as a bedroom to myself. . . . When the door of my study was opened and I saw my own fire, my own desk, my own easy chair and reading-lamp—nay even my own kettle—I was speechless with delight. . . . I did not know till then how much I had suffered from incessant interruptions of my home life. . . . What disturbed my mind were the claims my mother made on my attention, her appeals to my emotions and her resentment at my interest in matters outside the family circle.

Her mother, who had accompanied her to help her get settled, had a very different reaction. Turning to her daughter "with open arms and tears in her eyes," she declared, " 'You can come home again with me, Nell, if you like!' " As Helena remembered in her autobiography, "That which had enraptured me had struck her as so unutterably dismal that she was prepared to rescue me at all costs."[29]

This observation highlights a graphic example of a mother-daughter generation gap in perceptions and values. Helena also remembered that she and her mother were incompatible in other ways: "I was not at all the sort of girl my poor mother would have liked, and it was hard on her that her only daughter should be, as she put it, 'the worst boy of the lot.' . . . My mother hated red hair and only by degrees learnt to tolerate mine because painters made a fuss of it."[30] The combination of Mrs. Sickert's own personal history—she was the illegitimate daughter of a dancer and an astronomer—and the general discontinuity between Victorian expectations of conventionality and the new ideas about women's roles probably made conflict inevitable for this mother and daughter. But their relationship did improve eventually: "Once I had a husband, her whole attitude towards me changed and just as, formerly, I could do nothing right, so, latterly, I could do nothing wrong in her eyes," Helena noted.[31]

For most middle-class young women in late nineteenth- and early twentieth-century England, and for their mothers, as Helena Swanwick's experience indicates, marriage remained the major focus of the future. Margaret Nevinson's mother firmly maintained that "a bad husband was better than none," and this sentiment, described by her daughter as "the strange creed of my time," articulated a common point of view.[32] Margaret, who was an only daughter with five brothers, "hated being a girl." Her sympathetic father provided her with an early introduction to classical learning, but because her mother was afraid that no one would marry a girl who read Greek, a curriculum of French and drawing lessons replaced this instruction.[33] Margaret was appalled when a wealthy older bachelor proposed to her after her father's unexpected death, but her mother reacted differently: "Later, when I told my Mother as a private and excellent joke, I was amazed to find she took it most seriously. My Mother believed greatly in marriage. . . . She could not bear to see me suffering the poverty we were enduring, Mr. _____ was very rich, it was an excellent offer, and we could wait until I was a little older, girls used to marry quite young in her day, and I might never have such a good chance again." No doubt the shock of early widowhood and the ensuing financial problems partially influenced this maternal response. Nevertheless, mother and daughter clearly disagreed on the matter. The death of the suitor ended the conflict, but the episode troubled both women. Margaret turned against men for several years, and her mother continued to remind her about the "great career I had missed as a young and wealthy widow."[34]

While she never regretted this lost opportunity for marriage, Margaret Nevinson did regret her inability to acquire the kind of education she desperately wanted. Because her mother could not afford to send her to Girton, she was forced to accept a teaching position at South Hampstead High School, where she remained for four years until she married a man she had known since childhood.[35] Although she taught part-time, worked in girls' clubs, and even served as a rent collector in Whitechapel after her marriage, she never fulfilled the early intellectual aspirations that her mother had found so threatening. As an adult, she maintained that her father had influenced her life significantly: "A close affinity and resemblance, physical, mental, and spiritual, drew us together, and the memory of his love and sympathy has always remained with me, a cup of strength in the disillusions and disappointments of life." Her summary of her mother's influence expressed quite different sentiments: "The one maxim of life my Mother had taught me was: 'Never take back a maid, if she has given notice,' and I learnt by experience the wisdom of her words."[36]

Vera Brittain's mother, raising her daughter a generation later, would probably have agreed with Margaret Nevinson's mother regarding the relative importance of Greek and marriage in a woman's life. But Vera wanted to go to college as soon as she learned that women's colleges existed. While her mother would have preferred to have "an ordinary daughter," she eventually began to "secretly sympathise" with and support her daughter despite her husband's skepticism, and the disapproval of friends and neighbors who concluded that Mrs. Brittain had abandoned any hope of finding a husband for her eccentric offspring. Vera remembered that one particularly "lugubrious" lady had inquired: "How *can* you send your daughter to college, Mrs. Brittain! . . . *Don't you want her ever to get married?*"[37]

Feminism defined the central focus of Vera Brittain's life.[38] As a young woman, she resented the contrast between her parents' reluctance to support her aspirations and their expectations regarding her brother's education. She recalled that it was only when a male family friend seemed to accept as normal her desire to go to Oxford that her father changed his views on women's education and agreed to her plan to enroll at Somerville. In her diary she observed that "probably no ambitious girl who has lived in a family which regards the subservience of women as part of the natural order of creation ever completely recovers from the bitterness of her early emotions."[39] For her parents, as for society more generally, World War I resulted in the abandonment of many Victorian attitudes and the acceptance of newer values concerning marriage and women's roles. Her mother's "unobtrusive co-operation" when Vera decided to take a leave of absence from her studies to become a nurse, and her acceptance of her daughter's engagement to a "suitor whose brains were his [only] capital," suggests that this is so. Interestingly, Vera herself attributed these manifestations of maternal support to the fact that her mother could understand love more easily than she could understand ambition.[40]

This mother-daughter relationship seems to have been particularly complicated, undoubtedly in part because Vera was so fully committed to her feminist ideals while her mother remained entrenched in middle-class conventionality. Even as a young girl, Vera perceived a fundamental lack of understanding between her mother and herself which she attributed to her own resemblance to members of the Brittain side of the family. Several diary references to this incompatibility suggest that she found it a troubling problem. "It is characteristic of Mother that though I always want her to come home she always upsets me when she does come; one really feels it is not worth bothering to try & keep things straight in her absence," she observed on one occasion when her mother returned from a visit to her grandmother.[41] Vera also deplored her mother's general lack of assertiveness, her deference to an impatient husband, and her acceptance of a "dull level of mediocrity" as her lot in life.[42] Although her parents became reconciled to her desire to go to Oxford and even expressed pleasure in her educational achievements, she believed that they neither understood nor cared to understand "the spirit of the place" where she was so happy. As a result, she felt that she could not be herself when she went home for vacations. Perhaps the most poignant expression of Vera's feelings of alienation appears when she describes her reaction to her mother's efforts to offer condolence after her fiancé's death: "Mother was very nice—but I almost felt as if she were a stranger. One cannot pretend to live in any other than one's own atmosphere when one has reached the bed-rock of life."[43]

While the persistence of Victorian ideas and values concerning female roles and duties could make the "new woman's" aspirations completely incompatible with her mother's frame of reference, in Vera Brittain's case the concept of ambivalence rather than hostility best characterizes the intricacies of the mother-daughter relationship. Although Mrs. Brittain did not share her daughter's views and would have preferred to have a more traditional daughter (by her own admission), she apparently provided a certain amount of support for Vera's endeavors. She definitely recognized that her daughter was talented and able, as Vera recorded in her diary on November 15, 1913: "When we were talking about exams. & fame etc. this evening, Mother told me she has always felt that I shall succeed in everything I undertake & Edward [Vera's brother] will always just miss."[44] In turn, Vera understood that her mother's own "humdrum early life" and the circumstances of her marriage made it difficult for her to comprehend untraditional educational goals and feminist ideas about marriage. On one occasion, when Vera's anxiety over their lack of communication resulted in the discussion of "a variety of rather heart-rending explanations concerning difference of temperament," she found it comforting to realize that her mother did "seem to want" her and to want to make her feel less lonely. Despite their differences, she was relieved that they had talked openly to one another: "A few hours ago I couldn't have imagined myself either confessing my loneliness to Mother or letting her see my distress, but I am glad of it instead of sorry if only to prove how great a darling I always knew she could be."[45] Obviously, despite Vera's independent ideas, it was important to her to be able to feel positive about her mother and about their relationship.

While Vera Brittain consciously resented the negative impact of her mother's conventionality on their relationship, other young women worried about the impact of what they perceived as their own inadequacies. Conflict between the desire to be a good daughter and the desire for self-development, which she regarded as selfishness, was a source of great anxiety for Grace Hadow when she was offered a scholarship for teacher training in 1893. Although she felt guilty about doing so, she allowed her headmistress to plead her case with her mother: "I know it was frightfully selfish of me to let Miss Arnold write, I am very sorry now. It ought not to be so hard to give up anything for Mother. . . . Impress upon Mother that I am *glad* to come home at Christmas. . . . I think it must be best. It is no real sacrifice, it could not be to do anything for her. I should never forgive myself if I neglected any chance of making her life easier. I must leave. I *want* it."[46] Clearly here was a conflict between growing personal autonomy and Victorian ideals of selflessness. Six months later, the dilemma was resolved when Grace's brother convinced their mother that his sister should continue her education. She eventually enjoyed a successful career as a college teacher and administrator.

While Octavia Wilberforce never considered abandoning her ambitions to please her mother, her unpublished autobiography documents her sympathy with the latter's struggle to understand those ambitions. "I thought about my mother and realized how fond I was of her," she recalled. "She was a highly gifted, unique woman who treated me with sympathy and understanding except for her fanatical obsession about my future."[47] This young woman, who played golf competitively and associated with "golfing women" of whom her mother disapproved, refused a proposal of marriage from a relative of one of her friends, apparently at least in part because she hoped to become a doctor. She clearly recognized, with some apparent empathy, the degree to which this unconventional plan troubled her mother, but she did not allow herself to be deflected from the pursuit of her goal.[48]

It was not until the death of the young man whose proposal she had refused that Octavia was brave enough to ask her mother's permission to take the appropriate matriculation examinations for medical school. Even then she was afraid to reveal her real goal. When her mother finally learned the truth, she vehemently opposed her daughter's plan on the grounds that medical school would be "unsexing"; nursing school, she argued, would be a more appropriate choice. She maintained that Octavia had no need to earn a living; that she would lose all her friends; that she was too old (at the age of twenty-four) to begin to study; that the course would be too difficult; that she would have to associate with lower-class girls; and that she would ruin her chance ever to be a mother.[49]

Octavia was not deterred, and with financial support from a friend's family, entered medical school even before she had passed all the required examinations. She recorded that her mother remained unreconciled, as "once again [when she went home for Christmas vacation in 1915] I was submitted to every kind of abuse about my behaviour in not staying at home to look after my mother [who was by then a widow]."[50]

Molly Hughes's recollections suggest that like the mother of Octavia Wilberforce, her mother also espoused an essentially traditional view of women's roles. Unlike Octavia, however, Molly apparently internalized this frame of reference unconsciously. As the youngest of five children and the only daughter, she was expected to defer to her brothers while she was growing up. Her autobiography implies that she lived vicariously through their activities, but it portrays a happy rather than a frustrated childhood, and it describes a close, affectionate mother-daughter relationship. Molly was taught at home by her mother until the age of twelve, when she was sent to a nearby girls' school. Although she was anxious to go to school and she adjusted readily to formal education, she recalled her early learning fondly as the time when her mother's "outlook on life, her opinions on people, and her matured wisdom became a part of me."[51]

After her father was killed in an accident, Molly chose to prepare to support herself rather than to live with her mother and remain financially dependent on her brothers. With her mother's approval and her aunt's economic support, she entered the North London Collegiate School at the age of sixteen, continued her education at the Teacher Training College in Cambridge, and eventually received a degree from the University of London. When she secured her first teaching job, a resident post, in 1886, her mother accompanied her and rented a room near the school. This arrangement continued when Molly moved on to a second job. She shared both her professional experiences and her personal life—and even her love letters —with her mother.[52]

When her mother died in 1890 after a brief illness, she was only twenty-three, and she recalled the loss poignantly: "I was desolate. A mother's death must always make one feel cut away at the roots, and in my case it was worse, because she had always been like a sister as well as a mother in her complete comradeship and youthful outlook."[53] While Molly regarded her mother's outlook as "youthful," it was actually very conventional. She viewed men as "the important people," and she advised her daughter, "You must be ready to go anywhere in the world with your husband, from the Arctic to the Tropics."[54] The strength of her influence is manifestly clear in Molly's decision to give up her professional life as well as her independence when she married in 1897 (after a ten-year engagement). Although she was aware that some of her contemporaries chose to omit the promise of obedience from their wedding vows, she pledged to obey her husband "firmly, feeling the pleasure of having no longer to order other people's lives, but to be ordered myself."[55] Thus, after assuming the role of a "new woman," with her mother's ostensible blessing, Molly Hughes reverted to the traditional female role that her mother had both modeled and advocated.

It is difficult to ascertain precisely the effect of particular circumstances and individual personality characteristics on the mother-daughter relationship in any family. There is no way to determine whether or not Molly Hughes's mother would have encouraged her daughter to pursue an independent career before marriage if she had not experienced the sudden loss of her husband and the ensuing insecurity of a widow who was forced to depend on her sons and other relatives for financial support. Molly's childhood memories of her subordination to her brothers, and her recollections of her mother's ideas about men and marriage, indicate that her mother's behavior was dictated by pragmatic economic considerations. There is no evidence of personal commitment to the aspirations of the "new woman," or of any particular vision of a more fulfilling future for her daughter. Molly's adult decisions suggest that she recognized this and, consciously or unconsciously, she behaved in accordance with her mother's real beliefs. Her attachment to her mother and the internalization of the latter's intrinsically traditional point of view proved to be stronger influences than her own successful professional experiences, and these factors eventually produced a "new woman" *manqué* rather than a feminist.

The combination of a traditional point of view and a precarious family financial situation yielded different results for the relationship of Helen Corke and her mother. The wife of a grocer, Mrs. Corke had no intellectual interests, and she never understood her daughter's literary propensities.[56] Like many of her more affluent counterparts, she adhered rigidly to conventional middle-class beliefs and values that conflicted with her daughter's untraditional interests: "Girls expect to be married, says my mother. Do they? Who would choose conditions of married life such as hers!" Helen asked. "What *do* I want? Freedom, opportunity, education, varied experience."[57]

A series of business reverses exacerbated the incompatibility between Helen's desires, which effectively defined the creed of the "new woman," and her mother's vision of middle-class gentility. As the family was forced to live more and more frugally, Mrs. Corke "hugged her middle-class traditions and sense of superiority, avoided her neighbours (except when she might step down from her pedestal to *help* them), and cherished the pose of an exile."[58] Not surprisingly, this situation did not improve her relationship with her daughter. Helen remembered that when her mother told her they could not afford to feed a stray cat, the animal died and she blamed her mother. "I go cold with hate against my mother, as if she were the visible symbol of our poverty," she wrote. And she experienced that poverty and her mother's middle-class life-style as obstacles to her aspirations for a career as a writer: "Poverty is a prison, but its doors *can* open unless marriage locks them."[59]

While Helen never identified with her mother—"I never wished to be like Mamma, or to live her kind of life"—she remembered that her father, who liked poetry, provided "a sense of security, of rightness and justice, conveyed merely by his presence."[60] Both of her parents encouraged her to be a teacher so that she could earn her living, and as she prepared for her certification examinations, she found her mother somewhat more sympathetic than she had been earlier. "My mother's qualities were not so evident to me in childhood as in later years," she recalled.[61] Despite Helen's eventual acknowledgment of her mother's positive characteristics, their relationship remained basically incompatible. Mrs. Corke's strict middle-class frame of reference was too narrow to allow her to accept her daughter's unconventional relationship with a married man or to understand Helen's feelings of anger toward the husband of a cousin who had died in childbirth.[62] Here, as in the case of Molly Hughes and her mother, the family's economic struggle played a major role in the mother-daughter relationship, but the consequences were different.

The preceding examples certainly suggest that a young woman's untraditional aspirations could create serious obstacles for the mother-daughter relationship. Even where financial constraints were not a factor, for example, in the cases of Constance Maynard, Constance Jones, and Vera Brittain, "new women" in England could not depend on the sort of unconditional maternal support enjoyed by so many of their American counterparts. Indeed, mothers appear to have played the opposite role, often discouraging and inhibiting their daughters rather than enabling them to fulfill intellectual and professional ambitions. But this conclusion does not reflect the entire picture.

Although many English mothers neither understood nor sympathized with young women's desires for personal development, others served as important mentors for daughters. Three examples suggest that the performance of this function was not limited to any particular segment of the middle class. Lilian Faithfull, the second youngest in a large, affluent, upper-middle-class family, Sara Burstall, the eldest of three and the only daughter of a financially insecure family, and Sarah Marks, one of eight children in a lower-middle-class family, all attributed their successful academic and professional careers to unflagging maternal support.

Lilian Faithfull was educated at home by governesses and her mother until her intellectual ability was recognized. Mrs. Faithfull read widely, wrote magazine articles on the ethics of daily life, and attempted to write a history of England, in addition to managing a large country house and an active family. It was she who decided that Lilian should go to college, and although her husband "had no faith in higher education," he acceded to his wife's wishes. After preparatory studies at an all-male school of which her uncle was headmaster, Lilian entered Somerville in 1883. Subsequently, she had a distinguished career as an educator, serving for many years as headmistress of Cheltenham Ladies College.[63]

Lilian recognized and acknowledged her mother's support and direction in an autobiographic volume, *In the House of My Pilgrimage,* which she dedicated "To My Mother, Whose Foresight Made My Professional Life Possible, And To My Friends, Young and Old, Who Have Made It Happy." Her comments on the importance of mother-daughter communication might have come directly from the pages of the *Ladies Home Journal:*

As we grew older, the teacher and disciplinarian [her mother] turned naturally and easily into the comrade, discussing plans and politics, conduct and character with us all. In later life I have often noticed that the difficulties which arise between mother and daughter, so disastrous to home life when school is over, are due to the fact that this necessary readjustment of relationship has not taken place. The mother forgets that if she does not make a friend of her daughter some one else will do so, and become the confidante and counsellor at the most crucial point of her girl's development.[64]

The supportive, communicative relationship Lilian Faithfull described flourished in a context that was not particularly conducive to intimacy—an affluent and relatively formal household where the children spent more time in the company of servants than they did with their parents, whose rooms "they would not have dreamed of invading . . . at other than appointed times."[65]

In contrast, Sara Burstall spent more time with both of her parents. Her mother was an independent, unconventional woman who "had never followed fashion or even worn a crinoline." Although she had rendered important career assistance to each of her children, she believed that her own life had been a failure.[66] She regretted her own lack of education and regularly attended lectures at the institution that later became Birkbeck College. No doubt her example, in conjunction with her husband's progressive views, provided the impetus for Sara's interest in entering the Camden School for Girls in 1871 when she was twelve years old. Sara continued her education at the North London Collegiate School with a scholarship from the Camden School, and a second scholarship from that institution enabled her to enroll at Girton at the age of nineteen. Like Lilian Faithfull, Sara Burstall remained committed to women's education, serving for many years as headmistress of Manchester High School for Girls.[67]

Sarah Marks (who later adopted the first name Hertha and the married name Ayrton) was also influenced strongly by a broad-minded mother who encouraged her to question authority and launched her on an educational path that led to a Girton degree and a successful career as a physicist, wife, and mother. Mrs. Marks was widowed when Sarah was five years old. She managed to support her eight children with the help of relatives and her own skill as a seamstress. Raised in a Jewish family under difficult economic circumstances, Sarah's experiences differed substantially from those of young women like Constance Maynard, Octavia Wilberforce, and Lilian Faithfull who grew up in comfortable, secure families. Her mother's strong belief in the importance of a good education for women may have reflected her own financial struggles, as well as the recognition of her daughter's abilities. Nevertheless, she was committed to securing the best possible education for Sarah, although it meant sending her away from home to live with relatives in London so that she could attend a girl's private school.[68]

According to her friend and biographer, Evelyn Sharp, as an adult Sarah (by this time known as Hertha) consistently attributed her own considerable achievements to her mother's support and example. From the age of sixteen, when she went to work as a governess to help her mother financially, until Mrs. Marks died in 1898, she remained a devoted daughter, even setting aside her research to nurse her mother in the last stages of illness. This devotion apparently coexisted comfortably with a strong sense of personal autonomy, as illustrated in Sarah's communication of her intention to marry out of her faith:

MY DEAREST MOTHER,—I have something to tell you which will give you both pleasure and pain, but I hope for my sake you will let the pleasure overcome the pain. Yesterday evening Professor Ayrton asked me to marry him, and I accepted him. . . . He has promised to let me do, or to do himself, the same for you and Winnie [a younger sister] that I should have done if I had not married. . . . I am so happy, I hope you won't take away from my happiness by being unhappy yourself. You know how much I love you, dear Mother, and I would do anything I could to make you happy, but the one thing I could not do would be to give him up. Write me just one little word yourself Always and for ever, Your loving daughter, SARAH [69]

While she may have found it difficult to do so on religious grounds, Mrs. Marks accepted her daughter's decision, and their close relationship endured. No doubt the "perfect relations" attributed to Sarah and her daughter Barbara by her biographer reflected the supportive example offered by her own mother. Despite Barbara's temporary attack of conventionalism when she went to school—" 'I do wish mother had a boudoir, all filled with yellow satin furniture, instead of a laboratory—like the mothers of other girls!' "—their relationship was indeed distinguished by strong affection and friendship as well as a shared commitment to the suffrage movement.[70]

Obviously, as this example indicates, mothers who were themselves involved in women's rights issues could understand daughters' untraditional aspirations. In turn, their daughters, like Barbara Ayrton, might provide vital support for maternal endeavors, especially where other relatives and friends did not sympathize with militant activities.[71] Elsie Bowerman's mother, like Mrs. Ayrton, a dedicated suffragist, served as an important role model for her daughter, and their relationship was mutually supportive. Elsie's letters from Girton demonstrate her own commitment to her mother's political concerns.[72] While she also wrote about more mundane domestic matters, she obviously followed her mother's suffrage activities closely: "I suppose you must be very busy making all your arrangements for Tuesday," she wrote on November 17, 1910. "I *do* hope you won't get arrested." Three days later, she was still concerned about the same event: "Thank you so much for all your letters and telegrams. Needless to say I have been simply wild with excitement these last two days. . . . If you have time or energy left could you possibly send me a wire to-morrow night to tell me if you are arrested or not. I wish I could be there to help."[73] Their close communication continued after Elsie finished college. She was grateful for her mother's approval when she proposed to go to Europe as an ambulance driver in 1916—"It is good of you always to be so splendidly unselfish about letting me try my hand at the things I want to do"—and she wrote frequently from overseas.[74]

Like Elsie Bowerman, Margery Corbett Ashby enjoyed a close and mutually supportive relationship with her mother, who was also a women's rights activist. Mrs. Corbett encouraged her daughter's studies at Newnham and expressed pride in her achievements. "It was a very great pleasure to get your letters at last & to know that you had got through your ordeals well. They are excellent practice & I do hope you will never shun opportunities," she wrote. "You will get a splendid education . . . even though you do not take a first in classics. . . . Don't take after your stupid Ma who . . . always gave way the minute she did not swim to the front."[75] This support continued when Margery became a colleague in the women's movement: "You touch nothing but not dignify & exalt it. . . . Yours were the best speeches yesterday & not in my opinion only. . . . You have but one fault. You must put your chest up & your shoulders down!"[76] (This last piece of advice, reminiscent of Annie Winsor Allen's mother's anxiety over her daughter's posture, suggests that at least in some areas, English and American mothers shared identical concerns!)

Margery also wrote affectionate, supportive letters to her mother. She sought advice about social matters, confided her anxiety about academic matters, shared the ordinary details of her daily life, and apologized when she failed to write every day.[77] Her pride in, and affection for, her mother pervade her correspondence from Girton: "Your picture has come and is my great delight. People here like it very much and say I am like you and what more could I want? I do hope your speech will please as much as it will please your audience. You are bound to be a success you know."[78] The same esteem comes through in later frequent correspondence, after Margery's marriage, as the following example illustrates: "My dearest & best beloved Mother, . . . The more I see of other women, the more you stand out amongst them. I test you against the women of all lands & cant find a better all round one. Bless you."[79] The only hint of conflict in this relationship appears in maternal expressions of concern regarding the strength of Margery's commitment to her fiancé prior to their marriage:

Time seems to be getting on & no way is made apparently towards the great crisis in your life. You never speak except in the vaguest & most indifferent way about your marriage. . . . I sometimes wonder how much or rather how little you care for one another. . . . This makes me anxious & I want you to think seriously about your prospects & to make some plans concerning them if they are bright enough. . . . All I want to know is are you really fond enough of Brian & is he fond enough of you?[80]

Evidently, "a girl's best friend" could indeed be her mother, in England as well as in America.[81] On balance, however, middle-class English mothers appear to have functioned less frequently in this capacity than their American counterparts did. Differences in personality, self-image, and life experience undeniably affected women's perceptions of, and reactions to, the growing independence of their daughters in both countries. Financial pressures might exacerbate mother-daughter antagonism or facilitate understanding. Widowhood could make a mother less inclined to accept her daughter's views or induce her to be more tolerant of them. And a woman's personal interests and commitments, as in the case of those who actively embraced the cause of suffrage, could certainly facilitate a harmonious mother-daughter relationship. But the idiosyncrasies and personal predilections of individual women must be considered in a broader cultural context.

Despite the links between American and English culture and the transatlantic dialogue, national differences cannot be discounted as causal factors in the varying patterns of mother-daughter relationships. For example, demographic diversity may partially explain why American mothers could be more receptive to daughters' aspirations. Population statistics suggest that while fertility rates in the United States declined throughout most of the nineteenth century, this phenomenon was not significant in the English context until approximately 1880.[82] Thus middle-class English families continued to be large, and, at least during the first part of the period under consideration, mothers did not necessarily have the luxury of concentrating on and fostering the special hopes of daughters who had untraditional goals. In contrast, smaller families would permit their American counterparts to channel both time and emotional energy in this way.

A longer national tradition of secondary education for women, and a corollary belief in the importance of universal, free public schooling, may also account for stronger maternal support in America. When Sara Burstall traveled abroad to study the educational system, she was impressed to learn that "there was in America . . . a real belief in education. There she was no longer what she still is here —a Cinderella." She reported that a teacher in New York had told her: "We have no established Church; we have established Education."[83] In this American context, the "new woman's" educational aspirations did not represent a complete break with the past. In contrast, although the movement for women's secondary education originated in the 1850s in England, it did not really flourish until two decades later. Hence, even in the years preceding World War I, it was not unusual for upper-middle-class girls to be educated at home, and for parents to balk at the idea of spending as much to educate a daughter as they might to educate a son.[84] Thus, their own prior experiences with secondary schooling, and a cultural climate that valued education, enabled American mothers to support their daughters' aspirations. On the other hand, minimal personal exposure to secondary education, and the comparative absence of societal support for female schooling, deterred their English counterparts from providing similar support to their offspring.

National differences within the family setting were also important. The American middle-class family in the nineteenth century—and even earlier—offered considerably more freedom to children generally, and to girls specifically, than its English analogue did. English travelers consistently commented with disapproval on the tendencies of American parents to indulge their children and to treat them as equals.[85] They noted the close companionship between mothers and daughters: "Daughters are much with their mothers, and they become their companions younger than they do in Europe. At an age when the French girl, for instance, is still demurely attending her convent, or the English girl is in the hands of her governess, her more emancipated sister across the Atlantic is calling with her mother on her friends, or assisting her in the drawing-room on her reception days."[86] While these observations described the closeness between American mothers and daughters in conventional activities, this pattern of intimacy may have set the tone and provided the foundation for maternal support for the untraditional choices of "new women" as well. Other observations focused on the attitudes of English and American girls with regard to marriage. One such comparison emphasized that the latter were not trained to regard marriage as the ultimate goal in life; hence they could socialize with young men as friends rather than view them only as possible husbands.[87]

The observations of visitors who found American parent-child relationships noteworthy for their informality and friendship, mother-daughter relationships interesting for their closeness, and boy-girl relationships unique for their friendly quality underlined the fact that middle-class social life in England was highly ritualized and more rigid than in America. A major share of the responsibility for maintaining the family's standards and values, and thus its social standing, fell to wives and mothers, who must have experienced a good bit of tension in their efforts to fulfill their social roles, particularly if the reality of their circumstances conflicted with the ideal to which they aspired.[88]

Against the background of the economic and political upheavals that characterized the nineteenth century, women were expected to preserve the fabric of society through their positions as social gate-keepers and arbiters of social acceptance. To a great extent, their lives were directed by the concept of gentility, which integrated the behavioral codes of the earlier aristocratic and gentry classes with newer middle-class patterns and served as a powerful instrument of social control.[89] In the middle class, social duties were viewed as more urgent for women than for men. Hence wives who took the social code seriously might be concerned about avoiding the appearance of socializing with inappropriate people—either those of inferior social standing, or those of higher status to whom one might be accused of toadying. Men had more leeway in their connections.[90]

The social code placed heavy emphasis on maternal responsibility for grooming of daughters to be wives and mothers. Because late Victorian society established more formal etiquette for girls than had been the case earlier, the pressure on mothers in this area was particularly acute by the end of the nineteenth century.[91] At the upper levels of the middle class, this meant that daughters had to be oriented carefully to the formalities of the dinner party and the custom of paying calls, both of which were structured by rigidly prescriptive rules.[92]

Katherine Chorley's recollections of growing up in an affluent suburb of Manchester suggest that these customs could be a problem for some women and also a source of mother-daughter conflict. She remembered that her mother planned her calls carefully but hoped that most people would not be home so that she could just leave her cards. When Katherine and her contemporaries were old enough to participate in this ritual, they greeted the obligation with distaste: "The day was indeed a black one on which we found that our mothers had had their cards reprinted and that our names figured below theirs on the disgusting little white slips. But we, too, were drilled and disciplined," she commented.[93]

Strict rules applied to other areas of social life as well. Socially correct young people were expected to interact in prescribed ways; for example, a girl could not dance more than three dances with the same young man at a party.[94] Even dealings with tradesmen had to be conducted properly in an upper-middle-class household. When the grocer came to Ursula Bloom's home, the drawing room was prepared and the silver was polished. Her mother gave him the order, he wrote it down, and then they served him "cooking sherry and macaroons."[95] Rigid etiquette also surrounded the use of the lavatory. It was considered especially vulgar for a lady to appear to be aware of the existence of such a place, and thus a guest in the house was never told where it was. Eleanor Acland remembered that she and her siblings were required to stay in the lavatory until their nurse came to escort them out; they were not allowed to mention where they were going or to call out when they were finished because everyone in the house would then know where they had been.[96]

Other matters were also considered taboo—especially discussions of the facts of life, which posed problems for women at all levels of the English middle class as well as for American mothers and daughters. Vera Brittain remembered how difficult it was for her to extract information on these matters from her mother, and Ursula Bloom commented ironically: "Unmarried girls must be virginally innocent, and zealously guarded against emotions like passion and flirtations, yet married ladies from the moment they left the church as matrons knew the lot!"[97] Although Katherine Chorley was also sheltered, occasionally her mother felt compelled to tell her things that could not be kept from her.[98]

Clearly this complex social code could potentially engender the sort of intergenerational conflict that might impede the development of mother-daughter intimacy, particularly in an upper-middle-class family. But in other segments of the middle class, where a woman might aspire to gentility and respectability, possibly to mitigate the burdens of financial insecurity, a daughter's nonconformity could also introduce tensions into the relationship, as Helen Corke's experiences indicate. Some young women internalized the rules they were supposed to follow, and, for them, breaking those rules represented "conscious and premeditated rebellion."[99] Others, such as Vera Brittain, constantly chafed against these restraints. Certainly the aspirations of a budding "new woman" who was anxious to enroll at Girton or Newnham rather than to live the life of a "daughter at home" could exacerbate any existing tensions, especially where a mother whose own outlook remained firmly entrenched in a nineteenth-century framework of gentility and domesticity was committed to training her daughter to follow the same path.

Katherine Chorley readily conformed to her mother's training until the end of World War I, when she decided that the social pattern she had expected to follow was out of date. Neither of her parents was enthusiastic about her newly discovered desire to go to Cambridge, and her mother, who was "anything but a feminist," supported her husband when he vetoed this plan. It did not occur to their twenty-one-year-old daughter to challenge their decision, partially because her commitment to the pursuit of higher education was not completely serious.[100] When her mother relaxed her standards somewhat after her husband's death, Katherine viewed the change as an acknowledgment of the general trend toward more casual manners as well as evidence of a need for "the insurance policy of timely concessions." However, it may also have reflected a feeling of liberation from patriarchal constraints, since her mother, like Mrs. Brittain, had been completely dedicated to her husband's needs.[101] Ursula Bloom also described patriarchal practices in her family: when her father, who was a vicar, rang the bell in his study, her mother would rush out of the room to find one of the maids: "It's Mr. Bloom's bell! You simply *must* answer Mr. Bloom's bell, he has rung twice already." But, she observed ironically, no one would have cared if it had been "Mrs. Bloom's bell," since until World War I a woman was expected to be kept in her place, to produce a family, to bring it up without bothering her husband, and "to get the maids going in a big way and run the home well."[102] Mentoring an independent daughter did not fall under this rubric, nor did challenging male prerogatives on behalf of an aspiring "new woman" as many American mothers did.

If middle-class women in England differed from those across the Atlantic in this respect, they may have also differed in their interpretations of their maternal obligations. The mystique of motherhood that permeated American middle-class family ideology throughout the nineteenth century did not dominate the English middle-class home during this period. Recent scholarship on the family lives of upper-middle-class Victorian women has suggested that although both mothers and fathers were involved in the lives of their children, motherhood did not provide the central focus of English women's lives, nor was it expected to absorb all of their energies and prevent them from fulfilling their social obligations.[103] Certainly some upper-middle-class mothers played major roles in their children's lives, as Lilian Faithfull's experience illustrates. But, as her experience also suggests, it was not unusual for children in affluent families to spend more time with servants than they spent with their parents, and hence to share their problems and their joys with these people rather than with their mothers.[104]

The recollections of other women support this observation. Esther Stokes, who was born in 1895, remembered that her mother rarely spent any time in the nursery, although they always shared an hour together after tea. While her feelings about her mother were not completely negative, they reflected this distance: "I never really loved her. I had enormous respect for her and her judgment, and all she did and everything, but there was no warmth you know."[105] In Grace Fulford's family, the children also saw relatively little of their mother. Although both parents usually kissed them goodnight, they only dined with them on Sundays.[106] Eleanor Acland and her siblings treasured the hour they spent in the drawing room with their mother every day and the occasional opportunity to be alone with her if they were ill. Because the nursery effectively functioned as a world apart from the rest of the household, the harshness of an unsympathetic nurse was permitted to continue unnoticed for twenty years. While she was a threatening figure, the nurse also symbolized some form of security to her charges, who worried about the change in routine when their mother took over their care in her absence.[107]

Katherine Chorley's nurse also figured importantly in her life.

Unlike Eleanor Acland, Katherine thought her nurse was perfect, and although she recalled that she loved her mother more, she felt "more intimate and easy" with the nurse. As an adult, she believed that she had never suffered "quite the same feeling of desolation" as she had experienced at the age of nine when the nurse departed.[108] Winifred Peck's recollections of her childhood document similar experiences. She remembered that although she loved her mother, their worlds were totally separate. Looking back, she concluded that "modern children" who experienced closer parent-child interaction were more fortunate than their predecessors even though the latter had experienced their parents as more "special" because they saw less of them.[109]

Since only a small percentage of middle-class families could afford to employ nurses and governesses, such people had a relatively minor impact on the nature of mother-daughter relationships. Even where a household included more than one general servant, English Victorian and Edwardian motherhood did not necessarily produce alienated, angry children; indeed in some cases, as Winifred Peck's observations suggest, this structure invested both mothers and fathers with a kind of aura and mystique that made family interactions seem more like special occasions. Yet it seems plausible to assume that in some cases at least, these practices, like other middle-class social customs, impeded the development of the mutuality and support that typified relationships in American middle-class families. Because the same social ideology dictated the values, if not the actual practices, of other segments of the middle class, it is also likely that greater emotional distance between mothers and daughters characterized less affluent families as well.

The sources suggest that it was neither easy nor natural for a mother at any level of the English middle class to assume the role of mentor for a daughter whose aspirations for education and independence threatened to undermine the established social conventions, although in some cases those conventions were clearly outweighed by economic considerations.[110] The fact that the nineteenth-century tradition of feminism in England was less extensive and forceful than its analogue in America probably also served as an inhibiting factor.[111]

Gwen Raverat's recollections of her American mother, who married a son of Charles Darwin and raised her family in Cambridge, raise interesting questions about the potential ramifications of these cultural differences for the mother-daughter relationship. According to her daughter, Mrs. Darwin was "always on the side of progress," and her American belief in independence led her to expect her children to do things for themselves that properly socialized English children would not have done. She was casual, informal, fearless, and "a good deal of a feminist"; she believed that girls, as well as their brothers, should be educated to have an occupation, and that people could do anything they really wanted to do.[112] In a letter to her sister in America, she complained about the English tendency to overprotect daughters: "When Gwen grows up, it will be very hard to know how to treat her. If I let her be as independent as a girl at home, people will say in Cambridge she is fast."[113]

Despite her unconventional attitudes, Mrs. Darwin adhered to the upper-middle-class English custom of employing servants to care for her children. Gwen never remembered being bathed or having her hair brushed by her mother, and she would "not at all have liked it if she had done anything of the kind."[114] Interestingly, she found her mother more proper than her English counterparts in some respects: she described her as "more puritanical, in an old-fashioned early-American way, while they were more concerned with gentility and appearances."[115] She also recalled that her own shyness and lack of interest in social activities disappointed her gregarious, attractive mother and caused difficulties for them both. Because her mother thought that shyness was silly, she continued to encourage her daughter to be more sociable: "The kind of girl she understood was gay and pretty and charming, and had lots of love affairs and told her all about them; and she never understood that I could not—really *could* not—fill this role." When a cousin who enjoyed parties visited, Gwen found it "really pathetic" to observe her mother's pleasure.[116]

The apparent contradiction between Mrs. Darwin's support for women's education, her informality, and her preoccupation with the importance of frivolous social activities may reflect the contrasting influences of her American upbringing, her subsequent exposure to English middle-class culture, and her own negative school experiences. Although learning had not come easily to her, she respected education and culture. As a member of the Darwin family, she was surrounded by university faculty and exposed to their intellectual concerns. The family tradition of child-rearing differed from typical Victorian practice, and her husband accepted her relatively relaxed approach to family life.[117] Yet she never understood her daughter's wish to be a "really good painter," and she definitely did not assume the role of mentor for her.[118]

As an adult, Gwen believed that the English middle-class outlook from the mid-nineteenth century to 1914 was characterized by a sense of unreality and an attachment to false standards—that "the English middle classes were locked up in a great fortress of unreality and pretence."[119] Recent studies of nineteenth-century middle-class English social ideology lend credence to this opinion, and thus to the argument that this ideology defined a major difference between American and English culture, which helps to account for the different patterns of mother-daughter interactions.[120] The apparent conversion of Gwen Raverat's American-born mother attests to the power of the ideology as well.

To conclude merely that middle-class American mothers firmly supported their daughters' ambitions between 1880 and 1920, while their English counterparts generally declined to do so, runs the risk of failing to do justice to the complexity of mother-daughter interactions. The evidence also demonstrates that strong mother-daughter ties could exist even where pronounced differences separated the female generations in a middle-class family, and that some mothers and daughters readily expressed warm affection and admiration for one another.[121] Nevertheless, it appears that English middle-class society and culture foreclosed the development of the ability of many women to serve as mentors for untraditional daughters, and prevented them from even understanding the latter's aspirations. Certainly it was no coincidence that young women who managed to take advantage of the opportunity for higher education repeatedly articulated their profound satisfaction with the privacy and independence offered by their college accommodations, while their mothers often found it impossible to comprehend their desires for what Virginia Woolf would later label "money and a room of her own."[122]

A recent exploration of the interaction between the personal experiences and ideological perspectives of leading English feminists who were born during the nineteenth century revealed a slight correlation between feminist activism and difficult mother-daughter relationships. This study also suggested that with the exception of those who were feminists themselves, mothers were less likely to encourage untraditional behavior than fathers, who seem to have held more unconventional views about women's roles.[123] These findings support the evidence of maternal conventionality that has been documented in the preceding examples. They also suggest that even a small amount of paternal encouragement for a daughter's aspirations could be a crucial factor in her ability to persevere, as the cases of Constance Maynard and Margaret Nevinson illustrate. In this respect, the experiences of late nineteenth-century English daughters seem to resemble those of some earlier, ambitious young women in America who appear to have admired and identified with their fathers rather than their mothers.[124] Whereas many American mothers had assumed a mentoring role for untraditional daughters by the turn of the century, however, their English counterparts were slower to move in this direction.

How did the absence of maternal support ultimately affect the course of daughters' lives in England? As the available statistics on female college enrollments suggest, the failure of mothers to foster the aspirations of their offspring may have reduced the numbers of young women who felt they could attempt a new path in the face of the dominant social conventions. It also appears to have led at least some of those who did pursue untraditional goals to rely on the support of other women as mentors.[125] Like Helena Swanwick, Constance Jones, and Octavia Wilberforce, aspiring students might also be forced to accept financial assistance from friends or relatives. While some young women consciously expressed resentment over their mothers' rigidity, others apparently suppressed their anger and occasionally experienced health problems as a result of unresolved family conflicts over their intellectual interests.[126] More generally, it is possible that the militant tone of English feminism and the escalation of violence that characterized the suffrage campaign—including riots, arson, arrests, imprisonment, hunger strikes, and forced feedings—represented an expression of anger directed particularly against the conventional attitudes of middle-class women (including mothers) toward their own roles.[127]

The examination of middle-class English mother-daughter interactions in the era of the "new woman" has revealed significant variations from the pattern that characterized the interactions of American mothers and daughters during the same period. This comparative evidence underscores the intricacies of the relationship, and accentuates the complexity of the effort to understand it historically. The English evidence also reiterates the importance of attention to specific cultural differences, as well as to broader theoretical issues, for the analysis of mother-daughter relationships in the past. The addition of a comparative perspective, then, may qualify some aspects of the interpretation of the data on American mother-daughter relationships in important ways.

CHAPTER 8

"MOTHER DROVE US IN THE STUDEBAKER": AMERICAN MOTHERS AND DAUGHTERS AFTER 1920

LTHOUGH middle-class American mother-daughter relationships never replicated the English patterns exhibited in
the era of the "new woman," there is some evidence of
change during the decades following 1920. While in many ways, the
interactions of twentieth-century mothers and daughters resembled
those of previous generations of American women, the intensity of
the intimacy that had characterized earlier relationships apparently
lessened. A complete examination of the dynamics of the relationship
in the post-1920 period remains beyond the limits of the present
investigation, but the effort to develop the outlines of a historical
framework for the analysis of the interactions of middle-class American mothers and daughters would remain incomplete without some
consideration of the changes and continuities during those years.
Hence, while this chapter addresses this important task, it differs
from the preceding chapters, which offered a fuller interpretation
together with more extensive and detailed examples of both cultural
representations of the relationship and actual mother-daughter interactions.

In contrast, the following discussion explores the parameters of a
task that remains to be accomplished and suggests a direction for
further research. The decision to approach the post-1920 period in
this fashion was effectively dictated by the definition of the main
focus of the study, but it also reflects the nature of the available
sources. Although comprehensive collections of women's personal

documents offer extensive evidence regarding the character of the mother-daughter relationship during the late nineteenth and early twentieth centuries, similar material is far less accessible for the years that followed. With the advent of the telephone, mothers and daughters no longer needed to rely exclusively on lengthy letters to communicate with one another when they were separated. Diary and journal writing also declined in the course of the twentieth century. Even where relevant documents do exist, they are not necessarily obtainable for research. Understandably, families are less inclined to open more recent letters and other personal documents to public scrutiny, and even where such collections have been deposited in libraries, they often remain closed to researchers for a designated number of years. Hence, although some material is available, it is impossible to analyze later twentieth-century mother-daughter relationships as fully as those at the turn of the century. While the issues can be defined, the interpretation of women's responses to those issues remains to some extent impressionistic. This chapter then represents a more general treatment of the topic along with a call for further investigation.

The decades following 1920 encompassed a kaleidoscope of social and cultural change as America completed the transition to the modern age. The earlier tension between tradition and innovation was resolved with the defeat of the old order and the establishment in the twenties of new behavior and value patterns that still remain visible in contemporary American society. The era of "flaming youth" ended abruptly with the onset of the Depression, and the ensuing widespread suffering and deprivation. These economic difficulties, and the trauma of America's involvement in a world war barely twenty years after the "war to end all wars," brought issues of survival to the forefront of American consciousness. The return to "normalcy," with its stress on domesticity in the fifties, shortly gave way to the unrest of the sixties and seventies—the movements for civil rights and women's liberation and the rise of the counterculture. Against this variegated backdrop, it is possible to discern elements of both change and continuity in the middle-class American mother-daughter relationship.

The 1920s marked the beginning of modernity in the history of gender roles in America, as a new generation of middle-class women pursued equality in a new way. With the successful completion of the suffrage campaign and the subsequent fragmentation of the feminist movement, women's focus shifted from a public, political agenda that had centered on getting the vote to a quest for personal gratification and private rights. It was not the established leadership of the women's movement that formed the vanguard of this quest, but the modern young women of the "flapper" generation. These women rebelled overtly and decisively against the Victorian sexual mores that had survived the First World War in principle, if not in practice. Unlike their feminist predecessors, they sought to combine marriage and work. While earlier female students had engaged wholeheartedly in the intellectual life of the college campus, these young women engaged primarily in the social life it provided. In pursuit of personal satisfaction and fun, this generation smoked, danced, dated, and petted, and openly challenged traditional gender roles to an unprecedented degree.[1]

Thus, in the aftermath of World War I, the "flapper" replaced the "new woman" as the focus of social commentary and anxiety regarding female behavior. Like her predecessor, the "flapper" represented in the cultural discourse was a fictionalized composite image rather than a description of reality. As they were portrayed in the popular periodical literature, neither she nor her male counterpart resembled typical young people. Nevertheless, discussions of youth, defined by one contemporary observer as "Americans of both sexes who are in the adolescent period, particularly those of secondary school and college age," filled the pages of popular journals. While concern over children was not a new phenomenon in American cultural history, the extent of the pervasive anxiety over the younger generation distinguished the twenties. Perceived as fundamentally different from previous generations in their uninhibited, hedonistic, and defiant attitudes and behaviors, the young people of this era, particularly females, were portrayed as completely out of control and sexually demoralized. Like the "new woman," however, the "flappers" had their defenders as well as their detractors. Whether they were viewed negatively or positively, they clearly behaved differently from the women of the previous generation, and their attitudes and activities defined a focal point for much of the contemporary social and cultural discussion in the twenties.[2]

How did the mother-daughter relationship fare in the context of this new female generation gap? Despite the changes in women's lives during the late nineteenth and early twentieth centuries, middle-class mothers and daughters generally managed to maintain the bonds that had linked earlier female generations in American families. But the "flapper" threatened to go even further than her predecessors in the pursuit of equality. A daughter's aspirations for education and professional employment, even where these could also involve a conscious decision not to marry, might be understandable. Her aspirations for complete sexual freedom and the avowed intention to "have it all" could be far more threatening. Indeed, in their crusade for sexual freedom, the young women of the 1920s differed from their predecessors more than any of their successors in later generations differed from them.[3] It seems plausible, then, to assume that the anxiety expressed in the contemporary literature reflected the concerns of parents who confronted unconventional "flapper" attitudes and activities in their own families. While the popular literature evoked exaggerated and threatening images of licentious women, contemporary studies documented an unprecedented amount of freedom for both high school and college students as well as a dominant and influential peer culture.[4] Surely mothers would be uncomfortable with daughters who "bobbed" their hair, used cosmetics, socialized constantly, went out in automobiles, and openly defined their attitudes toward sex according to those of their peers rather than those of their parents.

Robert and Helen Lynd's *Middletown* suggests that middle-class parents were indeed concerned by the declining influence of the home in favor of the peer group, and the attendant early sophistication of their offspring. One mother interviewed reported that she had never been criticized by her children until they entered high school, but now both her daughter and an older son accused her of being old-fashioned. Another mother complained that her fourteen-year-old daughter accused her of being "cruel" if she did not permit her to stay at a dance until after 11 P.M.[5] A number of women also lamented the influence of domestic science classes, noting that their daughters had ridiculed the mothers' cooking and sewing practices.[6] Maternal anxieties like these were mirrored in the responses of high school daughters to a questionnaire concerning sources of disagreement with their parents. Out of a list of twelve possible problem areas, the two most frequently identified were: "Number of times you go out on school nights during the week" and "The hour you get in at night." Sources of disagreement mentioned in addition to those listed on the questionnaire included "Cigarettes," "Boys," "Petting parties," "Bobbed hair," "Playing cards," "Reading too many books," "Dancing," "Machine riding to other towns at nights with dates," and "Evolution."[7]

While mothers professed the desire to maintain or reassert traditional standards of discipline and obedience, even they were confused about what they ought to require of their children. As one worried woman expressed it, "You see other people being more lenient and you think perhaps that it is the best way, but you are afraid to do anything very different from what your mother did for fear you may leave out something essential or do something wrong. I would give anything to know what is wisest, but I don't know what to do."[8] Similar confusion surfaced in the results of a questionnaire that asked mothers to identify the most important traits to be stressed in child-rearing. The middle-class women sampled selected "independence," "frankness in dealing with others," and "strict obedience."[9] The obvious contradiction between independence and obedience suggests that mothers, like their daughters, were in the process of modernizing their values and expectations, and that they found their parental responsibilities perplexing.

The early age at which social life began in Middletown was clearly a major source of concern. A few parents chose to send their offspring away to school to avoid the dilemmas posed by social events such as school and church dances that lasted until midnight. One conscientious mother who had considered this solution described her efforts to solve the problem:

Last year we seriously considered sending our daughter away to school to get away from this social life. We try to make home as much a center as possible and keep refreshments on hand so that the children can entertain their friends here, but it isn't of much use any more. There is always some party or dance going on in a hotel or some other public place. We don't like the children to go out on school nights, but it's hard always to refuse. . . . Even as it is, we're a good deal worried about her; she's beginning to feel different from the others because she is more restricted and not allowed to go out as much as they do.

These observations certainly imply the possibility of mother-daughter conflict, but they also indicate that mothers could be responsive to their daughters' feelings about parental efforts to limit social freedom.

Mothers frequently found it necessary to compromise in the face of the prevailing conditions, and some, along with their children, apparently accepted the necessity and importance of social life and reacted accordingly. Thus, one woman complained that when her eleven-year-old son went to his first dance, his date's mother refused to tell her daughter that the couple should be home by 10:30: "Indeed, I'm not telling my daughter anything of the kind," she said. "I don't want to interfere with her good time!" Another mother reported that although she disapproved of people who permitted their children to join too many clubs, she decided to let her daughter join three high school organizations in addition to two groups outside of school. This choice reflected her desire "to minimize the boy interest" by filling her daughter's life with other activities.[10] Mothers also acknowledged the social realities through their support for the importance of teaching "sex hygiene" to their offspring and in their capitulation to daughters' urgent demands for expensive clothing, which was considered an essential prerequisite for social success.[11]

Certainly mothers and high school daughters disagreed on a variety of issues, and friction between them was not an unusual occurrence.[12] The Middletown data suggest that mothers found it very difficult to maintain traditional standards. Frequently they gave in to daughters' wishes or at least compromised in many situations that might otherwise have provoked serious conflict. Hence the dissension between adolescent girls and their mothers may have been mitigated to some extent by the tendency of the latter to succumb to the combination of social pressures and a genuine desire to make their daughters happy.

As the observations of the worried Middletown mother quoted above suggest, the potential for conflict might also be reduced when daughters were not enticed daily by the demands of social life in a coeducational high school. Sending a young woman to boarding school could eliminate many of the sources of disagreement that troubled mothers and their adolescent daughters who felt compelled to conform to a peer culture oriented primarily toward popularity with the opposite sex. For example, in stark contrast to the concerns articulated in Middletown, letters from Jessie Tarbox Beals to her daughter Nanette offer support regarding the latter's school work, urge her not to work too hard, and encourage her to have fun, do things with the other girls, and go out to Sunday Supper.[13]

College daughters, like their younger counterparts, engaged in a variety of untraditional behaviors that could provoke maternal concern. They explicitly rejected the established middle-class American social customs supported by the older generation in favor of the new norms of the powerful peer culture with which they identified. The encompassing influence of that culture fostered and supported a social life that redefined and restructured gender relationships. Experimentation with sex as well as cosmetics, bobbed hair, faddish clothing, cigarettes, alcohol, and wild dancing generated anxious adult criticism.[14] While their mothers might object to their attitudes and activities, the new orientation of the "flappers" reflected the increasingly democratic climate of middle-class family relationships, which encompassed a growing concern for children's emotional happiness as well as a tendency for mothers to focus their own needs for amusement and fulfillment on their children. In the democratic family, emotional ties and maternal indulgence took precedence over authority and discipline. Love, affection, and voluntary parenthood were the hallmarks of this institution.[15]

This family climate may have fostered the tendency of young people to reject their parents' values, but it could also support open communication between them. For example, one young woman casually teased her parents about their attitudes toward the activities of contemporary college students. She wrote that she and her cousin had concluded that "the tales our elders tell regarding the pranks played in their school days do very little toward proving that the modern college youth is in a state of rapid degeneration."[16] The sister of this young woman freely shared the details of her social life in her letters. On one occasion she mentioned that she had been spending time with the boyfriend of a good friend, a behavior that violated both traditional norms and new standards: "We both realize that we have no right because of Clara. Don't worry, Mother, I'm still fighting and as soon as we get back to school and he can be with her again, we'll just naturally forget each other." In another letter, this straightforward young woman commented: "There is one thing I have to be thankful for and that is that I've had a perfectly dandy time this year without getting in deep with anyone and I can go home or anywhere absolutely scot free to have a good time with anyone I please." When she finally decided to get married, she announced her engagement by writing "A Playlet in One Act," which she mailed to her parents.[17] The casual and outspoken attitude displayed by this young woman typified the college daughters of the twenties.

Conservative social observers, horrified by the frankness and the absence of inhibition on the part of young women, indicted the democratic family. Like their late nineteenth-century forerunners, critics frequently blamed maternal permissiveness and negligence for the problems they perceived.[18] As the compromises made by Middletown parents indicate, many mothers actually may have enabled daughters to follow the examples set by their peers. Data concerning the decades preceding the 1920s also support the suggestion that, like the "new woman," the "flapper" enjoyed maternal support, even though it was sometimes ambivalent. The years immediately before World War I had witnessed the blurring of age distinctions between middle-aged women and their daughters with regard to appearance, costume, and cosmetics. Women were encouraged to cultivate their figures, to wear more revealing styles, and to buy beauty aids such as powder, rouge, and lipstick—and they took this advice. Corset sales declined, and the cosmetics business flourished. Middle-aged matrons from the middle and upper classes followed the example of younger women. They started to smoke and drink cocktails. They also practiced birth control and sought divorces.[19] Magazine articles articulated the fear that mothers were rushing from one leisure activity to another in imitation of their daughters.[20] These earlier developments, followed by the liberalizing influences created by the war, suggest that middle-class women in the twenties were not necessarily shocked or distressed by all of the fads adopted by their daughters. Indeed the pervasiveness of some styles indicates at least the possibility of maternal cooperation with, if not explicit support for, certain fashions.[21]

Furthermore, despite their avowedly "naughty" conduct and their deviation from conventional standards of propriety, the young women of the "flapper" generation resembled their mothers in some basic ways. They were generally conservative politically, and they supported the same candidates their parents supported. They read the same magazines and watched the same films. Perhaps even more significantly, although they claimed the right to experiment with new sexual mores, they still regarded marriage as their destiny. Unlike the first two generations of women who pursued higher education, a majority of college alumnae in the 1920s—in some cases as high as 80 or 90 percent—married. And although many also took jobs, their goals were economic and practical rather than ideological, while their work commitments were typically short-term.[22] In some ways, then, the generation gap between the "flapper," whose crusade for sexual freedom ultimately led to marriage, and her mother was smaller than the distance between the "new woman," who often chose not to marry, and her mother. Indeed, where mothers disapproved of their daughters' actions, their concerns might be expressed in terms of a perceived betrayal of earlier feminist ideals as well as in more traditional terms.[23]

Such concerns were apparently well founded since by 1930 college students at both coeducational and women's institutions were requesting home economics courses, and middle-class young women were articulating their conscious rejection of the idea of a career in favor of marriage. Survey data revealed that 55 to 60 percent of those interviewed preferred marriage; a majority thought that it would be impossible to combine the two.[24] While the young women of the twenties were committed to asserting their freedom as individuals, they had rejected the ideology and structure of the earlier women's movement. In the absence of any formal organization, their efforts lost focus and momentum. Thus, the misgivings of the social commentators who deplored their shameless conduct and worried about the wider impact of their activities were never realized. Intergenerational conflict certainly plagued some families, but initial maternal confusion about how to deal with daughters evidently often yielded to an impulse to let them enjoy themselves. In other instances, middle-class mothers followed the trend toward more personal freedom that had emerged in the prewar years and accepted the idea that women could and should dress and behave in accordance with their personal preferences. Indeed, as Paula Fass has observed, for some adult women at least, "the path of the damned had become the way of the beautiful."[25]

Despite the apparent absence of a definitive break between mothers and daughters, the 1920s may have ushered in a less dramatic, but nevertheless significant change in the relationship. Certainly the cultural prestige of mothering and mothers declined in the context of the process of the professionalization of motherhood and the emphasis on behaviorist psychology that characterized much of the current child-rearing advice.[26] Possibly intergenerational understanding became more difficult to sustain as a result of the nature of the issues women confronted. While the "new woman's" mother may have felt perfectly comfortable supporting her daughter's college and work aspirations, the mother of the "flapper" may have found it much harder to accept notions of gender equality that encompassed complete sexual freedom as well as educational and career opportunities.[27]

Evidence of change in the dynamics of the mother-daughter relationship during and after the 1920s can be gleaned from various sources. Observations in Middletown suggested that the generation gap between parents and children had increased by 1935 and that adult control over the young had been weakened further as a result of the disillusionment engendered by the Depression. While women continued to worry about their efforts to guide and advise their precocious offspring, the latter became increasingly sophisticated. For example, when a group of Middletown mothers attempted to curtail the costs of the social functions sponsored by an exclusive high school sorority, their daughters united to oppose them and the mothers' effort failed.[28] Obviously no single incident or particular case study can be construed as documentation of a trend, but while individual examples remain quantitatively insignificant, they can be qualitatively important.[29] In this sense, then, the Middletown sorority episode may signal decreasing attention to maternal opinion, even a new tendency to disregard it completely, on the part of young women.

Personal documents also suggest that mother-daughter interactions were changing. A more relaxed, breezy, sometimes flippant tone appeared in daughters' letters. For example, a young woman who was working as a camp counselor wrote to her mother: "It was nice to hear from you, to put it mildly. I'd like to write often very much, and I consciously remember many interesting details to tell you, but alas and alack, when I have two minutes to sit down and write, I must write reports." This communication, and a marginal note appended to another letter from this young woman, provide a distinct contrast to the dedication reflected in the conscientious letter-writing habits characteristic of so many middle-class American daughters before 1920. "Father asked me to address letters to Mother," the marginal note revealed. "It would please her, he explained."[30] Previously most daughters would have directed their correspondence to their mothers almost automatically. The substance of this note, which implies that the writer herself felt no need to correspond privately with her mother, suggests that the dynamics of the relationship may indeed have changed in the direction of reduced intensity.[31] It may also reflect the availability of the telephone as a means of direct communication between mother and daughter, and a corresponding decline in the necessity for lengthy, detailed written communication at least from the daughter's point of view.[32]

Post-1920 daughters seem to have been less reticent as well as more casual than their predecessors were in their communications with their mothers. Jane Emmet, who suffered from diabetes, freely expressed her anger at what she considered maternal overprotectiveness when her mother sent the family's maid to accompany her on a return journey to boarding school: "Don't try to fool yourself that I'm sick because you know well that in our family I would not be returning to school if I had the slightest ailment. I think its selfish when you let your responsibility for me run away to such an extent that it seriously hampers my life. . . . I had a few hopes that you would have out grown some of this since I have been away, but maybe that's hoping to much from you."[33] This quotation expresses a more substantive and fully articulated anger than that represented, for example, by Mary Hills's girlish objections to her parents' leniency with her sister.[34] Although they undoubtedly felt similarly offended on occasion, few young women in the late nineteenth and early twentieth centuries would have been quite as outspoken in their criticisms of maternal behavior as Jane Emmet was. Nor perhaps would they have described their social conquests as graphically as the young woman who reported very forthrightly that all her friends were waiting to see whether she would have a "triumvirate" or choose one boyfriend over the other.[35]

A growing emphasis on peer group experiences, and sometimes a corresponding perception of mothers as serious adversaries to social life, offer further support for the claim of change in mother-daughter interactions. Diaries suggest that peers rather than mothers dominated young women's concerns. June Calender wrote mainly about her friends in the diaries she kept between the ages of twelve and nineteen. When she mentioned her mother, it was often in the context of matters involving young men and social life.[36] Adele Mongan Fasick was also intensely concerned about these matters. At the age of fifteen, she was ecstatic when a friend arranged a blind date for her, and her mother gave permission for her to accept: "Mom said I could go," she noted in her diary. "We'll probably go over to New York. I've never been on a date before. . . . I hope to heaven that I'll make a good impression and think of the right things, and enough of them to say." But she was furious when, on another occasion, her mother interfered with her plans to leave home early and "walk around" before attending a movie with friend: "Why the hell can't they leave me alone . . . I can be trusted in New York. Dammit," she complained.

Adele's objections to parental supervision were intensified by the perception that all her friends were allowed to "do things," while her parents always demanded a reason for everything: "To make it worse Mom of course gets mad when I demand to know why I can't do some things & then gets mad at me for getting mad. . . . The thing is they have all the authority & just ignore me so I not only have to obey them but also to shut up & I hat[e] to have to keep telling people 'My mother won't let me' My God! I can't do hardly anything."[37] Although friction between a teenaged daughter and her mother was hardly a new occurrence, the emphasis on the impor-

tance of peer group norms distinguished Adele's frame of reference
from that of adolescent girls in earlier generations. The intensity of
her concern over the opposite sex also reflected a new attitude.
Pondering her desire to love "one boy" completely, she wondered
whether she had ever really loved anyone and observed, "I very
seldom think of Dad & Mom though I'm of course fond of them."[38]
These introspective thoughts offer an interesting comparison to the
sentiments of Ella Lyman Cabot, whose love for her parents caused
her to hesitate for six years before accepting a proposal of marriage.[39]

If casual adolescent social life hampered mother-daughter communication in new ways, serious courtship matters could also be more
complicated in the decades following 1920 than they had been previously. A young woman might be less inclined to accept maternal
guidance and less likely to rely on maternal support. The diary of
Helene Harmon Weis recounts her resentment over her mother's
intrusion into her romance with a "cute photographer at Wanamak-
er's" whom she had met casually when he was commissioned to
photograph a pageant in which she participated. Helene had no
objection to her mother's accompanying her to meet the gentleman
in question when he invited her to join him for dinner, but she was
angry that her mother insisted on remaining with them: "We had a
good time but she monopolized the conversation so; they talked of
war and politics. I had wished to talk to him of quite different things.
It would have been the first time that I had ever gone out to dinner
with a man, just two of us. I suppose I shall never tell her how
disappointed I was."[40]

While she took exception to her mother's attempts to oversee this
relationship, on at least one occasion, she expressed the need for
some sort of guidance: "I said to her [her mother] that I would think
her justified in forbidding me to visit him and she said that then I
might deceive her and see him on the sly." Helene finally ended the
relationship, deciding that she could not "give in to him" because she
was afraid of "hell fire," the lack of control, and the possibility of
being snubbed by other people. She was also worried about hurting
her mother. Her distress and confusion were compounded by the
fact that she missed "being kissed and cuddled and considered and
admired," and she experienced difficulty reconciling herself to the

decision she had made: "Mother said that never to have loved was better than illicit love but it isn't, oh it isn't. I have done what she asked this time but another time I may not. Oh, if only my life were all my own to dispose of and so many people wouldn't be affected by what I do."[41]

When "another time" arrived, Helene persevered in her determination to get married despite her mother's adamant disapproval on economic and practical grounds: "She [her mother] said I wanted to get married because it was in the air," Helene complained.[42] After several stormy months during which even her fiancé became convinced that he was ruining her life, the troubled young woman confided to her diary: "I loved my mother for over 20 years but tonight I do not love her. I will love her again I know but the future is unforeseen." This entry continued: "Mother frightened me tonight —I really thought she might kill me. I looked into her face and it was the face of a stranger."[43] Helene's anguish over this conflict persisted, but it did not prevent the marriage, nor, apparently, did it result in any permanent mother-daughter estrangement.[44]

This young woman's situation offers a striking contrast to the comfortable confidences exchanged by mothers and daughters between 1880 and 1920, and to the credence formerly given to maternal advice on the subject of courtship. So does that of June Calender, whose diary recounts her agony over a broken engagement when she was twenty-one, with no mention of any discussion with her mother about it.[45] Yet neither of these mother-daughter relationships seems to have been essentially incompatible. Helene Harmon appreciated the fact that her friends felt welcome in her home: "That's so much Mother's fault, though, I am truly grateful," she noted. She enjoyed attending opera, concerts, and the theater with her mother, and she admired the latter's ability to cope with her new responsibilities when she was widowed. But she believed that they could not communicate about matters of the heart. "Mother said that no girl would wait 30 years with such an example of love and devotion before her," she observed after they had attended a production of Eugene O'Neill's Diff'rent. "We got talking about love but I quickly backed down for I saw that I could not talk to her about what I think love should mean."[46] June Calender also enjoyed her mother's company, and she looked forward to the times they spent alone, often while her father and brother attended a sports event or a movie together.[47] The marked contradictions in these mother-daughter interactions suggests a new complexity in the relationship that may have strained the limits of the kind of mutual understanding enjoyed by earlier mothers and daughters.

Changes in maternal conduct as well as in the behavior of daughters could also alter elements of the mother-daughter relationship. An apparently new maternal behavior, the overt expression of instrumental interest in expediting a daughter's success with the opposite sex, illustrates such a change. Thus, for example, June Calender's diary documents her mother's undisguised interest in her social life: "Mom says Elmer Pollard passes here just starring at the house"; "I'm sure Mom would be as pleased as I would if Jim should ask me for a date. She believes, and confidentially so do I, that Jim secretly likes me"; and "No sooner had Mom shut the door then she whispered quite loudly 'June he's cute. . . . . I hope he likes you.' "[48] This young woman was pleased by her mother's interest, and she was glad that they could discuss such things. "It is very wonderful that we are so alike," she noted.[49] But similar maternal behavior made Adele Mongan uncomfortable: "Mother was telling me today how Ursula O'Keefe always had 3 or 4 boys walking her home from school & she wonders why I don't. (at least she didn't come right out & say so but that's what she meant) Well so do I wonder but I wish she wouldn't because it makes me feel sorry for myself which is silly. I've got the notion that I'll make myself famous & thus in some way wipe out the stain (of unpopularity) on my honor."[50]

Turn-of-the-century mothers certainly expressed interest in their daughters' social lives, and sometimes participated quite actively, as in the case of Maud Rittenhouse's mother. But their involvement appears to have taken more of a reactive form rather than any proactive, explicit promotion of popularity with the opposite sex. While this new maternal behavior might delight a daughter, it could also generate uncomfortable pressure for social success and thus distress an insecure young woman, as the following example indicates: "When my mother got home tonight, I was up. We talked about the dance and she told me I should ask the boys to dance, and I should stay near the boys. I told her it wasn't so easy."[51]

Another potentially significant behavioral change, in the form of a role reversal, distinguished post-1920 mother-daughter interactions. While mutual support and understanding characterized earlier relationships, typically mothers served more overtly and consciously as the enabling figures, protecting daughters' interests and empowering them to expand their horizons. In the context of the changes in women's lives during the decades after 1920, daughters could also find themselves fulfilling these functions for their mothers. As a result of her parents' divorce, Jane Emmet acquired this responsibility while she was still in college. She wrote long, supportive letters to her mother, who had filed for divorce in Reno, Nevada, assuring her of the strength of their relationship as individuals and sympathizing with her situation: "I do hope time does not drag too much out there, & that you're not too lonesome." [52] She also encouraged her mother to pursue an apparent interest in moving to Washington to seek "a new and interesting job to set your teeth in." And she articulated her anxiety about her mother's welfare as well as her own feelings of responsibility for it. "Ma is tired & nervous I'm afraid. . . . She is still worried about what to do & where to go this winter. . . . I keep wishing I could do more to help her," she wrote to her brother. In another letter, she commented, "It doesn't seem quite fair when you think of Dad [who was remarried] with a wife and family, and Ma all alone, or in the Herter's maid's room [as a guest]." [53] The possibility of Mrs. Emmet's remarriage introduced another dilemma for Jane, who found her proposed stepfather "pompous and a bore," although she was pleased to see that her mother seemed happier. Eventually she conceded that he "really is damn *nice*," and after much emotional anguish and soul-searching, she accepted the situation as "a perfectly normal, natural thing." [54]

Daughters in the late twentieth century frequently find themselves required to provide moral support for mothers who are engaged in restructuring their lives after a divorce, but this situation was relatively uncommon until recently. Jane Emmet experienced emotional problems of her own, for which she consulted a therapist as opposed to her mother—another interesting change. She noted that she could not discuss her difficulties with either parent since "although they are only symptoms of my trouble, I guess they were contributory ones." [55] As this example indicates, a newly articulated maternal need for emotional and moral support might alter the mother-daughter relationship in at least two fundamental and related ways: it could place a daughter rather than her mother in the position of mentor, and it could cause her to seek support for her own problems from a source other than her mother.

The letters of Augusta Salik Dublin to Mary Dublin Keyserling offer another interesting example of role reversal. These letters reveal the fascinating case of a thoughtful middle-aged woman who turned to her daughter for support when she experienced what late twentieth-century Americans define as a midlife crisis. Anticipating Betty Friedan and the definition of the feminine mystique, Mrs. Dublin deplored the fact that as a result of her husband's "dominating tendencies," she had sacrificed her personal ambitions "on the altar of family peace." She lamented "the utter & complete frustration of my personal life, my life as an individual and as a member of society apart from my family relationships," which she blamed on her own failure to stand up for her "rights as an individual . . . no matter what it might lead to." And she summarized her situation in terms that strike the contemporary reader as all too familiar: "So here I am at the prime of life still with a mind that is not too bad and with a certain amount of ability, without an anchor in the world of affairs. . . . I am fifty and gray and have no references of work accomplished. So there is no place for me such as I want now."[56] While neither the conscious articulation of such concerns nor the graphic communication of them to daughters was necessarily typical during the middle decades of the century, Mrs. Dublin's reliance on Mary as her confidante in these matters illustrates the same direction of change suggested by Jane Emmet's experiences.

Mary apparently rose to the occasion. As her mother continued to confide her problems, she gratefully acknowledged her daughter's constructive advice. In one letter, for example, she reassured Mary that she felt "somewhat more inclined to see facts as such." Other letters noted that, at her daughter's suggestion, she was concentrating on "my further education just for the pleasure of it," and that the latter's interest in her "intellectual progress" was "most gratifying."[57] One can only imagine a nineteenth-century daughter's reaction to the candid maternal revelation that while her parents' relationship lacked the spiritual comradeship that characterized that of Elizabeth and Robert Browning, there was a certain "affection and devotion" between them![58] Where a woman formerly might have taken refuge from marital disappointments in illness or suppressed them through involvement in child care, clubs, and benevolent endeavors, this case suggests another avenue: now she might confide in a daughter whose own increasingly sophisticated and worldly experiences would enable her to offer relevant advice as well as a sympathetic ear.

Possibly the ability of daughters to adapt to this type of role reversal reflects some diminution of the overall intensity of the mother-daughter relationship in the context of post-1920 developments. The dominant influence of a powerful peer culture, the heavy emphasis on heterosexual companionship, and a putatively more extensive role assumed by fathers in middle-class child-rearing may have reduced somewhat the degree to which both mothers and daughters invested emotionally in the relationship. If young women looked primarily to their peers as role models, they may have distanced themselves from their mothers more than their predecessors had done. If they found fathers emotionally accessible, they no longer necessarily relied exclusively on maternal psychic support. In turn, these changes may have meant that women did not have to feel wholly responsible for meeting their daughters' needs, indeed that they could legitimately turn to them for support, and that daughters could view their mothers somewhat objectively, as individuals with interests and problems of their own.[59]

Objectivity of this sort might lead a daughter to question both the value of domesticity and the meaning of her mother's life in a new way. Adele Mongan pondered her mother's overt distaste for domestic tasks: "Mom often says she wishes she were teaching again and never had to keep house."[60] June Calender found it hard to understand how any woman could tolerate cooking and the other routine tasks of homemaking; she had no intention of marrying "any man who can't at least afford to hire a cook and housekeeper."[61] Perhaps most significantly, Helene Harmon wanted desperately to be different from her mother: "I have a fear of turning into the kind of person Mother is, who suddenly in middle age remembers all the things she wanted when she was young," she asserted.[62] Where earlier daughters' comments on their mothers' lives might reflect admiration for their managerial skills or concern about potential exhaustion from their duties, these examples convey a less positive, more skeptical tone and a sense of conscious distancing from maternal models. Here post-1920 daughters definitely differed from their predecessors. The "new women" who rejected marriage did so primarily because cultural constraints compelled them to choose between professional aspirations and traditional family life, rather than because their observations of their mothers resulted in any evaluation of domesticity as intrinsically negative—or even temporarily irrelevant, as Jane Emmet implied when she explained her decision to leave home after her mother's remarriage. Observing that "home" now meant something in the future for her, she commented: "I think this is a pretty prevalent feeling among those of my generation and the divorce, the War, and both your & Dad's marrying again are, in my case, only partly responsible." Assuring her mother that she did not feel "cut off" from her or from her stepfather, she maintained nevertheless that "the level of day-to-day life" with them "wouldn't be a very real way of pursuing my life."[63]

To some extent, articles in popular periodicals reiterated older themes concerning problems between mothers and daughters during the decades following 1920. But this literature also proffered some evidence of change. Like similar discussions published during the previous forty years, post-1920 articles suggested that the relationship was an important one and projected the expectation that mothers and daughters should be able to communicate with one another.[64] They also emphasized maternal responsibility for the health and strength of the relationship.[65] While earlier articles had reflected contemporary societal anxiety about the changes in women's lives in the era of the "new woman," this later commentary addressed the new problems generated by developments such as the advent of the "flapper" and the growing emphasis on dates and popularity with the opposite sex.[66] Mothers had once been held responsible for insuring that daughters were ladylike, but now they could be called upon to make them beautiful and popular, as well as moral, and they were still expected to train them to be good wives.[67]

Earlier periodical discussions had focused heavily on how women should improve themselves in order to maintain mother-daughter harmony, urging them, for example, to keep themselves young and approachable and to avoid nagging, while at the same time admonishing them to discipline their offspring properly. By the 1920s and beyond, articles seemed to concentrate more on prescribing appropriate maternal responses to specific external influences such as the pressure of dating mores.[68] This shift in emphasis reflects the new issues that confronted mothers and daughters during the post-1920 decades. It also highlights the possibility that, in response to these powerful outside forces, daughters were pulling away from the intensity that had characterized earlier mother-daughter interactions. Whereas young women and their mothers may have been relatively isolated within the parameters of the domestic sphere throughout much of the nineteenth century, and often allied with one another against conservative social forces (which could include husbands and fathers) during the era of the "new woman," now daughters might respond to external standards of conduct, particularly those of their peer group. And they might also turn to other sources, such as friends and, to some extent, fathers for support and validation.

Despite the evidence of differences between late nineteenth- and early twentieth-century mother-daughter interactions and those of succeeding generations, the diversity of experiences after 1920 suggests that claims of change in the relationship should not be overstated. Elements of traditional mother-daughter solidarity and mutuality persisted, even as new influences strained female intergenerational ties in unaccustomed ways. Although post-1920 relationships revealed patterns of change, clear evidence of continuity can also be discerned.

Like their turn-of-the-century predecessors, later mothers took particular pleasure in raising daughters. Helene Harmon Weis's mother documented that pleasure in a baby book where she recorded her daughter's early accomplishments and reproduced her conversations in baby talk. She also saved magazine articles dealing with various aspects of baby care and noted the names of relevant books on this subject.[69] Although Ruth Robinson had four sons, her two daughters held a special place in her life. Just before the older daughter's third birthday, her mother noted: "My days are so happy because of San [nickname for her daughter Anne]. She is so sweet—so loveable—so gentle and such fun. All my boys are at school and San is a comfort."[70] Shortly after her husband was killed while serving in the navy, she wrote: "Both my little girls are the greatest comfort—They hate to see me sad," and several months later she observed, "My little girls are my life here and I am so lucky to have them and their interests to keep me occupied." In a particularly eloquent tribute to Anne, she commented: "I love her terrifically. . . . Instead of my bringing San up I feel I learn something from her."[71]

Impelled by very traditional child-rearing goals, Ruth Robinson was anxious to raise her daughters properly, to avoid spoiling them, and to encourage them to be "unselfish."[72] She was distressed when Sally misbehaved in church, and when twelve-year-old Anne either wanted to go out or to invite friends to visit every evening. At the age of seventeen, Sally was a constant source of worry; she was thoughtless, and she stayed out all night without calling her mother, who lamented the fact that her younger daughter was "just going her own way hating me—It's hard and it hurts."[73] While typical adolescent resentment appears to have been involved here, Sally's behavior also suggested a new nonchalance about maternal opinion, and a disregard for it.

Mrs. Robinson's effort to understand her daughter's hostility clearly reflects a mid-twentieth century, psychologically oriented frame of reference: "I feel that the reason Sally dislikes me so much at the moment . . . is because she feels completely an adult. . . . In one sense she is independent but does not know how to control herself. . . . It takes practice and time and I believe when she is away from me she will see Alex [her stepfather] and me in a different light."[74] But in essence, her relationship with Anne and Sally differed very little from those of previous mothers and daughters. Despite their conflicts with her, Anne and Sally reciprocated their mother's affection. As teenagers, they wrote affectionate birthday poems for her. As adults, they expressed their appreciation for her love and support. And she continued to articulate her pride in her daughters, to praise their achievements, and to take comfort in their presence.[75] This family's experiences, then, illustrate strength and continuity in the mother-daughter relationship despite the challenges posed by new influences.

The experiences of Ruth Teischman, who recorded her relationship with her mother in a diary she kept when she was about twelve years old, also convey a sense of continuity with earlier patterns. An intense young woman who feared that her father was jealous because

she and her mother were so affectionate with one another, she articulated her strong attachment to her mother in expressive detail, as in
her description of a conversation about death: "Somehow it came out
(I said) that my mother would live until 144 and me 116. . . . Now it
has to come true. I have to show my mother that I wasn't kidding
what I said. I also want it to come true because I love her so much
and don't want to be sad when she dies and vice versa. So if you do a
little math, you'd find that we would die the same second, time and
place. I adore her so much."[76]

Ruth's diary contains other expressions of her affection for her
mother (and for her father) as well as evidence of typical mother-
daughter friction over trivial matters.[77] Nevertheless, intimacy and
harmony, rather than conflict and antagonism, clearly defined their
relationship. This young woman's mother was extremely important
to her; even minor disputes between them distressed her.[78] Possibly
their relationship changed significantly as Ruth grew up, but the
essential images reflected in her diary differ very little from the
images of typical interactions between middle-class mothers and early
adolescent daughters at the turn of the century and earlier.[79]

Other examples suggest a similar resemblance between post-1920
relationships and the experiences of earlier mothers and daughters.
An extensive collection of letters documents approximately thirty
years of close communication between Minnie Millette and her
daughter Nancy, and illustrates the same sort of mother-daughter
intimacy enjoyed by turn-of-the century women. Mrs. Millette, who
had lost her own mother as a child, wrote lengthy, frequent, and
affectionate letters to Nancy at Oberlin College and also after her
graduation and marriage.[80] Like earlier mother-daughter correspondence, these letters encompassed a wide range of domestic and social
concerns. Mrs. Millette missed her daughter and worried about her
health.[81] She offered typical maternal advice on clothing and etiquette with tact and humor. "This is advice, skip down to end of
parentheses if you wish," she wrote on one occasion.[82] Nancy sent
her laundry home from Oberlin as Hilda Worthington Smith had
done when she attended Bryn Mawr.[83] She also consulted her mother
about more serious matters, such as her desire to marry before she
finished college.

Although this desire clearly separates Nancy Millette from earlier generations of college students who would have found such a plan inconceivable, her reliance on maternal advice links her with them. Similarly, the content of her mother's fourteen-page response distances her from the mothers of the "new women," but her involvement in the decision connects her to them. Diplomatically presenting her reply as "merely my process of thinking put into words" rather than "advice," Mrs. Millette wrote: "I would consider my undergraduate work my first consideration . . . college is a privilege that will never come again. . . . Marriage can easily last for fifty years—college days—undergraduate days are so short." She also stressed the importance of being prepared to earn a living "if the future should bring such a necessity," on the grounds that there could be no guarantee of parental financial support, given current economic conditions.[84] While this advice clearly reflected the influence of contemporary social forces, particularly the Depression, the intimacy of the communication it represented did not differ fundamentally from interchanges between mothers and daughters in previous decades. Nor did Mrs. Millette's defense of Nancy's good judgment in the face of her husband's distress over this matter differ from the behavior of earlier mothers who had often aligned themselves with daughters.[85]

Mrs. Millette also followed Nancy's academic experiences carefully: "Every detail is of interest," she wrote. "Tell me everything—I am so interested."[86] Like the mothers of Hilda Worthington Smith and Louise Bosworth, she was enthusiastic about her daughter's scholastic efforts: "Remember, I want to read the papers for Political Science and for your Art course. Also the advanced Comp. papers." And like the mothers of Blanche Ames and other early college students, she provided moral support when Nancy became discouraged: "Your letter came today and even if it told about unsatisfactory blue books—and your loss of faith in yourself, my appraisal of you still remains as high as ever. So there!"[87]

This close relationship continued after Nancy's marriage. Like earlier mothers and daughters, they discussed domestic matters in detail. Mrs. Millette enjoyed Nancy's descriptions of her developing culinary expertise, assured her that it was not difficult to put a zipper into a garment, and urged her to treat herself to the new coat she wanted to buy.[88] They also exchanged opinions about world affairs.[89] Expressions of maternal concern about Nancy's welfare and advice on a wide variety of subjects appeared frequently in Mrs. Millette's letters.[90] Nancy was affectionate, attentive, and reassuring as her mother aged.[91] Despite obvious reflections of the specific societal context—the impact of the Depression on Mrs. Millette's frame of reference, for example—this relationship does not seem to have differed significantly from earlier mother-daughter interactions.

Minnie Millette was not unique in her adherence to the tradition of mother-daughter correspondence. Mary Tyng Higgins's mother, who was a missionary in China, closely followed the details of her daughter's life in the United States and offered advice on a variety of domestic matters in frequent letters addressed affectionately, "Darling Mary."[92] She appreciated Mary's weekly letters, and took great pleasure in her daughter's family.[93] Previously, when Mary and her husband (who was also a missionary) had been interned by the Japanese, her mother had kept a diary, "a letter a day," for her "so you will know we think of you everyday and pray for you always."[94]

The parallels between post-1920 relationships and those of the preceding decades extended beyond the comforts of sharing the details of daily life. As in the past, maternal advocacy and assistance could still be the crucial variable in a daughter's ability to pursue her own ambitions or to endure her lot in life. Despite her own midlife anxieties, Augusta Salik Dublin supported her daughter Mary's aspirations for postgraduate study even when the family's straitened financial circumstances made this very difficult. She took pride in Mary's successful career and praised the articles and speeches she wrote.[95] Barbara Wooddall Taylor's mother was "wonderful" to her pregnant daughter whose husband was overseas during World War II.[96] And Edna Rankin McKinnon's perpetual emotional and financial support bolstered her daughter Dorothy through years of frustration as she tried to cope with a disappointing marriage and the repeated failures of her efforts to write fiction.[97]

Thus daughters continued to rely on their mothers' help in both traditional and new contexts. As one nineteen-year-old daughter observed after having a tooth extracted, "Felt AWFUL—went 'home to Mother.' Ah me, no one can ease the discomfort better than she." On another occasion, this same young woman referred quite casually to a very different kind of maternal aid. Describing an excursion to the beach, she noted in her diary: "Mother drove us in the Studebaker."[98] The juxtaposition of this image of a completely new kind of maternal support with the more traditional one of comfort and nurture suggests an interesting combination of change and continuity within the same relationship. It also suggests that the social and cultural forces that influenced young women's lives after 1920 also changed the lives of their mothers and enabled at least some of them to bridge the generation gap discerned by the observers of Middletown families.

Despite the increased importance of peers, daughters still expressed affection for their mothers and confided in them. Jane Emmet addressed her mother fondly as "Mootzig," "Moo," and "Mootz," and shared her private concerns with her, urging "Please *don't* read this letter aloud."[99] Similarly in a "very personal" letter to her mother from camp, another young woman wrote: "When I get Home, I'm going to make you sit down by me and listen to things that I have to tell you, things that a person can't write a letter about."[100] And mothers confided in daughters as well, in new ways as suggested previously, and in more traditional ways, for example, sharing their worries regarding siblings and grandchildren.[101]

Both women's personal documents and other sources suggest that the traditional ties between mothers and daughters endured as new social and cultural issues arose during the post-1920 period. Frivolous and more substantive concerns continued to link the two female generations in middle-class families. Like those of their predecessors, their letters contained social gossip and discussions of new dresses. They still consulted one another about various traditional domestic matters, as well as about newer dilemmas. Mothers continued to offer both solicited and unsolicited advice, to worry about the health of their offspring, to complain to daughters about the behavior of siblings, and to disagree with their husbands on behalf of daughters. They supported and encouraged daughters in their academic and professional endeavors, and in their personal lives as well.

The evidence also suggests that at least some aspects of the middle-class mother-daughter relationship may have been altered in the course of the four decades following 1920. New influences apparently diffused some of the relationship's former intensity. Some daughters found themselves in the position of mentors for their mothers. These preliminary conclusions merit further study: it is important to determine whether the social and cultural changes that distinguished the post-1920 period from the four decades that preceded it actually distanced mothers and daughters from one another, or whether these changes represented more a change of venue than a disruption of fundamental connections.

Distinct evidence of continuity in certain aspects of mother-daughter interactions, along with wide variation in women's individual personalities and experiences, clearly precludes the claim that the 1920s ushered in any sort of complete reversal of earlier patterns. Nevertheless, it is important to recognize and acknowledge the signs of change that distinguished the middle-class mother-daughter relationship in the decades after 1920. Perhaps the erosion of the public sense of collective female community that had evolved in Victorian America and culminated in the successful campaign for suffrage affected women's private lives as well, and thus promoted the moderation of the earlier intensity in mother-daughter interactions. As the feminist movement experienced what has been described as "the doldrums" following the ratification of the Nineteenth Amendment, Americans generally turned their attention to other issues—the Depression and another war, for example—and this context may have been less conducive to the degree of intimacy that mothers and daughters had enjoyed previously.[102] The Cold War domestic ideology of the fifties, which emphasized "containment" and the security of family life as a bulwark against a variety of threatening forces, may have also contributed to a tendency on the part of young women to look elsewhere for confidantes as their mothers became increasingly enmeshed in the feminine mystique and a stifling domesticity.[103] The extent of the change in the mother-daughter relationship, and its precise origins must be pursued through further historical investigation.

CHAPTER 9

"THE ANCHOR OF MY LIFE": TOWARD A HISTORY OF MOTHER-DAUGHTER RELATIONSHIPS

T HE task of analyzing the nature of interpersonal relationships in the past poses a formidable challenge for the historian who must carefully peruse a range of personal, social,
and cultural documents in search of that which is not said as well as
that which is clearly articulated. Historically as well as in the contemporary era, the mother-daughter relationship has been characterized
by an intricate mix of social and personal expectations that have
rendered it exceedingly complex. In a sense, the historical examination of mother-daughter interactions raises more questions than it
answers, since it is impossible to fully explain the precise interaction
of particular historical circumstances, specific familial environments,
and the mercurial and unique qualities of individual human beings.
Nevertheless, the preceding chapters have presented a range of revealing data that clearly indicate the need for a reexamination of the
facile assumption that conflict, antagonism, and guilt necessarily define the modern mother-daughter relationship. While the experiences of middle-class American daughters between 1880 and 1920
frequently differed substantially from those of their mothers, this
divergence did not generally result in a relationship transformed by
fundamental antagonism. Although conflict certainly existed as
daughters evolved into "new women," and even when they followed
more traditional paths, the sources consistently reveal that middle-
class mothers were far more tolerant of untraditional choices and
activities than the contemporary periodical and advice literature suggested. Indeed, they appear to have provided essential support in

more than a few cases, which may actually explain why some young women's choices could be particularly untraditional. Even in the English context, where mother-daughter relationships were shaped by different social and cultural influences, this type of maternal support was not completely unusual.

Like the preceding forty years, the post-1920 decades witnessed developments that further segregated the experiences of daughters from those of their mothers and, according to some contemporary observers, produced an unprecedented female generation gap. During these years, an increased emphasis on social life and peer relations, as well as a closer father-daughter connection, may have moderated the intensity that had characterized earlier middle-class American mother-daughter relationships. But a less intense relationship is not necessarily a hostile relationship. Indeed, close interactions with other significant family members and friends may have contributed to the maintenance of harmony between mothers and daughters.[1]

Even in the context of the cataclysmic social and cultural events that followed the ostensibly "normal" 1950s, the mother-daughter relationship apparently was not defined primarily by conflict and hostility. For example, Kenneth Keniston has suggested that the activities of the radical students who actively opposed American involvement in Vietnam reflected the core values espoused by their parents rather than an effort to rebel against parental views.[2] Letters from middle-class female readers of Betty Friedan's best-selling 1963 critique of domesticity, The Feminine Mystique, articulated the hope that their daughters' lives would be different from their own. This correspondence suggested that these women, like their predecessors at the turn of the century, either explicitly or implicitly encouraged their offspring to pursue new options.[3] Correspondence that expressed the thoughts and feelings of Ms. readers testified to daughters' recognition of and appreciation for maternal accomplishments in the face of societally prescribed restrictions, and indicated that they had learned important lessons from their mothers' experiences.[4] Finally, personal correspondence and recollections also document the existence of strong and positive mother-daughter links in the latter half of the twentieth century.[5]

Recent empirical studies of various aspects of the mother-daughter relationship have underscored its complexity. Like the historical evidence, much of this work corroborates the argument that the relationship is not inherently and essentially negative nor has it deteriorated in the course of the twentieth century, although some studies describe serious intergenerational struggles.[6] Most of the research documents the presence of some form of mother-daughter conflict, but dissension is not typically the dominant characteristic of the relationship. Thus several investigations have underscored the primacy of attachment and connection as opposed to antagonism between adolescent daughters and their mothers. For example, despite a widespread general perception to the contrary, a follow-up study in Middletown produced no evidence that the generation gap between parents and their teenaged children had increased between 1924 and 1977.[7] Similarly, research conducted at the Emma Willard School illustrated the importance adolescent girls place on maintaining connectedness in the mother-daughter relationship, and the efforts they make, even under difficult circumstances, to preserve that connection.[8] Another study, which compared American and Austrian mother-daughter relationships, revealed more explicit acknowledgment of negative affect on the part of Austrian girls and more discussion of positive mother-daughter social interaction on the part of their American counterparts.[9] Apparently, despite the frequency of tension between adolescent girls and their mothers, the general impression of fundamental hostility in the relationship seriously exaggerates the reality of the situation, at least in part as a result of cultural prescriptions against anger between mothers and daughters.[10]

Studies of the relationship between adult women and their mothers have also underlined the enduring strength and importance of the ties between mothers and daughters as well as the intricacy of those bonds. One such examination concluded that the centrality of mothering and the continuity in the prevailing social arrangements for care-giving link the lives of women from generation to generation despite other factors that might distance mothers and daughters from one another, such as tension during a daughter's adolescence or constraints produced by changes in family structure —for example, the introduction of sons-in-law or grandchildren, or the role reversals that often occur as mothers age.[11] Other research produced evidence that despite social pressure to the contrary, highly educated women between the ages of twenty and forty remained firmly attached to their mothers, identified strongly with them, and considered it important to act in ways that would protect them from emotional distress.[12] Two additional investigations yielded findings that seem especially interesting in the context of the conclusions suggested by the late nineteenth- and early twentieth-century evidence. One of these, an examination of the relationship between midlife women and their mothers, indicated that maternal support remains vitally important to adult daughters and that its presence or absence may actually determine whether or not a daughter is satisfied with the relationship.[13] The second study, which examined the influence of the mother-daughter relationship on women's adult role choices, found no direct relationship between those choices and their mothers' primary roles. Instead, maternal influence was expressed through a daughter's sense of self and her attitudes toward the roles she had chosen. Apparently what mothers *said*, rather than what they actually *did*, made the difference.[14]

While a survey of contemporary research dealing with the mother-daughter relationship can only briefly highlight the dimensions of this subject, it is clear that these studies and the evidence gleaned from various other post-1920 sources do not describe an essentially negative relationship. Like the data concerning mother-daughter relationships between 1880 and 1920, this evidence displaces the shallow image of alienation and agony that has been assigned to women's interactions with their female offspring in favor of a more complex and complete image in which dissension is mitigated by powerful relational mutuality. Evidence of congruence between contemporary data and earlier findings does not account for the nature of mother-daughter relationships during the late nineteenth and early twentieth centuries, however. It is the remaining task of this final chapter to propose such an explanation and thus to define more fully a historical framework for the study and analysis of this basic family connection.

What explains the presence of strong maternal support for daughters' innovative aspirations and activities during the period 1880–1920? During this transitional time, daughters who pursued higher education certainly moved into a world their mothers had not known, or knew only in part. Those who did not attend college also encountered new influences. The "woman question" pervaded the social and cultural climate and placed new and difficult demands on their relationships, but it did not really divide middle-class mothers and daughters. Why did mutuality prevail over estrangement in a situation that appears to have been particularly conducive to conflict and hostility?

In the first place, as the evidence in chapter 1 illustrates, a reassessment of the earlier nineteenth-century background against which mother-daughter interactions between 1880 and 1920 have been measured suggests that the case for previously untroubled, harmonious relationships has been overstated. Contemporary observers, who were probably personally uncomfortable with the changes in the world of women, apparently exaggerated the novelty of the tensions between mothers and daughters as well as the extent of the conflict they perceived during the late nineteenth and early twentieth centuries.[15] Both the physical and the emotional aspects of puberty in young women had engaged the attention of various medical and educational advisers earlier in the nineteenth century. The extensive discussion of mother-daughter relationships after 1880, then, continued this trend in the context of the "invention" of adolescence as the concept was elaborated by G. Stanley Hall and others.[16]

Despite this continuity, however, evidence of a major intensification of mother-daughter discord after 1880 would not be surprising, particularly where daughters chose to pursue the option of higher education and the accompanying independence. However, the sources document the absence of systematic conflict. Hence a fuller explanation for this finding must be sought through the further exploration of the complex interaction of social, psychological, and cultural factors with the experiences of mothers and daughters between 1880 and 1920—both those experiences intrinsic to the relationship and those unique to the period.[17]

Certainly, women's varied personality characteristics and activities shape the mother-daughter relationship during any historical period. Not all turn-of-the-century mothers nagged and complained as Annie Winsor Allen's mother did; not all daughters were patient and tolerant as Annie was. Similarly, very few mothers were as sophisticated and open as Ethel Sturges Dummer was. Undoubtedly, conflict in the relationship, or its absence, was at least in part a function of the specific traits of individuals.

In the same way, women's particular life experiences help to account for the lack of conflict in specific instances. For example, certain widowed mothers may have felt that it was essential to remain in their daughters' good graces since they were otherwise alone in the world. They may have accepted what, in some sense, was unacceptable to them in the interests of preserving a relationship they needed for their own security. Such women may also have been able to fill the void left in their own lives by the loss of a spouse through their involvement in their daughters' lives. While this situation would seem more typical in the case of a married daughter with children, it may also describe mothers whose daughters chose less conventional options, for example, the mothers of Vida Scudder and Hilda Worthington Smith.

Likewise, mothers whose own educational and personal aspirations had not been fulfilled may have lived out those desires vicariously through the act of assisting their daughters to achieve their goals.[18] Relatedly, those who felt themselves constrained, either consciously or unconsciously, by the expectations placed on women in a male-dominated society may have been able to discharge their own psychic tensions by allying themselves with their daughters in opposition to their husbands, as in cases where maternal support overruled paternal skepticism regarding the necessity of higher education for women. On the other hand, mothers who were satisfied and fulfilled in their own lives, comfortable in their marriages and successful in club and charitable work, as Ethel Sturges Dummer was, may have found it perfectly natural and comfortable to support daughters' efforts to move even farther from traditional domestic roles. It is even possible that as a result of the sweeping changes in women's circumstances, discord between mothers and daughters was reduced during the late nineteenth century and beyond. Either consciously or unconsciously, many middle-class women may have reacted very positively to the liberating influences represented by the "new woman." Thus even mothers who espoused and/or modeled traditional female behavior may have accepted or applauded daughters' unconventional activities and desires.

In a psychoanalytically based examination of the mother-daughter relationship, Nini Herman has suggested that a good marriage could contribute directly to the maintenance of harmony, arguing that the presence of a supportive husband and father facilitated maternal support for untraditional daughters and mediated what she defines as inevitable conflicts between the two female generations in nineteenth-century middle-class nuclear families. Like the work of family-systems theorists, this suggestion underscores the fact that mothers and daughters do not interact with one another in isolation.[19] Indeed, several historical discussions have stressed the importance of fathers rather than mothers as major role models for nonconforming daughters before the late nineteenth century.[20] Other evidence indicates that middle-class paternal involvement with children increased significantly in the first decades of the twentieth century.[21] Increased paternal presence and participation in family interactions may have alleviated mother-daughter tensions, but this change could also have generated some new intergenerational rivalry for male attention within the family setting. Hence, although a full discussion of the father-daughter relationship remains beyond the scope of this investigation, it is clearly important to address its relevance as a factor in the historical mother-daughter equation.

Because the task of communicating about, and coping with, the concerns and needs of daughters has typically been assigned to mothers in the past, the available historical documents often reveal far more about mother-daughter interactions than about those between fathers and daughters. For example, although fathers and daughters certainly corresponded with one another, their letters frequently concentrated on practical and pragmatic matters such as train schedules and clothing allowances and thus did not reveal a great deal about their deeper feelings for one another.[22] While the absence of such evidence in no way indicates a dearth of affection, it limits the historian's ability to interpret the relationship as fully as is possible in the case of mother-daughter interactions.

A cursory survey of available evidence concerning father-daughter relationships documents the importance that some daughters placed on their relationships with their fathers during the years between 1880 and 1920. Clara Savage Littledale greatly enjoyed her father's company.[23] Eliza Coe Brown Moore and her daughter Dorothea May Moore corresponded extensively with their respective fathers, and their letters provide evidence of strong attachment, including expressions of affection and concern for paternal well-being, and appreciation for both moral and financial support.[24] Mary Kate Brewster's father accompanied her on the first leg of a journey from Boston to Australia, intending to disembark when the ship reached New York. She was delighted to have his company and was devastated by his sudden death on board the ship.[25] Affa Miner Tuttle was also devastated by the loss of her father. She treasured the desk she had inherited from him and reported to her mother that she cried when she saw the "postman" because "he has been so synonymous to me with a letter from Father." Her sister, Elizabeth Miner Garman, shared the same sense of loss, noting in her diary: "First Thanksgiving father was not there to welcome me oh, that he could have lived, Life is so different without him and we all missed him so much."[26]

Fathers also articulated their deep feelings for their daughters. "You my dear Florence, have largely met my ideal, and have daily helped to renew my life," Florence Bascom's father told her. Otto Auerbach looked forward to receiving letters from his daughter Lydia, admired his new son-in-law, and rejoiced over the birth of his granddaughter. "Life is worth while living when Mother and I can see in your children their noble character and the happiness they have given us," he wrote.[27] Post-1920 fathers also valued their interactions with daughters, as in the case of Louis Dublin, who carefully advised his daughter Mary regarding her graduate studies, urged her to tell him "more about yourself, what is happening to your own dear little soul," expressed his pride in her work, and missed her desperately when she was studying in England.[28]

The evidence concerning father-daughter interactions documents negative as well as positive relationships. For example, although Alice Hamilton's father took great interest in his daughters' education, his business failures and excessive drinking impeded his parental effectiveness. As young adults, his children regarded him "as an ineffective but disturbing presence who demanded more attention than they wanted to give."[29] Ethel Spencer found her nervous and troubled father similarly ineffective, particularly in contrast to her capable, dependable mother, and Marion Taylor, whose parents were divorced, bitterly resented the lack of paternal support, both moral and financial.[30]

Although it is clearly impossible to derive any conclusions about father-daughter relationships from a few examples, it is certainly appropriate to suggest that this aspect of familial interaction could influence the nature of the mother-daughter connection in various ways. Paternal indifference or absence might foster devoted maternal advocacy and a strong mother-daughter alliance. Alternatively, paternal involvement might promote mother-daughter harmony, as Nini Herman has proposed, but it could also reflect some form of mother-daughter incompatibility.[31]

Studies in the new field of the history of the emotions indicate that the collective emotional standards of the period, or "emotionology," as articulated in the prescriptive literature, also played a role in defining mother-daughter relationships between 1880 and 1920. This research suggests that definitions of emotional normalcy shift over time. Social influences as well as biological and psychological factors constrain emotional expression and also promote emotions that are consistent with societal interests.[32] In pre-Revolutionary America, for example, feminine emotion, including a mother's love for her children, was feared and suspected. A new appreciation for familial affection and a different conceptualization of motherhood, linked with republican political ideology and Christian theology, emerged in the late eighteenth and early nineteenth centuries. The emotionology surrounding anger and jealousy has also changed over the course of American history.[33]

In the context of mother-daughter relationships, it is particularly significant that throughout the nineteenth and twentieth centuries the suppression of female anger was specifically encouraged. This pattern probably explains the general absence of overt expressions of anger between mothers and daughters. Failure to express anger, however, certainly does not indicate that women did not feel this emotion throughout the nineteenth century and during the period 1880–1920.[34] Recent research has suggested that for some middle-class young women in the past, unexpressed family conflict, particularly mother-daughter tension, was manifested through serious illnesses, specifically anorexia nervosa and related eating disorders.[35] While relatively few daughters suffered these illnesses, the possible connection between these disorders and the repression of mother-daughter conflict encourages further consideration of the role of psychological issues in the historical interpretation of the mother-daughter relationship.

Current studies of the complex and subtle relationship between emotional standards and actual emotional experience indicate that emotionology may actually influence the experience, as well as the expression, of emotions. Socialization and societal perceptions of a particular state of emotional arousal may determine how that state is apprehended by an individual. Similarly, an individual's decision to think about an emotion or to express it may intensify or even create the actual experience of that emotion, while the choice to suppress it or not think about it may have the opposite effect. Hence changes in emotional standards in the past could have resulted in changes in the emotions themselves.[36]

While it is difficult to document explicitly the influence of collective emotional standards on individual women, the research on emotionology and emotional experience has interesting implications for the historical study of mother-daughter interactions. First, this research suggests that the nature of mother-daughter relationships between 1880 and 1920 reflects in part the stress on both the suppression of female anger and the importance of intergenerational harmony in the emotionology of the period. If mothers fully internalized the emotional standards prescribed for them, they may not have actually experienced significant negative emotions about their daughters' activities. Alternatively, they may have altered only their overt expressions of emotions in accordance with societal standards. In either case, maternal support rather than basic conflict was the manifest result.

The research also suggests a possible link between the matrophobia articulated by some late twentieth-century women and the feminist emotionology that accompanied the crusade for women's liberation. In the context of literary criticism, Elaine Showalter has commented that "hating one's mother was the feminist enlightenment of the 50's and 60's."[37] This observation can be construed historically as well as in literary terms. Mother-blaming was not a new phenomenon in the second half of the twentieth century. The feminist articulation of the notion that mothers should be held responsible for daughters' problems, and for problems in the relationship itself, represented a continuation of earlier negative maternal images (including those conveyed by the prescriptive literature between 1880 and 1920). But the explicit suggestion that mothers could be held directly responsible for the reproduction of women's subordination and the perpetuation of gender inequality added a new dimension. Hence the resentment and bitterness experienced and expressed by many contemporary daughters with regard to their mothers reflected the effect of the late twentieth-century emotionology.[38]

Women's collective experiences, both within and outside the home, also shaped their family relationships. Although the domestic role still dominated the lives of middle-class women in the late nineteenth and early twentieth centuries, their lives were not as narrowly circumscribed as that concept suggests. During most of the nineteenth century, women were active in various religious and social organizations and causes outside the home. Involvement in external activities was not a new idea to mothers between 1880 and 1920, nor was secondary education, which had been available earlier in the century in the form of private female academies and seminaries and even in girls' public high schools of the sort founded in Worcester, Massachusetts, in 1824. Thus while their daughters' aspirations may have extended beyond the boundaries of their own experiences, to encompass college and career goals, their own socialization included the concept that women's "sphere" reached beyond the home.[39]

Even within the home, evidence suggests that middle-class women experienced a significant increase in power and autonomy during the course of the nineteenth century. Suzanne Lebsock has argued that the first half of the century witnessed an ongoing general process of growth toward female freedom from total dependence on particular men.[40] This increase, expressed as a kind of "domestic feminism," has been documented with reference to women's exercise of control over sex and reproduction within marriage.[41] The theory of domestic feminism interprets the evolution of female domestic roles and the perceptions that developed from those roles, for example, women's presumed expertise in homemaking and child-rearing, as positive developments. In this context, it is possible that by the late nineteenth century, mothers had altered their own views of womanhood to such an extent that they felt comfortable supporting daughters' efforts to extend the feminism they had developed at home into the public sphere. Thus domestic feminism may have actually encouraged maternal support for daughters' activities, particularly where paternal opposition was involved, as, for example, in the case of M. Carey Thomas.[42] If, as Daniel Scott Smith has suggested, the eventual success of women outside the domestic setting can be construed as an extension of their earlier progress within the family, the connection between domestic feminism and mother-daughter relationships may have been a crucial component in that success.[43]

In addition to mirroring an evolving sense of autonomy within the domestic context, maternal support for daughters' untraditional choices may also reflect the subtle influence of a specifically middle-class frame of reference. Investigations of the nature of twentieth-century middle-class child-rearing values have discerned a tendency on the part of parents to value demonstrations of self-direction in accordance with internal standards as opposed to conformity in accordance with externally imposed standards. In comparison with working-class parents, their disciplinary practices seem to consider intent rather than to respond primarily to the consequences of a child's behavior. Middle-class mothers appear to punish daughters and sons equally while their working-class counterparts appear to distinguish between them, placing more stringent expectations on daughters.[44] Given the atmosphere of growth and expansion, and the sense of new possibilities that permeated middle-class life between 1880 and 1920, it is possible that some parents held similar attitudes about the importance of self-direction, and exercised them in relation to daughters as well as sons during that period too. The influence of this frame of reference, then, would also help to explain why mothers were able to support their daughters' aspirations and achievements.

Several related factors thus explain why the emergence of a generation gap in opportunity and aspirations did not prove to be the most powerful determinant of the nature of mother-daughter relationships in the late nineteenth and early twentieth centuries. Various other influences fostered a pattern of primarily positive, supportive interactions. However, a final point remains to be explored: the yawning discrepancy between the reality of mother-daughter relationships and the tone of the discussion in the contemporary periodicals and advice manuals.

Undoubtedly this discrepancy partly reflected the individual idio-syncrasies of writers and editors. For example, Edward Bok of *The Ladies Home Journal,* who was not known for his liberal views, even regarded the women's club movement as a threat to the family.[45] More significantly, however, the direction of the prescriptive litera-ture reflected the general social concerns of the era.[46] The reiteration of the importance of mother-daughter harmony and the insistence on maternal obligations for fostering that harmony addressed a growing anxiety about the stability of the middle-class family that spread as women articulated untraditional ambitions and responded to new opportunities. Thus, for example, *Harper's Bazar,* which sup-ported suffrage and other progressive causes, rejected feminist de-mands for the expansion of women's sphere and insisted that the obligations of wifehood and motherhood defined the proper profes-sion for a woman.[47] The pervasive emphasis on avoiding intergener-ational female conflict also mirrored contemporary cultural expecta-tions for women, particularly those regarding the inappropriateness of female anger.[48]

At least two other discernible and important cultural trends emerged in the prescriptive literature: the "professionalization" of mother-hood in the second half of the nineteenth century, and the develop-ment of formal public concern over adolescence at the beginning of the twentieth.[49] The growing emphasis on the importance of so-called expert advice as essential for proper child-rearing (which was exemplified in the proliferation of advice books) and the attendant tendency to preach to women partially explain the prevalence of literature that blamed mothers for intergenerational difficulties. With the development of the concept of expertise in mothering and the articulation of the social definition of adolescence as a period of storm and stress, tensions that had been viewed formerly as normal parts of family life—moody daughters or impatient mothers, for example—seem to have been upgraded or redefined as serious prob-lems for which properly professional mothers could and should find solutions. The prescriptive literature contributed to the growth of this perception by focusing extensively on mother-daughter issues.

It is difficult to estimate the relative contributions of each of these cultural strands to the creation of the generation gap painted by the prescriptive literature, and still more difficult to unravel the intricacies of the connections between that literature and the emotional and behavioral realities of individual women's lives. Yet the latter issue is particularly important to consider inasmuch as these women functioned as part of the culture that is reflected in the literature. Hence, while the magazines and advice manuals apparently did not express the explicit reality of the experiences of "new women" and their mothers, this literature was not necessarily totally irrelevant to their concerns. No doubt some middle-class mothers and daughters (whether or not they attended college) were troubled by aspects of their relationships. Probably some of them found an outlet in the periodical and advice literature for tensions that could not be directly expressed at the conscious level due to the influence of women's socialization patterns and the emotionology of the period. At the other end of the spectrum, readers who did not identify personally with the problems described may have enjoyed reading the advice and congratulating themselves for avoiding such difficulties. Finally, the data on women's actual experiences indicate that trivial disputes could arise even where mothers and daughters were basically compatible. In this sense, then, the prescriptive literature erred more with regard to the interpretation than the occurrence of such incidents. As these examples suggest, a complex range of possibilities defines the relation between prescription and behavior in the context of mother-daughter relationships, as in women's history more generally.[50]

Similarly, the links between the portrayal of mother-daughter interactions in late nineteenth- and early twentieth-century novels and the reality of middle-class family experiences between 1880 and 1920 can be characterized as subtle and oblique rather than immediately obvious. In any historical period, aspects of social and cultural issues that are construed as too sensitive to be discussed directly, even through prescriptive literature, can be articulated indirectly and addressed through works of fiction. Thus literary treatments of the mother-daughter relationship in the era of the "new woman" primarily described troubled situations rather than those in which unanimity of goals and desires prevailed. Rather than depict untroubled, comfortable relationships, popular novels explored the social and cultural causes of problematic mother-daughter interactions and examined the ramifications of potential solutions. And because they were "fiction" as opposed to "fact," these works represented a safe and unthreatening context within which readers could acknowledge and examine their own concerns about mother-daughter issues, whatever the nature of their personal experiences.

Despite the complexity of the connections between the portrayal of mother-daughter interactions in the prescriptive literature and novels of the period and the character of women's actual relationships, it is evident that mutual caring and support rather than conflict dominated the middle-class mother-daughter relationship between 1880 and 1920. Although the sources do reveal the presence of tensions surrounding both trivial and weightier issues, the striking absence of fundamental intergenerational conflict is what stands out.

A current and continuing reexamination of developmental theory as it pertains to women's psychological growth suggests the possibility of a link between this absence of major conflict and the ability of young women in the late nineteenth and early twentieth centuries to undertake new, untraditional behaviors. Most theories of the self describe development as an evolutionary process of separation and individuation, a progression through increasingly autonomous psychological levels toward an ultimate goal of personal independence. These theories acknowledge the importance of relationships to individual development in the early years of life, but they posit autonomy and separation as emblems of maturity and thus as preferable to relatedness and mutual interdependence. This conceptualization of the self does not appear to fit women's experience, which has more typically manifested a continuing emphasis on connection and affiliation as opposed to disengagement. Recognition of this discrepancy has resulted in a new approach that redefines female development in terms of relationship as opposed to separation.[51]

Relational development theory argues that women develop and strengthen a sense of self through their involvement in both external social relationships and in the internal experiences of relationships characterized by mutuality and affective connection. This development is initiated by the early mother-daughter relationship in which children identify with the mother as an active caretaker. In modern Western culture, the full evolution of the image of an interacting self, "a self whose emotional core is responded to by the other and who responds back to the emotions of the other," is discouraged in boys

but becomes the center of the self-image in girls.[52] This responsiveness, characterized as mutual intersubjectivity, involves empathy at
both the cognitive and the affective level. Over time, the mother-
daughter relationship becomes a mutually reciprocal process in which
each participant holds the other's subjectivity as central to the interaction with that individual, each remains open to change in the
interaction, and each views the process of relating as intrinsically
valuable. While mutuality will not distinguish every interchange in
such a relationship, sufficient mutuality must be present so that the
participants can feel that their needs are met.[53]

   According to this model, mother-daughter attachments foster the
development of positive capabilities such as motivation for action,
self-esteem, and self-affirmation, as the self is enhanced rather than
reduced or threatened by relationship. Thus the ongoing interdependence implied by mutuality produces positive as opposed to negative or even pathological outcomes, as some theorists have maintained.[54] Women develop agency and initiative in the context of the
mother-daughter relationship (and in other important relationships
as well).[55] Transitory conflicts between adolescent daughters and their
mothers represent a means of elaborating the continuity of connection to significant others, a way to work out differences within the
relationship rather than to separate.[56] While the adolescent does not
necessarily seek separation, she needs to modify the relationship in
order to affirm her own developmental changes and enable new
relationships to proceed. Such modification requires the capacity and
the willingness for change and growth on the part of both mother
and daughter. This suggests that at least some of the storm and stress
associated with adolescence may reflect parental difficulties in changing as much as it mirrors the characteristics of the adolescent.[57]

   The research findings that support this theory are based on the
experiences of late twentieth-century women rather than those of
mothers and daughters between 1880 and 1920. Nevertheless, it is
possible to discern elements of congruence between the contemporary model of relational development and earlier mother-daughter
interactions without claiming any sort of ahistorical universality for
the female experience.[58] Thus the self-in-relation research suggests
that the mutuality and support that typified late nineteenth- and
early twentieth-century mother-daughter relationships would gener-

ate an important positive effect upon daughters' psychological abilities to function successfully in new roles and settings—on their ability to venture beyond their mothers' worlds. Perhaps this also explains why their mothers were able to cope with their doing so. Yet the apparent congruence between the theory of relational development and middle-class mother-daughter interactions between 1880 and 1920 raises further questions. Does the theory describe a phenomenon that is characteristic of American women's psychological development over time—and if so, why? Or do the experiences of late nineteenth- and early twentieth-century mothers and daughters specifically link them psychologically with their late twentieth-century counterparts? These issues clearly merit further consideration.

As critiques of psychohistorical scholarship have demonstrated, the task of linking human psychology and social change is exceedingly complex.[59] Intrinsically, psychological theories tend toward universalistic claims concerning psychological commonalities rather than toward historical, social, or cultural specificity. Current studies in the emerging field of emotions history have underscored the inadequacy of any type of one-dimensional conceptualization that would posit an unchanging, ahistorical human psyche. Yet, as Nancy Chodorow has argued, the fact that a psychological theory has not been utilized in a culturally or socially specific manner does not preclude its application in that way.[60] Hence the interpretive potential of the theory of relational development for the historical study of mother-daughter interactions can encompass the effects of social and cultural variables as well as the influence of factors that do not change.

Some fundamental continuities that have characterized women's experiences historically are clearly pertinent to the use of this theory for the construction of a history of middle-class American mother-daughter relationships. For example, biological constants, such as the hormonal changes that accompany puberty and often produce increased aggressiveness in adolescent girls, link women across time. Certain social and cultural constants define similar connections. Typically in the past, as well as in contemporary society, daughters have been cared for and socialized primarily by their mothers, and middle-class women's roles have been tightly bound up with the lives of their offspring. Furthermore, both mothers and daughters have experienced the devaluation of their gender in a male-dominated, patriarchal society: as Marcia Westkott has observed, "the story of mothers and daughters takes place in the world of the father."[61] With relatively few exceptions, that world has effectively rendered womanhood and personhood mutually exclusive. It has also generated an enduring cultural heritage of mother-blaming.

Evidence of continuities of this sort certainly underscores the relevance of contemporary developmental psychological theory for the analysis of mother-daughter relationships in the past as well as in contemporary society. Such evidence also accentuates the obvious danger of historical misinterpretation as a result of positing any complete change in the patterns of mother-daughter interactions in modern American society. Nevertheless, social and cultural variables have changed women's experiences in ways that must be considered in the context of an analysis of those patterns. Although family issues are in one sense private, they are also socially and culturally constructed. Family forms, functions, roles, and relationships reflect the impact of diverse social and cultural factors that vary with time, place, and social class. Historical developments such as industrialization, the separation of the home and the workplace, alterations in emotional standards, and variations in social and cultural expectations of motherhood have all influenced patterns of mothering and thus may have affected the nature of middle-class American mother-daughter interactions in important ways.[62]

For example, in colonial America, fathers were primarily held responsible for the conduct of their offspring, but this responsibility was later transferred to mothers, first as part of the job of republican motherhood, then as an integral component of Victorian family life, and finally as a product of Freudian and post-Freudian ideology.[63] Women's perceptions of, and reactions to, their maternal roles have undoubtedly varied in conjunction with these changing expectations and have influenced the mother-daughter relationship accordingly. Similarly, shifting cultural norms regarding the identity and roles of women have affected daughters' personal perceptions of their own mothers as well as their concepts of motherhood more generally, and thus have also had an impact on the relationship.

A recent study of the impact of maternal death on midlife daughters concluded that women experienced more grief over their mothers' lives—for example, their unfulfilled potential, their unsatisfying marriages—than over their actual deaths. These daughters mourned the fact that their own culturally defined conceptions of the nature of an effective woman had prevented them from really knowing their mothers or had caused them to devalue their mothers' lives.[64] They expressed the same deep sense of loss articulated by daughters between 1880 and 1920.[65] But while the latter apparently grieved principally for themselves when their mothers died, for the loss of treasured companionship, guidance, and support, the bereavement of contemporary adult daughters clearly incorporated concerns engendered by the influence of feminist ideology in late twentieth-century American culture. This research illustrates the continuity of mother-daughter connection and mutuality as posited by relational development theory, but it also affirms the influence of social and cultural variables on the mother-daughter relationship.

Elaine Showalter has discerned and explored a number of political, social, and cultural parallels between the last decades of the twentieth century and the 1880s and 1890s.[66] Among the similarities that connect these two transitional eras she cites particularly a series of gender-based concerns that include the threat of sexual chaos, posed first by the "new woman" and then by contemporary feminism. Her comparison of *fin-de-siècle* crises suggests that although nearly a hundred years separate turn-of-the-century mothers and daughters from their contemporary counterparts, these female generations are linked psychologically by their shared experiences in two historical periods marked by major transitions in women's lives. Such a linkage would certainly help to explain the symmetry between contemporary relational development research and the history of middle-class mother-daughter relationships between 1880 and 1920.

Nevertheless, in some ways at least, these four decades appear to have been unusual. Previously American mothers and daughters had typically enjoyed compatible relationships, but at the same time they had shared essentially the same experiences and aspirations. When this traditional intergenerational continuity was disrupted in the late nineteenth century, no corresponding degeneration of the mother-daughter relationship ensued. On the contrary, the changes in women's lives may have actually strengthened the ties between middle-class mothers and their female offspring. Yet this had not been the case earlier in the century, when young women with unconventional interests were encouraged more frequently by fathers than by mothers. Possibly the trend toward smaller middle-class families in the late nineteenth century fostered greater mother-daughter intimacy and maternal support as women found themselves increasingly able to devote time and energy to the individual needs of their offspring. The period between 1880 and 1920 also differed clearly from subsequent decades, which witnessed a partial but discernible reduction in the interdependence of mothers and daughters. Likewise, this period in American mother-daughter history contrasted distinctly with the same chronological era in the history of English mother-daughter relationships, during which women served far more often as restrictive influences for ambitious daughters. In the context of this contemporaneous English pattern, the distinctive nature of American mother-daughter interactions stands out even more clearly.

Cultural variability and change in the mother-daughter relationship can be traced, at least in part, to complex cultural, social, and psychological factors, both within the American context and beyond. Thus, for example, the late nineteenth century witnessed the conjuncture of a cultural climate marked by a definite dichotomy between tradition and innovation in women's lives as well as more generally, and the culmination of a process of growing female autonomy within the home. This mixture created a unique context that nurtured a distinctive middle-class American mother-daughter relationship characterized by mutual understanding and female unity in the face of male domination. While English society experienced similar cultural confusion, the influence of a more rigid social code restricted middle-class women's abilities to challenge either established behavioral conventions or patriarchal authority on behalf of daughters, although economic exigency apparently led their working-class counterparts to do so.

Although the psychological realm is often cited as a source of continuity rather than variation in human experience, it too can partially explain historical evidence of change in the nature of mother-daughter interactions. According to the theory of relational development, an individual's early external social relationships and internal representations of such relationships are crucial to self-development. The fact that those early relationships most often are between mother and child determines the nature of the mother-daughter relationship. This circumstance suggests a psychological link between the differences in American and English mother-daughter relationships at the turn of the century and the different ideologies of motherhood that distinguished middle-class Victorian family culture in the two societies. While in America, middle-class women were expected to devote themselves fully, in both a physical and an emotional sense, to their offspring, in England this was not the case. The extent to which mothers implemented the expectations of their respective cultures influenced the frequency and the intensity of their interactions with daughters. These qualities, in turn, defined the degree to which the latter identified with and responded to mothers as active caretakers, and also determined the presence or absence of the sort of mutual intersubjectivity posited by relational development theory. Thus the interaction of psychological factors with social and cultural influences helps to explain why mutual interdependence and support typified middle-class American mother-daughter relationships, while these characteristics appeared less frequently in middle-class English families.

Despite its apparent exceptionality in the history of mother-daughter relationships, or perhaps because of it, the period between 1880 and 1920 has important implications for the history of American women. The closeness and mutual understanding enjoyed by middle-class mothers and daughters during the late nineteenth and early twentieth centuries enabled many women to move beyond the domestic world to take advantage of new educational and professional opportunities that emerged as American society completed the transition to modernity. The possibility that middle-class mothers and daughters may have been unusually close, and that this intimacy served to empower both of them to challenge male prerogatives within and beyond the family, identifies this period as a watershed in the history of American women. It also raises an important question about the impact of possible differences between the experiences of middle-class and various groups of working-class women as mothers and daughters, and highlights the need for focused historical investigation along these lines. Finally, the link between mother-daughter relationships and women's abilities to undertake new activities in the age of the "new woman" underscores the centrality of family as a major influence in women's lives at the same time as it challenges the assumption that family roles and relationships have necessarily fore-closed female development in the past. More generally, this link suggests the relevance of further historical examination of the connections between family life and individuals' capacities to respond to societal change.

At the age of ninety, in 1946, Mary Ezit Bulkley assessed her own worldview in comparison with that of her mother and her grandmother, and reached the following conclusions:

There has, I convince myself, been some betterment in my outlook. I am not quite so ready to accept Things As They Are as my grandmother was. I am not so much concerned with my soul's salvation as she and her mother were. I have other ideas than my mother as to what women should or should not do. But on the whole the change in my spirit is not marked, although it shows differently. If perhaps a group of my friends and I could go back the hundred odd years and settle in my grandmother's village, if we went to church on Sunday and kept our mouths shut on week days, we need be considered by them as only slightly cracked.[67]

This astute appraisal captures a daughter's personal sense of connection between the female generations in her own family as well as her recognition and acknowledgment of a certain degree of change in women's viewpoints. More broadly, it also suggests the power of continuity rather than disruption and change in women's feelings about the connections between mothers and daughters. Although middle-class American women of Mary Bulkley's generation experienced a different world from that of their predecessors, the mother-daughter relationship served as a vital and enduring source of support that enabled them to face and respond to the challenges they confronted during a period of rapid change in their lives. Connection rather than separation remained the hallmark of mother-daughter interactions during the period 1880–1920 and beyond, as it had been before the appearance of the "new woman."

Traditionally, middle-class American mothers have been charged with the responsibility for preparing daughters to assume their prescribed roles in a hierarchical, male-dominated society. However, many have been able to envision alternatives that would allow women to enjoy personal accomplishment and to take control of their own lives, and some have inspired and assisted their daughters to move forward toward that goal.[68] In an overview of research on women in American history, Barbara Sicherman identified one significant long-range trend: she concluded that supportive female networks in various institutional contexts have played a central and enduring role in fostering women's aspirations and their creativity, in assisting their efforts to overcome "the conflict between individual aspirations and cultural imperatives."[69] The history of middle-class American mother-daughter relationships illustrates the same trend, first through numerous, striking examples of maternal support for daughters' activities, and more recently through daughters' growing recognition and explicit acknowledgment of their mothers' strengths and needs. Mutuality and connection rather than tension and conflict defined the essence of mother-daughter interactions between 1880 and 1920, and these qualities have remained integral to the relationship despite some apparent changes in the succeeding decades. The sentiments expressed in the following Mother's Day greeting from an adult daughter to her ninety-six-year-old mother testify eloquently to the enduring, affirmative power of the "bonds of womanhood" as they have linked middle-class American mothers and daughters:

Your "light" must shine a great distance and with power! Your thoughts, if recorded, would make fascinating reading, I'm sure! Your long trip through the many years has been adventuresome and very challenging! *I* learned the *challenge lesson* early from you & it has helped me many times! I hope you have many more happy Mothers' Days! love, Doris [70]

NOTES

Preface

1. An investigation of the impact of black culture on mother-daughter interactions would also enhance the effort to understand the relationship historically. For an interesting discussion of this topic, see Patricia Hill Collins, "The Meaning of Motherhood in Black Culture and Black Mother-Daughter Relationships," *Sage* 4, 2 (Fall 1987): 3–9.

2. Tillie Olsen, ed., *Mother to Daughter, Daughter to Mother* (New York, 1984), 275.

3. A relevant discussion of diaries as sources for women's history is Judy Nolte Lensink, "Expanding the Boundaries of Criticism: The Diary as Female Autobiography," *Women's Studies* 14, 1/2 (1987): 39–53.

1. "The Central Problem of Female Experience"

1. Nikki Stiller, *Eve's Orphans: Mothers and Daughters in Medieval English Literature*, Contributions in Women's Studies, no. 16 (Westport, Conn., 1980), xi.

2. See Adrienne Rich's statement to this effect: "But in writing these pages, I am admitting, at least, how important her existence is and has been for me." *Of Woman Born: Motherhood as Experience and Institution* (New York, 1976), 224.

3. Ellen Bayuk Rosenman, *The Invisible Presence: Virginia Woolf and the Mother-Daughter Relationship* (Baton Rouge, 1986), ix.

4. Ruth Bloch, "American Feminine Ideals in Transition: The Rise of the Moral Mother, 1785–1815," *Feminist Studies* 4 (1978): 101–26; Ann Dally, *Inventing Motherhood: The Consequences of an Ideal* (New York, 1982); and Jan Lewis, "Mother's Love: The Construction of an Emotion in Nineteenth-Century America," in Andrew E. Barnes and Peter N. Stearns, eds., *Social History and Issues in Human Consciousness* (New York, 1989), 209–29.

5. See, for example, Lydia Maria Child's advice to mothers regarding the "want of confidence between mothers and daughters on delicate subjects" in *The Mother's Book* (Boston, 1831), 151–52, quoted in Barbara Welter, "The Cult of True Womanhood," in Michael Gordon, ed., *The Family in Historical*

Perspective (New York, 1973), 376; and Lydia Sigourney's suggestions about maternal responsibility for maintaining female health and strength "for the community's welfare," *Letters to Mothers* (Hartford, 1838), 72–73, microfilm, Reel 181, #1182, Schlesinger Library, Radcliffe College. For the turn-of-the-century advice literature, see chapter 2. See also Philip Wylie, *Generation of Vipers* (New York, 1946); David Levy, *Maternal Overprotection* (New York, 1943); and more recently, Selma N. Fraiberg, *Every Child's Birthright: In Defense of Mothering* (New York, 1977).

    6. Nancy Friday, *My Mother, My Self* (New York, 1977).

    7. Judith Arcana, *Our Mothers' Daughters* (Berkeley, 1979), 5. See also Marcia Westkott's observation that "the story of mothers and daughters takes place in the world of the father" in "Mothers and Daughters in the World of the Father," *Frontiers* 3, 2 (Summer 1978): 16–17.

    8. Arcana, *Our Mothers' Daughters*, 18, 9.

    9. Adrienne Rich, *Of Woman Born*, 236–37, 244. See also Dorothy Dinnerstein, *The Mermaid and the Minotaur* (New York, 1976).

    10. Rich, *Of Woman Born*, 248.

    11. Discussions of the problems engendered by maternal caretaking in a male-dominant society have not been limited to a focus on daughters. For more general commentary, see Dorothy Dinnerstein, *The Mermaid and the Minotaur*; Jane Lazarre, *The Mother Knot* (New York, 1976); and Shulamith Firestone, *The Dialectic of Sex* (London, 1972).

    12. Jane Flax, "The Conflict between Nurturance and Autonomy in Mother-Daughter Relationships and within Feminism," *Feminist Studies* 4, 2 (June, 1978): 171–89.

    13. Signe Hammer, *Daughters and Mothers: Mothers and Daughters* (New York, 1975), xv–xvi.

    14. Nancy M. Chodorow, *The Reproduction of Mothering: Psychoanalysis and the Sociology of Gender* (Berkeley, 1978). See also Chodorow's collected essays, *Feminism and Psychoanalytic Theory* (New Haven, 1989), especially "Family Structure and Feminine Personality" and "The Fantasy of the Perfect Mother" (with Susan Contratto); and Elizabeth J. Aries and Rose R. Olver, "Self-Other Differentiation and the Mother-Child Relationship," *Berkshire Review* 21 (1986): 31–52. For relevant examinations of object-relations theory, see Jay R. Greenberg and Stephen A. Mitchell, *Object Relations in Psychoanalytic Theory* (Cambridge, Mass., 1983), and Judith M. Hughes, *Reshaping the Psychoanalytic Domain* (Berkeley, 1989).

    15. Jean Baker Miller, *Toward a New Psychology of Women*, 2d ed. (Boston, 1987); Carol Gilligan, *In a Different Voice: Psychological Theory and Women's Development* (Cambridge, Mass., 1982). See also the essays by Judith V. Jordan, Alexandra G. Kaplan, Jean Baker Miller, Irene P. Stiver, and Janet L. Surrey in *Women's Growth in Connection: Writings from the Stone Center* (New York, 1991).

    16. See, for example, Paula J. Caplan, *Don't Blame Mother: Mending the*

Mother-Daughter Relationship (New York, 1989), and Evelyn Bassoff, *Mothers and Daughters: Loving and Letting Go* (New York, 1988).

17. Karen Payne, ed., *Between Ourselves: Letters between Mothers and Daughters, 1750–1982* (Boston, 1983), 5.

18. Signe Hammer, *Daughters and Mothers: Mothers and Daughters.* Hammer (p. xiii) suggests that the relationship's emotional power and importance may have been increased precisely because it has been ignored: "What is taken for granted, and therefore ignored, may be the most powerful." See also Payne, *Between Ourselves,* xiv–xv.

19. "The Female World of Love and Ritual," "Hearing Women's Words: A Feminist Reconstruction of History," and "The New Woman as Androgyne: Social Disorder and Gender Crisis, 1870–1936," in Carroll Smith-Rosenberg, *Disorderly Conduct: Visions of Gender in Victorian America* (New York, 1985), 53–76, 11–52, 245–96; and Peter G. Filene, *Him/Her/Self,* 2d ed. (Baltimore, 1986), 20–25.

20. For overviews of the changes in women's lives, see Carl Degler, *At Odds: Women and the Family in America from the Revolution to the Present* (New York, 1980); Margaret G. Wilson, *The American Woman in Transition: 1870–1920* (New York, 1979); Mary P. Ryan, *Womenhood in America* (New York, 1975); and Filene, *Him/Her/Self,* chap. 1.

21. Filene, *Him/Her/Self,* 18–19.

22. Carol Z. Stearns and Peter N. Stearns, *Anger: The Struggle for Emotional Control in America's History* (Chicago, 1986), especially chap. 4. For an interesting example of child-rearing advice regarding gender-specific socialization patterns, see George A. Hubbell, *Up through Childhood: A Study of Some Principles of Education in Relation to Faith and Conduct* (New York, 1904), especially chaps. 23 and 24.

23. John Higham, "The Reorientation of American Culture in the 1890s," in John Higham, *Writing American History: Essays in Modern Scholarship* (Bloomington, Ind., 1970); Peter Conn, *The Divided Mind: Ideology and Imagination in America, 1898–1917* (Cambridge, Mass., 1983), especially chap. 1; Filene, *Him/Her/Self,* 18–19. See also Sheila Rothman's characterization of the dichotomy created for women by the contrast between the impact of social and cultural changes and the continued existence of the ideology of virtuous womanhood: "There pervades throughout the period a sense of opportunity limited by obligation, of social reality limited by ideology," in Introduction to Marion Harland, *Eve's Daughters Or Common Sense for Maid, Wife and Mother,* reprint of 1882 ed. (New York, 1978).

24. Carolyn Forrey, "The New Woman Revisited," *Women's Studies* 2, 1 (1974): 38–39; Filene, *Him/Her/Self,* 6–25. See also Lucy Bland, "Marriage Laid Bare: Middle-Class Women and Marital Sex, 1880s–1914," in Jane Lewis, ed., *Labour and Love: Women's Experience of Home and Family, 1850–1940* (Oxford, 1986), 133.

25. Barbara Miller Solomon, *In the Company of Educated Women* (New

Haven, 1985). Joseph Kett has suggested that the growth of female secondary education in the nineteenth century reflected the fact that girls had less obvious economic value than their brothers in middle-class families. In a certain sense, they were superfluous. Hence, they were kept in school longer than boys. For some families, an educated daughter could represent "a sort of prestige symbol, a crude form of conspicuous consumption." Joseph F. Kett, *Rites of Passage: Adolescence in America, 1790 to the Present* (New York, 1977), 138.

26. Filene, *Him/Her/Self*, 26; Roberta Wein, "Women's Colleges and Domesticity," *History of Education Quarterly* 14 (Spring 1974): 31–47. For a contemporary discussion of the growth of women's higher education, see Earl Barnes, "The Feminizing of Culture," *Atlantic Monthly* 109 (June 1912).

27. Filene, *Him/Her/Self*, 26.

28. Ibid., 29. The marriage rates of college women were also affected by demographic factors. For example, in 1900 men outnumbered women in the western part of the country and in many rural areas, while in some areas of the East and in urban areas, women were more numerous. For an interesting analysis of the phenomenon of spinsterhood in the era of the "new woman," see Ruth Freeman and Patricia Klaus, "Blessed or Not? The New Spinster in England and the United States in the Late Nineteenth and Early Twentieth Centuries," *Journal of Family History* 9, 4 (Winter 1984): 394–414. Freeman and Klaus (398, 408) cite contemporary magazine articles that accept and justify spinsterhood, but they also find evidence of cultural ambivalence on this topic in the form of novels that affirm the importance of marriage even for the "new woman."

29. Filene, *Him/Her/Self*, 40.

30. Dorothy Dix, "The Girl of Today," *Good Housekeeping* 62 (March 1916): 288, 290–91. See also Carroll Smith-Rosenberg, "The New Woman as Androgyne: Social Disorder and Gender Crisis, 1870–1936," in *Disorderly Conduct*, 245–96.

31. E. S. Martin, "Mothers and Daughters," *Good Housekeeping* 64 (May 1917): 27. For another positive appraisal of the qualities of the "new woman," see Lillian Bell, *From a Girl's Point of View* (New York, 1897).

32. Mary Kelley, Introduction, and Ann Uhry Abrams, "Frozen Goddess: The Image of Woman in Turn-of-the-Century Art," in Mary Kelley, ed., *Woman's Being, Woman's Place: Female Identity and Vocation in American History* (Boston, 1979), 90, 94, 106. For an interesting, detailed discussion of cultural images of American womanhood in the late nineteenth and early twentieth centuries, see Martha Banta, *Imaging American Women: Idea and Ideals in Cultural History* (New York, 1987).

33. Undoubtedly more than a few young women would still have agreed with the observations of a young wife regarding the death of one of her peers: "It seems to me sad that any person,—especially a young person,— should die before having completely lived, and without marriage the depth & heigth [sic] of life cannot be reached"; Amy Aldis Bradley to her mother,

Mary Aldis, February 18, 1894, Series III, Folder 96, Carton 3, Bradley Family Collection, Schlesinger Library, Radcliffe College.

34. *Daughters and Mothers: Mothers and Daughters*, xiv.

35. James R. McGovern, "The American Woman's Pre-World War I Freedom in Manners and Morals," *Journal of American History* 55, 2 (September 1968): 315–33.

36. Mary Beth Norton, *Liberty's Daughters: The Revolutionary Experience of American Women, 1750–1800* (Boston, 1980), 12–18, 23–26, 102–4. Like Smith-Rosenberg, Norton (105–9) stresses the centrality of female friendship in women's lives.

37. Nancy F. Cott, *The Bonds of Womanhood: "Woman's Sphere" in New England, 1780–1835* (New Haven, 1977).

38. Norton, *Liberty's Daughters*, 276–78.

39. Terri L. Premo, *Winter Friends: Women Growing Old in the New Republic, 1785–1835* (Urbana and Chicago, 1990), 57–82; Marilyn Ferris Motz, *True Sisterhood: Michigan Women and Their Kin* (Albany, 1983).

40. See, for example, Deborah Norris Logan's observations: "I often think of my dear mother. This morning I thought that she would have been made more outwardly comfortable by some of the improvements which we now have; especially the defense from the cold. And as to her mental trials, as I have gone along in life I felt sympathy that she had so many and they were so severe. These great perplexities and difficulties were not monetary ones. She had a good fortune at her own command. And I rejoice that she had it." Diary of Deborah Norris Logan, February 13, 1833, quoted in Penelope Franklin, ed., *Private Pages; Diaries of American Women, 1830s–1970s* (New York, 1986), 459–60.

41. Suzanne Lebsock, *The Free Women of Petersburg: Status and Culture in a Southern Town, 1784–1860* (New York, 1984), 77–79, 136. The quotation is from an unidentified will. I am grateful to Professor Peter Karsten for suggesting this reference on the disposition of women's property.

42. See characterizations of that world in Smith-Rosenberg, "The Female World of Love and Ritual," in *Disorderly Conduct*, and Filene, *Him/Her/Self*.

43. The use of the term "valorization" to describe the nineteenth-century emphasis on the home comes from Glenna Matthews, *"Just a Housewife": The Rise and Fall of Domesticity in America* (New York, 1987), 89. For discussions of the evolution of concepts of women's sphere and motherhood, see Mary Ryan, *The Empire of the Mother: American Writing about Domesticity* (New York, 1982); Jan Lewis, "Mother's Love: The Construction of an Emotion in Nineteenth-Century America," in Barnes and Stearns, eds., *Social History and Issues in Human Consciousness*, 209–29; and Mary Beth Norton, "The Paradox of 'Women's Sphere,' " in Carol Berkin and Mary Beth Norton, eds., *Women of America: A History* (Boston, 1979).

44. Daniel Scott Smith, "Family Limitation, Sexual Control, and Domestic Feminism in Victorian America," in Mary S. Hartman and Lois Banner, eds., *Clio's Consciousness Raised* (New York, 1974), 119–36. On domestic feminism,

see also Degler, *At Odds*, chap. 11, 249–78; Cott, *The Bonds of Womanhood*; Norton, "The Paradox of 'Women's Sphere' "; Kathryn Kish Sklar, *Catharine Beecher: A Study in American Domesticity* (New York, 1973); Matthews, *"Just a Housewife"*; Dolores Hayden, *The Grand Domestic Revolution: A History of Feminist Designs for American Homes, Neighborhoods, and Cities* (Cambridge, Mass., 1981); and Barbara Harris, *Beyond Her Sphere: Women and the Professions in American History* (Westport, Conn., 1978).

45. For evaluative discussions of domestic feminism, see Smith, "Family Limitation, Sexual Control, and Domestic Feminism in Victorian America"; Harris, *Beyond Her Sphere;* Norton, "The Paradox of 'Women's Sphere' "; and Cott, *The Bonds of Womanhood*.

46. Aurelia Smith to her mother, July 1, 1850, and July 21, 1850, Box 1, Folder 48, Hooker Collection, Schlesinger Library, Radcliffe College.

47. Maria Avery to Mrs. Asenath Avery, January 10, 1846, Box 2, Folder 83; Fannie Russell to Mrs. E. Augustine Russell, July 1, 1848, Box 2, Folder 82. Both in Hooker Collection, ibid.

48. Fran Myra (unclear: Egan?) to her mother, July 9, 1852, and August 31, 1852, Box 2, Folder 103, Hooker Collection, ibid.

49. Lemira (no last name) to her mother, May 1, 1853, Box 2, Folder 104, Hooker Collection, ibid.

50. See letters from Aurelia Smith, September 8, 1850, Box 1, Folder 48, Hooker Collection, ibid., and from Augusta Sewall to Abby Morgridge Sewall, February 17, 1862, March 22, 1862, May 8, 1862, September 9, 1865, December 30, 1865, Box 1, Folder 9, Sewall Family Papers, Schlesinger Library, Radcliffe College.

51. See, for example, letters from Sallie Joy White, who became the first woman journalist in Boston when she was appointed a special reporter for the Boston *Post* in 1870, to her mother. Sallie Joy White Papers, Box 1, Folder 5, Schlesinger Library, Radcliffe College.

52. Augusta Sewall to Abby Morgridge Sewall, December 4, 1862, Box 1, Folder 9, Sewall Family Papers.

53. Emily Perkins Hall to Mary Perkins, postscript dated February 22, 1857, and letter dated February (unclear), 1857, both in Box 32b, Folder 807, Hale Family Collection, Sophia Smith Collection, Smith College. See also Emily's letter dated March 23, 1857, which describes a dream that her mother had returned home early "from some mistaken idea that we had insisted upon it," and when she realized that she could have stayed longer, "instead of making the best of it and being glad to see us," had been "downcast and doleful," in Box 32b, Folder 807.

54. Hannah Chandler to her mother, December 16, n.d., Box 2, Folder 135, Hooker Collection. (This entire collection consists of nineteenth-century correspondence.)

55. Sarah Watson Dana to her mother, Sarah Watson Dana, April 9, 1858, Box 16, Folder 37, Dana Family Papers, Schlesinger Library, Radcliffe College.

56. Augusta Sewall to Abby Morgridge Sewall, February 19, 1873, and December 13, 1873, Box 1, Folder 12, Sewall Family Papers.

57. Abby Morgridge Sewall to Augusta Sewall, December 14, 1856, Box 1, Folder 6, Sewall Family Papers. For additional expressions of her affection for her daughter, see also letters from Mrs. Sewall to her sister Serena Brown, July 23, 1854, and July 1, 1855, in Box 1, Folder 4.

58. Abby Morgridge Sewall to her sister Serena Brown, July 17, 1853, Box 1, Folder 3, Sewall Family Papers. For Hammer's concept, see above, p. 9.

59. Letter to Anna M. Weston from her mother, May 20, 1843, Box 2, Folder 71, Hooker Collection.

60. Diary of anonymous farm woman, vol. 1, Ada Carter Hopson Collection, Schlesinger Library, Radcliffe College. See also other diary entries for 1871.

61. See entries for 1871 and 1873, Diary of Melissa Carter, vols. 2 and 3, Ada Carter Hopson Collection, ibid.

62. February 6, 1871, and February 17, 1871, Diary of Melissa Carter, vol. 2, Ada Carter Hopson Collection, ibid.

63. For another example of similar diary evidence regarding close and frequent mother-daughter interaction, see Elizabeth Crowinshield Hammond's diary for 1856–64, Schlesinger Library, Radcliffe College.

64. For additional examples, see Smith-Rosenberg, "The Female World of Love and Ritual"; Marilyn Ferris Motz, *True Sisterhood*; and Nancy M. Theriot, *The Biosocial Construction of Femininity: Mothers and Daughters in Nineteenth-Century America* (Westport, Conn., 1988), 76–77. For a useful, general discussion of the early nineteenth century, see Cott, *The Bonds of Womanhood*, especially chap. 5.

65. Frances Willard, *Glimpses of Fifty Years: The Autobiography of an American Woman* (Chicago, 1889; reprinted 1970).

66. Rebeccah Root to Weltha Brown, August 7, 1815, Hooker Collection, quoted in Cott, *The Bonds of Womanhood*, 178.

67. Theriot, *The Biosocial Construction of Femininity*, 77.

68. Ellen K. Rothman, *Hands and Hearts: A History of Courtship in America* (New York, 1984), 118, 120–22, 214, 217.

69. Mrs. George Hodges to Kate Hodges, April 3, 1861, and October 22, 1861, Folder 2, Hodges Family Papers, Schlesinger Library, Radcliffe College.

70. Mrs. George Hodges to Kate Hodges, n.d. (probably 1860); April 18 and 23, 1860; May 11, 1860; July 9, 1860; Folder 1, Hodges Family Papers, ibid. See especially her comment, July 9, 1860: "There is an old adage which I think you would do well to remember it is 'don't ride a horse to death' Your father has I think been very indulgent indeed & has denied you scarce anything you have asked for. I think you should be a little modest about asking for more favors."

71. Mrs. George Hodges to Kate Hodges, April 23, 1860, Folder 1, Hodges

Family Papers, ibid. See also another exchange on the same subject, May 11, 1860, Folder 1: "The remark you quoted about my showing my affection was not particularly polite in the young lady who said it & still less so in you to repeat it. I write as much and as often as I can & in liew [sic] of writing the news myself got Lizzie Paine to write you."

72. The nineteenth century also witnessed the development of what has been described as the Cult of Single Blessedness, the notion that the single life could represent a socially and personally valuable alternative to marriage, another way to serve God and do God's work. Lee Virginia Chambers-Schiller, *Liberty A Better Husband. Single Women in America: The Generations of 1780–1840* (New Haven, 1984); Freeman and Klaus, "Blessed or Not?"

73. Cornelia Hancock to Rachel Hancock, May 9, 1871, Friends Historical Library, quoted in Chambers-Schiller, *Liberty A Better Husband*, 107.

74. Emily Howland to Hannah Howland, July 29, 1857, Cornell University, quoted in Chambers-Schiller, *Liberty A Better Husband*, 118.

75. Daniel T. Fiske, *The Cross and the Crown; or Faith Working by Love: as Exemplified in the Life of Fidelia Fiske* (Boston, 1868), 54–58, quoted in Chambers-Schiller, *Liberty A Better Husband*, 120–21.

76. Gail Hamilton [pseudonym for Mary A. Dodge], *A New Atmosphere* (Boston, 1865), 41–43, 45, quoted in Chambers-Schiller, *Liberty A Better Husband*, 113.

In the same vein, see a later statement by Charlotte Perkins Gilman: "A duty is a duty, but there is more than one way of doing it! A girl can take care of her mother as an independent householder and wage earner, providing her with the same delicate generosity, let us hope with which the mother once 'supported' her; or she can take care of her as a subordinate, a nurse, a companion, upper servant. Why is not the first better? . . . The object of this is to suggest to the Daughter that she is also an Individual and a Human Being, and has duties as an individual to herself, and as a human being to her race, as well as the duty of a daughter to her mother." See "A Daughter's Duty," written in the early 1890s, quoted in Mary A. Hill, *Charlotte Perkins Gilman: The Making of a Radical Feminist, 1860–1896* (Philadelphia, 1980), 195–96.

77. Harris, *Beyond Her Sphere*, 102–3.

78. Jean Strouse, *Alice James: A Biography* (Boston, 1980), 46, 202–3.

79. Marilla Turrill to Myron Buck, November 1, 1857, Field Family Collection, Michigan Historical Collections, Bentley Historical Library, University of Michigan, quoted in Motz, *True Sisterhood*, 116.

80. Electa Loomis to Ann Gennette Loomis Preston, January 8, 1865, Preston Family Collection, Michigan Historical Collections, ibid., quoted in Motz, *True Sisterhood*, 68.

81. Motz, *True Sisterhood*, 117. Motz found only one example of a mother who complained explicitly about abuse. Martha Cole recorded such complaints in her diary on January 5, 16, and 25; March 31, June 21, and July 5 and 24, 1901; Martha Cole Collection, Michigan Historical Collections, ibid.

82. *The Letters of Emily Dickinson,* ed. Thomas H. Johnson II (Cambridge, Mass., 1958), 475, quoted in Barbara Ann Clarke Mossberg, "Reconstruction in the House of Art: Emily Dickinson's 'I Never Had A Mother,' " in Cathy N. Davidson and E. M. Broner, eds., *The Lost Tradition: Mothers and Daughters in Literature* (New York, 1980), 128. In addition to her letters, which document her relationship with her mother, the voluminous literature on Dickinson includes two studies that focus extensively on Mrs. Dickinson's role in her daughter's life and work: John Cody, *After Great Pain: The Inner Life of Emily Dickinson* (Cambridge, Mass., 1971), and Jean Mudge, *Emily Dickinson and the Image of Home* (Amherst, Mass., 1975).

83. Mossberg, "Reconstruction in the House of Art," and Mabel Collins Donnelly, *The American Victorian Woman: The Myth and the Reality* (Westport, Conn., 1986), 23–26.

84. Mossberg, "Reconstruction in the House of Art."

85. Margo E. Horn, "Family Ties: The Blackwells. A Study in the Dynamics of Family Life in Nineteenth-Century America" (Ph.D. diss., Tufts University, 1980), 106–8, 176–77; Diary of Elizabeth Blackwell, February 23, 1838, and December 4, 1838, quoted in ibid., 106.

86. Ibid., 107–8; Diary of Emily Blackwell, March 25, 1851, quoted on 108. One daughter, Marian, managed to maintain a closer relationship with her mother; ibid., 106.

87. On the issue of financial support, see Marilyn Ferris Motz's discussion of the role played by the female family network, in *True Sisterhood.*

88. Joan Jacobs Brumberg, "Chlorotic Girls, 1870–1920: A Historical Perspective on Female Adolescence," *Child Development* 53, 6 (December 1982): 1468–77.

89. Barbara Welter, "The Cult of True Womanhood." See, for example, Charlotte Perkins Gilman's classic short story, "The Yellow Wallpaper," in *The Yellow Wallpaper and Other Writings by Charlotte Perkins Gilman,* ed. Lynne Sharon Schwartz (New York, 1989). Gilman's own experiences, as well as those of other assertive, ambitious nineteenth-century women, also illustrate this problem. See Hill, *Charlotte Perkins Gilman.*

90. Sharon O'Brien, "Tomboyism and Adolescent Conflict: Three Nineteenth-Century Case Studies," 351–72. A recent study by Frances Cogan challenges the cultural dominance of the passive ideal of "true womanhood" in Victorian America. Cogan maintains instead that a more resourceful, active image, which she terms "real womanhood," distinguished the mid-nineteenth-century popular fiction and advice literature; this argument suggests the possibility that a second and completely different set of expectations could have created additional confusion and stress for middle-class wives and mothers during this period. See *All-American Girl: The Ideal of Real Womanhood in Mid-Nineteenth-Century America* (Athens, Georgia, 1989).

91. Steven Mintz, *A Prison of Expectations: The Family in Victorian Culture* (New York, 1983).

2. *"My Girls' Mothers"*

1. E. S. Martin, "Mothers and Daughters," *Good Housekeeping* 64 (May 1917): 27.

2. Louise Collier Willcox, "Mothers and Daughters," *Harper's Bazar* 44 (July 1910): 452.

3. "Maybell," *Ladies Home Journal* 1 (October 1884).

4. Mrs. Emma C. Hewitt, *Ladies Home Journal* 3 (February 1886); "A Plea for Boarding Schools," *Ladies Home Journal* 6 (September 1889): 10.

5. Ruth Ashmore, "My Girls' Mothers," *Ladies Home Journal* 7 (October 1890): 12; Alan Cameron, "A Woman's Most Grievous Mistake," *Ladies Home Journal* 14 (October 1897): 10.

6. Mrs. Burton Kingsland, "Daughter at Sixteen," *Ladies Home Journal* 11 (March 1894): 4.

7. Madeline Vinton Dahlgren, "Liberties of Our Daughters," *Ladies Home Journal* 7 (November 1890): 2.

8. Ada E. Hazell, "True Relationship of Mother and Daughter," *Ladies Home Journal* 5 (October 1888): 7.

9. Grace H. Dodge, "Between Mother and Daughter," *Ladies Home Journal* 9 (February 1892).

10. Fanny Fern, "Tell Your Mother," *Ladies Home Journal* 5 (June 1888): 16; Ruth Ashmore, "A Girl's Best Friend," *Ladies Home Journal* 8 (May 1881): 12.

11. Kate Tannatt Woods, "Letters to Beth," no. 11, *Ladies Home Journal* 7 (January 1890): 10.

12. Ruth Ashmore, "Side Talks with Girls," *Ladies Home Journal* 9 (April 1892): 16. See also Ruth Ashmore, "Your Own Familiar Friend," *Ladies Home Journal* 11 (March 1894): 16.

13. Helen Ayre, "Mother's Birthday," *Ladies Home Journal* 1 (January 1884).

14. Helen Ayre, "An Open Letter to the Girls," *Ladies Home Journal* 1 (July 1884).

15. Mrs. Burton Kingsland, "A Daughter at Home: Helping Her Mother Socially," *Ladies Home Journal* 11 (September 1894): 14.

16. Ruth Ashmore, "The Sweetest Word in the Language," *Ladies Home Journal* 2 (May 1890): 10.

17. M.E.W. Sherwood, "How Shall Our Girls Behave?" *Ladies Home Journal* 5 (October 1888): 2.

18. Ella Wheeler Wilcox, "An Evil of American Daughters," *Ladies Home Journal* 7 (April 1890): 3.

19. "How Girls Deceive Their Parents," *Ladies Home Journal* 1 (November 1884).

20. Louise Collier Willcox, "Mothers and Daughters," *Harper's Bazaar* 44 (July 1910): 452.

21. Edward Bok, "The American Skeleton," *Ladies Home Journal* 20 (May

1903): 14; "The American Girl: An Editorial," *Ladies Home Journal* (May 1908): 5; Guest Editorial, "An Open Letter to the American Girl Who Was Born between January 1, 1892, and January 1, 1899," *Ladies Home Journal* (September 1910): 5; "Editorial," *Ladies Home Journal* 33 (November 1916): 42.

22. Elizabeth Robinson Scovil, "Mother and Daughter," *Ladies Home Journal* 8 (August 1891): 16.

23. Alice Preston, "A Girl's Preparation for Marriage," *Ladies Home Journal* 25 (March 1908): 22; William Lee Howard, M.D., "Why Didn't My Parents Tell Me," *Ladies Home Journal* 24 (August 1907): 32. See also Mrs. Woodallen Chapman, "How Shall I Tell My Child: A Little Talk as Mother with Mother," *Ladies Home Journal* 28 (January 1, 1911): 39, and "Personal Experiences of Mothers," *Ladies Home Journal* 29 (May 1912): 28.

24. "My Mother Didn't Tell Me," *Harper's Bazaar* 46 (October 1912): 484, 523.

25. See, for example, Charles Nelson Crittendon, "From Lips Usually Sealed to the World," *Ladies Home Journal* 26 (January 1909): 23; Emily Calvin Blake, "A Girl's Letter to Her Mother," *Good Housekeeping* 58 (January 1914): 57–62; Hon. John J. Freschi, "How Strict Are You with Your Daughter," *Good Housekeeping* 57 (July 1913): 70–74; and "Where One Girl Began," *Ladies Home Journal* 34 (January 1917): 7.

26. Marion Harland, "The Passing of the Home Daughter," *The Independent* 71 (July 13, 1911): 88–91.

27. Alice Bartlett Stimson, "When the College Girl Comes Home," *Harper's Bazar* 42 (August 1908): 797–99; Clara E. Laughlin, "The Girl and Her Own Way," *Ladies Home Journal* 26 (February 1909): 34; Margaret E. Sangster, "When the Daughter Comes Home," *Woman's Home Companion* 39 (June 1912): 4; and E. S. Martin, "Mothers and Daughters," *Good Housekeeping* 64 (May 1917): 106.

28. Lillie Hamilton French, "Mothers and Stay-at-Home Daughters," *The Delineator* 63 (June 1904): 1016–18; "The Case of the Elderly Mother," *Ladies Home Journal* 36 (March 1919): 112; Harriet Brunkhurst, "The Girl Whose Mother Is 'Old,' " *Ladies Home Journal* 35 (June 1919): 132; Helen C. Candee, "The Habit of Being a Girl," *Ladies Home Journal* 18 (May 1901): 34; Helen Watterson Moody, "The Trying Time between Mother and Daughter," *Ladies Home Journal* (February 1901): 20; Emily Calvin Blake, "The Girls I Knew," *Ladies Home Journal* 28 (March 1, 1911): 20, 75; Lillie Hamilton French, "The Girl Who is Irritable at Home," *Harper's Bazar* 43 (May 1909): 480–83; Katherine Ferguson, "Ninety-nine Girls Out of a Hundred," *Woman's Home Companion* 43 (August 1916): 8.

29. Charles Edward Jefferson, "A Sermon to Grown-up Daughters," *Woman's Home Companion* 43 (February 1916): 7.

30. Margaret E. Sangster, "Girls' Problems," *Ladies Home Journal* 19 (March 1902): 29; "Mrs. Sangster's Girls' Problems," *Ladies Home Journal* 20 (April 1903): 34; "Mrs. Sangster's Heart to Heart Talks with Girls," *Ladies Home*

Journal 20 (November 1903): 42; (January 1904): 30; (April 1904): 32; and (May 1904): 26.

31. Ruth Ashmore, "Side Talks with Girls," *Ladies Home Journal* 10 (July 1893): 3. See also Amelia E. Barr, "Mothers as Match-Makers," *Ladies Home Journal* 8 (April 1891): 8.

32. Editorial, *Ladies Home Journal* 28 (March 15, 1911): 5.

33. Ruth Ashmore, "The Mother of My Girl," *Ladies Home Journal* 11 (September 1894): 16; "Antagonism between Mothers and Daughters," *The Independent* 53 (September 26, 1901): 2310–11.

34. Mrs. Pelham, "A Daughter of Today," *Ladies Home Journal* 32 (January 1915): 26; Margaret E. Sangster, "Mrs. Sangster's Home Page: Mother and Daughter," *Woman's Home Companion* 36 (March 1909): 44.

35. Edward Bok, "Dedicated to the American Parent," *Ladies Home Journal* 19 (January 1902): 18; "Mothers' Meetings," *Ladies Home Journal* 19 (April 1902): 22; Edward Bok, "The Social Life of a Young Girl," *Ladies Home Journal* 19 (September 1902): 16; Nellie Comins Whitaker, "The Mother's Part," *Woman's Home Companion* 40 (June 1913): 32; Sarah Comstock, "Today's Schoolgirl, Tomorrow's Mother," *Good Housekeeping* 63 (September 1916): 44–45, 148–50.

36. See, for example, the series of editorial articles published in *Woman's Home Companion* 36 (1909), which argued that American girls would eventually lead primarily domestic lives even if they worked for several years before marriage, and the editorial in *Ladies Home Journal* 29 (October 1912): 5–6, which criticized mothers who were opposed to "newfangled notions" and thus would not allow their daughters to practice new domestic approaches at home.

37. Editorial, *Ladies Home Journal* 30 (November 1913): 5–6; Edward Bok, "The Social Life of a Young Girl," *Ladies Home Journal* 19 (September 1902): 16.

38. Ruth Harding, "How I Blundered as a Mother," *Woman's Home Companion* 37 (May 1910): 16; "How I Nearly Ruined My Two Daughters as Told by One Mother for the Benefit of Other Mothers," in "Life Stories from the Experiences of Real Women," *Ladies Home Journal* 27 (January 1910): 11, 48; "The Mistake I Made With 'My Little Daughter,' " in "Personal Experiences of Mothers," *Ladies Home Journal* 31 (February 1914): 28; Ruth Harding, "How I Blundered as a Daughter," *Woman's Home Companion* 36 (July 1909): 9; "The Lesson My Children Have Taught Me. By a Mother," *Ladies Home Journal* 36 (May 1919): 108.

39. See above, p. 28.

40. Theodore Peterson, *Magazines in the Twentieth Century* (Urbana, Ill., 1964), 11–12.

41. Jay Mechling, "Advice to Historians on Advice to Mothers," *Journal of Social History* 9 (1975): 45–63.

42. Peterson, *Magazines in the Twentieth Century*, 6, 11–12, 14, 85.

43. Ibid., 14.

44. Ibid., 140–41, 165, 219–20; Frank Luther Mott, *A History of American Magazines,* vol. 3, 1865–1885 (Cambridge, Mass.), 388–90.

45. For example, Gertrude Battles Lane, who joined the staff of *Woman's Home Companion* in 1903, assumed the editorship in 1912. Under her leadership, the magazine was competing with the *Ladies Home Journal* for first place in the field of women's magazines by the 1930s. Other prominent editors included Theodore Dreiser and Honore Willsie Morrow, both of whom edited the *Delineator* between 1907 and 1921; Peterson, *Magazines in the Twentieth Century,* 118–19, 140–41, 166.

46. Christopher Lasch, *The New Radicalism in America, 1889–1963* (New York, 1965), 47–50.

47. Marion Harland, *Eve's Daughters, or Common Sense for Maid, Wife and Mother,* reprint of 1882 ed. (New York, 1978), 311–12.

48. Gabrielle E. Jackson, *Mother and Daughter* (New York and London, 1905), 3, 63, 81–82, 104, 114, 129.

49. Ibid., 85–86.

50. Gabrielle E. Jackson, *A series of don'ts for mothers, who may, or may not, stand in need of them* (Boston, 1903), 65, 80–81, 89, 76–77.

51. Caroline W. Latimer, *Girl and Woman, a Book for Mothers and Daughters* (New York and London, 1910), 32–33.

52. Ibid., 76.

53. Dorothy Canfield Fisher, *Mothers and Children* (New York, 1914), 161–62.

54. Ibid., 205–6.

55. Ibid., 247–49, 262.

56. Ibid., 266.

57. Jackson, *Mother and Daughter,* 137–38, 135–36.

58. Helen Ekin Starrett, *After College, What? For Girls* (New York, 1896), 13, 15–17, 24.

59. Ibid., 16–17, 9, 19.

60. Margaret Sangster, *Radiant Motherhood: A Book for the Twentieth-Century Mother* (Indianapolis, 1905), 189–90.

61. Margaret Sangster, *The Little Kingdom of Home* (New York, 1905), 415.

62. *The Little Kingdom of Home,* 430–31; *Radiant Motherhood,* 194–95.

63. Latimer, *Girl and Woman,* 138–44; Harland, *Eve's Daughters,* 79, 83.

64. *Eve's Daughters,* 83.

65. *A series of don'ts for mothers,* 85.

66. Latimer, *Girl and Woman,* 261–62.

67. Aline Lydia Hoffman, *The Social Duty of Our Daughters: A Mother's Talke with Mothers and Their Grown Daughters* (Philadelphia, 1908), 7, 9, 64–65, 34, 38.

68. Ibid., 59–60.

69. James C. Fernald, *The New Womanhood* (Boston, 1891), 127–28.

70. Ibid., 197, 235–36.

71. Frederic William Farrar, *Woman's Work in the Home as Daughter, as Wife, and as Mother* (Philadelphia, 1895), 16, 23–24, 31.

72. Ellen Key, *The Renaissance of Motherhood*, trans. Anna E. B. Fries (New York and London, 1914), v–vi, 115.

73. Elizabeth Macfarlane Chesser, *Women, Marriage and Motherhood* (New York and London, 1913), 226–43.

74. *After College, What? For Girls*; also Helen Ekin Starrett, *The Charm of Fine Manners. Being a Series of Letters to a Daughter* (Philadelphia and London, 1920).

75. Helen Ekin Starrett, *Letters to Elder Daughters, Married and Unmarried* (Chicago, 1892), 127–29.

76. Jessica G. Cosgrave, *Mothers and Daughters* (New York, 1925), 22.

77. Ibid., 80–81, 42.

78. Bernard Wishy, *The Child and the Republic: The Dawn of Modern American Child Nurture* (Philadelphia, 1968), 105–7, 115–20. Other such groups included the Mothers' Club of Cambridge and the Mothers' Discussion Club of Cambridge, established respectively in 1878 and 1899. The records of both of these organizations are in the Schlesinger Library, Radcliffe College.

79. Peter Conn, *The Divided Mind: Ideology and Imagination in America, 1898–1917* (Cambridge, Mass., 1983), especially chap. 1.

80. Mary P. Ryan, *Womanhood in America* (New York, 1975), 12.

81. Carroll Smith-Rosenberg has noted the importance of examining the relationship between prescriptive literature and unpublished personal documents specifically for the development of knowledge about women's experiences in the past; "The New Woman and the New History," *Feminist Studies* 3, 1/2 (Fall 1975): 185–98. For a more general example, see the discussion of the relationship between the rise of sibling jealousy in the early twentieth century and the treatment of the topic in the prescriptive literature in Peter N. Stearns, "The Rise of Sibling Jealousy in the Twentieth Century," in Carol Z. and Peter N. Stearns, eds., *Emotion and Social Change: Toward a New Psychohistory* (New York, 1987), 193–222. On the pitfalls of assuming correspondence between prescriptive literature and family behavior, see Jay Mechling, "Advice to Historians on Advice to Mothers," *Journal of Social History* 9 (Fall 1975): 45–63. Mary Beth Norton has commented on this topic, specifically with regard to the probable discrepancy between the diverse experiences of nineteenth-century women and the social norms formulated mainly by men and articulated in advice manuals; see "The Paradox of 'Women's Sphere,'" in Carol Ruth Berkin and Mary Beth Norton, eds., *Women of America: A History* (Boston, 1979), 140–46. See also Ernest Earnest, *The American Eve in Fact and Fiction* (Urbana, Ill., 1974).

3. "Cultural Work"

1. Dorothy Canfield Fisher, *The Bent Twig* (New York, 1915), 442–43.
2. Ibid., 475.
3. *Mary Olivier: A Life* (New York, 1919), 249–50.
4. Jane Tompkins, *Sensational Designs: The Cultural Work of American Fiction, 1790–1860* (New York, 1985), xi, 200, xvi. See also the parallel interpretation of the nature and function of the novel suggested by Alfred Habegger in the preface to his book, *Gender, Fantasy, and Realism in American Literature* (New York, 1982). I am grateful to Professor William Lenz for calling these sources to my attention.
5. Tompkins, *Sensational Designs*, xvi–xix, 3–39. Traditionally, popular novels have been effectively disregarded as objects of literary study on the grounds that their content and conventions render them suspect as works of art. Hence literary critics have ignored most of the nineteenth-century bestsellers that were bought and read by a wide audience of middle-class Americans.
6. With regard to the history of women's lives, Patricia Branca has pointed to the misconceptions fostered by historians' reliance on the images of helpless, dependent females conveyed in the fiction of Jane Austen; see *Silent Sisterhood: Middle-Class Women in the Victorian Home* (London, 1975), 11. See also Ernest Earnest's observations regarding the discrepancy between the portrayal of women in the fiction of the late eighteenth and nineteenth centuries and the characteristics of real women in *The American Eve in Fact and Fiction, 1775–1914* (Urbana, Ill., 1974), 62, 81, 140; and Peter Laslett's concern about the tendency to infer generalizations about a society from the presentation of a novel's central character and its story in *The World We Have Lost* (London, 1965), 87.
7. Cathy N. Davidson, *Revolution and the Word: The Rise of the Novel in America* (New York, 1986), 260. I am grateful to Professor William Lenz for suggesting the relevance of Davidson's work for my study.
8. Ibid., 260. For a discussion of the similarities between fiction and history, see Hayden White, "The Fictions of Factual Representation," in Angus Fletcher, ed., *The Literature of Fact* (New York, 1976), 21–44. For a discussion of the use of literature specifically for the writing of social history, see Harry Payne, "The Novel as Social History: A Reflection on Methodology," *The History Teacher* 11, 3 (May 1978): 341–51. A particularly interesting discussion of the relationship between books and their readers is Barbara Sicherman, "Sense and Sensibility: A Case Study of Women's Reading in Late-Victorian America," in Cathy N. Davidson, ed., *Reading in America: Literature & Social History* (Baltimore, 1989), 201–25.
9. The work of Tompkins and Cathy Davidson represents a current trend in literary studies toward placing more emphasis on the interaction of the novel and its social and cultural context as opposed to stressing primarily the formal principles of literary discourse. For an examination of the rela-

tionship between the development of Victorian family patterns and imaginative literature, see Stephen Mintz, *A Prison of Expectations: The Family in Victorian Culture* (New York, 1983). Other relevant studies include Mary Kelley, *Private Woman, Public Stage: Literary Domesticity in Nineteenth-Century America* (New York, 1984), and Nina Baym, *Woman's Fiction: A Guide to Novels by and about Women in America, 1820–1870* (Ithaca, N.Y., 1978), and *Novels, Readers, and Reviewers; Responses to Fiction in Antebellum America* (Ithaca, N.Y., 1984). Focusing specifically on the work of the authors she terms the "literary domestics," Kelley suggests that their novels integrated the private, domestic side of their own lives into their published prose, thus providing valuable insights into the lives of nineteenth-century women. Baym maintains that nineteenth-century domestic fiction was designed both to instruct and to entertain. She argues that these novels reflected and contributed to the changes occurring in women's lives, and finds in their tremendous popularity a significant indication that they spoke directly to the concerns of their readers. Judith Rowbotham also discusses the didactic nature of nineteenth-century women's fiction in *Good Girls Make Good Wives* (Oxford, 1989).

10. Mary P. Ryan, *The Empire of the Mother: American Writing about Domesticity, 1830–1860* (New York, 1982), 10–12. See also Carol Dyhouse's observation that novels by feminist authors are useful sources for understanding the nuances and the complexity of family relationships, particularly mother-daughter interactions, in *Feminism and the Family in England, 1880–1939* (Oxford, 1989), 185–86.

11. Baym, *Woman's Fiction*, 11–12, 28, 35; Marianne Hirsch, *The Mother/ Daughter Plot* (Bloomington, Ind., 1989), 10–11. Absent, silent, and flawed mothers are characteristic of nineteenth-century English novels as well. See Susan Peck Macdonald, "Jane Austen and the Tradition of the Absent Mother," in Cathy N. Davison and E. M. Broner, eds., *The Lost Tradition: Mothers and Daughters in Literature* (New York, 1980), 58–69.

12. Baym, *Woman's Fiction*, 37. See, for example, Susan Warner's *The Wide, Wide World*, first published in 1850. One interesting exception to these generalizations appears in Louisa May Alcott's *Little Women*, first published in 1868, where the mother serves as a major source of guidance and moral support for all four of her daughters. See Nina Auerbach's comments on her character in *Communities of Women: An Idea in Fiction* (Cambridge, Mass., 1978), 62–63.

13. Jan Lewis, "Mother's Love: The Construction of an Emotion in Nineteenth-Century America," in Andrew E. Barnes and Peter N. Stearns, eds., *Social History and Issues in Human Consciousness: Some Interdisciplinary Connections* (New York, 1989), 209–29.

14. Joan Manheimer, "Murderous Mothers: The Problem of Parenting in the Victorian Novel," *Feminist Studies* 5, 3 (Fall 1979): 530–46; Sandra M. Gilbert and Susan Gubar, *The Mad Woman in the Attic* (New Haven, 1979), 59. This is a complicated issue that has been discussed at length in the critical literature. See, for example, Marianne Hirsch's contention that maternal

absence and silence create the necessary conditions for the heroine's development in *The Mother/Daughter Plot: Narrative, Psychoanalysis, Feminism* (Bloomington, Ind., 1989), 47. See also Carol Martin, "No Angel in the House: Victorian Mothers and Daughters in George Eliot and Elizabeth Gaskell," *Midwest Quarterly* 24, 3 (Spring 1983): 297–314.

15. Carroll Smith-Rosenberg, "The Female World of Love and Ritual," in *Disorderly Conduct: Visions of Gender in Victorian America* (New York, 1985), 53–76. For examples of actual women's experiences which also contradict Smith-Rosenberg's interpretation, see chapter 1, pp. 16–19.

16. Sally Allen McNall, *Who Is in the House?* (New York, 1981).

17. Lee R. Edwards, "Flights of Angels: Varieties of a Fictional Paradigm," *Feminist Studies* 5, 3 (Fall 1979): 547–70; Mary Suzanne Schriber, *Gender and the Writer's Imagination: From Cooper to Wharton* (Lexington, Ky., 1987), 9.

18. Carolyn Forrey, "The New Woman Revisited," *Women's Studies* 2, 1 (1974), and Cathy N. Davidson, "Mothers and Daughters in the Fiction of the New Republic," in Davidson and Broner, eds., *The Lost Tradition*, 126.

19. For a list of relevant novels, see Gail M. Rudenstein, Carol Farley Kessler, and Ann M. Moore, "Mothers and Daughters in Literature: A Preliminary Bibliography," in Davidson and Broner, eds., *The Lost Tradition*, 309–22. In general, women's fiction in the era of the "new woman" placed more emphasis on the intricacies of heterosexual relationships than on mother-daughter interactions. Until later in the twentieth century, most narratives stressed courtship and romance rather than the mother-daughter relationship, although recent scholarship has highlighted a continuing but recessive concern with mothers and daughters in women's texts. Elizabeth Abel, "Narrative Structure(s) and Female Development: The Case of *Mrs. Dalloway*," in Elizabeth Abel et al., *The Voyage In: Fictions of Female Development* (Hanover, N.H., 1983).

20. The novels were selected from a bibliography of works that either treat the mother-daughter relationship centrally or portray it to some degree. Twenty-seven American titles are listed for the period between 1880 and 1920. The slight variation in the time frame for the novels chosen permits the discussion of several works that contain particularly interesting treatments of the mother-daughter relationship and effectively represent the cultural transitions at the beginning and end of the period under study. One English novel was also chosen. See Rudenstein, Kessler, and Moore, "Mothers and Daughters in Literature: A Preliminary Bibliography," in Davidson and Broner, eds., *The Lost Tradition*, 309–22. For a discussion of transatlantic literary connections, see chapter 8.

21. Abel, "Narrative Structure and Female Development," in Abel et al., *The Voyage In.*

22. Elizabeth Stuart Phelps [Ward], *The Story of Avis* (New York, 1977; reprint of 1879 ed.), 61–63.

23. Ibid., 318.

24. Ibid., 264, 268.

25. Ibid., 273.

26. See, for example, Harriet Burton's comments on her mother's death, chapter 4, p. 74, and Ethel Spencer's recollections of her feelings when she lost her mother: "When she died, one of the things that must have saddened all of us was that there never again would be anyone who so wholeheartedly thought we were wonderful"; see *The Spencers of Amberson Avenue: A Turn-of-the-Century Memoir,* ed. Michael P. Weber and Peter N. Stearns (Pittsburgh, 1983), 131.

27. *The Story of Avis,* 63.

28. Ibid., 456–57.

29. Mary E. Wilkins Freeman, *Pembroke* (New York, 1899; first published in 1894), 16, 41, 44, 78.

30. Ibid., 125.

31. Ibid., 188, 145.

32. Sarah Orne Jewett, *The Country of the Pointed Firs* (London, 1927; first published in 1896), 58–60.

33. Ibid., 62–63.

34. Ibid., 78.

35. Josephine Donovan, *New England Local Color Literature: A Woman's Tradition* (New York, 1983), 116, 113, 118, 107. See also an intriguing examination of the use of symbolic and presymbolic language in the novel in Jean Rohloff, " 'A Quicker Signal': Women and Language in Sarah Orne Jewett's *The Country of the Pointed Firs,*" *South Atlantic Review* 55, 2 (May 1990): 33–46; and another interesting analysis of Jewett's work in Elaine Orr, "Reading Negotiation and Negotiated Reading: A Practice with/in 'A White Heron' and 'The Revolt of Mother,' " *The CEA Critic* 53 (Spring/Summer 1991): 49–65. I am grateful to Professors Robert Corber and William Lenz respectively for calling these articles to my attention.

36. Willa Cather, *The Song of the Lark* (Boston, 1963; copyright 1915 and 1943), 82–83.

37. Ibid., 192, 194, 198.

38. Ibid., 281–83.

39. Ibid., 298, 301–2.

40. Ibid., 491–92.

41. Ibid., 559.

42. *The Bent Twig,* 189, 219–20, 267.

43. Ibid., 410, 442–43, 472.

44. Ibid., 472.

45. Ibid., 475.

46. Mary Austin, *A Woman of Genius* (New York, 1912, reprinted 1977), 66–67, 126.

47. Ibid., 202, 206.

48. Ibid., 213.

49. A recent analysis of the novel argues that Mrs. Bart views herself as a

commodity also and regards her daughter's beauty as an extension of her own. Thus Lily has not learned to separate her identity from her mother's, although she has destructive impulses that represent rebellions against her mother's fantasies; see Dale M. Bauer, *Feminist Dialogics: A Theory of Failed Community* (Albany, 1988), 101–4.

50. Edith Wharton, *The House of Mirth* (New York, 1905), 46–47, 53, 55–56.

51. Linda W. Wagner, "Ellen Glasgow: Daughter as Justified," in Davidson and Broner, eds., *The Lost Tradition*, 140.

52. Ellen Glasgow, *Virginia* (Garden City, N.Y., 1913), 54.

53. Ibid., 310.

54. Ellen Glasgow, *Life and Gabriella: The Story of a Woman's Courage* (London, 1916), 7.

55. *Virginia*, 397–98; *Life and Gabriella*, 85–86, 348.

56. *Virginia*, 415, 438, 424–25.

57. Ibid., 429–31, 453.

58. *Life and Gabriella*, 372–73, 336–37, 375.

59. Edith Wharton, *The Old Maid* (New York, 1924).

60. Ibid., 175–76, 177–79, 182–83, 189.

61. Edith Wharton, *The Mother's Recompense* (New York, 1925), 75–76, 82–83, 87, 96–97, 156–57.

62. Ibid., 202.

63. Adeline R. Tintner has suggested that Kate is unable to tolerate her daughter's marriage to her former lover because she views Chris as a husband-figure. Hence, even as sophisticated and unconventional as she is, she sees the marriage as incestuous; see "Mothers, Daughters, and Incest in the Late Novels of Edith Wharton," in Davidson and Broner, eds., *The Lost Tradition*, 147–56. See also Marianne Hirsch's analysis of the conflict between Kate's sexuality and her daughter's sexuality in *The Mother/Daughter Plot*, 118–21.

64. Mary Wilkins Freeman, *The Portion of Labor* (New York, 1901), 257–58.

65. Ibid., 15, 255.

66. Ibid., 255.

67. Ibid., 363.

68. Ibid., 219–20, 488, 439, 562.

69. Anzia Yezierska, *Bread-Givers* (New York, 1925).

70. Ibid., 257.

71. See chapter 8 for a discussion of the connections between American and English culture during the late Victorian era and the early twentieth century. While it is obviously impossible to generalize from one example, it is interesting to consider whether the depth and intensity of the mother-daughter portrait in this work as compared to the portrayals in the American novels might reflect any differences between American and English experiences.

72. Ibid., 124, 229.

73. See, for example, Nancy Friday, *My Mother, My Self* (New York, 1977).

74. *Mary Olivier*, 324–25.

75. *The House of Mirth*, 45.

76. *A Woman of Genius*, 18–19, 21.

77. *The Bent Twig*, 6.

78. *The Portion of Labor*, 337, 488.

79. See chapter 1, pp. 6–7.

80. In this regard, see Marianne Hirsch's observation that "the silence of mothers about their own fate and the details of their lives, insures that those lives, those stories will be repeated by daughters. . . . Ironically, if daughters knew the mothers' stories, they might *not* repeat them"; see *The Mother/Daughter Plot*, 67.

81. For an interesting essay on the value of biographical context in studying the work of women writers, see Barbara Clarke Mossberg, "A Rose in Context: The Daughter Construct," in Jerome J. McGann, ed., *Historical Studies and Literary Criticism* (Madison, Wisc., 1985), 199–225.

82. Kelley, *Literary Domestics*; Auerbach, *Communities of Women*; Elaine Showalter, *Sexual Anarchy: Gender and Culture and the Fin de Siècle* (New York, 1990).

83. The precise circumstances surrounding this event are unclear, but its occurrence is certainly significant. The introduction to *The Story of Avis* (1977 reprint ed.) notes that when Ward became a writer, she took her mother's name in response to her obsessive resentment and grief over the loss. However, other evidence suggests that she was given the name immediately after her mother died, and thus summarily lost her own identity and her mother at a young and vulnerable age. See Elizabeth T. Spring, "Elizabeth Stuart Phelps," *Our Famous Women, An Authorized Record of the Lives and Deeds of Distinguished American Women of Our Times* (Hartford, 1884), 561–62, quoted in Habegger, *Gender, Fantasy and Realism in American Literature*, 53.

84. Elizabeth Hardwick, "Introduction," in *The Story of Avis*. Alfred Habegger suggests that the portrayal of Avis reflects Ward's perception of her mother as much less successful and much more of a victim than she actually was; *Gender, Fantasy and Realism in American Literature*, 53.

85. Mary Austin, "Woman Alone," in Elaine Showalter ed., *These Modern Women: Autobiographical Essays from the Twenties* (New York, 1989), 78–86; Sharon O'Brien, *Willa Cather: The Emerging Voice* (New York, 1987), 104.

86. Wagner, "Ellen Glasgow: Daughter as Justified," in Davidson and Broner, eds., *The Lost Tradition*, 139. See, for example, Fisher's *Mothers and Children* (New York, 1914).

87. R.W.B. Lewis, *Edith Wharton: A Biography* (New York, 1975).

88. Ibid., 152. I am grateful to Professor William Lenz for calling my attention to this occurrence, which supports the suggestion that contemporary readers identified with the women portrayed in these novels.

89. The essays in Broner and Davidson, eds., *The Lost Tradition*, address this issue.

90. See note 63.

91. Judith Gardiner, "A Wake for Mother: The Maternal Deathbed in Women's Fiction," *Feminist Studies* 4, 2 (June 1978): 146–65; and Elinor Lenz, "The Generation Gap: From Persephone to Portnoy," *New York Times Book Review*, August 30, 1987. For an interesting overview of the treatment of the mother-daughter relationship in contemporary American literature, see the essays in Mickey Pearlman, ed., *Mother Puzzles: Daughters and Mothers in Contemporary American Literature* (Westport, Conn., 1989).

92. Laslett, *The World We Have Lost*, 87.

4. *"A Girl's Best Friend"*

1. February 7, 1892, Diary of Edna Ormsby, Folder 1, Edna Ormsby Papers, Schlesinger Library, Radcliffe College. Mrs. Ormsby's emphasis on the fact that her own mother liked the name she and her husband chose for their daughter suggests that as a daughter herself, she attributed great importance to the mother-daughter relationship.

2. September 22, 1895, Diary of Edna Ormsby, ibid.

3. September 22, 1895; June 16, 1896; November 4, 1896; October 7, 1898; December 22, 1898; November 9, 1899; February 12, 1900; September 24, 1902; August 25, 1905; September 18, 1905; and October 1, 1910; Diary of Edna Ormsby, ibid. The diary does not describe the precise nature of Esther's difficulties.

4. September 24, 1902, Diary of Edna Ormsby, Folder 2, ibid.

5. October 1, 1910, ibid.

6. June 14, 1903, ibid.

7. Entry dated only 1904–5; August 25, 1905; September 18, 1905; October 31, 1905; and October 1, 1910; ibid.

8. Like Edna Ormsby's diary, other sources do offer some evidence about the relationship between women and younger daughters, primarily from the maternal point of view. For example, letters from mothers who traveled illustrate their efforts to monitor their daughters' activities from a distance and to reassure them of their love and affection. Such correspondence recalls Mrs. Ormsby's careful attention to Esther's upbringing and her devotion to her child. See Sallie Joy White's letters to her daughter Grace, January 22, 1889, and July 27, 1891, Box 1, Folder 9, Sallie Joy White Papers; and Eliza Coe Brown Moore's letters to Dorothea May Moore, October 20, 1902, Carton 3, Folder 62; and July 12, 1903, and September 15, 1904, Carton 3, Folder 63, Dorothea May Moore Collection. Both in Schlesinger Library, Radcliffe College.

9. December 3, 1890; December 4, 1890; and June 19, 1891; Diary of

Mary Anderson Boit, Box 10, vol. 17, Hugh Cabot Family Papers, Schlesinger Library, Radcliffe College.

10. June 22, 1891, ibid.

11. August 27, 1891, ibid.

12. September 1, 1891, and November 7, 1891, ibid.

13. May 16, 1892, ibid.

14. November 7, 1891, ibid.

15. February 29, 1890, Harriet Burton Diary, Box 1, Folder 4, Harriet Wright Burton Laidlaw Papers, Schlesinger Library, Radcliffe College.

16. Maud Nathan, *Once Upon a Time and Today* (New York, 1974; reprint of 1933 ed.), 304–5.

17. Mary Hills to her mother, September 17, 1886, Series I, Box 9, Folder 1, Hills Family Papers, Amherst College Archives.

18. Mary Hills to her mother, October 31, 1886, ibid.

19. Mary Hills to her mother, November 4, 1886, and December 1, 1886, ibid.

20. Emily Hills to her mother, January 11, 1887, and January 15, 1888, Series I, Box 10, Folder 1, ibid.

21. Emily Hills to both parents, November 3, 1887, ibid.

22. January 20, 1888, Series I, Box 10, Folder 2, ibid.

23. See, for example, Emily's letters of April 23, 1889, and May 7, 1889, ibid.; and Mary's letters of November, n.d., 1886, and April 15, 1887, Series I, Box 9, Folders 1 and 3.

24. See, for example, Mary's letters of October 23, 1886; October 30, 1886; December 8, 1886; May 8, 1887; May 29, 1887; and February 9, 1888; and Emily's letters of November 13, 1887, and November 15, 1887, in Series I, Box 9, Folders 1, 3, and 5, and Box 10, Folder 1, ibid.

25. Mary Hills to her mother, March 6, 1887. See also her letter of March 23, 1887: "I am very jealous of Emily for I think she has more than her share of gaiety when I am away," in Series I, Box 9, Folder 2, ibid. For an interesting and pertinent analysis of sibling jealousy in the nineteenth century, see Peter N. Stearns, *Jealousy: The Evolution of an Emotion in American History* (New York, 1989), 49–65.

26. Mary Hills to her mother, February 9, 1888, Series I, Box 9, Folder 5, Hills Family Papers. See also her letter of February 26, 1888: "I thought it very strange you should have written Emily first but you probably had some good reason as you would not allow her to show me the letter," in ibid.

27. Emily Hills to her mother, February 15, 1888, and January 20, 1888, Series I, Box 10, Folder 2, ibid.

28. *Growing Up in Boston's Gilded Age: The Journal of Alice Stone Blackwell, 1872–1874*, ed. Marlene Deahl Merrill (New Haven, 1990), April 5, 1872, 57; Alice Stone Blackwell to Kitty Barry Blackwell, October 29, 1872, quoted in *Growing Up in Boston's Gilded Age*, 244. Alice's biography of her mother was published in 1930.

29. February 11, 1872, 31; May 13, 1872, 73; September 21, 1872, 109; *Growing Up in Boston's Gilded Age.*

30. February 10, 1873, *Growing Up in Boston's Gilded Age,* 150. See also Alice's resentment when she was asked to "empty the slops" while she was reading and her description of a dispute with her mother about going to school in bad weather; June 8, 1872, 81–82, and November 19, 1873, 206, ibid.

31. July 28, 1873, *Growing Up in Boston's Gilded Age,* 188.

32. March 8, 1872, 42; April 18, 1872, 64; Introduction, 6–7; and December 16, 1873, 212; in ibid.

33. Marion Taylor [pseudonym] recorded her adolescent experiences in detailed, introspective diaries that eventually came into the possession of the psychologist Gordon Allport and were donated to the Schlesinger Library, Radcliffe College, after his death. See July 16, 1916, Marion Taylor Diary excerpts, Box 1, Folder 7. See also her comments about a favorite teacher: "Altogether she is the most adorable, lovable, nicest person, *next to my mother,* in the world" [emphasis added], April 6, 1915, Box 1, Folder 4.

34. July 13, 1916, Box 1, Folder 7, ibid.

35. October 16, 1915, Box 1, Folder 4, ibid.

36. August 7, 1915; December 18, 1915; August 25, 1915; Box 1, Folder 4, ibid.

37. January 21, 1916, Box 1, Folder 7, ibid. See also the entry for January 24, 1916: "The other girls are all going and they laughed at me when I told them what mother said"; Box 1, Folder 7. This complaint foreshadows the emphasis on the peer group that would characterize the orientation of young people in the decade of the 1920s. See Paula Fass, *The Damned and the Beautiful* (New York, 1977).

38. Marion Taylor Diary excerpts, August 19, 1916, Box 1, Folder 7.

39. Helen Jackson Cabot Almy to Mary Almy, June 20, 1909; July 6, 1909; and August 3, 1909; Box 2, Folder 25, Almy Family Papers, Schlesinger Library, Radcliffe College.

40. Josephine Herbst, notebook dated 1906–7, quoted in Elinor Langer, *Josephine Herbst* (Boston, 1983, 1984), 31.

41. Anne Bent Ware Winsor to Annie Winsor Allen, February 10, 1885, Series III, Box 23, Folder 380, Annie Winsor Allen Papers, Schlesinger Library, Radcliffe College.

42. Eugenie Andruss Leonard, *Concerning Our Girls and What They Tell Us: A Study of Some Phases of the Confidential Relationship of Mothers and Adolescent Daughters* (New York, 1930).

43. Diary of Maud Rittenhouse, April 12, 1882; May 17, 1881; July 27, 1884; in Isabelle Rittenhouse Mayne, *Maud,* ed. Richard Lee Strout (New York, 1939), 78, 9, 322.

44. See, for example, Mary Hills to her mother, April 15, 1887: "Had I better get my French kid shoes in Rochester, or wait and get them in Northampton?" Series I, Box 9, Folder 3, Hills Family Papers.

45. Autobiographical fragment, *The Making of a Feminist: Early Journals and Letters of M. Carey Thomas*, ed. Marjorie Dobkin (Kent, Ohio, 1979), 312.

46. Anne Bent Ware Winsor to Annie Winsor Allen, October 18, 1885, Series III, Box 23, Folder 380, Allen Papers.

47. Carl Degler, *At Odds: Women and the Family in America from the Revolution to the Present* (New York, 1980), 102.

48. Carroll Smith-Rosenberg, "Puberty to Menopause: The Cycle of Femininity in Nineteenth-Century America," in *Disorderly Conduct: Visions of Gender in Victorian America* (New York, 1985), 188–89. Smith-Rosenberg offers the example of a woman who reported that it had taken her an entire lifetime to forgive her mother for the fear and loneliness she had experienced as a result of her reticence on this matter.

49. See chapter 2.

50. *The Mosher Survey: Sexual Attitudes of 45 Victorian Women*, ed. James Mahood and Kristine Wenburg (New York, 1980), cited in Ellen K. Rothman, *Hands and Hearts: A History of Courtship in America* (New York, 1984), 256–57; Mary Ezit Bulkley, "Mother, Grandmother, and Me," 67, typescript, Schlesinger Library, Radcliffe College.

51. Langer, *Josephine Herbst*, 31.

52. The quotation is an excerpt from a letter to her favorite teacher that was never sent, October 29, 1916, Marion Taylor Diary excerpts, Box 1, Folder 8.

53. July 29, 1882, in *Maud*, 119. Despite their very close relationship, apparently Maud's mother had not broached the subject with her daughter, although she was greatly interested in her daughter's social life. See pp. 82–83.

54. Frances Parkinson Keys, *All Flags Flying: Reminiscences* (New York, 1970), 7, quoted Rothman, *Hands and Hearts*, 256.

55. R.W.B. Lewis, *Edith Wharton: A Biography* (New York, 1975), 53–54. According to Lewis, Wharton claimed that her mother's failure to give her even a rudimentary education about sex " 'did more than anything else to falsify and misdirect my whole life.' "

56. April 7, 1878, *The Making of a Feminist*, 142.

57. *Maud*, 542.

58. Childless Wife [pseud.], "Why I Have No Family," *Independent* 58 (March 23, 1905): 655, quoted in Peter G. Filene, *Him/Her/Self; Sex Roles in Modern America*, 2d ed. (Baltimore, 1986), 86.

59. Letter from Helen Swett to Charles Ernest Schwartz, July 2, 1899, Charles Ernest Schwartz Papers, Bancroft Library, University of California at Berkeley, quoted in Rothman, *Hands and Hearts*, 258.

60. Mary Smith Costelloe to her mother, quoted in Barbara Strachey, *Remarkable Relations: The Story of the Pearsall Smith Women* (New York, 1982), 103.

61. Rothman, *Hands and Hearts*, 218–19.

62. May 17, June 1, June 29, July 1, and August 25, 1881; February 19, May 22, June 3, and June n.d., 1882; September 10 and October 7, 1883; July 4, 1884; and September 25, 1885. All in *Maud*, 8, 14, 20–21, 35, 55, 95, 100, 109, 179, 216, 227, 320, 355.

63. Diary of Maud Rittenhouse, September 25, 1885, and letter to Maud from her mother, in *Maud*, 358, 347.

64. October 30 and November 3, 1889, in *Maud*, 494, 496.

65. Ella Lyman Cabot to her mother, Ella Lowell Lyman, August 18, 1892, and August 23, 1892, Series III, Box 3, Folder 65, Ella Lyman Cabot Papers, Schlesinger Library, Radcliffe College.

66. Ella Lyman to her mother, n.d., and February 28, 1894, ibid.

67. Mrs. D. W. Miner to Elizabeth Miner Garman, April 14, 1884, Box 13, Folder 1, Charles Edward Garman Papers, Amherst College Archives.

68. Ellen D. Hale to her mother Emily Perkins Hale, December 16, 1884, Box 45a, Folder 1064, Hale Family Papers, Sophia Smith Collection, Smith College. In the same letter, she also commented on her discomfort when a female friend expressed her affection: "I must say I don't like to have people say spoony things, and kiss me, even if they are of my own sex! I think more than ever that she is crazy, and I don't like to be alone with her very much. I believe you will think that I am crazy too."

69. Emily Perkins Hale to Ellen D. Hale, May 3, 1895, Box 32a, Folder 798, ibid.

70. Mary Hills to her mother, October 15, 1886; January 16, 1887; February 26, 1888; Box 9, Folders 1, 2, and 5, Hills Family Papers.

71. Emily Hills to her mother, May 8, 1894, and May 14, 1894, Box 10, Folder 4, ibid.

72. Emily Hills to her mother, October 3, 1894, ibid.

73. For a discussion of these expectations, see John S. Haller, Jr., "From Maidenhood to Menopause: Sex Education for Women in Victorian America," *Journal of Popular Culture* 6, 1 (1972): 49–69. Haller suggests the presence of a link between the aspirations of the growing middle class and social attitudes toward sex in the late nineteenth century.

74. Anne Bent Ware Winsor to Annie Winsor Allen, March 3, 1892, Series III, Box 24, Folder 383, Allen Papers.

75. Mary Herbst to Josephine Herbst, quoted in Langer, *Josephine Herbst*, 25.

76. For a fuller discussion of Mrs. Dummer's relationship with her four daughters, see chapter 5.

77. Frances Dummer to Ethel Sturges Dummer, February 16, 1919, Box 12, Folder 185, Ethel Sturges Dummer Papers, Schlesinger Library, Radcliffe College.

78. James R. McGovern, "The American Woman's Pre-World War I Freedom in Manners and Morals," *Journal of American History* 55, 2 (September 1968): 315–33. The quotation appears on p. 326. On the ideal of youth,

see also Elaine Tyler May, *Great Expectations: Marriage & Divorce in Post-Victorian America* (Chicago, 1980), 60–65.

79. June Sochen, *The New Woman: Feminism in Greenwich Village, 1910–1920* (New York, 1972), especially ix–xi and 137–38. For a discussion of new sexual behavior during the late nineteenth and early twentieth centuries, and the distinction between sexual behavior and societal norms, see May, *Great Expectations*, 92–96.

80. A study of "girls, their sweethearts and their families" published in 1926 suggested that the latter was the case. Arguing that "necking" and "petting," variously defined, were the key to popularity for young women, Eleanor R. Wembridge maintained that mothers lived vicariously through their daughters' social lives and did not want them to be wallflowers. "Do not listen to what their mothers *say*, but *watch* them, if you want to know how they feel about their daughters petting! Their protests are about as genuine as the daughter's 'Aren't you terrible?' when a young man starts to pet." See *Other People's Daughters* (Boston and New York, 1926), 195–97.

81. See diary entries of October, n.d., 1918, and November 26, 1919, Marion Taylor Diary excerpts, Box 1, Folders 11 and 14. When she learned that her father planned to remarry, Marion noted that "it is only on the 8th of this month and he gets the final divorce decree and *can* get married! Do you wonder that I am determined to be a Bachelor maid?" June 14, 1915.

82. Diary entry, October 29, 1916, and letter dated July 17, 1916, both in Marion Taylor Diary excerpts, Box 1, Folder 8; diary entry, July n.d., 1919, Box 1, Folder 11; diary entries, May 5, 1920, and January 31, 1921, in Box 1, Folder 14, typescript.

83. Anne Bent Ware Winsor to Joseph Allen, March 6, 1900, Series III, Box 24, Folder 392, Allen Papers.

84. Anne Bent Ware Winsor to Annie Winsor Allen, March 6, 1900, ibid.

85. *Hands and Hearts*, 221–23. For a pertinent discussion of the development of the youth culture of the 1920s, see Paula Fass, *The Damned and the Beautiful: American Youth in the 1920s* (New York, 1977). Chapter 7 offers a fuller consideration of the connection between the influence of peer culture and the nature of the mother-daughter relationship in the decades following 1920.

86. Ruth Ashmore, "A Girl's Best Friend," *Ladies Home Journal* 8 (May 1881): 12.

87. Paula Caplan, *Don't Blame Mother; Mending the Mother-Daughter Relationship* (New York, 1989).

88. Degler, *At Odds*, chap. 5, 86–110.

89. Sharon O'Brien, "Tomboyism and Adolescent Conflict: Three Nineteenth-Century Case Studies," in Mary Kelley, ed., *Woman's Being, Woman's Place: Female Identity and Vocation in America* (Boston, 1979), 351–72.

5. "I Am So Glad You Could Go to College"

1. Eleanora Wheeler Bosworth to Louise Marion Bosworth, Carton 1, Folder 42, Louise Marion Bosworth Papers, Schlesinger Library, Radcliffe College.

2. Judith Murray, *The Gleaner: A Miscellaneous Production in Three Volumes*, vol. 2 (Boston, 1798), 6, quoted in Barbara Miller Solomon, *In the Company of Educated Women* (New Haven, 1985), 13.

3. The percentage of college women among females aged eighteen to twenty-one in 1870 was only 0.7 percent; it rose to 2.8 percent in 1900 and reached 7.6 percent by 1920; Solomon, *In the Company of Educated Women*, 62–63. An interesting exception to the generalization that the female college student population was comprised of middle-class young women is the case of Alice Duer Miller, who was the daughter of an established, socially prominent New York family. She not only chose to go to college, but decided to work her way through Barnard when her father experienced financial reverses. Her husband recalled that this decision "shocked society and alienated her friends"; Henry Wise Miller, *All Our Lives: Alice Duer Miller* (New York, 1945), 30.

4. Eleanora Bosworth to Louise Marion Bosworth, Carton 1, Folder 40, Bosworth Papers.

5. Eleanora Bosworth to Louise Marion Bosworth, November 24, 1901, ibid.

6. Eleanora Bosworth to Louise Marion Bosworth, November 23, 1902, November 17, 1902, Carton 1, Folder 42, ibid.

7. See, for example, Louise's letter of December 2, 1903, Carton 1, Folder 19, and Mrs. Bosworth's letters of January 29, 1903, February 16, 1903, Carton 1, Folder 43; May 21, 1903, January 12, 1904, and February 23, 1904, Carton 1, Folder 47, ibid.

8. Eleanora Bosworth to Louise Marion Bosworth, August 8, 1912, Carton 1, Folder 63, ibid. See also extensive correspondence concerning Louise's clothing in Carton 1, Folder 54.

9. See, for example, extensive correspondence in Carton 1, Folder 38, and letter from Mrs. Bosworth to Louise on August 20, 1909, ibid.

10. Eleanora Bosworth to Louise Marion Bosworth, July 31, 1928, Carton 2, Folder 72, ibid.

11. For example, the mothers of other Wellesley women between 1880 and 1920 provided comparable support for their daughters' aspirations; Patricia A. Palmieri, "Patterns of Achievement of Single Academic Women at Wellesley College, 1880–1920," *Frontiers* 5 (Spring 1980), 63–67.

12. Alice Duer Miller remembered that, despite the disapproval of members of her social circle, her mother took great interest in her college life: "She used to know exactly what my courses were, where I could be reached by a message." Mrs. Astor called on Mrs. Duer to explain how she felt about

the situation, and her expression, "What a pity, that lovely girl going to college," became a treasured family joke; Miller, *All Our Lives*, 30.

13. Annie Winsor Allen to Ann Bent Ware Winsor, August 7, 1886, Series III, Box 25, Folder 397, Annie Winsor Allen Papers, Schlesinger Library, Radcliffe College.

14. Annie Winsor Allen to Ann Bent Ware Winsor, November 11, 1893, Series III, Box 25, Folder 400, ibid.

15. Ann Bent Ware Winsor to Annie Winsor Allen, Fragment, c. 1899, Series III, Box 24, Folder 390, ibid.

16. See extensive mother-daughter correspondence, Series III, Boxes 23, 24, 25, and 27, ibid.

17. January 11, 1879, in *The Making of a Feminist; Early Journals and Letters of M. Carey Thomas*, ed. Marjorie Dobkin (Kent, Ohio, 1979), 152.

18. See, for example, the entry for February 13, 1878: "Last night I went to the theatre for the first time. Father and Mother of course disapproved but I was twenty-one last month and I went entirely on my own responsibility. . . . I could see no imaginable harm in it and oh it is such a mighty pleasure! . . . I feel deprived all these years," in *The Making of a Feminist*, 131–32. Carroll Smith-Rosenberg has also noted the presence of tension and conflict in this particular mother-daughter relationship, but she has not considered the equally strong presence of mutual support and caring. See "The New Woman as Androgyne: Social Disorder and Gender Crisis, 1870–1936," in Carroll Smith-Rosenberg, *Disorderly Conduct; Visions of Gender in Victorian America* (New York, 1985), 257.

19. July 16, 1875, in *The Making of a Feminist*, 100. An earlier journal entry also documents Mrs. Thomas's commitment to education: "An English man Joseph Beck was here to dinner the other day and he don't believe in the Education of Women. Neither does Cousin Frank King and my such a disgusson *[sic]* they had. *Mother of course was for* . . ." [emphasis added]; see February 26, 1871, in ibid., 50.

20. *The Making of a Feminist*, 209, note 3; also Carey Thomas to Mary Whitall Thomas, November 21, 1880, and November 25, 1882, in ibid., 230, 263.

21. Carey Thomas to Mary Whitall Thomas, October 2, 1883, in ibid., 284. An earlier expression of Carey's regard for her mother appears in a letter to her friend Julia Rogers that was written on July 10, 1879, after she had spent a few days alone with Mrs. Thomas in Atlantic City: "I have had a lovely time with her. I tell her my ideal of happiness would be to have her born a widow and be her only child and travel about"; see ibid., 10, note 7.

22. "Mothers with a Job," autobiographic fragment, quoted in ibid., 9.

23. December 11, 1903, Box 3, Volume 61; January 21, 1906, Box 3, Volume 63; Hilda Worthington Smith Papers, Schlesinger Library, Radcliffe College. Other similar examples appear in journal entries for January 3, 1905, Box 3, Volume 62; October 14 and 15, 1905, December 16, 1905, and January 14, 1906; Box 3, Volume 63.

24. May 16, 1907, Box 3, Volume 64, Book 6, ibid.

25. It was not unusual for a mother who had been deprived of the opportunity to fulfill her own educational and/or professional ambitions to provide strong support and actually urge her daughter to pursue those goals. See also Phyllis Blanchard, "The Long Journey," Kate L. Gregg, "One Way to Freedom," and Lorine Livingston Pruette, "The Evolution of Disenchantment," in Elaine Showalter, ed., *These Modern Women; Autobiographical Essays from the Twenties* (New York, 1989), 105–9, 73–78, 68–73.

26. Mary Helen Hall Smith to Hilda Worthington Smith, October 3, 1909, Box 2, Folder 49; April 29, 1910, Box 3, Folder 50, Smith Papers. See also Mrs. Smith's letters of October 14, 17, and 24, 1909, Box 2, Folder 49, and February 27, 1910, in Box 3, Folder 50, for examples of practical advice regarding Hilda's laundry and clothing, and her letter of November 20, 1910, in Box 3, Folder 50, for her interest in a proposed visit from one of her daughter's friends: "It is all right about asking Miss Klein, We shall be very glad to see her—tho' being the great granddaughter of Hegel sounds rather awe-inspiring."

27. January 9, 1915, Box 4, Volume 78, Book 20, ibid. See also Hilda's description of her mother's objection to her overnight visit with friends: "I was shaking in my shoes when I went into our kitchen. . . . We talked matters over & both wept. I said other girls decided little matters like staying away for a night for themselves, & if they did it, no one accused them . . . of not loving their homes. M. *[sic]* said perhaps she was very selfish in grudging every minute I didn't spend at home, but it was only because she was so lonely without father & because she loved me so. I had never seen it that way, & would have given all I possessed if I had come home last night"; April 21, 1908, Box 3, Volume 66, Book 8, ibid.

28. Mary Helen Hall Smith to Hilda Worthington Smith, May 16, 1909, Box 2, Folder 49, ibid.

29. December 25, 1917, Box 4, Volume 81, Book 23, ibid.

30. M. Carey Thomas to Hilda Worthington Smith, Box 10, Folder 171, ibid.

31. Vida Scudder, *On Journey* (New York, 1937), 66–67, 88. After a few weeks, Vida "wrestled" with her own hair, and her mother returned to Boston.

32. Ibid., 57–58.

33. Ibid., 177, 112, 96, 66–67, 272–73, 292. With regard to these living arrangements, Vida commented, "Miss Converse had for years shared my life in all ways except in living under the same roof"; ibid., 275.

34. Mary Kingsbury Simkhovitch, *Neighborhood: My Story of Greenwich House* (New York, [1938]), 47.

35. Mary Kingsbury Simkhovitch, *Here Is God's Plenty: Reflections on American Social Advance* (New York, 1949), 12; *Neighborhood*, 41.

36. *Neighborhood*, 28.

37. Ibid., 41. Mary eventually left teaching to pursue a career in settle-

ment work in Greenwich Village, where she founded Greenwich House, but there is no evidence that her mother's criticism was responsible for that decision!

38. Joyce Antler, " 'After College, What?': New Graduates and the Family Claim," *American Quarterly* 32 (Fall 1980): 428; Lynn D. Gordon, "Co-Education on Two Campuses: Berkeley and Chicago, 1890–1912," in Mary Kelley, ed., *Woman's Being, Woman's Place: Female Identity and Vocation in American History* (Boston, 1979), 181; Rosalind Rosenberg, *Beyond Separate Spheres: Intellectual Roots of Modern Feminism* (New Haven, 1982), 18–27; Marion Talbot, *More Than Lore* (Chicago, 1936), 3, quoted in Rosenberg, *Beyond Separate Spheres*, 27.

39. Alice Hamilton, *Exploring the Dangerous Trades* (Boston, 1943), 32. She eventually became the first woman on the faculty at Harvard, where she taught in the school of public health.

40. Ibid., 92; Barbara Sicherman, *Alice Hamilton: A Life in Letters* (Cambridge, Mass., 1984), 20–21, 182–83.

41. Ethel Puffer Howes to her mother, January 4, 1896, Box 7, Folder 140, and January n.d., 1898, Box 7, Folder 141, Morgan-Howes Family Papers, Schlesinger Library, Radcliffe College.

42. Laura Puffer Morgan to her mother, n.d., probably 1897, Box 1, Folder 6, ibid.

43. Laura Puffer Morgan to her mother, n.d., 1897, Box 1, Folder 7, ibid. See also a letter written in 1902 concerning the proposed redecoration of a new family home and Laura's desire to be involved in the relevant decisions: "Get some of the new things in papers, not the ordinary kind. . . . How are the rooms painted? In White I hope. . . . Are there any fireplaces? . . . I wish you would consult me about any subject of importance regarding the house. Can't you send me samples of the paper under discussion"; n.d., Box 1, Folder 7.

44. Blanche Ames Ames to Blanche Butler Ames, January 20, 1895; September 22, 1895; October 28, 1895; and December 12, 1895; Series IV, Box 21, Folder 222, Ames Family Papers, Sophia Smith Collection, Smith College.

45. Blanche Ames Ames to Blanche Butler Ames, January 5, 1895, Series IV, Box 21, Folder 222, and January 7, 1896, Box 21, Folder 223, both in ibid.

46. Blanche Ames Ames to Blanche Butler Ames, January 13, 1895, Series IV, Box 21, Folder 222, ibid.

47. See, for example, her letters of October 1, 1896, and November 18, 1896, Series IV, Box 21, Folder 223, ibid.

48. See, for example, "We are anxiously waiting for another letter from you. It is possible we are more Blanche-sick than you are homesick"; "It seems to me that you have not been writing very much lately. I shall look for a letter this afternoon from my college-girlie" (January 11, 1896); and "Be

sure to write at once. . . . All your badly treated family send love and here is a kiss from Mother" (February 14, 1897), all in Series IV, Box 26b, Folder 331, ibid.

49. Blanche Butler Ames to Blanche Ames Ames, September 27, 1895, and March 20, 1897, ibid.

50. Blanche Butler Ames to Blanche Ames, January 22, 1896, ibid. For a similar expression of wholehearted support, see Ella Lowell Lyman's letter to her daughter Ella Lyman Cabot while the latter was enrolled as a special student at Radcliffe: "Darling Ella I must write a line since I cannot fall upon your neck & kiss you, to tell you how delighted Papa & I are with your success. And I am sure you deserved it for your patient steadfast industry. . . . May God ever help & guide you my darling, Most lovingly Your Mother"; June 24, 1890, Series III, Box 3, Folder 65, Ella Lyman Cabot Papers, Schlesinger Library, Radcliffe College.

51. Josephine Dunlap Wilkin to her mother, November 25, 1891, and October 25, 1891, Smith College Archives, Class of 1895, Box 1440.

52. Josephine Dunlap Willkin to her mother, June 15, 1894, ibid.

53. Charlotte Coffyn Wilkinson to her mother, Charlotte May Wilkinson, December 20, 1891, Smith College Archives, Class of 1894, Box 1424.

54. Charlotte Coffyn Wilkinson to Charlotte May Wilkinson, January 24, 1892, and May 19, 1892, ibid.

55. Charlotte Coffyn Wilkinson to Charlotte May Wilkinson, April 24, 1892. See also letters of April 22, 1892 and May 19, 1892, especially the latter: "I do hope you will think that I have improved this year. . . . I only want to be a good and noble woman, worthy of my dearest, old mum." All in ibid.

56. Alice Mason Miller to her mother, January 27, 1878, Smith College Archives, Class of 1883, Box 1345.1.

57. Helen Lyman Miller to her mother, September 21, 1877, Smith College Archives, Class of 1880, Box 1317.

58. Helen Lyman Miller to her mother, February 24, 1878, ibid.

59. Alice Mason Miller to her mother, October 19, 1882. Alice went so far as to copy a letter from a friend's sister in which the young woman described her first call from a young man and sent the copy to her mother so she could see how bright the sister was; November 18, 1877, Smith College Archives, Class of 1883, Box 1345.1.

60. See, for example, Alice's letter of November n.d., 1877, which explained that there was no money left for Helen's gym suit because she had been forced to replace a new pair of gloves that had torn. Apologetically asking her mother to send them more money, she promised: "We will try to be more economical, but going through college is a very expensive thing"; see also Alice's letter of November 25, 1877. Both in ibid. See also Helen's letter of January 15, 1878, in Smith College Archives, Class of 1880, Box 1317.

61. Helen Lyman Miller to her mother, October 17, 1877; October 28, 1877; December 23, 1877; February 12, 1878; and April 28, 1878. All in Smith College Archives, Class of 1880, Box 1317.

62. Helen Lyman Miller to her mother, November 13, 1877, ibid.

63. See Helen's letter of February 12, 1878, in ibid.: "You ask about Mr. Harris and Tom Creighton, and then say 'Don't have any secrets from your mother.' Dear Mamma, I don't want to have any, and if I have not written you about these two boys, it is rather because I forgot it than because I did not wish you to know everything."

64. Helen Lyman Miller to her mother, December 11, 1877; March 8, 1878; and May 19, 1878; all in ibid.

65. Inventory, Helen Lyman Miller Correspondence, in ibid.

66. Another interesting example of maternal pressure for a daughter to pursue higher education appears in a note to Annie Winsor Allen, whose mother felt that she was not preparing adequately to take the entrance examinations for Radcliffe: "I have been sorry to see you so dilatory and flabby about it all—it has seemed as if you really didn't care to do it, after all, or else as if you were so discouraged that you thought it not worthwhile to try. I am sure this last is a perfectly unnecessary feeling—you have sufficient ability and although your education has not been what I could have wished, still it has had its advantages." Anne Bent Ware Winsor to Annie Winsor Allen, August 29, 1882, Series III, Box 23, Folder 380, Allen Papers. See also Joseph Kett's observation regarding the nineteenth-century middle-class tendency to keep girls in high school longer than boys: "Possession of an educated daughter became a sort of prestige symbol, a crude form of conspicuous consumption"; *Rites of Passage: Adolescence in America, 1790 to the Present* (New York, 1977), 138.

67. Solomon, *In the Company of Educated Women*, 67–68.

68. For examples of letters from Ethel Sturges Dummer to Katharine Dummer Fisher at Radcliffe, see Box 44, Folders 911–20, and Box 45, Folders 922–23, Ethel Sturges Dummer Papers, Schlesinger Library, Radcliffe College.

69. Katharine Dummer Fisher to Ethel Sturges Dummer, December 4, 1910, Addendum, Box 42, Folder 886, ibid.

70. Katharine Dummer Fisher to her family, January 22, 1911, ibid.; Katharine to Ethel Sturges Dummer, November 14, 1912, Box 42, Folder 891; and Ethel Sturges Dummer to Katharine, Box 44, Folder 911, ibid.

71. Ethel Sturges Dummer to Mabel Fisher, June 28, 1915, Box 45, Folder 924, ibid. The letter is marked in pencil, "I believe this was never sent." Mrs. Dummer's suggestion that sexual repression could be unhealthy reflected a new, twentieth-century emphasis on the importance of sexual satisfaction in marriage; Elaine Tyler May, *Great Expectations: Marriage and Divorce in Post-Victorian America* (Chicago, 1980), 92.

72. Ethel Sturges Dummer to "Happy" (Ethel) Dummer Mintzer, February 13, 1918, Box 10, Folder 164, Dummer Papers.

73. Ethel Sturges Dummer to "Happy" (Ethel) Dummer Mintzer, July 8, 1920, Box 10, Folder 165a, ibid. See also her encouraging letter of December 27, 1921: "Do not let any feeling of inferiority, the thought that you are too human, hold you from taking in the world the big place for which you are fitted"; Box 3, Folder 42, ibid.

74. See detailed correspondence between Marion and her mother, Box 3, Folder 37, ibid.

75. See, for example, letters to Ethel Sturges Dummer from Katharine Dummer Fisher, Box 43, Folder 895; letters from "Happy" (Ethel) Dummer Mintzer, Box 10, Folder 162; and letters from Frances Dummer Logan, Box 12, Folder 185. All in ibid.

76. Frances Dummer Logan to Ethel Sturges Dummer, January 27, 1918, Box 12, Folder 184, ibid. See also a letter dated February 27, 1921, which expressed Frances's dismay that her mother had told her sister Happy something she had asked her not to mention, in Box 12, Folder 185, ibid.

77. Frances Dummer Logan to Ethel Sturges Dummer, March 2, 1919, Box 12, Folder 185, ibid.

78. Eliza Coe Brown Moore to Dorothea May Moore, April 28, 1912, Dorothea May Moore Papers, Box 3, Folder 69, Schlesinger Library, Radcliffe College.

79. Margaret Lesley Bush-Brown to Lydia Bush-Brown, Box 6, Bush-Brown Family Papers, Sophia Smith Collection, Smith College.

80. Helen Landon Cass to her mother, January 5, 1917; October 13, 1916; October n.d., 1916; January 23, 1917; and January 29, 1917; Smith College Archives, Class of 1920, Box 1810.

81. A recent study by Lynn D. Gordon suggests that the second generation of young women who attended college were portrayed as a type of Gibson Girl in the popular literature of the Progressive era, which described college life in terms of pranks and amusing social activities. Gordon argues that this portrayal responded to societal concerns about the possible effects of higher education on young women by depicting them in socially acceptable settings that provided reassurance that drastic social change was not taking place. Cultural reassurance of this sort could also increase maternal comfort with regard to daughters' untraditional choices. "The Gibson Girl Goes to College: Popular Culture and Women's Higher Education in the Progressive Era, 1890–1920," *American Quarterly* 39, 2 (Summer 1987): 211–30. See also Lynn D. Gordon, *Gender and Higher Education in the Progressive Era* (New Haven, 1990).

82. Sharon O'Brien, *Willa Cather: The Emerging Voice* (New York, 1987), 104.

83. Joyce Antler, *Lucy Sprague Mitchell: The Making of a Modern Woman* (New Haven, 1987); Sara Alpern, *Freda Kirchwey, a Woman of the Nation* (Cambridge, Mass., 1987), 11. Maternal values also contributed to Christine Ladd-Franklin's ability to pursue a career in the male-dominated world of scientific psychology; see Laurel Furumoto, "Joining Separate Spheres—

Christine Ladd-Franklin, Woman Scientist (1847–1930)," *American Psychologist* 47, 2 (February 1992): 175–82.

84. Abbie Blaisdell Queneau to Marguerite Queneau, May 18, 1922, Carton 1, Folder 15, Marguerite Queneau Papers, Schlesinger Library, Radcliffe College.

85. Abbie Blaisdell Queneau to Marguerite Queneau, December 5, 1920; March 28, 1921; August 11, 1921; and October 27, 1921; Carton 1, Folder 14, ibid. Although Mrs. Queneau had attended college, she never graduated. See interview with Marguerite Queneau, 1983, Transcript I, p. 5, Carton 1, Folder 20, ibid.

86. See, for example, letters written October 27, 1921; November 15, 1921; February 22, 1923; April 27, 1923; and March 31, 1924, Carton 1, Folder 14, ibid.

87. Abbie Blaisdell Queneau to Marguerite Queneau, October 31, 1924, Carton 1, Folder 15, ibid. Marguerite Queneau's observations in an interview many years later suggested that she felt close to her mother as an adult, and that the ties between them remained strong even after the latter's death. She noted especially that because her mother had been "very New England," she felt that she had roots in Boston. "So although I'm telling you this in 1982, and mother died in 1933, I feel mother close to me, around me. Whenever there's something really fine, it just seems 'mother would have agreed with that.'" Interview with Marguerite Queneau, 1982, Carton 1, Folder 19, ibid.

88. See the lengthy correspondence from Lucile Burdette Tuttle to Frances Davidson Tuttle, Series IIA, Box 8, Folders 156 and 157, and Box 9, Folders 158–62, Tuttle Family Papers, Schlesinger Library, Radcliffe College.

89. Lucile Burdette Tuttle to Frances Davidson Tuttle, June 25, 1922, Series IIA, Box 9, Folder 158, ibid.

90. Lucile B. Tuttle to Frances D. Tuttle, May 7, 1922. See also her similar sentiments: "There are so many of the girls whom I am looking forward to having you meet when you come back, and whom I want to meet you. Just think of Mother's Day at the Kappa Phi House. Its [sic] going to be great believe me" (June 25, 1922). Both in Series IIA, Box 9, Folder 158, ibid. See also an earlier letter: "Not only will I be meeting other mothers, but they and their sons and daughters will be meeting *my mother,* and oh how proud I'll be. . . . I know the time is just going to fly" (May 26, 1918??), in Series IIB, Box 8, Folder 154. (As the question marks indicate, the 1918 date is probably incorrect as Lucile was not a Denison student in that year.)

91. Unpublished writing by Max Eastman, quoted in Karen Payne, ed., *Between Ourselves: Letters Between Mothers & Daughters, 1750–1982* (Boston, 1983), 140.

92. Annis Ford Eastman to Crystal Eastman, 1899; Crystal Eastman to her mother, March 6, 1907; quoted in Payne, ed., *Between Ourselves,* 140, 142.

93. See letters from Crystal Eastman to Annis Ford Eastman, March 6, 1907, and June 25, 1907, and from Annis Ford Eastman to Crystal Eastman, March 7, 1907, and May 3, 1909, in Payne, ed., *Between Ourselves,* 143–48.

94. "Mother Worship," *The Nation*, March 16, 1927, reprinted in Elaine Showalter, ed., *These Modern Women: Autobiographical Essays from the Twenties* (New York, 1989), 87–92. Two decades earlier she had told her mother, "No one really knows how passionately I love you. . . . I simply can't imagine my life without you"; Crystal Eastman to Annis Ford Eastman, n.d., 1907, quoted in Payne, ed., *Between Ourselves*, 140.

95. Oral interview, *The Twentieth-Century Trade Union Woman: Vehicle for Social Change Oral History Project*, Institute of Labor and Industrial Relations, University of Michigan–Wayne State University (Ann Arbor, 1978), 43. Ms. Luscomb was eighty-nine when she was interviewed.

96. Virginia Gildersleeve, *Many a Good Crusade* (New York, 1954), 39.

97. Ibid., 48.

98. Ibid., 40–41, 50–53, 63, 199–200.

99. Ibid., 204.

100. A recent reappraisal of the literature on Victorian sexuality suggests that a female generation gap in attitudes and beliefs about sex may have separated young women and their mothers during this perod. This could also contribute to heightened tensions between college-educated daughters (and other middle-class daughters as well) and their mothers; see Stephen Seidman, "The Power of Desire and the Danger of Pleasure: Victorian Sexuality Reconsidered," *Journal of Social History* 24 (Fall 1990): 47–67.

101. See, for example, the use of expressions such as "scared to death," "it was screaming," "I think it is perfectly killing," "I got a spiffy bid to class day from Sam Lawrence," and "P.D.Q.," in letters written from Smith College by Mary Antoinette Clapp to her mother between 1908 and 1911; Smith College Archives, Class of 1912, Box 1700.

102. *My Thirty Years' War* (New York, 1969), first published in 1930. See, for example, Margaret's characterization of her mother's emotional make-up, 9–10, and her discussion of hostile interactions, 17 and 25–27.

Other examples of troubled, although not necessarily completely hostile mother-daughter interactions include Charlotte Perkins Gilman's problems with her mother, who was not particularly supportive of her daughter's ambitions at first, in Mary A. Hill, *Charlotte Perkins Gilman: The Making of a Radical Feminist, 1860–1896* (Philadelphia, 1980); Jane Addams's conflict with her stepmother regarding family obligations, in Jane Addams, "Filial Relations," in *Democracy and Social Ethics* (New York, 1902), 71–101; Genevieve Taggard's efforts to escape from her mother's authoritarianism, in Genevieve Taggard, "Poet Out of Pioneer," in Showalter, ed., *These Modern Women*, 63–68; and Mary Heaton Vorse's complicated yet distant relationship with her mother, in Dee Garrison, *Mary Heaton Vorse: The Life of an American Insurgent* (Philadelphia, 1989).

103. *My Thirty Years' War*, 64–65.

104. In a letter to her sister, Clara commented on this issue: "I see her position *perfectly*. I can understand how it is very natural for your mother to want to 'warn' you and 'suggest' as she says and it must be very hard to

realize that you haven't your daughter's confidence. But I have yet to see the mother who has! It's *impossible!*" February 18, 1915, Box 3, Folder 55, Clara Savage Littledale Papers, Schlesinger Library, Radcliffe College.

105. February 15, 1915, Box 1, Volume 17, Journal for 1915, ibid.

106. Clara Savage Littledale to her sister Marion, August 2, 1918, Box 3, Folder 56, ibid.

107. See, for example, journal entries for 1914, 1915, and 1916, Volumes 16, 17, 18, Box 1, in ibid.

108. February 2, 1916, *Lella Secor: A Diary in Letters, 1915–1922*, ed. Barbara Moench Florence (New York, 1978), 33.

109. March 20, 1916, in ibid., 54–55.

110. Election Day, November, 1916, in ibid., 109–10.

111. See, for example, letters written by Lella's secretary which assured her mother that she would write soon, January 16, 1917, and March 21, 1917, and her own letter, September n.d., 1918: "I am so sorry that you felt I was ungrateful for the dear things you have made for the baby, and also for your characteristic thoughtfulness in sending the cakes and corn. I thought you would understand that that hastily scribbled note on yellow paper was not meant as a reply to your letter or as an acknowledgment of the gifts, but rather as a makeshift to let you know how I was until I could get off a better letter"; ibid., 122, 137, 177.

112. In a letter to her sisters, March n.d., 1921, she wrote: "It is so hard for me to realize that Mother is really gone. . . . She is constantly in my thoughts, and often in the midst of the very strenuous activities which have filled my days in the past few weeks, I have found myself weeping without really knowing why at first—just a sense of irretrievable loss. . . . I used to be afraid that memories of the unhappy times which we sometimes had would finally predominate. But this isn't so at all. She was so much that was good and clever and tender and fine that all her foibles seem swallowed up and forgotten. I would so love to have seen her once more"; ibid., 247.

113. "The Female World of Love and Ritual"; "Hearing Women's Words: A Feminist Reconstruction of History"; and "The New Woman as Androgyne: Social Disorder and Gender Crisis, 1870–1936," in Carroll Smith-Rosenberg, *Disorderly Conduct*, 53–76, 11–52, 245–96. For an interesting discussion of the positive contribution of families, particularly mothers, to the continuing growth and development of college-educated daughters, see Joyce Antler, " 'After College, What?': New Graduates and the Family Claim."

114. Lydia Maria Child to "Louise," November 9, 1863, Loring Papers, Schlesinger Library, Radcliffe College, quoted in Carl Degler, *At Odds: Women and the Family in America from the Revolution to the Present* (New York, 1980), 106.

115. Hannah Whitall Smith, aunt of M. Carey Thomas, to Mary Berenson, her daughter, September 28, 1910, in Logan Pearsall Smith, ed., *Philadelphia Quaker: The Letters of Hannah Whitall Smith* (New York, 1950), 210.

116. Journal entry, October 22, 1916, Box 1, Volume 18, Littledale Papers.

6. *"We Need Each Other"*

1. Recollections of Lucy Wilson Peters, Box 1, Folder 5, Elizabeth Millar Wilson Papers, Schlesinger Library, Radcliffe College.

2. Blanche Ames Ames to her parents, June 24, 1900. See numerous additional letters written while she was on her honeymoon, all in Box 21, Folder 226, Ames Family Papers, Sophia Smith Collection, Smith College.

3. Annis Ford Eastman to Crystal Eastman, March 3, 1907, in Karen Payne, ed., *Between Ourselves: Letters Between Mothers and Daughters* (Boston, 1983), 146.

4. Caroline Judson Hitchcock to Mary L. Hitchcock, October 21, 1897, Box 4, Folder 3, President Edward Hitchcock Papers, Amherst College Archives.

5. Caroline Judson Hitchcock to her mother, February 28, 1892, and October 1, 1893, Box 2, Folder 27, and Box 3, Folder 2; and Mary Hitchcock to Bess Hitchcock, November 4, 1893; all in ibid. See also other letters about clothing from Caroline and Bess Hitchcock, Box 2, Folders 26 and 27, and letters from Lucy Hitchcock, November 23, 1893: "I am cross as can be— disgusted too. Why? Because all my clothes are wearing out." Box 3, Folder 2; February 10, 1893, Box 3, Folder 1; and March 9, 1893, Box 3, Folder 1.

6. Mary Elizabeth Homer to Eugenie Homer Emerson, July 10, 1896, Series I, Box 2, Folder 19, Emerson-Nichols Family Papers, Schlesinger Library, Radcliffe College; Sophia Bledsoe Herrick to Louise Herrick Wall, August 5, 1900, Box 3, Folder 50, Bledsoe-Herrick Family Papers, Schlesinger Library; and letters from Eleanora Bosworth to Louise Bosworth, Carton 1, Folder 54, Louise Marion Bosworth Papers, Schlesinger Library, Radcliffe College.

7. Lulu Perry Fuller to her mother, Mary Alice Rice Perry, January 1, 1896, and January 27, 1896, Folder 6, typescripts, Perry Family Papers, Schlesinger Library, Radcliffe College.

8. Mary Alice Rice Perry to her mother, Mary Howe Rice, June 3, 1900, Box 1, Folder 4, ibid.

9. Helen Jackson Cabot Almy to her daughter Mary, June 8, 1908, Helen Jackson Cabot Almy Papers, Schlesinger Library, Radcliffe College.

10. Anne Bent Ware Winsor to Annie Winsor Allen, May 23, 1892, Series III, Box 24, Folder 383, Annie Winsor Allen Papers, Schlesinger Library, Radcliffe College.

11. Addendum to letter written May 23, 1892, dated May 24, and Anne Bent Ware Winsor to Annie Winsor Allen, April 28, 1893, Series III, Box 24, Folder 384, Allen Papers. In the same folder, see her letter dated April 28, 1893, in which she expressed her objections to Jane's engagement to a

man who was "distinctly beneath her, in age and thought and ideas and understanding" and her fears about the eventual outcome of this unsuitable alliance. Regarding her concerns about her daughter Mary, see her letter of February 25, 1892, which reports that Mary never sees anyone except "at some meeting or lecture occasionally. . . . I can't go and ask people for invitations for her. And I don't see why they leave her out so unanimously. I lie awake nights over it"; Series III, Box 24, Folder 383.

12. Bess Hitchcock to Mary L. Hitchcock, n.d., 1896, Box 4, Folder 1, President Hitchcock Papers.

13. Eugenie Homer Emerson to Mary Elizabeth Homer, February 6, 1897, Series I, Box 1, Folder 6, Emerson-Nichols Family Papers. See also a letter from Dorothea May Moore to her parents, November 2, 1926, reassuring them that they had done the right thing in their treatment of another daughter whose life-style they found unsuitable; Box 4, Folder 97, Dorothea May Moore Papers, Schlesinger Library, Radcliffe College.

14. February 9, 1886, in *Maud*, ed. Richard L. Strout (New York, 1939), 370.

15. Mary L. Hitchcock to Bess Hitchcock, November 4, 1893, Box 3, Folder 1, President Hitchcock Papers; Emily Perkins Hale to Ellen D. Hale, January 22, 1893, Box 32a, Folder 797, Hale Family Papers, Sophia Smith Collection, Smith College.

16. Carroll Smith-Rosenberg, "The Female World of Love and Ritual," in *Disorderly Conduct: Visions of Gender in Victorian America* (New York, 1985), 53–76; Marilyn Ferris Motz, *True Sisterhood: Michigan Women and Their Kin, 1820–1920* (Albany, 1983); Nancy F. Cott, *The Bonds of Womanhood: "Woman's Sphere" in New England, 1780–1835* (New Haven, 1977).

17. Mary A. Hill, *Charlotte Perkins Gilman: The Making of a Radical Feminist, 1860–1896* (Philadelphia, 1980), 124–25, 127.

18. Eliza Coe Brown Moore to Mary Elizabeth Adams Brown, October 21, 1893, Box 1, Folder 8, Dorothea May Moore Papers.

19. Frank Fuller to Mary Alice Rice Perry, February 17, 1898, typescript, Folder 6, Perry Family Papers.

20. Frances Tuttle to her mother, March ??, 1902, Series II, Box 4, Folder 50, Tuttle Family Papers, Schlesinger Library, Radcliffe College.

21. Frances Tuttle to her mother, March 1, 1903, Series II, Box 4, Folder 52, ibid.

22. Frances Tuttle to her mother, March 13, 1903, Series II, Box 4, Folder 55, ibid. See also a letter to her mother and her sister in which she repeats that she is not sorry to be pregnant and that she hopes the baby will live; May 7, 1903, Series II, Box 4, Folder 53, ibid.

23. Frances Tuttle to her mother, June 1, 1903, Series II, Box 4, Folder 53, ibid.

24. Lydia Auerbach to Lydia Marie Parsons, n.d., 1917, Box 1, Folder 4, Lydia Marie Parsons Papers, Schlesinger Library, Radcliffe College. Mrs. Auerbach's desire for her daughter to come home for the birth of her child

recalls the feelings of connection between female family members described by both Marilyn Ferris Motz and Carroll Smith-Rosenberg in their analyses of nineteenth-century women's lives in *True Sisterhood* and "The Female World of Love and Ritual."

25. Lydia Auerbach to Lydia Marie Parsons, January 4, 1918, Box 1, Folder 4, Parsons Papers.

26. Lydia Auerbach to Lydia Marie Parsons, August 2, 1928, Box 1, Folder 5, ibid.

27. See, for example, letters written in 1895, 1902, and 1903, Section I, Correspondence, Box 18, Folder 6, Charles Edward Garman Papers, Amherst College Archives. The note dictated by Affa's daughter was enclosed in a letter dated November 13, 1903, Section I, Correspondence, Box 18, Folder 7.

28. July 24, 1893; March 6, 1894; and November 25, 1895; Series III, Carton 3, Folders 95 and 96, Bradley Family Papers, Schlesinger Library, Radcliffe College. See extensive correspondence from Amy Aldis Bradley to her mother, Mary T. Aldis, 1892–1909, Folders 93–134, which describes the affluent middle-class life-style of a devoted wife and mother.

29. Annie Winsor Allen to Ann Bent Ware Winsor, March 13, 1904, and n.d., 1904, Series III, Box 27, Folder 411, Allen Papers.

30. Whatever the subject might be, sharing daughters' letters was a way of nurturing the network of connections between mothers and their offspring. See, for example, Mary Hitchcock's instructions to her daughter Caroline: "I send all these letters on to you for I know you will be interested in them all please send back to me . . . but send Bessie's letter to Mabel & ask her to return it to us after she has read it" (January 20, 1901), Box 4, Folder 7, President Hitchcock Papers; Mary Elizabeth Homer's advice to Eugenie Homer Emerson: "Anything you want *me* to see and *no one* else put 'private' on the back" (November 26, 1896), Series I, Box 2, Folder 19, Emerson-Nichols Family Papers; and Emily Perkins Hale's assurance that her own mother took "the greatest pleasure" in having her granddaughter's letters read to her, in Letter to Ellen Hale, February 19, 1895, Box 32a, Folder 798. Mrs. Hale read the letters "with a tube" because her mother was hard of hearing. She felt guilty because she did not want to just give her the letters to read for herself, but, as she put it, "somehow I can't bear to." She also shared Ellen's letters with other interested female friends and relatives.

31. Mary Pierce Poor to her unmarried daughters Agnes Blake Poor and Lucy Poor, January 28, 1888, and to Agnes, Lucy, and Mary Poor Chandler, the "boys' " mother, July 1, 1895, Box 12, Folders 185 and 186, Poor Family Collection, Schlesinger Library, Radcliffe College.

32. Mary Pierce Poor to Mary Poor Chandler, July 9, 1895, and July 15, 1898, Box 15, Folders 242 and 243, ibid.

33. Ann Bent Ware Winsor to Annie Winsor Allen, March 8, 1901, and March 7, 1901, Series III, Box 24, Folder 393, Allen Papers.

34. Anne Bent Ware Winsor to Annie Winsor Allen, August 29, 1902, Series III, Box 25, Folder 394, ibid.

35. See, for example, various affectionate letters written in 1904, which describe the details of her life and her children's activities, Series III, Box 27, Folder 411, ibid.

36. See chapter 5, pp. 96, 98–99.

37. Autobiographical typescript and unpublished biography, "My Little Mother," Mary Williams Dewson Papers, Schlesinger Library, Radcliffe College.

38. Caroline Hitchcock to Mary L. Hitchcock, October 15, 1893, and Lucy Hitchcock to Mary L. Hitchcock, n.d., 1893, both in Series III, Box 2, President Hitchcock Papers.

39. Helen Brewster to Anna Williams Brewster, April 16, 1903, and September 11, 1904, Box 4, Folder 25, Brewster Family Papers, Sophia Smith Collection, Smith College.

40. For evidence of their devotion to family matters, see letters from their mother, Mary Pierce Poor, to Agnes, Box 13, Folders 194, 196, 199, and to Lucy, Box 13, Folders 208, 209, 210, 211, Poor Family Collection.

41. Elizabeth Ellery Dana to Sarah Watson Dana, April 10, 1885, Box 16, Folder 51, Dana Family Papers, Schlesinger Library, Radcliffe College.

42. Anna Gertrude Brewster to Anna Williams Brewster, February 11, 1907, Box 4, Folder 16, Brewster Family Papers.

43. See examples of their letters to one another, Box 45a, Folders 1064, 1066, 1069, 1070, and Box 32b, Folders 799 and 800, Hale Family Papers. Ellen eventually served as her father's hostess during his term as chaplain of the U.S. Senate, from 1904 until his death in 1907.

44. Chapter 1, pp. 12–14, and in Smith-Rosenberg, "The Female World of Love and Ritual."

45. Ellen D. Hale to Emily Perkins Hale, December 2, 1887, Box 45a, Folder 1064, and December 15, 1900, Box 45a, Folder 1070, Hale Family Papers. See also her letters of May 10, 1894: "I've been having . . . quiet days (I wrote you on the first) owing to the Friend" and August 18, 1901: "I am feeling much better, it is a *much* less trying bout than the last. It was several days late"; Box 45a, Folders 1067 and 1070, ibid.

46. Emily Perkins Hale to Ellen D. Hale, August 26, 1901, Box 32b, Folder 800, and November 18, 1896, Box 32b, Folder 799; Ellen D. Hale to Emily Perkins Hale, January 22, 1893, Box 45a, Folder 1066, ibid.

47. Affa Miner Tuttle to Mrs. D. W. Miner, November n.d., 1903, Section I, Correspondence, Box 18, Folder 6, Garman Papers. See also her letter of December 1, 1905, Box 18, Folder 7, ibid.

48. Letter from Affa Miner Tuttle, addressed to "dear Ones at Home," November 29, 1903, Section I, Box 18, Folder 7, Garman Papers.

49. Eugenie Homer Emerson to Mary Elizabeth Homer, November 11, 1896, Series I, Box 1, Folder 4, Emerson-Nichols Family Papers.

50. Sophia Bledsoe Herrick to Louise Herrick Wall, August 5, 1900, Box 3, Folder 50, Bledsoe-Herrick Family Papers.

51. Ruth Gordon to her daughter, March 13, 1886, and November 11, 1887, Folder 1, Ruth Gordon Papers, Schlesinger Library, Radcliffe College. See also references to both her daughter's health and her own in letters dated October 22, 1884; February 27, 1885; and April 5, 1886; all in Folder 1.

52. Mary Elizabeth Homer to Eugenie Homer Emerson, January 25, 1897, Box 2, Folder 18, Emerson-Nichols Family Papers.

53. Mary Elizabeth Homer to Eugenie Homer Emerson, March 24, 1897, and Eugenie Homer Emerson to her mother, March 24, 1898, Series I, Box 2, Folder 19, and Box 1, Folder 7, Emerson-Nichols Family Papers. See, for example, letters from Frances Tuttle to her mother in Series II, Box 4, Folders 50, 52, 53, 55, and 64, Tuttle Family Papers.

54. The Bledsoe-Herrick Family Papers contain eighty-three folders of Mrs. Herrick's letters to her daughter. See, for example, those contained in Series II, Boxes 2 and 3.

55. Sophia Bledsoe Herrick to Louise Herrick Wall, February 12, 1899, Box 3, Folder 45, Bledsoe-Herrick Family Collection. A letter to Virginia, who lived nearby, suggests that Mrs. Herrick also enjoyed a warm relationship with her: "My precious little girl I want to tell you that I have felt intensely all your love and tenderness these last years of my life. And that I love you very dearly" (October 8, 1908); Box 6, Folder 110. Nevertheless, it is not difficult to understand why Virginia found her mother "lugubrious" in her constant yearning for Louise, whom she regarded as "the nearest of the children"; Sophia Bledsoe Herrick to Louise Herrick Wall, July 17, 1917, Box 6, Folder 107, Bledsoe-Herrick Family Papers.

56. Sophia Bledsoe Herrick to Louise Herrick Wall, December 27, 1889, Box 2, Folder 29, ibid.

57. Sophia Bledsoe Herrick to Louise Herrick Wall, July 17, 1917, Box 6, Folder 107, ibid. Interestingly, a note on an envelope in Box 6, Folder 107, records the fact that Louise spent eighteen months with her mother just before the latter's death on October 9, 1919.

58. Catherine Booth-Clibborn to Victoria Booth Demarest, n.d., 1910, and Fragment, n.d., both in Carton 1, Folder 25, Victoria Booth Demarest Papers, Schlesinger Library, Radcliffe College.

59. Catherine Booth-Clibborn to Victoria Booth Demarest, Fragment, n.d., 1913; February 26 (probably), 1909; August 3, 1907; March 21, 1908; and March 15, 1910, all in Carton 1, Folder 25; and two letters written in n.d., 1913, in Carton 1, Folder 26, Victoria Booth Demarest Papers.

60. Catherine Booth-Clibborn to Victoria Booth Demarest, August 3, 1907, Carton 1, Folder 25, and n.d., probably 1915, Carton 1, Folder 26, ibid. Victoria was eighteen when the first letter was written and probably twenty-six when she received the second one.

61. See, for example, letters written in n.d., 1903, and on March 21, 1908, and February 26 (probably), 1909, all in Carton 1, Folder 25, ibid.

62. Notation on a manila envelope in Carton 1, Folder 25, and a slip of paper in Folder 26, ibid.

63. January 25, March 18, May 6, and June 13, 1914; Diary of Victoria Booth Demarest, Carton 1, Folder 19, ibid. Occasional apologetic comments suggest that Mrs. Booth-Clibborn felt she asked too much of her daughter— for example, her statement, "I am unjust to *you because this constant irritation wears me*" (n.d., 1914); Carton 1, Folder 26, ibid.

64. R. A. Field to her aunt, March 31, 1890, Field Family Collection, Michigan Historical Collection, Bentley Library, University of Michigan, quoted in Motz, *True Sisterhood*, 116.

65. Blanche Ames Ames to Blanche Butler Ames, n.d., 1900, Box 21, Folder 226, Ames Family Papers; Jean Miner to her sister, Elizabeth Miner Garman, May 25, 1901, Garman Papers, Series I, Box 14, Folder 1, and also letters dated February 28, 1884, Series I, Box 13, Folder 8; July 3, 1901; and July 5, 1901, Box 14, Folder 2; and Lucy Hitchcock to Caroline Hitchcock, n.d., 1899, Box 4, Folder 5, President Hitchcock Papers. See also a letter from Mary Colton Boies to her mother, March 8, 1888: "I am not aware that either Abbie . . . or I are in the habit of concealing *anything* from you or Father, or misrepresenting affairs for there is nothing to conceal. When I was so sick three years ago and you were sick at the same time, I did not think it advisable to say anything about it, to aggravate your worry but that has been all"; Box 3, Folder 30, Bessie Boies Cotton Papers, Sophia Smith Collection, Smith College.

66. See, for example, letters from Mrs. D. W. Miner to her daughter, Elizabeth Miner Garman, which urge her to visit—"I am afraid if you do not come down in term time you won't come at all"—and to write every day so that her parents will know she is healthy; June 6, 1893; January 28, 1896; December 2, 1905; and n.d., 1905, all in Series I, Box 13, Folder 2, Garman Papers.

67. See, for example, Maud Rittenhouse's comments on her parents' opposition to her desire to try teaching: "I'm perfectly determined to teach school next year and Mama won't have me do it and says it'll break my health and Papa is a fraud and says I couldn't teach and there isn't any vacancy and I couldn't go to parties and rehearsals and have company all the time" (May 27, 1883); in *Maud*, 204.

68. See, for example, letters from Ella Reeve Bloor to Helen Ware, August 7, 1911, and August 9, 1911. The quotation is from a letter dated February 17, 1912, all in Series IV, Box 8, Folder 36, Ella Reeve Bloor Papers, Sophia Smith Collection, Smith College. See also her comments on Mother's Day, 1926: "I need you *more* as I grow older—and it's quite natural that you should need me less with so many around you to love you and so many dear interests to work for—Just a little word from you helps a lot"; Box 8, Folder 37, ibid.

69. See correspondence from Ella Reeve Bloor to Helen Ware, Mother's Day, 1926, Series IV, Box 8, Folder 37, and other letters in Folders 38, 39, and 40, especially one, n.d., 1935, Folder 39, and one, n.d., 1936, in Folder 40, ibid.

70. Anita Clair Fellman, "Laura Ingalls Wilder and Rose Wilder Lane: The Politics of a Mother-Daughter Relationship," *Signs: Journal of Women in Culture and Society* 15, 3 (1990): 535–61.

71. See, for example, the case of Annie Winsor Allen, who was patient and sympathetic with the whims of a demanding and irascible mother, while her sister Jane had great difficulty with her. Anne Bent Ware Winsor to Annie Winsor Allen, May 23, 1892, and October 30, 1892, Series III, Box 24, Folder 383; and October 3, 1893, Series III, Box 24, Folder 384, Allen Papers.

72. The paucity of evidence regarding conflict between late nineteenth and early twentieth-century mothers and adult daughters may reflect a perception that such disputes should not be discussed. The findings of a contemporary oral history project suggest that it is not unusual for adult women to regard family conflict of this sort as a private matter; see Corinne Azen Krause, *Grandmothers, Mothers, and Daughters: Oral Histories of Three Generations of Ethnic American Women* (Boston, 1991).

73. In this context, it is especially interesting to note that Mrs. Bulkley had never discussed anything "except very external experiences" with her children and had seldom found time to read to them; see Mary Ezit Bulkley, "Grandmother, Mother and Me," mimeographed manuscript, Schlesinger Library, Radcliffe College, 112–14, 27.

74. Mary Pierce Poor to Agnes Blake Poor, November 5, 1883, Box 13, Folder 196, Poor Family Collection; Ellen D. Hale to Emily Perkins Hale, November 20, 1890, Hale Family Papers. See also a letter from Eugenie Homer Emerson to Mary Elizabeth Homer, on the latter's eightieth birthday, March 24, 1898, Series I, Box 1, Folder 7, Emerson-Nichols Family Papers, and a letter in which Dorothea May Moore acknowledged her mother's birthday greetings: "Thank you so dear, for all your loving words—for past present and future" (May 15, 1926), Carton 4, Folder 97, Dorothea May Moore Papers.

75. Affa Miner Tuttle to Mrs. D. W. Miner, March 28, 1904, Section I, Box 18, Folder 7; Diary of Elizabeth Miner Garman, Section III, Box 43, Folder 2, Garman Papers; May 6, 1912, Journal of Elizabeth Ellery Dana, Box 5, Volume 141, Dana Family Papers. Like Affa Miner Tuttle, Eugenie Homer Emerson wrote on her own birthday to tell her mother that she was thinking about her, and that she felt that her mother was thinking of her; April 27, 1898, Series I, Box 1, Folder 7, Emerson-Nichols Family Papers.

76. Peter Uhlenberg, "Death and the Family," *Journal of Family History* 5, 3 (Fall 1980): 313–20; and "Cohort Variations in Family Life Cycle Experiences of United States Females," *Journal of Marriage and the Family* 36, 2 (May 1974): 284–92.

77. See evidence regarding the relationship between the existence of old-age pensions and the maintenance of harmonious relations between working-class adults and elderly parents, in Michael Young and Peter Willmott, *Family and Kinship in East London* (Baltimore, 1962), 192–93.

78. Daniel Scott Smith, "Life Course, Norms, and the Family System of Older Americans in 1900," *Journal of Family History* 4, 3 (Fall 1979): 285–98.

79. While the mother of Annie Winsor Allen appears to have been financially independent, she definitely made increased emotional demands on her children after her husband's death. See, for example, Anne Bent Ware Winsor to Annie Winsor Allen, March 1 and March 22, 1890, Series III, Box 23, Folder 381; February 24, 1893, Series III, Box 24, Folder 384; January 28, 1895, Series III, Box 24, Folder 386; and February 28, 1896, Series III, Box 24, Folder 387, Allen Papers.

80. Carl N. Degler, *At Odds; Women and the Family in America from the Revolution to the Present* (New York, 1980), 106–7. See also Marilyn Ferris Motz's emphasis on the enduring ties between mothers and adult daughters in *True Sisterhood.*

81. Young and Willmott, *Family and Kinship in East London,* and Peter N. Stearns, "Old Women: Some Historical Observations," *Journal of Family History* 5, 1 (Spring 1980), 44–57. But Stearns also notes the strength of the connections between elderly, middle-class women and their daughters.

82. Young and Willmott, *Family and Kinship in East London,* 190–96.

83. March 24, 1913, Box 1, Folder 3, Elizabeth Millar Wilson Papers.

7. *"The Revolt of the Daughters"*

1. Several efforts to develop comparative perspectives on feminism and suffrage represent interesting exceptions to this generalization. See, for example, Olive Banks, *Faces of Feminism: A Study of Feminism as a Social Movement* (New York, 1981); David Bouchier, *The Feminist Challenge: The Movement for Women's Liberation in Britain and the United States* (London, 1983); Richard J. Evans, *The Feminists: Women's Emancipation Movements in Europe, America and Australasia, 1840–1920* (London, 1977); William O'Neill, *The Woman Movement: Feminism in the United States and England* (London, 1969); and Ross Evans Paulson, *Women's Suffrage and Prohibition: A Comparative Study of Equality and Social Control* (Glenview, Ill., 1973).

For general discussions of comparative approaches to history, see George M. Fredrickson, "Comparative History," in Michael Kammen, ed., *The Past Before Us: Contemporary Historical Writing in the United States* (Ithaca, N.Y., 1980), 457–73, and Raymond Grew, "The Case for Comparing Histories," *American Historical Review* 85, 4 (October 1980): 763–78. See also the examples of comparative history in this issue of the *American Historical Review* and in the subsequent issue, 85, 5 (December 1980).

2. Patricia Branca, *Silent Sisterhood: Middle-Class Women in the Victorian Home* (London, 1975), 38–48, 53–57. Branca's findings indicate that approximately three-quarters of the late-Victorian middle class had incomes well below the level of three hundred pounds or more that would have enabled them to retain two or three servants.

3. Jane Lewis, *Women in England, 1870–1950: Sexual Divisions and Social Change* (Bloomington, Ind., 1984), 81, 114.

4. Like the composition of the English middle class, the nature of the available sources defines another issue of comparability. In terms of both quantity and accessibility, the data pertaining to the experiences of American mothers and daughters are more extensive. Obviously this situation reflects in part the larger American population, but it also reflects the general state of women's archives in the two countries. For example, the Schlesinger Library alone maintains over four hundred manuscript collections devoted to women's history, many of which document family life extensively, and other libraries also contain large collections of similar materials, for example, the Sophia Smith Collection at Smith College. The primary resource for women's history in England, the Fawcett Library, contains more published than archival sources. Much of the material in the Fawcett collection emphasizes women's public lives, such as their activities in the suffrage movement, rather than their family experiences. Although other materials, college archives and local history collections also exist, they are not always fully indexed and readily accessible to the researcher. As a result, this comparative chapter relies more on published biographical and autobiographical material than chapters 4, 5, and 6. As noted in the Preface, these sources can be less dependable than other types of documents, which suggests an additional issue that should be acknowledged.

5. Maria G. Grey, "The Women's Educational Movement," in Theodore Stanton, ed., *The Woman Question in Europe* (New York, 1884), 31.

6. David Rubinstein, *Before the Suffragettes: Women's Emancipation in the 1890s* (Brighton, England, 1986), 186; Joan N. Burstyn, *Victorian Education and the Ideal of Womanhood* (London, 1980), 26.

7. B. R. Mitchell, *British Historical Statistics* (Cambridge, England, 1988), 775, 811; B. R. Mitchell, *European Historical Statistics, 1750–1975*, 2d rev. ed. (New York, 1980), 62; Barbara Miller Solomon, *In the Company of Educated Women* (New Haven, 1985), 64.

One estimate suggests that in 1914, English and Welsh institutions other than Oxford and Cambridge (where women were not yet permitted to study as degree candidates) enrolled 2,900 females out of 11,000 full-time students; see Rita McWilliams Tullberg, "Women and Degrees at Cambridge University, 1862–1897," in Martha Vicinus, ed., *A Widening Sphere: Changing Roles of Victorian Women* (Bloomington, Ind., 1977), 293, note 1. The addition of the figures for Oxford and Cambridge would obviously raise the totals slightly, but not significantly; for example, figures from another source suggest that 437 female students were attending the women's colleges at Oxford and Cambridge in 1897; see Martha Vicinus, *Independent Women: Work and Community for Single Women, 1850–1920* (Chicago, 1985), 127.

8. Vicinus, *Independent Women*, 123, 139–40.

9. Alice M. Gordon, "The After-Careers of University-Educated Women," *Nineteenth Century* 37 (1895): 958; 960. See also Carol Dyhouse, *Girls Growing*

Up in Late Victorian and Edwardian England (London, 1981), 159–60; and Burstyn, *Victorian Education,* 148.

10. For discussions of the transatlantic cultural connections, see Daniel Walker Howe, "American Victorianism as a Culture," and David D. Hall, "The Victorian Connection," both in *American Quarterly* 27, 5 (December 1975): 502–32, 561–74; Stephen Mintz, *A Prison of Expectations: The Family in Victorian Culture* (New York, 1983); Elizabeth K. Helsinger et al., *The Woman Question: Defining Voices, 1837–1883* (New York, 1983), Introduction, xiii; Erna Olafson Hellerstein et al., *Victorian Women: A Documentary Account of Women's Lives in Nineteenth-Century England, France, and the United States* (Stanford, Calif., 1981), Introduction, 1; Stephen Spender, *Love-Hate Relations: English and American Sensibilities* (New York, 1975), Introduction, xvi; and Samuel Hynes, *The Edwardian Turn of Mind* (Princeton, N.J., 1968), 172–211. Christina Hardyment's study of child-rearing advice in England suggests that cross-cultural influences can be discerned in this context as well; see *Dream Babies: Three Centuries of Good Advice on Child Care* (New York, 1983).

11. Jane Mackay and Pat Thane, "The Englishwoman," in Robert Colls and Philip Dodd, eds., *Englishness: Politics and Culture, 1880–1920* (London, 1986), 200.

12. "The Girl of the Period," *Saturday Review* 25 (1868): 338–40, reprinted in *Living Age* 97 (1868): 188–90. The essay appeared under Linton's name for the first time in *The Girl of the Period and Other Social Essays,* in 1883. For an overview of the controversy, see Helsinger et al., *The Woman Question,* 103–25.

13. B. A. Crackanthorpe, "The Revolt of the Daughters," *Nineteenth Century* 35 (January 1894): 23–31. In the same volume, see also E. B. Harrison, "Mothers and Daughters" (February 1894): 313–22; and B. A. Crackanthorpe, "A Last Word on the Revolt," Alys Pearsall Smith, "A Reply from the Daughters," and Kathleen Cuffe, "A Reply from the Daughters" (March 1894): 424–36, 437–42, 443–50.

14. Sarah Grand, "The New Aspect of the Woman Question," *North American Review* 158 (1894): 271–73; Ouida [Louise Rame], "The New Woman," *North American Review* 158 (1894): 610–19. See also Mary Jeune, "The Revolt of the Daughters," *Fortnightly Review* 55 (1894): 267–76; Gertrude Hemery, "The Revolt of the Daughters: An Answer—By One of Them," *Westminster Review* 141 (1894): 679–81; and Sarah M. Amos, "The Revolution of the Daughters," *Contemporary Review* 65 (1894): 515–20.

15. For a summary of the commentary on the "new woman," see Rubinstein, *Before the Suffragettes,* 12–23.

16. Helsinger et al., *The Woman Question,* 113, 125; Rubinstein, *Before the Suffragettes,* 18.

17. Samuel Hynes addresses these issues at length in *The Edwardian Turn of Mind.* See also Philip Dodd, "Englishness and the National Culture," in Colls and Dodd, eds., *Englishness,* 1–28.

18. Mackay and Thane, "The Englishwoman," in Colls and Dodd, eds., *Englishness*, 202–5.

19. See, for example, in the column titled " 'Between Ourselves.' A Friendly Chat with the Girls," in *The Young Woman*, "The Sins of the Mothers," 3: 394; "On Leaving Home," 7: 197–98; "Tired Mothers," 8 (1900): 37–38; and, in a series of articles entitled "Letters to My Girl Friends" also in *The Young Woman*, "The Girl Who Knows More Than Her Mother," 4: 274–76. Also L.M.H. Soulsby, "Friendship and Love," in *Stray Thoughts for Girls* (London, 1910), 188, quoted in Vicinus, *Independent Women*, 176; and Florence Bell, "Concerning the Relation between Mothers and Daughters," *The Living Age*, 7th ser., 12, 230 (September 7, 1901), 593–602. Carol Dyhouse comments on the discussion of mother-daughter conflict in advice literature written for adolescent girls in "Mothers and Daughters in the Middle-Class Home c. 1870–1914," in Jane Lewis, ed., *Labour and Love: Women's Experience of Home and Family, 1850–1940* (Oxford, 1986), 43–44. See also Martha Vicinus, " 'One Life to Stand Beside Me': Emotional Conflicts in First-Generation College Women in England," *Feminist Studies* 8, 3 (Fall 1982): 603–28, and *Independent Women*, 10–45; also Crackanthorpe, "The Revolt of the Daughters."

20. Victor Gollancz, Preface, in Victor Gollancz, ed., *The Making of Women: Oxford Essays in Feminism* (London, 1917), 20; Josephine Pitcairn Knowles, *The Upholstered Cage* (London, 1913).

21. Constance found her father "always easier than Mother to manage when a request was on hand"; see C. B. Firth, *Constance Louisa Maynard, Mistress of Westfield College: A Family Portrait* (London, 1949), 54, 93, 102.

22. Constance Maynard, unpublished autobiography, Westfield College Archives, quoted in Vicinus, *Independent Women*, 137.

23. For example, her commitment to the idea of accepting God's will, her concern with self-control, her strict avoidance of novels and the theater, and her unsuccessful effort to communicate with and help a young woman she had adopted clearly reflected aspects of her mother's influence; see Firth, *Constance Louisa Maynard*, 141, 150.

24. Constance Jones apparently enjoyed an international reputation as a logician. When Sara Burstall, a respected educator in her own right, visited an American university in the Midwest in 1907, she was very much interested to find that the only knowledge her hosts had of Girton was the fact that Jones taught there. Burstall also noted the difficulties Constance Jones faced as a result of her family's lack of support for her ambitions. See *Retrospect and Prospect: Sixty Years of Women's Education* (London, 1933), 68–70.

25. E. E. Constance Jones, *As I Remember: An Autobiographical Ramble* (London, 1922), 1–6, 8, 49, 43.

26. Ibid., 3.

27. "Mary Lynda Dorothea Grier (1880–1967): A Memoir," *Brown Book*, May 1968, 2–10, 23–25, cited in Vicinus, *Independent Women*, 137.

28. Helena M. Swanwick, *I Have Been Young* (London, 1935), 84, 115–16, 117–18, 138–39.

29. Ibid., 118.

30. Ibid., 58.

31. Ibid., 58, 82–83.

32. Margaret W. Nevinson, *Life's Fitful Fever: A Volume of Memories* (London, 1926), 44–45.

33. Ibid., 17–18.

34. Ibid., 44.

35. Ibid., 71.

36. Ibid., 1, 112.

37. Vera Brittain, *Chronicle of Youth: The War Diary, 1913–1917*, ed. Alan Bishop with Terry Smart (New York, 1982), 84; and *Testament of Youth* (New York, 1980 [1933]), 32–33, 59–60, 73.

38. Deborah Gorham, " 'Have We Really Rounded Seraglio Point?': Vera Brittain and Inter-War Feminism," in Harold L. Smith, ed., *British Feminism in the Twentieth Century* (Amherst, Mass., 1990), 84.

39. *Testament of Youth*, 59.

40. Ibid., 146.

41. April 8 and April 24, 1913, *Chronicle of Youth*, 33, 34.

42. April 24, 1913; October 21, 1913; November 15, 1913; and September 4, 1914; ibid., 34–35, 39–40, 103.

43. December 12, 1914, and January 2, 1916, ibid., 130, 304.

44. November 29, 1913, ibid., 46.

45. April 24, 1913, ibid., 34–35.

46. Helena Deneke, *Grace Hadow* (London, 1946), 20, quoted in Vicinus, *Independent Women*, 173.

47. Octavia Wilberforce, "The Eighth Child," unpublished autobiography, I, 90, Fawcett Library, City of London Polytechnic, London.

48. Ibid., I, 89, 122.

49. Ibid., I, 139, 167.

50. Ibid., I, 191; II, 219.

51. M. V. Hughes, *A London Child of the 1870s* (Oxford, 1977 [1934]), 44.

52. Molly Hughes described the moment when she showed her first love letter to her mother as follows: "One of my most pleasing memories is the look on her face when I handed her my first love-letter, with the words, 'Would you like to read it, mother?' 'Do you really mean it?' she said in astonishment. She must have known how much it cost me to do this, and she took it as though it was a sacrament she was receiving. So it was—a kind of benison on all the restraint, absence of persuasion or interference, absence of all inquisitiveness, that she had maintained towards her only daughter." M. V. Hughes, *A London Girl of the 1880s* (Oxford, 1978 [1946]), 161.

53. M. V. Hughes, *A London Home in the 1890s* (Oxford, 1978 [1946]), 2.

54. Hughes, *A London Girl in the 1880s*, 240.

55. Hughes, *A London Home in the 1890s*, 138.

56. Helen noted that her mother "had little use for books, and during my school-days believed I should sleep better if I read less—which was probably true"; Helen Corke, *In Our Infancy: An Autobiography. Part I: 1882–1912* (Cambridge, England, 1975), 139.

57. Ibid., 96.

58. Ibid., 88.

59. Ibid., 97.

60. Ibid., 139.

61. Ibid., 131, 139.

62. Ibid., 148–55, 168.

63. Lilian M. Faithfull, *In the House of My Pilgrimage* (London, 1924), 30.

64. Ibid., 24.

65. Ibid., 17–18.

66. *Retrospect & Prospect*, 33–34, 41–42.

67. Ibid., 23–24, 43–47.

68. Evelyn Sharp, *Hertha Ayrton, 1854–1923: A Memoir* (London, 1926), 4–11.

69. Ibid., 4, 20–22, 134, 113.

70. Ibid., 125, 154, 198, 204, 216. The biographer's acknowledged friendship and admiration for her subject almost certainly account for her choice of this adjective to characterize the mother-daughter relationship, but apparently the relationship was a very compatible one.

71. Ibid., 198.

72. See, for example, her enthusiastic comments about the crusade for suffrage in letters dated July 15 and 16, 1910. She wrote: "Dearest Mother. . . . I am awfully glad the bill passed with such a good majority"; Box 395, Elsie Bowerman Papers, Fawcett Library, City of London Polytechnic, London. See also letters from Dorothea Taylor to her mother, who was arrested and jailed for her activities, for example, March 3, 1912: "Dearest Mother, We are all so very proud of you . . . I do hope you will be treated well," and April 11, 1912: "We are always thinking about you & I know you are about us"; both on microfiche, Autograph Collection, 26B, Fawcett Library.

73. November 17 and 20, 1910, Box 395, Bowerman Papers. In the November 20 letter, she also described in considerable detail her own participation in a hockey match at Girton. For other examples of the more conventional matters Elsie discussed with her mother, see her letters of August 21, October 13, 16, 20, and 30, and November 6, 1910, also in Box 395, Bowerman Papers.

74. July 5, 1916. See letters dated July 17, September 30, October 24, and November 27, 1916, Box 396, Bowerman Papers.

75. Marie Corbett to her daughter, October 18, 1901, Box 474, Dame Margery Irene Corbett Ashby Papers, Fawcett Library Archives, City of London Polytechnic, London.

76. Marie Corbett to her daughter, June 6, 1910, Box 475, Folder A 25, Ashby Papers.

77. See, for example, letters dated October 5, 10, and 15, and 19, 1901; February 15, 1902; and several letters written in January and February 1904; Box 474, Ashby Papers.

78. Margery Corbett Ashby to Marie Corbett, November 13, 1903, Folder 21, Box 474, Ashby Papers.

79. Margery Corbett Ashby to Marie Corbett, April 26, 1923, Box 477, Folder A 32, Ashby Papers.

80. Marie Corbett to Margery Corbett Ashby, May 27, 1910, Box 475, Folder A 25, Ashby Papers. Similarly, no evidence of conflict appears in Kathleen Courtney's frequent and lengthy correspondence with her mother. Although the tone of her letters is less intense than those of Elsie Bowerman and Margery Corbett Ashby, their contents suggest that she too enjoyed her mother's approval and support while she was in college, and later as well. See, for example, her letters from a school in Dresden in 1896, Box 454, A-2, and Box 474, A-2; from Oxford in 1897, Box 454, A-3, and Box 474, A-3; and from Europe, where she did relief work after World War I, Box 454, C-2; Dame Kathleen D'Olier Courtney Papers, Fawcett Library Archives, City of London Polytechnic, London. On one occasion, Kathleen felt compelled to apologize for the length of a twenty-four-page letter: "I am afraid you will be rather horrified on receiving it, but there is really a good deal to say" (February 14, 1897); Box 454, A-3.

81. Ruth Ashmore, "A Girl's Best Friend," *Ladies Home Journal* 8 (May 1881): 12.

82. Carl N. Degler, *At Odds: Women and the Family in America from the Revolution to the Present* (New York, 1980), 180; J. E. Goldthorpe, *Family Life in Western Societies: A Historical Sociology of Family Relationships in Britain and North America* (New York, 1987), 38.

83. Burstall, *Retrospect and Prospect*, 114. Another contemporary observer commented in 1889 that "the provision for women's education in the United States is ampler and better than that made in any European countries"; James Bryce, *The American Commonwealth*, vol. 2 (London and New York, 1889), 589–90, quoted in Ernest Earnest, *The American Eve in Fact and Fiction, 1775–1914* (Urbana, Ill., 1974), 236.

84. Rubinstein, *Before the Suffragettes*, 185; Dyhouse, *Girls Growing Up*, 3, 40, 55–57; Burstyn, *Victorian Education and the Ideal of Womanhood*, 22–24; Sara Delamont, "The Contradictions in Ladies' Education," in Sara Delamont and Lorna Duffin, eds., *The Nineteenth-Century Woman: Her Cultural and Physical World* (New York, 1978), 134–63; and Winifred Peck, *A Little Learning or a Victorian Childhood* (London, 1952), 104, 127–28.

85. Earnest, *The American Eve in Fact and Fiction*, 84, 47; Richard L. Rapson, "The American Child as Seen by British Travelers," in Michael Gordon, ed., *The American Family in Social-Historical Perspective* (New York, 1973), 192–208. With regard to criticism of the freedom granted to American girls, see also the observations of Alice Corkran, editor of the popular periodical, *Girl's Realm*, that "a frivolous American is perhaps one of the most

frivolous beings in the world," in "On Being Engaged," *Girl's Realm* 1 (1898–99): 954, quoted in Mackay and Thane, "The Englishwoman," 202.

86. A. M. Low, *America at Home* (London, 1905), 74, quoted in Rapson, "The American Child," 201–2.

87. "English and American Girlhood," *Harper's Weekly* 54 (October 22, 1910): 8–9.

88. Dyhouse, "Mothers and Daughters in the Middle-Class Home." See also Leonore Davidoff, *The Best Circles: Society Etiquette and the Season* (London, 1973). In her memoirs of middle-class life during this period, Ursula Bloom observed: "The whole of England remorselessly followed a complacent pattern of living in a niche above their own, for the desire of every head of the family, of his stoutening wife and his growing family, was to be the someone who was spoken of as being 'a little better' "; *Sixty Years of Home* (London, 1960), 13.

89. Leonore Davidoff and Catherine Hall, *Family Fortunes: Men and Women of the English Middle Class, 1780–1850* (Chicago, 1987). Also see Davidoff, *The Best Circles*.

90. Katherine Chorley, *Manchester Made Them* (London, 1950), 156.

91. Davidoff and Hall, *Family Fortunes*, 385.

92. For example, during the first course at dinner, a lady spoke to the man who had escorted her to the dining room; when the fish course arrived, she turned to the man on her left, and this pattern continued throughout the meal. After dessert, ladies left the dining room in the order of seniority, with married women first. Bloom, *Sixty Years of Home*, 109. The rules for calling were equally specific. Calling cards of the correct size had to be properly printed; the right corner was turned down if the call was personal, but if a servant took the card, no corner was turned down. A lady left one card, but her husband left two—one for his wife and a smaller one for himself. Chorley, *Manchester Made Them*, 152–53.

93. The drill and discipline to which she referred included attention to the necessity for proper attire as well as a firm grasp of the intricacies regarding whom one might appropriately visit and receive, and when; Chorley, *Manchester Made Them*, 152–53, and Bloom, *Sixty Years of Home*, 109–10.

94. Chorley, *Manchester Made Them*, 263.

95. Bloom, *Sixty Years of Home*, 50–51.

96. Bloom, *Sixty Years of Home*, 96–97; Chorley, *Manchester Made Them*, 101; Eleanor Acland, *Good-bye for the Present: The Story of Two Childhoods. Milly, 1878–88, & Ellen, 1913–24* (New York, 1935), 146–47. As a result of this practice, one of Eleanor Acland's siblings was accidentally left in the lavatory from teatime until bedtime.

97. Bloom, *Sixty Years of Home*, 116; Brittain, *Chronicle of Youth*, March 4, 1913, 30–31. See also Corke, *In Our Infancy*, 93.

98. For example, they discussed a young woman who had disappeared and been disowned by her parents, and a man who had fallen in love with someone during the war and never returned to his family. Katherine was

embarrassed by these conversations, and her mother was even more embarrassed. Chorley, *Manchester Made Them*, 269–70.

99. Ibid., 102.

100. Ibid., 246, 160, 252–53.

101. It is interesting that Katherine only recognized her mother's strength after her father's death; ibid., 110–11.

102. Bloom, *Sixty Years of Home*, 116–17. This mandate recalls Margaret Nevinson's observations about her mother's legacy of advice on the subject of hiring maids. See above, p. 144.

103. M. Jeanne Peterson, *Family, Love, and Work in the Lives of Victorian Gentlewomen* (Bloomington, Ind., 1989), 104; Dyhouse, "Mothers and Daughters in the Middle-Class Home," 29–30; Davidoff, *The Best Circles*, 53.

104. Paul Thompson, *The Edwardians: The Remaking of British Society* (London, 1977), 62; Thea Thompson, *Edwardian Childhoods* (London, 1981), 169–70. This distance between parents and children was also typical of upper-class families. See, for example, the experiences of Joan Poynder, in Thea Thompson, *Edwardian Childhoods*, 216, 219, 223–34, 226, 228–29, and Lady Violet Brandon, in Paul Thompson, *The Edwardians*, 98.

105. Thea Thompson, *Edwardian Childhoods*, 180, 174.

106. In this case, however, the lines of mother-daughter communication remained open; Grace found her mother easy to talk to, and she felt comfortable discussing her worries about the opposite sex with her. Paul Thompson, *The Edwardians*, 103–5.

107. Acland, *Good-bye for the Present*, 68, 27, 118, 25, 150, 196. As an adult, Eleanor Acland remembered her mother as a source of pure love for her children, and she took great pleasure in observing her behavior as a grandmother; see pp. 86–87.

108. Chorley, *Manchester Made Them*, 38–39.

109. Peck, *A Little Learning*, 31.

110. For lower-middle class mothers, economic security was clearly more important than social prescriptions, and thus they understood and supported daughters' aspirations, for example, their efforts to seek teaching jobs; see Frances Widdowson, " 'Educating Teacher': Women and Elementary Teaching in London, 1900–1914," in Leonore Davidoff and Belinda Westover, eds., *Our Work, Our Lives, Our Words: Women's History & Women's Work* (London, 1986), 99–123.

111. Bouchier, *The Feminist Challenge*, 13; Branca, *Silent Sisterhood*, 10–11.

112. Gwen Raverat, *Period Piece: A Cambridge Childhood* (London, 1952), 40, 48, 51.

113. She also objected to the custom of mothers chaperoning girls at parties. "I hope that when Gwen grows up there will be a revolution in this respect, and I hope that she will help to bring it around," she wrote on another occasion; ibid., 99–100.

114. Ibid., 76.

115. Ibid., 100.

116. Ibid., 276–77.

117. Ibid., 154. As Leonore Davidoff has pointed out, intellectuals functioned more as an alternative society than as participants in conventional middle-class society, and the Darwin family offers an example of this phenomenon; *The Best Circles*, 77.

118. Raverat, *Period Piece*, 129.

119. Ibid., 104. Ursula Bloom also commented on the hypocrisy of a society in which everything was "socially catalogued"; *Sixty Years of Home*, 13.

120. Davidoff, *The Best Circles*.

121. For additional examples, see the feelings expressed by Mrs. C. Hutton Beale, who feared that she would never recover from the loss of her mother, and Rebecca Solly Shaen, who experienced her mother's death as " 'a very bitter grief' " because "with every feeling gratified as a Wife and Mother, I have felt most keenly that I was also a daughter"; Mrs. C. Hutton Beale, *Reminiscences of a Gentlewoman of the Last Century* (Birmingham, England, 1891), 116, and Rebecca Solly Shaen, unpublished commonplace book, John Johnson Collection, Bodleian Library, Oxford University, 266, both quoted in Davidoff, *The Best Circles*, 341. For a discussion of mother-daughter relationships as revealed in women's personal diaries from the late sixteenth century to the twentieth century, see Harriet Blodgett, *Centuries of Female Days: Englishwomen's Private Diaries* (New Brunswick, N.J., 1988), particularly 223–31.

122. Virginia Woolf, *A Room of One's Own* (New York, 1929, 1957), 4. See, for example, the experiences of Helena Swanwick, Lynda Grier, and Winifred Peck, above, pp. 142–43, and Peck, *A Little Learning*, 156.

123. Olive Banks, *Becoming a Feminist: The Social Origins of "First Wave" Feminism* (Brighton, England, 1986), 25–31, 33, 144.

124. See discussions of the experiences of Mercy Otis Warren in Earnest, *The American Eve in Fact and Fiction*, 13–15, and Jane Addams, Sarah and Angelina Grimke, Catharine Beecher, and Emily Dickinson in Mabel Collins Donnelly, *The American Victorian Woman: The Myth and the Reality* (New York, 1986), 21–35.

125. See, for example, the cases of Mary Frances Buss of the North London Collegiate School, who encouraged her most capable students to enroll at Girton, loaned them money, and helped them to prepare for the scholarship examination; Clare Arnold, who intervened on behalf of her student, Grace Hadow, to help her get permission to continue her studies; and the comments of Emily Davies regarding the pleasures of college life as compared with the lives of young women at home; in Vicinus, *Independent Women*, 140, 173, 128.

126. Ibid., 138.

127. See Carol Dyhouse's interpretation of the relationship between feminism and the family between 1880 and 1939, especially her observation: "Indeed it was precisely their dissatisfaction with the family that fuelled their feminism"; *Feminism and the Family in England*, 3. As the English suffrage

campaign became increasingly militant in the early years of the twentieth century, it served as a model for American suffragists who closely monitored the progress of their counterparts across the Atlantic; Sara M. Evans, *Born for Liberty: A History of Women in America* (New York, 1989), 165.

8. *"Mother Drove Us in the Studebaker"*

1. Peter G. Filene, *Him/Her/Self: Sex Roles in Modern America*, 2d ed. (Baltimore, 1986), 115–35; Jane Sherron De Hart, "The New Feminism and the Dynamics of Social Change," in Linda K. Kerber and Jane Sherron De Hart, eds., *Women's America: Refocusing the Past*, 3d ed. (New York, 1991), 493–521.

2. Paula S. Fass, *The Damned and the Beautiful: American Youth in the 1920s* (New York, 1977), 13–52. The definition of "young people" is from George A. Coe, *What Ails Our Youth?* (1924), quoted in ibid., 13.

3. Nancy F. Cott, *The Grounding of Modern Feminism* (New Haven, 1987), 149.

4. Fass, *The Damned and the Beautiful*.

5. Robert S. Lynd and Helen Merrell Lynd, *Middletown: A Study in Contemporary American Culture* (New York, 1929), 135.

6. Ibid., 133.

7. Ibid., Appendix, Table 13: Sources of Disagreement between 348 Boys and 382 Girls and Their Parents, 522.

8. Ibid., 143.

9. Ibid., Appendix, Table 14: Traits to Be Stressed in Rearing Children as Rated by Housewives for Themselves in 1924 and for Their Mothers in the Nineties, 523.

10. Ibid., 136.

11. Ibid., Table 14, 523; also 162–63.

12. Ibid., Table 13, 522. See also John Modell, *Into One's Own: From Youth to Adulthood in the United States, 1920–1975* (Berkeley, 1989), for additional discussion of the newly sophisticated high school social life of this period.

13. See letters from Jessie Tarbox Beals to Nanette Beals, October and November 1926, Carton 1, Folder 8, Jessie Tarbox Beals Collection, Schlesinger Library, Radcliffe College.

14. One contemporary investigation determined that while 80 percent of daughters surveyed approved of smoking, only 26 percent of their parents agreed; Phyllis Blanchard and Carolyn Manasses, *New Girls for Old* (New York, 1930), quoted in Dorothy M. Brown, *Setting A Course: American Women in the 1920s* (Boston, 1987), 142.

15. Fass, *The Damned and the Beautiful*, 92–94; Elaine Tyler May, *Great Expectations: Marriage & Divorce in Post-Victorian America* (Chicago, 1980), 89; Brown, *Setting A Course*, 102–3, 112.

16. Lucille Palmer Cavender to her mother and father, December 29,

1921, Box 4, Folder 58, Elsie Miller Palmer Collection, Schlesinger Library, Radcliffe College.

17. E. Gertrude Palmer Gaines to her parents, n.d.; June 3, 1927; n.d., 1929 (between January and May); Box 5, Folders 74, 76, and 79, ibid.

18. Fass, *The Damned and the Beautiful*, 37.

19. James R. McGovern, "The American Woman's Pre-World War I Freedom in Manners and Morals"; May, *Great Expectations*, 63.

20. Brown, *Setting a Course*, 31.

21. For example, a 1923 survey revealed that in the freshman, sophomore, junior, and senior classes at Little Falls, Minnesota, High School, more than three girls in four had bobbed hair. While this figure could reflect daughters' determined opposition to maternal wishes, mothers' weary capitulation in the face of overwhelming odds, or their recognition that this fad was less dangerous than other manifestations of the contemporary peer culture, it may also illustrate that adult women actually found this new hairstyle attractive. See Modell, *Into One's Own*, 102.

22. Fass, *The Damned and the Beautiful*, 365–66; Filene, *Him/Her/Self*, 122–3.

23. Filene, *Him/Her/Self*, 132.

24. *New York Times*, April 6, 1930; Blanchard and Manasses, *New Girls for Old*, 174–75, quoted in Filene, *Him/Her/Self*, 128.

25. Fass, *The Damned and the Beautiful*, 376.

26. See, for example, John B. Watson, *Psychological Care of Infant and Child* (New York, 1928).

27. There is a hint of this in Ethel Sturges Dummer's dialogue with her daughter Frances on the subject of flirting. See chapter 4, pp. 85–86.

28. Robert S. Lynd and Helen Merrell Lynd, *Middletown in Transition; A Study in Cultural Conflicts* (New York, 1937), 168–71.

29. See Elaine Tyler May's observations concerning the relevance of individual divorce cases in the study of changing expectations and experiences of marriage: "Each unique testimony itself serves as a microscope through which it is possible to examine the effects of historical change on individual lives"; *Great Expectations*, 11.

30. The quotations are from letters dated July 23, 1933, and June 5, 1928, Adele Siegel Rosenfeld Papers, unprocessed collection, Schlesinger Library, Radcliffe College. The second letter is also dated as follows: (July ! 1928); the notation concerning the form of address appears in turquoise ink. See also a letter dated July 13, 1930, which illustrates the same casual tone. The conditions of use for this collection require that the writers' names be omitted. For contrasting examples, see chapters 4 and 5.

31. The note could also indicate that the writer had a troubled relationship with her mother, but other evidence suggests that this was not the case. See below, pp. 190–91.

32. See, for example, this young woman's comments in another letter, January 16, 1934: "I've just finished speaking to you, and last night father

was here, and Sunday Marion was with me all afternoon. Nevertheless you want a letter, and I'm willing to oblige." In Carton 1, Rosenfeld Papers.

33. Jane Emmet Drake to her mother Helen Pratt Emmet, n.d., 1938, Folder 1, Box 5, unprocessed collection, Alan Summersby Emmet Papers, Schlesinger Library, Radcliffe College.

34. See chapter 4, p. 75.

35. July 23, 1933, Carton 1, Rosenfeld Papers.

36. See, for example, entries dated February 7, June 12, July 7, 1953; January 25, August 12, October 24, 1954; and June 9, 1958; June Calender Diaries, June Calender Papers, Schlesinger Library, Radcliffe College.

37. February 11, January 23, and April 19, 1945, Adele Mongan Fasick Diary, Schlesinger Library, Radcliffe College.

38. March 4, 1945, ibid.

39. See chapter 4, p. 83.

40. December 23, 1940, Helene Harmon Weis Diary, Schlesinger Library, Radcliffe College. See also Helene's comments of December 28, 1940: "Mother felt called upon to give me talk about going off with him alone. Good Hoot! He didn't fascinate me as much as he did her. She is nuts about him." The resentment expressed here contrasts distinctly with Maud Rittenhouse's obvious pleasure over her mother's interest in her suitors. See chapter 4, pp. 82–83.

41. April 22 and August 25, 1941, Helene Harmon Weis Diary.

42. March 29, 1943, ibid.

43. N.d. (June or July), 1943, ibid.

44. See diary entries of July 2, 1943: "I love my Mother so much; if only she didn't think I was doing this just to anger her"; and July 19, 1943: "Mother took it rather badly but we went back to visit her on Friday evening and she was just lovely to us"; in ibid.

45. With regard to the engagement, see, for example, a reference to her reliance on the support of friends: "Thank heaven I have a friend like Keith, I have needed him so much at times"; September 15, 1959, June Calender Diaries, Calender Papers.

46. September 7 and November 18, 1941; August 3, 1942; May 12, 1942; and September 6, 1940; Helene Harmon Weis Diary.

47. See, for example, her comments about one such occasion: "Mom and I are at home alone. We had quite a talk. I love to talk for a while like we did. It makes me feel real daughterish"; February 12, 1953, June Calender Diaries, Calender Papers.

48. October 11 and February 27, 1953, and January 25, 1954, ibid. See also an entry on July 7, 1953: "Mom said to me that she thought who ever that boy was I danced with last night was the cutest one there."

49. June 12, 1953, ibid.

50. May 30, 1945, Adele Mongan Fasick Diary.

51. November 2, 1959, Ruth Teischman [pseudonym] Diary, Schlesinger

Library, Radcliffe College. The original diary is closed until January 1, 2043, but a copy with names removed is available for research.

52. Jane E. Emmet to Helen Pratt Emmet, May 23, 1942, and June 8, 1942, Box 4, Emmet Papers.

53. Jane E. Emmet to Richard S. Emmet, Jr., n.d., 1943, and n.d., 1943 or 1944, Box 4, ibid.

54. December 9, 1945, and February 6, 1946, ibid.

55. January 20, 1946, ibid. Jane Emmet suffered from diabetes, which created special problems for her as an adolescent seeking to develop independence.

56. Augusta Salik Dublin to Mary Dublin Keyserling, November 26, 1931, Carton 1, Folder 8, Mary Dublin Keyserling Papers, Schlesinger Library, Radcliffe College. Mrs. Dublin's problems exemplify the frustration experienced by "postmaternal women," nonworking women with adult children, whose plight was highlighted by early twentieth-century discourses that emphasized their loneliness, their "potential," their superannuation, and their economic helplessness and social uselessness—and this convinced them that they were objects of pity. See Margaret Morganroth Gullette, "Inventing the Postmaternal Woman (1898–1926): Idle, Unwanted, and Out of a Job," unpublished manuscript.

57. Mrs. Dublin continued to share her problems with her daughter through the 1940s. Noting that she spent her time gardening, mending, sewing, and knitting, she commented: "What a stupid life for an intelligent person!" She also complained of boredom and the fact that her husband remained "stubborn as you know, domineering as ever and completely inconsiderate of me." See letters to Mary Dublin Keyserling, June 28, 1944; August 8, 1949; and August 19, 1949; Carton 1, Folders 11 and 15, Keyserling Papers.

58. Augusta Salik Dublin to Mary Dublin Keyserling, June 26, 1932, Carton 1, Folder 8, ibid. It is interesting to note that in addition to serving as her mother's confidante and mentor, Mary managed to maintain a close relationship with her father; see letters from Louis Dublin to Mary Dublin Keyserling, in Carton 1, Folders 24, 25, 26, 27, and 28. Mrs. Dublin believed that Mary was her husband's favorite of their four children although she thought he would never admit the fact to himself; Augusta Salik Dublin to Mary Dublin Keyserling, July 12, 1932, in Carton 1, Folder 8.

59. Paula Fass cites evidence from several studies in support of the idea that fathers were becoming more involved in child-rearing. She argues that men's new interest in aspects of child care indicates that a new concept of parenthood was replacing the previous dichotomy between the role of the mother and that of the father; The Damned and the Beautiful, 86–87.

60. December 2, 1945, Adele Mongan Fasick Diary.

61. May 14, 1953, June Calender Diaries, Calender Papers.

62. March 8, 1943, Helene Harmon Weis Diary.

63. Jane Emmet Drake to Helen Pratt Emmet, n.d. (Fall 1945), Folder 2, Box 5, Emmet Papers. See also her candid observation to her brother: "To be frank, I'm sure I would fight like hell if I lived with Ma anyway"; n.d. (1943 or 1944), to Richard S. Emmet, Jr., in Box 4.

64. J. H. Cosgrave, "Mothers and Daughters," *Good Housekeeping* 81 (September 1925): 34–35; (October 1925): 70–71; (November 1925): 36–37; "Why I Do Not Confide in My Mother," *Woman's Home Companion* 53 (June 1926): 34; F. Howitt, "Do You Know Everything in Your Daughter's Head?" *Good Housekeeping* 120 (January 1945): 28; M. Riddell, "Girl's Best Friend," *Atlantic* 196 (October 1955): 99–100.

65. A. S. Duryea, "Revaluing Motherhood: Mothers Who Devour and Mothers Who Develop Their Children," *Century* 109 (April 1925): 737–43; B. Barmby, "Smother Love," *Pictorial Review* 29 (August 1928): 1; G. Woodcock, "Are Our Daughters Overprotected?" *Parents Magazine* 10 (October 1935): 25; E. A. Whitman, "Twelve Ways to Be a Friend to Your Daughter," *Parents Magazine* 19 (June 1944): 72; E. K. Morse, "Wanted: Mothers, Not Imitation Sisters," *Parents Magazine* 23 (September 1948): 161; D. Barclay, "How Girls Judge Mother's Role," *New York Times Magazine* (June 21, 1953): 32.

66. B. B. Creel, "Job or Joy Ride: Is It Harder Work to be a Mother Than a Daughter?" *Century* 115 (November 1927): 41–46; W. O. Saunders, "Me and My Flapper Daughter," *American Magazine* 104 (August 1927): 27; E. Boykin, "Should Mothers Be Matchmakers?" *Parents Magazine* 11 (August 1936): 20–21; C. Wheeler and M. Nelson, eds., "What A Mother Should Tell Her Daughter," *Parents Magazine* 25 (March 1950): 36–37.

67. I. H. Irwin, "Insuring Your Daughter's Success," *Woman's Home Companion* 63 (December 1936): 22; I. S. Hunter, "Raising American Beauties," *Ladies Home Journal* 53 (October 1936): 89; G. D. Schultz, "Mother Answers a Morals SOS from her Daughter," *Better Homes and Gardens* 22 (March 1944): 15; M. L. Runbeck, "Suitcase and the Key: Remember When You Were 16," *Woman's Home Companion* 71 (August 1944): 29; M. Holmes, "Are You Helping Your Daughter to be Popular?" *Better Homes and Gardens* 27 (February 1949): 80; "Are You Training Your Daughter to be a Good Wife?" *Better Homes and Gardens* 27 (April 1949): 192–93; L. P. Benjamin, "Is Your Little Girl a Good Wife?" *Ladies Home Journal* 64 (November 1947): 34–35; D. Francis, "Unpopular Daughter," *Good Housekeeping* 129 (November 1949): 43; "How to Bring Up a Beauty," *Good Housekeeping* 146 (May 1958): 56.

68. "When Should She Start Dating," *Woman's Home Companion* 74 (November 1947): 7–8.

69. See, for example, entries for January 13, February 10, and March 14, 1923; March 3 and May 16, 1924; Baby Book, Box 1, Helene Harmon Weis Papers. One clipping consisted of a picture of a smiling baby and the following brief homily that may have characterized her own identifiably traditional feelings about being a mother: "Happy Motherhood is founded on Right

Living, Right Thinking, Right Loving. . . . Right Loving means the belief that parenthood is a divine gift and that little children are the crowning joy of living." After Helene's second birthday, regular entries became less frequent, and they ended with a full description of her third birthday. However, her mother continued to save various mementoes and clippings.

70. October 31, 1935, Box 1, Ruth Slocum Tilghman Smith Robinson Diaries, Schlesinger Library, Radcliffe College. She particularly enjoyed dressing Anne up and watching her play with her dolls; Introduction, January 11, 15, 19, and May 12, 1935. At this time, Ruth Robinson's husband was the head of a boys' school in Morristown, New Jersey. Thus they were surrounded by boys in addition to their own sons. Probably the birth of her two daughters seemed even more of a novelty in this context.

71. February 14, 1944, and Introduction, 1944, ibid.

72. April 3, 1935; Introduction; and September 4, 1944; all in ibid. She seems to have been more concerned about raising unselfish daughters than unselfish sons, although she had twice as many of the latter to deal with.

73. February 20 and August 4, 1944, and June 8, 1954, Box 1, ibid. It is interesting that where Anne's active social life was concerned, it was not the impropriety of preteens socializing nightly that distressed her mother, but the fact that these activities might threaten her health: "Its [sic] staying up late I object to—I must keep her strong and well and sleep is so important," she explained; see August 4, 1944.

74. These comments are contained in a note, apparently to herself, dated January 18, n.d. (probably 1954), ibid.

75. For the birthday poems, see the diary entry for November 19, 1944. For expressions of her daughters' feelings, see several undated letters written in 1954 by Anne and Sally to their mother. For examples of Ruth Robinson's feelings about her daughters, see diary entries January 16, February 2, March 3 and 18, May 5, 1954, all in Box 1; and December 8, 1964, February 4 and March 3, 1972, in Box 2, ibid.

76. September 7 and September 12, 1959, Teischman Diary. Ruth expressed a similar sentiment on another occasion when she wrote: "I think life is great and I never want to die—except with my mother"; October 25, 1959.

77. September 6, December 1, and October 23, 1959, ibid.

78. See, for example, her comments after she argued with her mother about drinking a glass of milk: "We had a fight and I was very mad at her. But now I've forgiven her and we're friends again . . . I know my mother really does love me, and I love her!" (October 24, 1959), and her reaction when her mother joked about not really loving her: "She made me feel very bad. But then I told her to say she didn't really mean it and she said it. I felt so much better!" (November 6, 1959), both in Teischman Diary.

79. See, for example, the striking resemblance between Ruth's anxiety about the prospect of her mother's death and similar concerns expressed by Mary Anderson Boit over fifty years earlier, in chapter 4, p. 73.

80. See, for example, the letters in Box 1, Folders 6, 7, 8, and 9; Box 2, Folders 10, 11, and 12; and Box 3, Folder 20, Minnie Florence Roop Millette Papers, Schlesinger Library, Radcliffe College.

81. For examples of concern about Nancy's health, see letters dated September 9, November 4 and 18, 1929, and October 5, 1930. See, for example, "Thanksgiving without you is dreadful," November 26, 1928, and "I miss you like the dickens," Box 1, Folder 7, ibid.

82. Minnie Millette to Nancy Millette Mosher, October 15, 1929, ibid.

83. See chapter 5, p. 96.

84. Minnie Millette to Nancy Millette Mosher, May 16, 1932, Box 2, Folder 10, Millette Papers. See also another letter in which Mrs. Millette noted that the Depression had made parents especially anxious to insure that their offspring would be able to earn a living: "Three months on a paper [newspaper] might show you whether you cared for that sort of work. And too, it would serve after you get out of college—in showing that you had had experience in some line of work. . . . Whatever you do will be all right with me just so you do not overdo yourself," December 8, 1931, Box 1, Folder 9.

85. Minnie Millette to Nancy Millette Mosher, November 20, 1930, Box 1, Folder 8, ibid.

86. Minnie Millette to Nancy Millette Mosher, September 21 and October 9, 1929, Box 1, Folder 7, ibid.

87. Minnie Millette to Nancy Millette Mosher, January 21, 1932, Box 2, Folder 10; November 14 and December 6, 1930, Box 1, Folder 8; January 21, 1932, Box 2, Folder 10; November 14 and December 6, 1930, Box 1, Folder 8. All in ibid. For earlier examples of maternal interest in daughters' academic experiences, see chapter 5.

88. "When you recite your menu it sounds better than anything we ever have," January 16, 1935, Box 2, Folder 12; April 3, 1939, and May 16, 1939, both in Box 3, Folder 20, ibid.

89. See, for example, Mrs. Millette's reply to Nancy's comments on Hitler and her observations about the relationship between Russia and England in letters dated February 2, 1939, and April 20, 1939, Box 3, Folder 20, ibid.

90. See her advice regarding the importance of checking for bed bugs in a vacation accommodation, July 3, 1935, and her comments on Nancy's shopping habits: "I feel better since you mentioned that you have your hamburger ground from perfectly fresh meat. That way you can cook it rare if you choose—of course I am glad that you are thrifty, but I can't feel good about your buying unsafe meat—or decaying fruit or wilted old vegetables," August 4, 1935, ibid.

91. Minnie Millette to Nancy Millette Mosher, April 8, 1939, Box 3, Folder 20, and n.d., 1958, Box 1, Folder 6, ibid.

92. See, for example, advice from Ethel Arens Tyng to Mary Tyng Higgins about Mary's son: "I am not trying to run you or him, just suggesting," June 5, 1948; comments regarding a proposed trip, "I don't like to dictate you a mode of travel, but it seems to me . . . that it will be a very hectic

journey. . . . Did you consider flying?" October 10, 1948; and discussions of a miscarriage and possible pregnancy, September 16 and October 29, 1948; all in Series I, Folder 10, Mary Tyng Higgins Papers, Schlesinger Library, Radcliffe College.

93. Ethel Arens Tyng to Mary Tyng Higgins, September 6, 1952; November 14, 1956; and January 17, 1957; Series I, Folder 12, ibid.

94. January 2, 1942, Ethel Arens Tyng Diary, Series I, Higgins Papers.

95. Augusta Salik Dublin to Mary Dublin Keyserling, February 25, 1932, Carton 1, Folder 8; May 19, 1947, Carton 1, Folder 13; April 3, 1960, Carton 1, Folder 23; Keyserling Papers.

96. Judy Barrett Litoff and David Smith, eds., *Miss You: The World War II Letters of Barbara Wooddall Taylor and Charles E. Taylor* (Athens, Georgia, 1990), 145.

97. Dorothy's letters to her mother suggest that this was a particularly complicated relationship. Edna Rankin McKinnon traveled all over the world in her professional capacity as a family-planning advocate, while her daughter appears to have suffered a classic case of what Betty Friedan called "the problem that has no name." Mrs. McKinnon seems to have tried to alleviate Dorothy's anguish by providing financial assistance and generous gifts. The letters document the latter's unhappiness, her gratitude to her mother, and her feelings of guilt and regret. For illustrative examples, see Box 1, Folders 13–23, Edna Rankin McKinnon Collection, Schlesinger Library, Radcliffe College.

98. December 9, 1935, and July 21, 1931. Both quotations are from diaries in Carton 1, Rosenfeld Papers.

99. See, for example, Jane Emmet to Helen Pratt Emmet, January 25, 1937; July 8, 1937; n.d., 1937; n.d., 1938; n.d., 1940; April 1940; Box 5, Folder 1, Emmet Collection.

100. August 24, 1928, Carton 1, Rosenfeld Papers. An explanatory note in the margin of this letter explains "I was very homesick. [My sister] often teased me. I wouldn't ever write this."

101. See, for example, letters from Augusta Salik Dublin to her daughter Mary concerning another daughter, July 31, 1929, and August 6, 1929, Carton 1, Folder 7, Keyserling Papers; May 4, 1943, and July 14, 1943, Carton 1, Folder 10, Keyserling Papers; and a letter dated August 10, 1937, Carton 1, Rosenfeld Papers.

102. Leila Rupp and Verta Taylor, *Survival in the Doldrums* (New York, 1987). See also Filene, *Him/Her/Self,* chapter 6: "The Long Amnesia: Depression, War, and Domesticity," 148–76.

103. Elaine Tyler May, *Homeward Bound: American Families in the Cold War* (New York, 1988).

9. "The Anchor of My Life"

1. Carroll Smith-Rosenberg has argued that existence of a network of intimate female relatives and friends during the first two-thirds of the nineteenth century served to defuse mother-daughter tensions. "The Female World of Love and Ritual," in Smith-Rosenberg, *Disorderly Conduct: Visions of Gender in Victorian America* (New York, 1985), 53–76.

2. Kenneth Keniston, *Young Radicals: Notes on Committed Youth* (New York, 1968), 112–16, and *Youth and Dissent: The Rise of a New Opposition* (New York, 1971), 172.

3. Friedan Manuscript Collection, Schlesinger Library, Radcliffe College, quoted in Elaine Tyler May, *Homeward Bound: American Families in the Cold War Era* (New York, 1988), 209–17.

4. Mary Thom, ed., *Letters to Ms., 1972–1987* (New York, 1987), 64–77.

5. See, for example, letters written in 1967 and 1968 by Fredelle Maynard to her daughter Rona at Middlebury College, Fredelle Maynard Papers, and diaries kept by Catherine Bly Cox during the 1960s, Catherine Bly Cox Papers (one box), both in Schlesinger Library, Radcliffe College. The Maynard letters document the same sorts of concerns and the same close mother-daughter communication that typified correspondence between earlier mothers and their college-student daughters. The Cox diaries suggest mothers and young adolescent daughters also remained close despite the increased influence of peers and the pressures of teen social life. See also examples of contemporary mother-daughter relationships illustrated in Karen Payne, ed., *Between Ourselves: Letters between Mothers and Daughters, 1750–1982* (Boston, 1983), and Julie Kettle Gundlach, *My Mother before Me: When Daughters Discover Mothers* (Secaucus, N.J., 1986). For an interesting analysis from the maternal point of view, see the essay titled "On Being Raised by a Daughter," in Nancy Mairs, *Plaintext* (Tucson, 1986). I am grateful to Dr. Ellen Rothman for calling this reference to my attention.

6. For example, the research of Judith Pildes and that of Shere Hite has documented a strong desire on the part of daughters not to be like their mothers, that is, to avoid assuming the subordinate roles and the status to which the latter have been relegated in a male-dominated culture. See Judith Pildes, "Mothers and Daughters: Understanding the Roles," *Frontiers* 3, 2 (Summer 1978): 1–11; and Shere Hite, "I Hope I'm Not Like My Mother," in Jane Price Knowles and Ellen Cole, eds., *Woman-Defined Motherhood* (New York, 1990), 13–30. Hite and others have suggested that the fear of aging which characterizes American culture generally is also implicated in women's fear of being like their mothers.

See also a recent volume by Victoria Secunda, *When You and Your Mother Can't Be Friends* (New York, 1990), which offers a worst-possible-case scenario through examples of strongly negative long-term effects of mother-daughter conflict.

7. Theodore Caplow et al., *Middletown Families: Fifty Years of Change and*

Continuity (Minneapolis, 1982), 138–57, and Appendix A, Tables 7.1 through 7.8, 371–77. See also Joseph Adelson's argument that the widely perceived generation gap between parents and children in the late 1960s was no greater than it had been in any other period, in "Adolescence and the Generation Gap," *Psychology Today* 12 (February 1979).

8. See Carol Gilligan, Prologue, 1–5, and Preface, "Teaching Shakespeare's Sister: Notes from the Underground of Female Adolescence," 6–29; Lori Stern, "Conceptions of Separation and Connection in Female Adolescents," 73–87; Judith P. Salzman, "Save the World, Save Myself: Responses to Problematic Attachment," 110–46; Janet Mendelson, "The View from Step Number 16: Girls from Emma Willard School Talk about Themselves and Their Futures," 233–57; and Sharon Rich, "Daughters' Views of Their Relationships with Their Mothers," 258–73; all in Carol Gilligan et al., eds., *Making Connections: The Relational Worlds of Adolescent Girls at Emma Willard School* (Cambridge, Mass., 1990).

9. Ruth Wodak and Muriel Schulz, *The Language of Love and Guilt: Mother-Daughter Relationships from a Crosscultural Perspective* (Amsterdam and Philadelphia, 1986). While the American subjects clearly emphasized the closeness of their ties to their mothers, the authors of the study noted the difficulty of distinguishing between the influence of prescriptive notions of the ideal family and the young women's actual experiences; see pp. 147–49.

10. Anne C. Petersen, "Those Gangly Years," *Psychology Today* (September 1987): 28–34; Paula J. Caplan, *Don't Blame Mother: Mending the Mother-Daughter Relationship* (New York, 1989), 11.

11. Lucy Rose Fischer, *Linked Lives: Adult Daughters and Their Mothers* (New York, 1986).

12. Natalie Low, "Mother-Daughter Relationships: The Lasting Ties," *Radcliffe Quarterly* (December 1984): 1–4.

13. Angela M. Rosenberg, "Equity and Satisfaction in the Midlife Woman's Relationship with Her Mother," poster presentation, Gerontological Society of America Annual Meeting, San Francisco, November 1988.

14. Diane Sholomskas and Rosalind Axelrod, "The Influence of Mother-Daughter Relationships on Women's Sense of Self and Current Role Choices," *Psychology of Women Quarterly* 10, 2 (June 1986): 171–82. See also Barbara Engel's observations about the connection between maternal discontent and daughters' desires to defy established societal standards in nineteenth- and early twentieth-century Russia, in *Mothers and Daughters: Women of the Intelligentsia in Nineteenth-Century Russia* (New York, 1983), 13.

15. See, for example, discussions of the dangers of too much education for women contained in E. H. Clarke, *Sex in Education: or, A Fair Chance for the Girls* (Boston, 1873).

16. Joseph F. Kett, *Rites of Passage: Adolescence in America, 1790 to the Present* (New York, 1977): 133–43, 215–38.

17. An interesting analysis of the relationship among cultural, social, and psychological factors and the dynamics of family life is Stephen Mintz, *A*

Prison of Expectations: The Family in Victorian Culture (New York and London, 1983).

18. See, for example, the articulation of one mother's recognition of such unfulfilled aspirations: " 'Some day I shall get reckless and do all the things I have been debarred from doing all my life almost.' " Mary Herbst to her daughter Helen, quoted in Elinor Langer, *Josephine Herbst* (Boston, 1983, 1984), 26. Peter Filene suggests that mothers lived vicariously through their daughters' rebellious and emancipated behavior during the late nineteenth century, in *Him/Her/Self: Sex Roles in Modern America*, 2d ed. (Baltimore, 1986), 23. See also Barbara Miller Solomon, *In the Company of Educated Women* (New Haven, 1985), 67–68. For an interesting and more complex example of the potential impact of unfulfilled maternal aspirations on an Australian mother-daughter relationship, see Jill Ker Conway's autobiographic recollections in *The Road from Coorain* (New York, 1989).

19. Nini Herman, *Too Long a Child: The Mother-Daughter Dyad* (London, 1989), 212. An overview of the principles of family systems theory is contained in Paula Marantz Cohen, *The Daughter's Dilemma: Family Process and the Nineteenth-Century Domestic Novel* (Ann Arbor, Mich., 1991), chapter 1. See also Augustus Y. Napier and Carl A. Whitaker, *The Family Crucible* (New York, 1978), and Lynn Hoffman, *Foundations of Family Therapy: A Conceptual Framework for Systems Change* (New York, 1981). For an overview of some of the issues pertaining to the interactions of mothers, daughters, and fathers, see David Lynn, *Daughters and Parents: Past, Present, and Future* (Monterey, Calif., 1979).

20. See, for example, Barbara Welter, *Dimity Convictions: The American Woman in the Nineteenth Century* (Athens, Ohio, 1976), 6–7; Earnest, *The American Eve in Fact and Fiction* (Urbana, Ill., 1974), 23–24, 85; and Mabel Collins Donnelly, *The American Victorian Woman: The Myth and the Reality* (New York, 1986), 21–24. Elaine Showalter has made similar observations regarding female novelists and their fathers in the nineteenth-century English context, in *A Literature of Their Own: British Women Novelists from Brontë to Lessing* (Princeton, N.J., 1977), 62–64. See also observations by John Demos on the father's role in providing moral supervision for daughters as well as sons in early America, "The Changing Faces of Fatherhood," in *Past, Present, and Personal: The Family and the Life Course in American History* (New York, 1986), 46; evidence that emphasizes the role of paternal influence in encouraging the aspirations of leading English feminists, above, chapter 8; and Olive Banks, *Becoming a Feminist: The Social Origins of "First Wave" Feminism* (Brighton, England, 1986), 25–31.

21. Paula S. Fass, *The Damned and the Beautiful; American Youth in the 1920's* (New York, 1977), 86–87; Margaret Marsh, "Suburban Men and Masculine Domesticity, 1870–1915," in Mark C. Carnes and Clyde Griffen, eds., *Meanings for Manhood: Constructions of Masculinity in Victorian America* (Chicago, 1990), 111–27. I am grateful to Professor Peter N. Stearns for bringing the Marsh essay to my attention.

The putative increase in paternal involvement around the turn of the century offers an interesting contrast to Mary Bulkley's recollections of the nineteenth-century paternal role. In her memoirs, she observed that while fathers were the official family heads, disbursed the money, and occasionally had to "speak to" a child, wives were actually in charge of the household. With regard to her own father, she commented: "I was always very close to my father; yet he does not take a major place until my adolescence. Now, I can see that this was according to the pattern of the time and because of this pattern most fathers were deprived of the pleasures as well as the proper duties"; see Mary Ezit Bulkley, "Grandmother, Mother and Me," 33, mimeographed manuscript, Schlesinger Library, Radcliffe College.

22. Examples of this type of correspondence are contained in the letters of Mary Hills, Box 9, Folder 3, Hills Family Papers, Special Collections, Amherst College Library, and in those between Lousie Marion Bosworth and her father, Carton 2, Folders 76 and 77, Louise Marion Bosworth Papers, Schlesinger Library, Radcliffe College. A recent commentary regarding the difficulties experienced by college psychology students who were asked to assume their fathers' voice suggests that a similar situation also characterizes contemporary father-daughter communication: "Everyone could tell *about* their fathers . . . but to *speak* as our fathers was a huge problem for most of us. We discovered that most of our information came from hints and outward behavior and what our mothers had told us. Only a few of us felt we really knew our dads, and even fewer could remember times their fathers had actually confided to them"; quoted in Linda Weltner, "A Father Puts His Philosophy on Paper," *Boston Globe* (June 19, 1987): 28.

23. April 27, 1907, Diary of Clara Savage Littledale, Box 1, Volume 15, Littledale Papers, Schlesinger Library, Radcliffe College.

24. Eliza Coe Brown to John Crosby Brown, May 20, 1888, Folder 7; August 17, 1890, Folder 8; August 7, 1900, Folder 9, all in Carton 1; Dorothea May Moore to Edward Moore, April 15 and July 27, 1903; September 10, and September 14, 1904, Folder 64; June 22 and August 10, 1910, Folder 66; November 6, 1911, Folder 68, all in Carton 3. See also letters from Eliza Coe Brown to her mother while she was traveling in Europe with her father in 1900, in Folder 9, and those of November 9, 1913, Folder 10, and May 24, 1914, Folder 11, all in Carton 1; and letters from Edward Moore to his daughter, July 22, 1910, Folder 67, and October 10, 1911, Folder 69, in Carton 3. All in Dorothea May Moore Papers, Schlesinger Library, Radcliffe College.

25. Interestingly, despite this tragedy, the young woman decided to continue her journey. Her family unanimously approved the decision, and her mother assured her that her father would have agreed. See Mary Kate Brewster to her mother, October 5, 1893, Box 5, Folder 38; Mrs. Brewster to Mary Kate, October 15, 1893, and November 8, 1893, Box 5, Folder 35, Brewster Family Papers, Sophia Smith Collection, Smith College. See especially Mrs. Brewster's comments of November 8: "I hope also that you realize

... that he would wish you to get as much enjoyment as possible out of this trip and that it is part of your education to see what you can of foreign society."

26. Affa Miner Tuttle to her mother, February 5, 1895, and February 6, 1895, Box 18, Folder 6, and Diary of Elizabeth Miner Garman, Section III, Box 43, Folder 2, both in Charles Edward Garman Papers, Special Collections, Amherst College Library. See also affectionate letters to Elizabeth Garman from her father, D. W. Miner, in Box 13, Folder 1, in ibid.

27. John Bascom to Florence Bascom, October 2, 1884. See also letters dated October 7, 1884, and November 29, 1884, all in Box 10, Folder 7, Florence Bascom Papers, Sophia Smith Collection, Smith College. This folder contains numerous other encouraging, loving letters. Otto Auerbach to Lydia Marie Parsons, February 27, 1910; n.d., 1917; June 5, 1917; September 20, 1923; all in Box 1, Folder 3, Lydia Marie Parsons Papers, Schlesinger Library, Radcliffe College. The quotation is from a letter dated September 17, 1915, which was written in honor of Lydia's twenty-eighth birthday. Annie Winsor Allen also received affectionate letters from her father, who was a physician and occasionally included health advice along with comments about his grandchild. See, for example, a letter dated September 16, 1885, Series III, Box 23, Folder 380, Annie Winsor Allen Papers, Schlesinger Library, Radcliffe College.

28. Louis Dublin to Mary Dublin Keyserling, regarding her research, October 27, 1931, November 13, 1931, January 6, 1932, and June 21, 1932, all in Folder 25, and how much he missed her, October 13, 1931, in Folder 24. The quotation is from January 22, 1932, also in Folder 25. Expressions of pride in Mary's work are contained in letters written during the period 1941–61, contained in Folders 26 and 27, all in Carton 1, Mary Keyserling Papers, Schlesinger Library, Radcliffe College.

29. Barbara Sicherman, *Alice Hamilton: A Life in Letters* (Cambridge, Mass., 1984), 19.

30. *The Spencers of Amberson Avenue: A Turn of the Century Memoir*, ed. Michael P. Weber and Peter N. Stearns (Pittsburgh, 1983), 122–23; Marion Taylor Diary excerpts, September 18, 1918, October 18, 1918, and July n.d., 1919, Box 1, Folder 11; November 26, 1919, and June 7, 1920, Box 1, Folder 14, all in typescript, Schlesinger Library, Radcliffe College.

31. Judith Bardwick, *Psychology of Women: A Study of Bio-Cultural Conflicts* (New York, 1971), 138–39.

32. Peter N. Stearns with Carol Z. Stearns, "Emotionology: Clarifying the History of Emotions and Emotional Standards," *American Historical Review* 90 (October 1985): 813–36; Shula Sommers, "Understanding Emotions: Some Interdisciplinary Considerations," in Carol Z. Stearns and Peter N. Stearns, eds., *Emotion and Social Change: Toward a New Psychohistory* (New York and London, 1988), 23–38 (see also the essays and works cited in the bibliography therein).

33. Jan Lewis, "Mother's Love: The Construction of an Emotion in Nine-

teenth-Century America," and Peter N. Stearns, "Suppressing Unpleasant Emotions: The Development of a Twentieth-Century American Style," in Andrew E. Barnes and Peter N. Stearns, eds., *Social History and Issues in Human Consciousness: Some Interdisciplinary Connections* (New York, 1989), 209–29, 230–61; Carol Z. Stearns and Peter N. Stearns, *Anger: The Struggle for Emotional Control in America's History* (Chicago, 1986); Carol Z. Stearns, " 'Lord Help Me Walk Humbly': Anger and Sadness in England and America, 1570–1750," and Peter N. Stearns, "The Rise of Sibling Jealousy in the Twentieth Century," in Stearns and Stearns, eds., *Emotion and Social Change*, 39–68, 193–222; and Peter N. Stearns, *Jealousy: The Evolution of an Emotion in American History* (New York, 1989).

34. Stearns and Stearns, *Anger*, chapter 4, and Introduction in *Emotion and Social Change*, 12. The suppression of female anger reflects a cultural construction of "femininity" in which women's expressions of anger and aggression are essentially unacceptable; Jean Baker Miller, "The Construction of Anger in Women and Men," in Judith V. Jordan et al., *Women's Growth in Connection: Writings from the Stone Center* (New York, 1991), 181–96.

35. Joan Jacobs Brumberg, *Fasting Girls: The Emergence of Anorexia Nervosa as a Modern Disease* (Cambridge, Mass., 1988), 126–40, and Nancy M. Theriot, *The Biosocial Construction of Femininity: Mothers and Daughters in Nineteenth-Century America* (Westport, Conn., 1988), 119–32. A possible connection between mother-daughter conflict and eating disorders in the late twentieth century has also been articulated by Kim Chernin, *The Hungry Self: Women, Eating and Identity* (New York, 1985). For a different view of this connection, see Kathleen M. Pike and Judith Rodin, "Mothers, Daughters, and Disordered Eating," *Journal of Abnormal Psychology* (May 1991): 198–201. This study links eating disorders in teen-aged girls to their mothers' eating and dieting behavior and also to their attitudes regarding their daughters' weight and appearance.

36. For discussions of the relationship between emotional standards and actual emotions, see Shula Sommers, "Understanding Emotions: Some Interdisciplinary Considerations," in Stearns and Stearns, *Emotion and Social Change*, 23–38; Margaret S. Clark, "Historical Emotionology: From a Social Psychologist's Perspective," in Barnes and Stearns, eds., *Social History and Issues in Human Consciousness*, 262–69; and Miller, "The Construction of Anger in Women and Men," especially 193–96.

Recent research in emotions history includes Stearns and Stearns, *Anger*; Lewis, "Mother's Love," 209–29; and Stearns, "Suppressing Unpleasant Emotions," 230–61; all cited in note 33. See also the essays and works cited in the bibiliography in Stearns and Stearns, *Emotion and Social Change*.

37. Elaine Showalter, "Toward a Feminist Poetics," in *The New Feminist Criticism: Essays on Women, Literature, Theory* (New York, 1985), 135, quoted in Marianne Hirsch, *The Mother/Daughter Plot* (Bloomington, Ind., 1989), 125.

38. For a discussion of the cultural heritage of mother-blaming, see Caplan, *Don't Blame Mother*. For a brief overview of nineteenth-century commen-

tary on the failures of mothers to fulfill their responsibilities, see Bernard Wishy, *The Child and the Republic: The Dawn of Modern American Child Nurture* (Philadelphia, 1968), 28–29. Mid-twentieth-century examples of mother-blaming include Philip Wylie, *Generation of Vipers* (New York, 1955), and Edward A. Strecker and Vincent T. Lathbury, *Their Mothers' Daughters* (Philadelphia and New York, 1956).

39. Ethel Sturges Dummer, for example, was involved in a wide variety of activities outside her home. See Carl Degler, *At Odds: Women and the Family in America from the Revolution to the Present* (New York, 1980), chapter 13, for a discussion of women's world beyond the home. Smith-Rosenberg also comments on the activities of women outside the confines of domesticity in "The New Woman as Androgyne" in Carroll Smith-Rosenberg, *Disorderly Conduct: Visions of Gender in Victorian America* (New York, 1985), 256–57.

40. Suzanne Lebsock, *The Free Women of Petersburg: Status and Culture in a Southern Town, 1784–1860* (New York, 1984), xvi.

41. Daniel Scott Smith, "Family Limitation, Sexual Control, and Domestic Feminism in Victorian America," in Mary S. Hartman and Lois Banner, eds., *Clio's Consciousness Raised* (New York, 1974), 119–36. See also Degler, *At Odds*, chapter 11, 249–78; Nancy F. Cott, *The Bonds of Womanhood: "Woman's Sphere" in New England, 1780–1835* (New Haven, 1977); Mary Beth Norton, "The Paradox of 'Women's Sphere,' " in Carol R. Berkin and Mary Beth Norton, eds., *Women of America: A History* (Boston, 1979); Kathryn Kish Sklar, *Catharine Beecher: A Study in American Domesticity* (New York, 1973); Glenna Matthews, *"Just a Housewife": The Rise and Fall of Domesticity in America* (New York, 1987); Dolores Hayden, *The Grand Domestic Revolution: A History of Feminist Designs for American Homes, Neighborhoods, and Cities* (Cambridge, Mass., 1981); and Barbara Harris, *Beyond Her Sphere: Women and the Professions in American History* (Westport, Conn., 1978). I am grateful to Professor Peter N. Stearns for suggesting a possible connection between domestic feminism and maternal support.

42. See chapter 5, p. 95.

43. Smith, "Family Limitation, Sexual Control, and Domestic Feminism."

44. Melvin L. Kohn, *Class and Conformity: A Study in Values*, 2d ed. (Chicago, 1977), especially xxxiv, 17, 35, 43, 46, 71–72, 101, 105–6, 114. The findings reported in this study reflect research conducted primarily in the late 1950s and early 1960s. Kohn also cites cross-cultural data from an Italian study, which document a middle-class tendency to value characteristics that reflect self-direction, and data from Middletown, which indicate that working-class mothers stressed obedience more than their middle-class counterparts did during the 1920s. Data from both classes suggest that fathers are less supportive of daughters than are mothers. See also Jonas Frykman and Orvar Lofgren, *Culture Builders: A Historical Anthropology of Middle-Class Life* (New Brunswick, N.J., 1987), which examines the evolution of the Swedish middle-class worldview between 1880 and 1910. I am grateful to Professor Richard Schoenwald for calling my attention to these sources.

A recent exploration of the interactions of single mothers and adolescent daughters in early twentieth-century Los Angeles also lends credence to the suggestion that middle-class parents accepted nonconformity more readily than their working-class counterparts did. This study found that when daughters engaged in untraditional behavior such as leaving home, frequenting dance halls, refusing to turn over their wages to parents, and engaging in premarital sex, single mothers frequently turned to the juvenile court system for assistance in resolving the ensuing family conflicts. See Mary Odem, "Single Mothers, Delinquent Daughters, and the Juvenile Court in Early 20th Century Los Angeles," *Journal of Social History* 25, 1 (Fall 1991): 27–43. Clearly, further work is needed in order to substantiate the existence of this potential class-based difference in mother-daughter relationships.

45. See "My Quarrel with Women's Clubs," *Ladies Home Journal* 27 (January 1910): 5–6, quoted in Christopher Lasch, *The New Radicalism in America, 1889–1963* (New York, 1965), 47–49. Carroll Smith-Rosenberg has commented on the lack of congruence between the perspectives of male authors and the experiences of women: "I ceased to search in men's writings for clues to women's experiences"; "Hearing Women's Words: A Feminist Reconstruction of History," in *Disorderly Conduct*, 27. See also Norton, "The Paradox of Women's Sphere," in Berkin and Norton, eds., *Women of America.*

46. Maxine L. Margolis, *Mothers and Such: Views of American Women and Why They Changed* (Berkeley, 1984), 39.

47. See, for example, Mrs. Burton Harrison, "Home Life as a Profession," *Harper's Bazar* 33 (May 19, 1900): 148–50, quoted in Lasch, *The New Radicalism*, 49.

48. Stearns and Stearns, *Anger*, chapter 4.

49. For an analysis of the effects on the family of the emphasis on outside experts, see Christopher Lasch, *Haven in a Heartless World: The Family Besieged* (New York, 1977).

50. Carroll Smith-Rosenberg, "The New Woman and the New History," *Feminist Studies* 3, 1/2 (Fall 1975): 185–98. See also the discussion of the influence of culture on an individual's interpretation of mothering as distinguished from that of the specific model provided by her own mother, in Arlie Hochschild with Anne Machung, *The Second Shift* (New York, 1989), 155–57.

51. Introduction and Jean Baker Miller, "The Development of Women's Sense of Self," in Jordan et al., *Women's Growth in Connection*, 1–7, 11–26.

52. Alexandra G. Kaplan and Rona Klein, "The Relational Self in Late Adolescent Women," in Jordan et al., *Women's Growth in Connection*, 123. Carol Gilligan's model of female development also emphasizes the role of affective connectedness in women's concepts of self; see *In a Different Voice: Psychological Theory and Women's Development* (Cambridge, Mass., and London, 1982).

53. Judith V. Jordan, "The Meaning of Mutuality," in Jordan et al., *Women's Growth in Connection*, 82–83, 87.

54. Ibid., 84.

55. Janet L. Surrey, "The Relational Self in Women: Clinical Implications," in Jordan et al., *Women's Growth in Connection*, 35–43.

56. Kaplan and Klein, "The Relational Self in Late Adolescent Women," 125.

57. Janet L. Surrey, "The Self-in-Relation: A Theory of Women's Development," in Jordan et al., *Women's Growth in Connection*, 60. See Nancy Mairs's comments on her own experience of the mutual growth and change that occurs in the mother-daughter relationship in her essay, "On Being Raised by a Daughter" (see note 5).

58. For examples of current studies that support this theory, see Nancy A. Gleason, "Daughters and Mothers: College Women Look at Their Relationships," in Jordan et al., *Women's Growth in Connection*, 132–40, and Terri Apter, *Altered Loves: Mothers and Daughters during Adolescence* (New York, 1990). The issue of the application of ahistorical, psychological theories to the analysis of the family in past periods is considered in Nancy M. Theriot, *The Biosocial Construction of Femininity: Mothers and Daughters in Nineteenth-Century America* (Westport, Conn., 1988), 12. See also Jane Flax, "The Conflict between Nurturance and Autonomy in Mother-Daughter Relationships and within Feminism," *Feminist Studies* 4 (June 1978): 171–89.

59. See, for example, Jacques Barzun, *Clio and the Doctors: Psycho-History, Quanto-History, and History* (Chicago, 1974); Saul Friedlander, *History and Psychoanalysis: An Inquiry into the Possibilities and Limits of Psychohistory* (New York, 1978); Gerald Izenberg, "Psychohistory and Intellectual History," *History and Theory* 14 (1975): 139–55. A useful discussion of the issues surrounding psychohistory and a relevant bibliography may be found in Richard L. Schoenwald, "The Psychological Study of History," in Georg G. Iggers and Harold T. Parker, eds., *International Handbook of Historical Studies: Contemporary Research and Theory* (Westport, Conn.), 71–86.

60. Nancy Chodorow, Introduction, *Feminism and Psychoanalytic Theory* (New Haven and London, 1989), 3–4.

61. Marcia Westkott, "Mothers and Daughters in the World of the Father," *Frontiers* 3, 2 (Summer 1978): 16–17. Strong mother-daughter relationships also characterized the experiences of immigrant women at the turn of the century and women who participated in the nineteenth-century westward movement. On the former, see Sydney Stahl Weinberg, *The World of Our Mothers* (Chapel Hill, N.C., 1988); Elizabeth Stern, *My Mother and I* (New York, 1937 [1916]); and H. M. Bannan, "Warrior Women: Immigrant Mothers in the Works of Their Daughters," *Women's Studies* 6 (1979): 165–77. On frontier women, see Elizabeth Hampsten, ed., *To All Inquiring Friends: Letters, Diaries and Essays in North Dakota, 1880–1910* (Grand Forks, N.D., 1979); *A Victorian Gentlewoman in the Far West: The Reminiscences of Mary Hallock Foote*, ed. Rodman W. Paul (San Marino, Calif., 1972); Lillian Schlissel, *Women's Diaries of the Westward Journey* (New York, 1982); and Eliane Silverman, "In Their Own Words: Mothers and Daughters on the Alberta Frontier, 1890–

1920," *Frontiers* 2, 2 (1977): 37–44. Black women have also relied on maternal support as well as the support of a wider female network. See, for example, Jacqueline Jones, *Labor of Love, Labor of Sorrow: Black Women, Work, and the Family from Slavery to the Present* (New York, 1985); Carol Stack, *All Our Kin: Strategies for Survival in a Black Community* (New York, 1974); and Patricia Hill Collins, "The Meaning of Motherhood in Black Culture and Black Mother/Daughter Relationships," *Sage* 4, 2 (Fall 1987): 3–9.

62. For examples of the impact of cross-cultural and class-based differences on mother-daughter interactions, see the analysis of English mother-daughter relationships in chapter 7 and the discussion of variations in mother-daughter interactions across social classes in nineteenth-century Russia in Barbara Alpern Engel, *Mothers and Daughters*, 7–14.

63. Demos, "The Changing Faces of Fatherhood"; Mary Beth Norton, *Liberty's Daughters: The Revolutionary Experience of American Women* (Boston, 1980); Jan Lewis, "Mother's Love"; and Nancy Chodorow, "Family Structure and Feminine Personality," in *Feminism and Psychoanalytic Theory*, 63.

64. Martha A. Robbins, "Mourning the Myth of Mother/hood: Reclaiming Our Mothers' Legacies," in Knowles and Cole, *Woman-Defined Motherhood*, 41–59; and idem, *Midlife Women and Death of Mother: A Study of Psychohistorical and Spiritual Transformation* (New York, 1990).

65. See chapter 4, pp. 73–74, and chapter 6, pp. 125, 133, for expressions of daughters' feelings about maternal death.

66. Elaine Showalter, *Sexual Anarchy: Gender and Culture at the Fin de Siècle* (New York, 1990).

67. Mary Ezit Bulkley, "Grandmother, Mother and Me," mimeographed manuscript, Schlesinger Library.

68. Carolyn G. Heilbrun, *Writing a Woman's Life* (New York, 1988), 118–19.

69. Barbara Sicherman, "American History," *Signs* 1, 2 (Winter 1975): 480.

70. Doris Parsons Rose to Lydia Marie Parsons, May 8, 1983, Box 1, Folder 18, Lydia Marie Parsons Papers.

INDEX

Acland, Eleanor, 159, 161–62
Affection between mothers and daughters, 95–98, 186–88, 244 n. 21, 247 n. 50, 251 n. 94, 257 n. 55, 275 n. 55
Allen, Annie Winsor, 77, 79, 85, 87, 94–97, 116, 120–21, 155, 197
Almy, Helen Jackson Cabot, 116
Almy, Mary, 77, 116
Ames, Blanche Ames, 101–2, 114–15, 127, 132, 184
Anderson, Margaret, 110–12
Anger, socialization regarding, 6–7, 201–2
Anorexia nervosa, 201. *See also* Health issues
Arcana, Judith, 2–3
Ashby, Margery Corbett, 155–56
Association of Collegiate Alumnae (American Association of University Women), 99
Austin, Mary, 55, 67
Avery, Maria, 12, 14
Ayrton, Barbara, 154

Barnard College, 106, 109
Bascom, Florence, 200
Beals, Jessie Tarbox, 173
Bent Twig, The, 41, 52, 54–55, 61, 64, 66
Blackwell, Alice, 75–76
Blackwell, Elizabeth, 19
Blackwell, Hannah, 19
Blackwell, Lucy Stone. *See* Stone, Lucy
Bloom, Ursula, 159–60
Bloor, Ella Reeve, 127–28
Boit, Mary Anderson, 72–74, 89
Bok, Edward, 26, 29–30, 205
Booth-Clibborn, Catherine, 125–26

Boston University, 99
Bosworth, Eleanora Wheeler, 91–93, 116
Bosworth, Louise Marion, 91–93, 105, 189
Bowerman, Elsie, 154–55
Bradley, Amy Aldis, 119
Bread-Givers, 62, 64–67
Brewster, Anna Gertrude, 122
Brewster, Helen, 122
Brewster, Mary Kate, 200
Brittain, Vera, 144–47, 151, 159, 160
Bryn Mawr College, 95, 96, 188
Bulkley, Mary Ezit, 79, 129, 214
Burstall, Sara, 151–52, 156
Burton, Harriet Wright, 74
Bush-Brown, Lydia, 105

Cabot, Ella Lyman, 83–84, 179
Cabot, Richard, 83
Calender, June, 178, 180–81, 184
Cambridge University, 137, 160
Carter, Melissa, 15
Cass, Helen Landon, 106
Cather, Willa, 52, 67, 106
Chandler, Hannah, 13
Change in mother-daughter relationships, 21, 86, 176–78, 179–86, 192
Chessler, Elizabeth Macfarlane, 38, 113
Child, Lydia Maria, 113
Chodorow, Nancy, 3–4, 209
Chorley, Katherine, 158–61
Communication between mothers and daughters, 31–33, 74–75, 264 n. 52, 278 n. 5; regarding domestic tasks, 116; in England, 148–50; regarding the facts of life, 26–27, 35–36, 79–81, 89, 159, 240 nn. 48, 55, 267–68 n. 98;